Honoré de Balzac

The Lily of the Valley

Honoré de Balzac

The Lily of the Valley

ISBN/EAN: 9783744743853

Printed in Europe, USA, Canada, Australia, Japan

Cover: Foto ©ninafisch / pixelio.de

More available books at **www.hansebooks.com**

H. DE BALZAC

THE
LILY OF THE VALLEY

(LE LYS DANS LA VALLÉE)

AND OTHER STORIES

TRANSLATED BY

JAMES WARING

WITH A PREFACE BY

GEORGE SAINTSBURY

PHILADELPHIA
THE GEBBIE PUBLISHING CO., Ltd.
1898

CONTENTS

	PAGE
PREFACE	ix
THE LILY OF THE VALLEY	1
ANOTHER STUDY OF WOMAN	304
THE GREAT BRETÈCHE	347
A MAN OF BUSINESS	371

LIST OF ILLUSTRATIONS

THE LADY GAVE A PIERCING CRY . . . . *Frontispiece*

HE STARTED UP, THREW THE TABLE OVER ME AND THE LAMP ON THE GROUND 67

I RAISED THE POOR WOMAN IN MY ARMS 122

MADELEINE, JACQUES, AND THE ABBÉ DE DOMINIS ALL KNEELING AT THE FOOT OF A WOODEN CROSS 263

"WHEN ARE YOU TO MARRY THE DUKE?" 317
Drawn by D. Murray-Smith.

PREFACE.

"THE LILY OF THE VALLEY" ("Le Lys dans la Vallée") has considerable importance in the history of Balzac's books, and not a little in that of his life, independently of its intrinsic merit. It brought on a lawsuit between him and the "Revue de Paris," in which the greater part of it was published, and in which he refused to complete it. As the actual suit was decided in his favor, his legal justification is not matter of dispute, and his adversaries put themselves hopelessly in the wrong by reviewing the termination of the book, when it appeared elsewhere, in a strain of virulent but clumsy ridicule. As to where the right or wrong lay, independent of questions of pure law on one side and pure taste on the other, it is not so easy to come to any conclusion. Balzac published an elaborate justification of his own conduct, which does not now appear with the book, but may be found, by any one who is curious, among the rejected prefaces which fill a large part of the twenty-second volume (the third of the "Œuvres Diverses") of his Works. It is exceedingly long, not by any means temperate, and so confused that it is difficult to make head or tail of it. What is clear is that the parties went on the dangerous and unsatisfactory plan of neither complete performance of the work before payment nor complete payment beforehand, but of a *per contra* account, the author drawing money as he wanted it, and sending in copy as he could or chose. Balzac seems to allow that he got into arrears, contending that if he paid those arrears the rest of the work was his own property. But there were complicating disagreements in reference to a simultaneous publication at St. Petersburg; and, on the whole, we may fairly conclude in the not very original terms of "faults on both sides." The affair, however, evidently gave him much annoyance, and seems to have brought him into some discredit.

The other point of personal interest is that Madame de Mortsauf is very generally said to represent Madame de Berny, his early friend and his first instructress in aristocratic ways. Although there are strong expressions of affection in his letters with regard to this lady, who died early in his career, they do not definitely indicate what is commonly called love. But the whole scenery and atmosphere of "The Lily of the Valley" ("Le Lys dans la Vallée") are those of his own early haunts. Frapesle, which is so often mentioned, was the home of another platonic friend, Madame Zulma Carraud, and there is much in the early experiences of Félix de Vandenesse which has nearly as personal a touch as that of "Louis Lambert" itself.

Dismissing this, we may come to the book itself. Balzac took so much interest in it—indeed, the personal throb may be felt throughout—that he departed (according to his own account, for the second time only) from his rule of not answering criticism. This was in regard to a very remarkable article of M. Hippolyte Castillès (to be found in M. de Lovenjoul's invaluable bibliography, as is the answering letter in the "Œuvres Diverses" *) reflecting upon the rather pagan and materialist "resurrection of the flesh" in Madame de Mortsauf on her death-bed. His plea that it was the disease, not the person, though possessing a good deal of physiological force, is psychologically rather weak, and might have been made much stronger. Indeed, this scene, though shocking and disconcerting to weak brethren, is not merely the strongest in the novel, but one of the strongest in Balzac's works. There is farther to be noted in the book a quaint delineation, in the personage of M. de Mortsauf, of a kind of conjugal torment which, as a rule, is rather borne by husbands at the hands of wives than *vice versa*. The behavior of the

* Sundry Works.

"lily's" husband, sudden rages and all, is exactly that of a shrewish and valetudinarian woman.

This, however, and some minor matters, may be left to the reader to find out and appreciate. The most interesting point, and the most debatable, is the character of the heroine with, in a lesser degree, that of the hero. Of M. Félix de Vandenesse it is not necessary to say very much, because that capital letter from Madame de Manerville (one of the very best things that Balzac ever wrote, and exhibiting a sharpness and precision of mere writing which he too frequently lacked) does fair, though not complete, justice on the young man. The lady, who was not a model of excellence herself, perhaps did not perceive—for it does not seem to have been in her nature to conceal it through kindness—that he was not only as she tells him, wanting in tact, but also wanting, and that execrably, in taste. M. de Vandenesse, I think, ranks in Balzac's list of good heroes; at any rate he saves him later from a fate which he rather richly deserves, and introduces him honorably in other places. But he was not a nice young man. His "pawing" and timid advances on Madame de Mortsauf, and his effusive "kissing and telling" in reference to Lady Dudley, both smack of the worst sides of Rousseau: they deserve not so much moral reprehension as physical kicking. It is no wonder that Madeleine de Mortsauf turned a cold shoulder on him; and it is an addition to his demerits that he seems to have thought her unjust in doing so.

As for the "lily" we come once more to one of those ineradicable differences between French and English taste—one of those moral fosses not to be filled which answer to the physical Channel. I have said that I do not think the last scene unnatural or even repulsive: it is pretty true and rather terrible, and where truth and terror are there is seldom disgust. But, elsewhere, for all her technical purity, her shudderings, and the rest of it, I cannot help thinking that, without insular narrowness or prudery, one may find Madame de

Mortsauf a little rancid, a little like stale cold-cream of roses. And if it is insular narrowness and prudery so to find her, let us thank God for the narrowness which yet leaves room for Cleopatra, for Beatrix Esmond, and for Becky Sharp. I should myself have thought Madame de Mortsauf a person of bad taste in caring at all for such a creature as Félix. But if she did care, I should have thought better of her for pitching her cap over the very highest mill in her care for him, than for this fullsome hankering, this "I would, but dare not," platonism. Still, others may think differently, and that the book is a very powerful book they cannot hold more distinctly than I do.

Some bibliographical details about *Le Lys* (The Lily) have been anticipated above. It need only be added that the appearances in the "Revue de Paris" were in the numbers for November and December, 1835, and that the book was published by Werdet in June of next year. The date of the "Envoi" (afterward removed), August 8, 1827, may have some biographical interest. Charpentier republished the book in a slightly different form in 1839, and, five years later, it was installed in the "Comédie."

The stories of the "Autre Étude"* (other study) are called in the Repertoire of MM. Christophe and Cerfberr "D'Exquises Causeries" ("Choice Chit-chats"). . It is not certain that all readers will acquiesce in this epithet, which is used several times in the piece by Balzac himself, though I do not remember that the combination of it with *causerie* is textual. In the first place, the discourses of Marsay and Blondet might be called by unfriendly critics rather sermons than *causeries* (chats). In the second, though Marsay is rather less of a "tiger" than in some of his other performances, the coxcombry of the exhibition exceeds its charm, while Blondet's discussion of womankind has the unreality of all these discussions. Montriveau's story is considerably better than

* "A Study of Woman" is in vol. of "Wild Ass' Skin."

either of these; and it leads up very well to "La Grande Bretêche."

This latter is one of the best known of Balzac's short stories, and may rank among the half-dozen best of all. Contrary to a habit which, though not invariable, is too common with him, he is not long in "getting under way," and he does not waste a single stroke in drawing the actual catastrophe. Bianchon, who generally has a good part assigned him, is here unusually lucky. Indeed, the piece is so short and so good that critical dwelling on it is almost an impertinence.

"A Man of Business" ("Un Homme d'Affaires"), in the eyes of some readers, does not stand very high. La Palférine reappears, and that more exalted La Palférine Maxime de Trailles, "Balzac's pet scoundrel," as some one has called him, though not present, is the hero of the tale, which is artificial and slight enough.

G. S.

Note.—It may be barely necessary for me to protect myself and the translator from a possible charge of mistaking *Lilium candidum* for *Convallaria majalis*. The French for our " lily-of-the-valley " is, of course, *muguet*. But "Lily *in* the Valley" would inevitably sound in English like a worse mistake or a tasteless variation on a consecrated phrase. And " Lily of the Valley " meets the real sense well.

THE LILY OF THE VALLEY.

To Monsieur J. B. Nacquart,
Member of the Royal Academy of Medicine.

Dear Doctor:—Here is one of the most highly wrought stones of the second story of a literary edifice that is being slowly and laboriously constructed; I wish to set your name here, as much to thank the physician who once saved my life as to do honor to the friend of every day. DE BALZAC.

To Madame la Comtesse Natalie de Manerville.

"I YIELD to your wish. It is the privilege of the woman whom we love more than she loves us that she can at any moment make us forget the laws of good sense. To spare ourselves the sight of a wrinkle on your brow, to dissipate a pout on your lips—which so small a contradiction saddens—we work miracles to annihilate distance, we give our blood, we mortgage the future.

"You, to-day, want my past: here it is. But understand this, Natalie: to obey you I have had to trample under foot a repugnance I never before have conquered. Why must you be suspicious of the long and sudden reveries which come over me when I am happiest? Why show the pretty tempers of a woman beloved because I fall silent? Could you not play with the contrasts of my nature without knowing their causes? Have you in your heart secrets which must have mine to gain absolution?

"Well, you have guessed rightly, Natalie, and it is better

perhaps that you should know everything: yes, my life is overshadowed by a phantom; it asserts itself vaguely at the least word that evokes it; it often hovers over me unbidden. I have, buried within my soul, astounding memories, like those marine growths which may be seen in calm waters and which the surges of the storm fling in fragments on the shore.

"Though the travail needed for the utterance of ideas has controlled the old emotions which hurt me so much when they are suddenly aroused, if there should be in this confession any outbreaks that offend you, remember that you threatened me in case of disobedience, and do not punish me for having obliged you.

"I only wish my confidence might increase your tenderness twofold.

"Till this evening.   FELIX."

To what genius fed on tears may we some day owe the most touching elegy—the picture of the tortures suffered in silence by souls whose roots, while still tender, find nothing but hard pebbles in the soil of home, whose earliest blossoms are rent by the hands of hate, whose flowers are frost-bitten as soon as they open? What poet will tell of the sorrows of the child whose lips suck the milk of bitterness, whose smiles are checked by the scorching fire of a stern eye? The fiction that should depict these poor crushed hearts, down-trodden by those who are placed about them to encourage the development of their feelings, would be the true story of my childhood.

What vanities could I, a new-born babe, have fretted? What moral or physical deformity earned me my mother's coldness? Was I the offspring of duty, a child whose birth is fortuitous, or one whose existence is a standing reproach?

Sent to be nursed in the country and forgotten by my parents for three years, when I returned to my father's house

I counted for so little that I had to endure the pity of the servants. I know not to what feeling nor to what happy chance I owed it that I was able to rally after this first disaster; as a child I did not understand, and as a man I do not know. My brother and my two sisters, far from mitigating my fate, amused themselves by tormenting me. The mutual compact, in virtue of which children hide each other's peccadilloes and learn an infant code of honor, was null and void as regarded me; nay more, I often found myself in disgrace for my brother's misdeeds, with no power of appeal against the injustice; was it that insidious self-interest, of which a germ exists even in children, prompted them to add to the persecution that weighed on me, so as to win the good graces of the mother whom they feared no less? Was it the result of their imitative instinct? Was it a desire to try their power, or a lack of fellow-feeling? All these causes combined perhaps to deprive me of the comfort of brotherly kindness. Cut off already from all affection, I could love nothing, and nature had made me loving! Is there an angel who collects the sighs of such ever-repressed feeling? If misprized sentiments turn to hatred in some souls, in mine they became concentrated, and wore a channel from whence at a later date they gushed into my life. In some characters the habit of shrinking relaxes every fibre and gives rise to fear; and fear reduces us to perpetual subjection. Hence proceeds a weakness which debases a man and gives him an indescribable taint of servility.

But this constant torment gave me the habit of exerting a force which increased with exercise, and predisposed my soul to moral fortitude. Always on the lookout for some new misery, as martyrs expect a fresh blow, my whole being must have expressed a gloomy dejection which stifled all the graces and impulses of childhood, a condition which was regarded as a symptom of idiocy, justifying my mother's ominous prognostics. A sense of this injustice gave rise in my spirit to a premature feeling of pride, the outcome of reason, which, no doubt, was a check on the evil disposition fostered by such a manner of education.

Though completely neglected by my mother, I was occasionally the cause of some scruples in her mind; she sometimes talked of my learning something, and expressed a purpose of teaching me; then I shuddered miserably at the thought of the anguish of daily contact with her. I blessed my deserted loneliness, and was happy in being left in the garden to play with pebbles, watch the insects and gaze at the blue sky.

Though isolation made me dreamy, my love of meditation had its rise in an incident which will give you an idea of my first woes. I was so entirely overlooked that the governess often forgot to put me to bed. One evening, peacefully sitting under a fig tree, I was looking at a star with the passionate curiosity known to children, to which, in me, precocious melancholy gave a sort of sentimental intuition. My sisters were playing and shouting; I heard the remote clatter like an accompaniment to my thoughts. The noise presently ceased; night fell. By chance my mother then noticed my absence. To avert a scolding, our governess, a certain terrible Mademoiselle Caroline, justified my mother's affected fears by declaring that I had a horror of home; that if she had not watched me narrowly, I should have run away before then; that I was not weak of intellect, but sly; that of all the children she had ever had care of, she had never known one whose disposition was so vile as mine.

She then pretended to search for me, and called me; I replied; she came to the fig tree where she knew that I was.

"What have you been doing here?" she asked.

"I was looking at a star."

"You were not looking at a star," cried my mother, who was listening from her balcony, "as if a child of your age could know anything of astronomy!"

"Oh, madame," cried Mademoiselle Caroline, "he turned on the tap of the cistern, the garden is flooded!"

There was a great commotion. My sisters had amused themselves with turning the tap to see the water flow; but startled by a spurt sideways that had wetted them all over, they lost their heads, and fled without turning the water off again. Accused and convicted of having devised this piece of mischief, and of lying when I asserted my innocence, I was severely punished. But, worst of all, I was mocked at for my love of star-gazing, and my mother forbade my staying in the garden in the evening.

Tyrannical prohibitions give zest to a passion, even more in children than in men; children have the advantage of thinking of nothing else but the forbidden thing, which then becomes irresistibly fascinating. So I was often caned for my star. Unable to confide my woes to any human being, I told my griefs to the star in that exquisite internal warbling by which a child lisps its first ideas as he has already lisped his first words. At the age of twelve, a boy at school, I still contemplated it with a sense of unspeakable rapture, so deep are the marks set on the heart by the impressions received in the dawn of life.

My brother Charles, five years my senior, was not less handsome as a child than he is as a man; he was my father's favorite, my mother's darling, the hope of the family, and consequently the king of the household. Well made and strong, he had a tutor. I, frail and sickly, was sent, at the age of five, to a day-school in the town, whither I was taken in the morning by my father's valet, who fetched me home in the afternoon. I took my midday meal in a basket but scantily filled, while my comrades brought ample supplies. This contrast of my necessity with their abundance was the source of much suffering. The famous *rillettes* and *rillons* of Tours (a kind of sausage meat) formed the larger part of our midday luncheon, between breakfast in the morning and late dinner at the hour of our return home. This preparation, highly prized by some epicures, is rarely seen at Tours on any genteel table; though I may have heard of it before going to school, I had never been so happy as to see the brown confection spread on a slice of bread for my own eating; but even if it had not been a fashionable dainty at school, my longing for it would have been no less eager, for it had become a fixed idea in my brain, just as the stews concocted by her porter's wife inspired a longing in one of the most elegant of Paris duchesses, who, being a woman, gratified her fancy.

Children can read such a longing in each other's eyes just as you can read love: thenceforth I was a standing laughing-stock. My school-fellows, almost all of the storekeeper class, would come to display their excellent *rillettes*, and ask me if I knew how they were made, where they were sold, and why I had none. They would smack their lips as they praised their *rillons*, fragments of pork fried in their own fat and looking like boiled truffles; they took stock of my basket, and, finding only Olivet cheeses or dried fruit, struck me dumb by saying, "Why, you have nothing at all!" in a way that taught me to estimate the difference made between my brother and myself.

This comparison of my own misery with the good fortune of others dashed the roses of my childhood and blighted my blossoming youth. The first time that I, taken in by a semblance of generosity, put out my hand to take the longed-for treat from a hypocrite who offered it, the boy snatched it away, raising a shout of laughter among the others who were aware of the practical joke.

If the loftiest minds are accessible to vanity, we may surely pardon a child for crying when he finds himself despised and made game of. Treated thus, most children would become greedy, sneaking, and mean. To avoid persecution, I fought my foes; the courage of despair made me formidable, but I was detested, and remained without defense against treachery. One evening, as I left school, a handkerchief, tightly rolled and full of stones, struck me on the back. When the valet, who avenged me amply, told my mother about it, she only said—

"That dreadful child will never be anything but a trouble to us!"

I then suffered the most miserable distrust of myself, discerning at school the same repulsion as was felt for me by my family. I was thrown in on myself at school and at home. A second fall of snow checked the blossoming of the germs sown in my soul. Those who were loved were, I saw, sturdy rascals; with this I comforted my pride, and I dwelt alone. Thus there was no end to the impossibility of pouring out the feelings which swelled my poor little heart. Seeing me always alone, hated and dejected, the master confirmed my parents' unjust notions as to my evil nature.

As soon as I could read and write, my mother had me exiled to Pont-le-Voy, a school managed by Oratorians, who received children of my age into a class designated as that of the *Pas latins* (Latin steps), which also included scholars whose defective intelligence had precluded the rudiments. There I remained for eight years, seeing no one, and leading the life of a Pariah. And this was why: I had but three francs a month for pocket-money, a sum which barely sufficed for the pens, knives, rulers, ink and paper, with which we had to provide ourselves. And so, being unable to buy stilts, or ropes, or any of the things needed for school-boy amusements, I was banished from every game; to gain admittance I must either have toadied the rich or have flattered the strong boys in my division. Now the least idea of such meanness, which children so often drift into, raised my gorge.

I used to sit under a tree reading the books given out to us once a month by the librarian. How much anguish lay hidden in the depths of this unnatural isolation, what misery this desertion caused me! Imagine what my tender soul must have felt when, at the first distribution of prizes, I was awarded the two most anxiously looked for—that for composition and that for translation! When I went up to the platform to receive them, in the midst of applause and cheers, I had neither father nor mother to rejoice with me, while the room was full of my comrades' parents. Instead of kissing the visitor who distributed the prizes, as was usual, I threw myself on his breast and melted into tears. In the evening I burnt my laurel crowns in the stove. The other boys' parents stayed in the town during the week of examinations preceding the prize-giving, so that my school-fellows went off next morning in high glee; while I, whose parents were only a few leagues away, remained at school with the "*Outre-mers*" (over the seas), a name given to boys whose families lived in the islands or abroad. In the evening, while prayers were read, the barbarous little wretches would boast of the good dinners they had had at home.

You will see that my misfortunes went on growing in proportion to the circumference of the social spheres in which I moved. How many efforts have I not made to invalidate the sentence which condemned me to live in myself alone! How many hopes long cherished, with a thousand soul-felt aspirations, have been destroyed in a single day! To induce my parents to come to the school, I wrote them letters full of feeling, rather emphatically worded perhaps—but should these letters have drawn down on me my mother's reproaches and ironical comments on my style? Still, not discouraged, I promised to do all my parents insisted on as the conditions of a visit; I implored my sisters' aid, writing to them on their name-days and birthdays with the punctuality of a hapless, deserted child—but with vain persistency.

As the day for prize-giving approached, I made my entreaties more urgent, and wrote of my hopes of success. Deceived by my parents' silence I expected them with exultant hopes, telling my school-fellows that they were coming; and when, as family parties began to arrive, the old porter's step echoed along the passages I felt sick with anticipation. But the old man never uttered my name.

One day when I confessed that I had cursed my existence, the priest spoke to me of heaven, where the palm branch grows that the Saviour promised to the *Beati qui lugent.* So in preparing for my first communion, I threw myself into the mystic gulf of prayer, bewitched by religious notions, whose spiritual fairy dreams enchant the youthful mind. Fired with eager faith I besought God to renew in my favor the fascinating miracles of which I read in the history of martyrs. At five I had gone forth to a star; at twelve I was knocking at the door of the sanctuary. My ecstasy gave rise to unutterable dreams which supplied my imagination, gave fervor to my tenderness, and strengthened my thinking powers. I often ascribed these sublime visions to angels charged with fashioning my soul to divine ends, and they gave my eyes the power of seeing the inmost soul of things; they prepared my heart for the magic which makes the poet wretched when he has the fatal power of comparing what he feels with what exists, the great things he craves after with what he obtains; they wrote in my brain a book in which I have read what I was required to express; they touched my lips with the fire of the *improvisatore.*

My father having conceived some doubts as to the tendency of the Oratorian teaching, came to fetch me from Pont-le-Voy, and placed me in a boarding-house for boys in Paris, situated in the Marais. I was now fifteen. On examination as to my acquirements, the pupil from Pont-le-Voy was judged capable of entering the third class. The miseries I had endured at home, at day-school, and at Pont-le-Voy were renewed under a new aspect during my life at the pension Lepître. My father gave me no money. When my parents had ascertained that I could be fed, clothed, crammed with Latin and stuffed with Greek, that was enough. In the whole course of my career at school and college, I have known perhaps a thousand fellow-students, and I never heard of a case of such utter indifference.

Monsieur Lepître, a fanatical adherent of the Bourbons, had been thrown in my father's way at the time when some devoted royalists tried to rescue Queen Marie Antoinette from the Temple; they had since renewed their acquaintance. Hence Monsieur Lepître conceived it his duty to remedy my father's oversight; but the sum he allowed me monthly was small, for he did not know what my parents' intentions might be.

M. Lepître occupied a fine old house, the Hôtel Joyeuse, where, as in all the ancient residences of the nobility, there was a lodge for a gate-porter. During the hour of recreation, before the usher took us in a file to the Lyceum of Charlemagne, the wealthy boys got breakfast at the lodge, provided by the porter named Doisy. Monsieur Lepître either knew nothing of Doisy's business or he winked at it. The man was a perfect smuggler, made much of by the boys in their own interest; he was the screen for all our mischief, our confidant when we stole in after hours, our go-between with the lending library for prohibited books. Breakfast with a cup of coffee was in the most aristocratic taste, in consequence of the exorbitant price to which colonial products rose under Napoleon. If the use of coffee and of sugar was a luxury to our parents, in us it was a sign of such arrogant superiority as was enough to give us a passion for it, if the tendency to imitation, greediness, and the infection of fashion had not been enough. Doisy gave us credit; he supposed that every schoolboy must have sisters or aunts who would uphold his honor and pay his debts.

For a long time I resisted the blandishments of the coffee-bar. If my judges could have known the force of temptation, the heroic efforts of my soul to attain to such stoicism, and the suppressed rages of my long resistance, they would have dried away my tears instead of provoking them to flow.

But, boy as I was, could I have acquired the magnanimity which leads us to scorn the scorn of others? And I was also feeling, perhaps, the temptations of various social vices whose power was increased by my longing.

At the end of the second year my father and mother came to Paris. The day of their arrival was announced to me by my brother; he was living in Paris, but had not paid me a single visit. My sisters were to come, too, and we were all to see Paris together. The first day we were to dine at the Palais-Royal to be close to the Théâtre Français. In spite of the intoxicating delight of such a programme of unhoped-for joys, my glee was mitigated by the sense of a coming storm, which so easily blights those who are inured to troubles. I had to confess a debt of a hundred francs to the Sieur Doisy, who threatened to apply to my parents for the money. I determined to make use of my brother as Doisy's dragoman, to plead my repentance and mediate for forgiveness. My father was in favor of mercy; but my mother was relentless; her dark-blue eye petrified me, and she fulminated terrible forecasts.

"If I allowed myself such licenses at seventeen, what should I become later? Could I be a son of hers? Did I want to ruin the family? Was I the only child to be thought of? The career on which my brother Charles had embarked required an independent income, and he deserved it, for he had already done the family credit, while I should disgrace it. Did I know nothing of the value of the money I cost them? What benefit to my education would come of coffee and sugar? Was not such conduct an apprenticeship to every vice?" Marat was an angel as compared with me, so it seemed to me.

After enduring the shock of this torrent, which filled my soul with terrors, my brother took me back to the boarding-house, I lost my dinner at the café of the "Three Provençal Brothers," and was deprived of seeing Talma in "Britannicus." This was my interview with my mother after a parting of twelve years.

When I had gone through the "humanities," my father still left me in the care of Monsieur Lepître. I was to study higher mathematics, to work at law for a year, and begin the advanced branches.

Now, as a private boarder, and free from attending classes, I hoped for a truce between misery and me. But notwithstanding that I was now nineteen—or perhaps because I was nineteen—my father continued the system which had of old sent me to school without sufficient food, to college without pocket-money, and had run me into debt to Doisy. I had very little money at command, and what can be done in Paris without money? My liberty, too, was ingeniously fettered. Monsieur Lepître always sent me to the law-schools with an usher at my heels, who handed me over to the professor, and came again to escort me back. A girl would have been watched with less care than my mother's fears devised for my protection. Paris had justifiable terrors for my parents. Students are secretly interested in the self-same thoughts as fill the heads of school-girls; do what you will, a girl always talks of lovers, a youth of women.

But in Paris at that time the conversation of fellow-students was tinged by the Oriental and Sultan-like world of the Palais-Royal. The Palais-Royal was an Eldorado of love where ingots ready coined were current every evening. Virgin doubts were there enlightened, and there our curiosity might find gratification. The Palais-Royal and I were asymptotes, ever tending to meet, but never meeting.

This is how fate thwarted my hopes. My father had introduced me to one of my aunts, who lived in the Ile Saint-Louis, and I was to dine there every Thursday and Sunday, escorted thither by Madame or Monsieur Lepître, who went out themselves on those days, and called for me on their way home in the evening. A singular form of recreation! The

Marquise de Listomère was a very ceremonious fine lady, to whom it never occurred to make me a present of a crown-piece. As old as a cathedral, as much painted as a miniature, and magnificently dressed, she lived in her mansion just as though Louis XV. were still alive, seeing none but old ladies and gentlemen, a company of fossils among whom I felt as if I were in a cemetery. No one ever spoke to me, and I had not the courage to speak first. Cold looks of aversion made me feel ashamed of my youth, which was so annoying to all the others.

I hoped for the success of an escapade based on their indifference, making up my mind to steal off one evening directly after dinner and fly to the wooden galleries. My aunt, when once she was absorbed in whist, paid no further heed to me. Jean, her manservant, cared little enough for Monsieur Lepître; but those ill-starred dinners were, unfortunately, lengthy in consequence of the antiquity of the jaws or the weakness of the teeth of that ancient company.

At last, one evening between eight and nine, I had reached as far as the stairs, as tremulous as Bianca Capello when she made her escape; but just as the porter had let me out, I saw Monsieur Lepître's cab in the street, and the worthy man asking for me in his wheezy tones. Three times did fate come between the hell of the Palais-Royal and the paradise of my youth. On the day when, ashamed of being so ignorant, and already twenty, I determined to defy every peril to gain my end—at the very moment when I was about to evade Monsieur Lepître as he got into a hackney coach (a difficult matter, for he had a club-foot, and was as stout as Louis XVIII.)—who should appear but my mother, arriving in a post-chaise. I was riveted by her eye, and stood like a bird fascinated by a serpent.

What chance had led to this meeting? Nothing could be simpler. Napoleon was making a last effort. My father, foreseeing the return of the Bourbons, had come to explain matters to my brother, who was already embarked in diplomacy under the imperial rule. He had come from Tours with my mother. My mother had undertaken to convey me home, to remove me from the dangers which, to those who were keen enough to follow the advance of the enemy, seemed to threaten the capital.

Thus, in a few minutes I was snatched from Paris, just as my residence there would have proved fateful.

The torments of an imagination for ever agitated by thwarted desires, and the weariness of a life saddened by constant privations, had thrown me into study, just as in former times men weary of life shut themselves up in cloisters. Study had become a passion with me, which might have blighted me utterly by imprisoning me at an age when young men ought to be free to enjoy the activities of their natural springtime.

This slight sketch of my early years, in which you can imagine much sadness, was necessary to give you some idea of the effect of that training on my later life. Bearing the stamp of so many adverse influences, at the age of twenty I was stunted, thin, and pale. My spirit, full of cravings, struggled with a body which was frail indeed in appearance, but which—as an old doctor of Tours was wont to say— was going through the last annealing process of an iron temperament. Young in body and old in mind, I had read and thought so much, that I was metaphysically familiar with life in its highest summits, just when I was about to explore the tortuous difficulties of its narrow passes and the sandy ways of its plains. Exceptional chances had kept me late in that delightful phase when the soul is conscious of its first agitation, when it is opening to its first raptures, when everything is fresh and full of savor. I was standing between boyhood prolonged by study and manhood late in showing its green shoots. No young man was ever more fully prepared than I to feel and to love.

To fully understand my narrative, think of me at the charming age when the lips are pure from falsehood, when the eyes are honest though veiled by lids weighed down by shyness in conflict with desire, when the spirit is not yet abject before jesuitical worldliness, and when the heart is as timid as its first impulses are vehemently generous.

I need say nothing of my journey from Paris to Tours with my mother. Her cold demeanor crushed the effusiveness of my affection. As we started afresh after each relay, I resolved to talk to her; but a look or a word scared away the phrases I had composed as a beginning. At Orleans, where we were to sleep, my mother reproached me for my silence. I fell at her knees and clasped them, shedding hot tears; I poured out my heart to her, bursting with affection; I tried to soften her by the eloquence of my pleading; starving for love, my words might have stirred the soul of a stepmother. My mother told me I was acting a farce. I complained of her neglect; she called me an unnatural son. There was such a cold grip about my heart that at Blois I went out on the bridge to throw myself into the Loire. I was put off from suicide simply by the height of the parapet.

On my arrival, my two sisters, who scarcely knew me, showed more surprise than warmth; later, however, by comparison they seemed to me full of kindliness. I was given a bedroom on the third floor. You will understand the extent of my wretchedness when I tell you that my mother left me, a grown man, with no linen but my shabby college outfit, and no wardrobe but what I had brought from Paris.

When I flew from one end of the drawing-room to the other to pick up her handkerchief, she gave me thanks as cold as she might have granted to a servant. Watching her anxiously as I did, to discover whether there were in her heart a friable spot where I could insert some buds of affection, I saw her a tall, parched, thin woman; a gambler, selfish and insolent—like all the Listomères, in whom impertinence is part of their dower. She saw nothing in life but duties to be performed; every cold-hearted woman I have ever met has made duty her religion, as she did; she accepted our adoration as a priest accepts incense at mass; my elder brother seemed to have absorbed the modicum of maternal feeling her heart could contain. She was constantly inflicting small stings of biting irony, the weapon of heartless people, which she freely used on us who could not retort.

In spite of all these thorny barriers, instinctive feeling is held by so many roots, the pious terror inspired by a mother includes so many ties—indeed, to give her up as hopeless is too cruel a shock—that the sublime blunder of loving her lasted till a day when at a riper age we judged her truly. Then began her children's reprisals. Their indifference, resulting from the disenchantment of the past, enhanced by the slimy wreckage they have rescued from it, overflows her tomb even.

This frightful despotism drove out the voluptuous dreams I had madly hoped to realize at Tours. I flung myself desperately into my father's library, where I read all the books I did not already know. My long hours of study spared me all contact with my mother; but they left me, morally, worse off than ever. My eldest sister, who has since married our cousin the Marquis de Listomère, sometimes tried to comfort me without being able to soothe the irritation from which I suffered. I longed for death.

Great events, of which I knew nothing, were then in the air. The Duc d'Angoulême, having left Bordeaux to join Louis XVIII. in Paris, was to be the recipient of the ovations prepared by the enthusiasm that possessed France on the return of the Bourbons. Touraine in a ferment round its legitimate princes, the town in a turmoil, the windows hung with flags, the residents all in their best, the preparations for the fête, the indefinable something in the air which mounted to my head, all made me long to be present at the ball that was to be given to the Prince. When, greatly daring, I expressed this wish to my mother—at that time too ill to go out—she was extremely wroth. Had I dropped from the Congo, that I knew nothing of what was going on? How could I imagine that the family would not be fitly represented at the ball? In the absence of my father and brother, of course it would be my part to go. Had I no mother? Did she never think of her children's happiness? In a moment the almost disowned son had become a person of importance. I was as much amazed by finding myself of consequence as by the deluge of ironical reasoning with which my mother received my request.

I questioned my sisters, and heard that my mother, who liked theatrical surprises, had necessarily considered the matter of my dress. The tailors of Tours, in the sudden rush of customers, could none of them undertake to fit me out. So my mother had sent for a needlewoman, who, as usual in provincial towns, was supposed to be able to do every kind of sewing. A blue coat was secretly made for me, more or less successfully. Silk stockings and new pumps were easly procured; men wore their waistcoats short, and I could have one of my father's; for the first time in my life I donned a shirt with a goffered frill that gave importance to my figure and was lost in the folds of my cravat. When I was dressed, I was so little like myself that my sisters' compliments gave me courage to make my appearance before the whole of assembled Touraine.

It was a formidable enterprise! But too many were called to this festivity to allow of there being many elect. Thanks to my slender figure, I was able to creep into a tent in the gardens of the Maison Papion, and got close to the armchair in which the Prince was enthroned. In an instant I was stifled by the heat, dazzled by the lights, by the crimson hangings, the gilt ornaments, the dresses and the diamonds of the first public function I had ever attended. I was pushed about by a throng of men and women, all hustling and crowding each other in a cloud of dust. The blatant brass and Bourbon strains of the military band were drowned by shouts of—

"Hurrah for the Duc d'Angoulême! Long live the King! Hurrah for the Bourbons!"

The fête was an outbreak of enthusiasm in which every one vied with the rest in his vehement eagerness to hail the rising sun of the Bourbons, a display of party selfishness that left me cold, made me feel small, and shrink into myself.

Carried away like a straw in a whirlpool, I was childishly wishing that I were the Duc d'Angoulême, and could mingle with these princes thus made a show of to the staring crowd. This silly provincial fancy gave rise to an ambition dignified by my character and by circumstances. Who might not have coveted this worship, repeated on a more splendid scale a few months later when all Paris rushed to greet the Emperor on his return from the island of Elba? This supreme power over the masses, whose feelings and vitality discharge themselves into one soul, made me a sudden devotee to Glory, the goddess who puts the French to the sword nowadays, as the Druidess of old sacrificed the Gauls.

And then, as suddenly, I saw the woman who was fated to goad perpetually my ambitious hopes and to crown them by throwing me into contact with royalty.

Too shy to ask any one to dance with me, and fearing, too, that I might make confusion in the figures, I naturally felt very awkward, not knowing what to do with myself. Just when I was most conscious of the fatigue of constantly moving under the pressure of the crowd, an officer trod on my feet, which were swollen by the pressure of my shoes and by the heat. This crowning annoyance disgusted me with the whole affair. It was impossible to get away and I took refuge in a corner at the extreme end of a vacant bench, where I sat down, my gaze fixed, motionless, and sulky. A woman, misled by my delicate looks, took me for a boy half-asleep while awaiting my mother's pleasure, and seated herself by me with the light movement of a bird settling on its nest. I was at once aware of a feminine fragrance which flashed upon my soul as Oriental poetry has flashed upon it since. I looked at my neighbor, and was more dazzled by her than I had been by the ball.

If you have at all entered into my previous life, you can guess the emotions that swelled my heart. My eyes were suddenly fascinated by white rounded shoulders that made me long to bury my face in them, shoulders faintly pink, as if they were blushing to find themselves bare for the first time, bashful shoulders with a soul of their own and a satin skin shining in the light like a silken fabric. Between these shoulders ran a furrow which my eyes, bolder than my hand, glided into. My heart beat as I stood up to look over them, and I was entirely captivated by a bosom modestly covered with gauze, perfect in roundness, and bluely veined as it lay softly bedded in lace frills. The least details of the charming head were allurements stirring me to endless delight: the sheen of the hair knotted above a neck as peach-like as a little girl's, the white partings made by the comb along which my imagination played as in a new-made path—everything together turned my brain.

Looking around to make sure that no one saw me, I buried my face in that back as a baby hides in its mother's breast, and kissed those shoulders all over, rubbing my cheek against them. The lady gave a piercing cry, inaudible above the music; she turned sharply round, saw me, and said, "Monsieur!"

If she had said, "My good boy, what possesses you?" I should perhaps have killed her; but this word *Monsieur* brought hot tears to my eyes.

I was petrified by a look fired with righteous anger, and an exquisite face crowned with a plait of fair brown hair, in harmony with those adorable shoulders. The crimson of offended modesty flamed in her face, which was already softening with a woman's forgiveness for a mad act when she is the cause of it, and when she sees a passion of worship in the tears of repentance. She arose and walked away with the dignity of a queen.

Then I understood how ridiculous was my position; then, and not till then, I felt that I was dressed like a Savoyard's monkey. I was ashamed. I sat there quite stupefied, relishing the apple I had stolen, feeling on my lips the warmth of the blood I had scented; quite unrepentant, and following with my eyes this being come down from heaven. Then, overpowered by this first physical indulgence of my heart's wild fever, I wandered through the ball-room, now a desert, without finding the unknown vision. I went home and to bed, an altered creature.

A new soul, a soul with iridescent wings, had burst its chrysalis within me. My favorite star, dropping from the blue waste where I had admired it, had become woman, while preserving its light, its sparkle, and its brilliancy. Suddenly, knowing nothing of love, I had fallen in love. Is not this first irruption of the most intense feeling a man can know a very strange thing? I had met some pretty women in my aunt's drawing-room; they had not made the slightest impression on me. Is there an hour, a conjunction of the stars, a combination of fitting circumstances, a particular woman above all other women, which seal a passion as exclusive at the age when passion includes the whole female sex?

As I thought that my chosen lady dwelt in Touraine, I inhaled the air with rapture; I saw a blue in the sky which I have never since perceived elsewhere.

Though mentally I was in ecstacy, I seemed to be very ill; my mother was at once alarmed and remorseful. Like animals aware of approaching distemper, I would creep into a corner of the garden to dream of the kisses I had stolen. A few days after the memorable ball my mother began to ascribe my neglect of study, my indifference to her searching looks, my heedlessness of her irony, and my gloomy behavior to the natural development of a growing man. Country air, the universal remedy for every malady of which science can give no account, was regarded as the best means of curing me of my apathy. My mother decided that I should spend a few days at Frapesle, a château on the Indre, between Montvazon and Azay-le-Rideau, with a friend of hers, to whom, no doubt, she gave her private instructions.

On the day when I was thus given the key of the fields, I had plunged so deeply into the ocean of love that I had crossed it. I knew not my fair one's name; what could I call her or where could I find her? To whom, indeed, could I speak of her? My natural shyness increased the unaccountable terrors which possess a young heart at the first flutter of love, and made me begin with the melancholy which is the end of a hopeless passion. I was quite content to come and go and wander about the country, with the childlike spirit that is ready for anything and has a certain tinge of chivalry; I was prepared to hunt through all the country-houses of Touraine, wandering on foot, and saying at each pretty turret, "It will be there!"

So one Thursday morning I left Tours by the Saint-Eloy gate, I crossed the bridges of Saint-Sauveur, I reached Poncher, my nose in the air in front of every house I passed, and was on the road to Chinon. For the first time in my life I could rest under a tree, walk fast or slowly as I wished without being called to account by any one. To a poor creature so utterly crushed by the various despotisms which weigh more or less on every young life, the first taste of freedom, though exerted in trifles, brought unspeakable expansion to my soul.

Several reasons combined to make that a high day full of delights. In my childhood my walks had never taken me more than a league out of the town. My excursions in the neighborhood of Pont-le-Voy and the walks I had taken in Paris had not surfeited me with rural beauty. Nevertheless, I had retained from the earliest impressions of my life a strong feeling of the beauty inherent in the scenery round Tours, with which I was familiar. Thus, though I was new to what constitutes the poetry of a site, I was unconsciously exacting, as men are who have conceived of the ideal of an art without ever having practiced it.

To go to the château of Frapesle, those who walk or ride shorten the way by crossing the common known as the Landes de Charlemagne, a waste lying at the top of the plateau which divides the valley of the Cher from that of the Indre, and which is reached by a cross-road from Champy. This flat and sandy down, depressing enough for about a league, ends in a coppice adjoining the road to Saché, the village nearest to Frapesle. This country-lane, leading into the Chinon road at some distance beyond Ballan, skirts an undulating plain devoid of remarkable features as far as the hamlet of Artanne. Thence a valley opens down to the Loire, from Montvazon at the head; the hills seem to rebound under the country-houses on each range of slopes; it is a glorious emerald basin, and at the bottom the Indre winds in serpentine curves. I was startled by the view into a rapturous astonishment for which the dullness of the Landes or the fatigue of my walk had prepared me: If this woman, the flower of her sex, inhabits a spot on earth, it must be this!

At the thought I leaned against a walnut tree; and now, whenever I revisit that beloved valley, I go to rest under its boughs. Under that tree, the confidant of all my thoughts, I examine myself as to the changes that may have taken place during the time that has elapsed since last I left it.

My heart had not deceived me: it was there that she dwelt;

the first château I could see on a shelf of the down was her home. When I sat down under my walnut tree, the noonday sun struck sparks from the slates of *her* roof and the glass panes of *her* windows. Her cambric dress was the white spot I could see among some vines under a pleached alley. She was, as you know already, though as yet you know nothing, the Lily of this Valley, where she grew for heaven, filling it with the fragrance of her virtues. I saw an emblem of infinite love with nothing to keep it alive but an object only once seen, in the long watery ribbon which glistens in the sun between two green banks, in the rows of poplars which deck that vale of love with moving tracery, in the oak woods thrust forward between the vineyards on the hillsides rounded by the river into constant variety, and in the soft outlines crossing each other and fading to the horizon.

If you wish to see nature fair and virginal as a bride, go thither some spring day; if you want to solace the bleeding wounds of your heart, return in the late days of autumn. In spring love flutters his wings under the open sky; in autumn we dream of those who are no more. Weak lungs inhale a healing freshness, the eye finds rest on golden-hued groves from which the soul borrows sweet peace.

At the moment when I looked down on the valley of the Indre, the mills on its falls gave voice to the murmuring vale; the poplars laughed as they swayed; there was not a cloud in the sky; the birds sang, the grasshoppers chirped, everything was melody. Never ask me again why I love Touraine. I do not love it as we love our childhood's home, nor as we love an oasis in the desert; I love it as an artist loves art. I love it less than I love you; still, but for Touraine, perhaps I should not now be alive.

Without knowing why, my eyes were riveted to the white spot, to the woman who shone in that garden as the bell of a convolvulus shines among shrubs and is blighted by a touch. My soul deeply stirred, I went down into this bower and presently saw a village, which to my highly strung poetic mood seemed matchless. Picture to yourself three mills, charmingly situated among pretty islets with imbayed banks, and crowned with clumps of trees, in the midst of a meadow of water; for what other name can I give to the aquatic vegetation, so brightly tinted, which carpets the stream, floats on its surface, follows its eddies, yields to its caprices, and bends to the turmoil of waters lashed by the mill-wheels. Here and there rise shoals of pebbles on which the river breaks in a fringe of surf reflecting the sun. Amaryllis, water-lilies, white and yellow, reeds, and phlox dress the banks with glorious hues. A crumbling bridge of rotting timbers, its piles hung with flowers, its balustrade covered with herbage and velvety mosses, and hanging over the stream, but not yet fallen; time-worn boats, fishing-nets, the monotonous song of a shepherd, ducks paddling from isle to isle, or preening themselves on the shoals—*le jard*, as the coarse gravel deposited by the Loire is called; miller's men, a cap over one ear, loading their mules; every detail made the scene strikingly artless. Then, beyond the bridge, imagine two or three farms, a dovecote, sundry turrets, thirty houses or more, standing apart in gardens divided by hedges of honeysuckle, jessamine, and clematis; heaps of manure in front of every door, and domestic fowls in the road—and you see the village of Pont-du-Ruan, a pretty hamlet crowned with an old church of characteristic style, a church of the time of the Crusades, such as painters love for their pictures. Set it all in the midst of ancient walnut trees, of young poplars with their pale, gold foliage, add some elegant dwellings rising from broad meadows where the eye loses itself under the warm misty sky, and you will have some idea of the thousand beauties of this lovely country.

I followed the lane to Saché along the left bank of the river, noting the details of the hills that broke the line of the opposite shore. At last I reached a park of venerable trees which showed me that I was at Frapesle. I arrived exactly as the bell was ringing for late breakfast. After this meal, my host, never suspecting that I had come from Tours on foot, took me all over his grounds, and from every part of them I could see the valley under various aspects; here through a vista and there spread out before me. In many places my gaze was attracted to the horizon by the broad golden tide of the Loire, where between the rolling hills sails showed their fantastic shapes flying before the wind. As I climbed a ridge I could admire for the first time the château of Azay, a diamond with a thousand facets with the Indre for a setting, and perched on piles buried in flowers. There in a dell I saw the romantic mass of the château of Saché, a melancholy spot, full of harmonies too sad for superficial minds, but dear to poets whose spirit is stricken. I myself at a later time loved its silence, its huge hoary trees and the mystery that seemed to hang over that deserted hollow. And still, each time I caught sight, on the shoulder of the next hill, of the pretty little château I had seen and chosen at a first glance, my eye lingered on it with delight.

"Oh, ho!" said my host, reading in my eyes an eager desire such as a youth of my age expresses without guile, "you scent a pretty woman from afar as a dog scents game."

I did not like the tone of this remark, but I asked the name of the place and of the owner.

"It is Clochegourde," said he, "a pretty house belonging to the Comte de Mortsauf, the representative of a family noted in the history of Touraine, whose fortune dates from the time of Louis XI., and whose name reveals the adventure to which he owes his arms and his fame. He is descended from a man who survived hanging. The arms borne by the Mortsaufs are: *Or*, on a cross potent and counter-potent, *sable*, a fleur-de-lys rooted, of the field. Motto, *Dieu saulve le Roi notre Sire* (God save our Sire the King).

"The Count came to settle here on the return of the

émigrés. The house of Lenoncourt-Givry becomes extinct in his wife, who was a Demoiselle de Lenoncourt; Madame de Mortsauf is an only child. The small wealth of this family is in such strong contrast to the splendor of their names that from pride—or perhaps from necessity—they always live at Clochegourde, and see no one. Hitherto their devotion to the Bourbons may have justified their isolation; but I doubt whether the King's return will change their way of living. When I settled here last year I paid them a call of politeness; they returned it and asked us to dinner. Then the winter kept us apart for some months and political events delayed our return, for I have only lately come home to Frapesle. Madame de Mortsauf is a woman who might take the first place anywhere."

"Does she often go to Tours?"

"She never goes there. Yes," he added, correcting himself, "she went there quite lately, on the occasion when the Duc d'Angoulême passed through, and was very gracious to Monsieur de Mortsauf."

"It is she!" I cried.

"She! Who?"

"A woman with beautiful shoulders."

"You will find many women with beautiful shoulders in Touraine," said he, laughing; "but if you are not tired, we can cross the river and go up to Clochegourde, where you may possibly recognize your fine shoulders."

I agreed, not without reddening from pleasure and shyness. By about four o'clock we reached the house on which my eyes had so fondly lingered. This little château, which looked well in the landscape, is, in fact, a modest building. It has five windows in front; that at each end of the south front projects by about two yards, giving the effect of wings and adding to the importance of the house. The middle window serves as the door, whence double steps lead to a garden extending in terraces down to a meadow bordering the Indre.

Though this meadow is divided by a lane from the lowest terrace shaded by a row of ailanthus and acacia trees, it looks like part of the grounds, for the lane is sunk between the terrace on one side and a thick hedge on the other. The slope between the house and the river is taken advantage of to avoid the inconvenience of being so near the water without losing the pretty effect. Under the dwelling-house are the stables, coach-houses, storerooms, and kitchens, with doors under archways.

The roof is pleasingly curved at the angles, the dormer windows have carved mullions, and finials of lead over the gables. The slates, neglected no doubt during the revolution, are covered with the rust-colored and orange, clinging lichens that grow on houses facing the south. The glazed door at the top of the steps has above it a little campanile on which may be seen the achievement of the Blamont-Chauvrys: Quarterly *gules*, a pale *vair* between two hands proper, and *or*, two lances *sable* in chevron. The motto, *See, but touch not*, struck me strangely. The supporters, a griffin and a dragon chained *or*, had a good effect in sculpture. The revolution had damaged the ducal coronet and the crest, a palm branch *vert* fruited *or*. Senart, secretary to the Committee of Public Safety, was bailiff of Saché till 1781, which accounts for this destruction.

The decorative character gives an elegant appearance to this country-house, as delicately finished as a flower, and hardly seeming to weigh on the ground. Seen from the valley, the first floor looks as if it were the second floor; but on the side toward the courtyard it is on the same level as the wide path ending in a lawn graced with raised flower-beds. To right and left vineyards, orchards, and some arable land dotted with walnut trees slope away steeply, surrounding the house with verdure down to the brink of the river, which is bordered on this side with clumps of trees whose various tints of green have been grouped by the hand of nature.

As I mounted the winding road to Clochegourde, I admired these well-assorted masses, and breathed an atmosphere redolent of happiness. Has our moral nature, like physical nature, electric discharges and swift changes of temperature? My heart throbbed in anticipation of the secret events which were about to transform it once for all, as animals grow sportive before fine weather. This, the most important day in my life, was not devoid of any circumstance that could contribute to sanctify it. Nature had dressed herself like a maiden going forth to meet her beloved; my soul had heard her voice for the first time, my eyes had admired her, as fruitful, as various as my imagination had painted her in those day-dreams at school of which I have told you something, but too little to explain their influence over me, for they were as an apocalypse, figuratively predicting my life; every incident of it, happy or sad, is connected with them by some whimsical image, by ties visible only to the eye of the soul.

We crossed an outer court, enclosed by the outbuildings of a rural habitation—a granary, a winepress, cow-houses, and stables. A servant, warned by the barking of a watchdog, came out to meet us, and told us that Monsieur le Comte, who had gone to Azay in the morning, would presently return, no doubt, and that Madame la Comtesse was at home. My host looked at me. I trembled to think that he might not choose to call on Madame de Mortsauf in her husband's absence, but he bade the servant to announce our names.

Driven by childish eagerness, I hurried into the long anteroom which ran across the house.

"Come in, pray," said a golden voice.

Although Madame de Mortsauf had spoken but one word at the ball, I recognized her voice, which sank into my soul and filled it as a sunbeam fills and gilds a prisoner's cell. Then, reflecting that she might recognize me, I longed to fly; it was too late; she appeared at the drawing-room door, and our eyes met. Which of us reddened most deeply I do not know. She returned to her seat in front of an embroidery frame, the servant having pushed forward two chairs; she finished drawing her needle through as an excuse for her silence, counted two or three stitches, and then raised her head, that was at once proud and gentle, to ask Monsieur de Chessel to what happy chance she owed the pleasure of his visit.

Though curious to know the truth as to my appearance there, she did not look at either of us; her eyes were fixed on the river; but from the way she listened, it might have been supposed that she had the faculty of the blind, and knew all the agitations of my soul by the least accent of speech. And this was the fact.

Monsieur de Chessel mentioned my name and sketched my biography. I had come to Tours some few months since with my parents, who had brought me home when the war threatened Paris. She saw in me a son of Touraine, to whom the province was unknown, a young man exhausted by excessive work, sent to Frapesle to rest and amuse myself, and to whom he had shown his estate, as it was my first visit. I had told him, only on reaching the bottom of the hill, that I had walked from Tours that morning; and fearing overfatigue, as my health was feeble, he had ventured to call at Clochegourde, thinking she would allow me to rest there. Monsieur de Chessel spoke the exact truth. But a genuinely happy chance seems so elaborate an invention, that Madame de Mortsauf was still distrustful; she looked at me with eyes so cold and stern that I lowered mine, as much from a vague sense of humiliation as to hide the tears I withheld from falling. The haughty lady saw that my brow was moist with sweat; perhaps, too, she guessed the tears, for she offered me any refreshment I might need with a comforting kindness which restored my powers of speech.

I blushed like a girl caught in the wrong, and in a voice,

quavering like an old man's, I replied with thanks, but declining anything.

"All I wish," I said, raising my eyes, which met hers for the second time, but for an instant as short as a lightning-flash, "is that you will allow me to remain here; I am so stiff with fatigue that I cannot walk."

"How can you doubt the hospitality of our lovely province?" said she. "You will perhaps give us the pleasure of seeing you at dinner at Clochegourde?" she added to her neighbor.

I flashed a look at my friend, a look so full of entreaty that he beat about the bush a little to accept this invitation, which, by its form, required a refusal.

Though knowledge of the world enabled Monsieur de Chessel to distinguish so subtle a shade, an inexperienced youth believes so firmly in the identity of word and thought in a handsome woman that I was immensely surprised when, as we went home in the evening, my host said, half-jokingly, to me—

"I stayed because you were dying to do so; but if you cannot patch matters up, I may be in a scrape with my neighbors."

This "if you cannot patch matters up" gave me matter for thought. If Madame de Mortsauf liked me, she could not be annoyed with the man who had introduced me to her. So Monsieur de Chessel thought I might be able to interest her —was not this enough to give me the power? This solution confirmed my hopes at a moment when I needed such support.

"That is hardly possible," replied Monsieur de Chessel, "my wife expects us."

"She has you every day," replied the Countess, "and we can send her a message. Is she alone?"

"She has the Abbé de Quélus with her."

"Very well, then," said she, rising to ring the bell, "you will dine with us."

This time Monsieur de Chessel thought her sincere, and gave me a look of congratulation.

As soon as I was certain of spending a whole evening under this roof, I felt as if eternity were mine. To many an unhappy wretch to-morrow is a word devoid of meaning, and at this moment I was one of those who have no belief in tomorrow; when I had a few hours to call my own, I crowded a lifetime of rapture into them.

Madame de Mortsauf then began to talk of the country, of the crops, of the vines—subjects to which I was a stranger. In the mistress of a house this behavior argues want of breeding, or else contempt for the person she thus shuts out of the conversation, but in the Countess it was simply embarrassment. Though at first I fancied she was affecting to regard me as a boy, and envied the privilege of thirty years, which allowed Monsieur de Chessel to entertain his fair neighbor with such serious matters, of which I understood nothing, and though I tormented myself by thinking that everything was done for him; within a few months I knew all that a woman's silence can mean and how many thoughts are disguised by desultory conversation.

I at once tried to sit at my ease in my chair; then I perceived the advantage of my position, and gave myself up to the delight of hearing the Countess' voice. The breath of her soul lurked behind the procession of syllables, as sound is divided in the notes of a keyed flute; it died undulating on the ear, whence it seemed to drive the blood. Her way of pronouncing words ending in *i* was like the song of birds; her pronunciation of *ch* was like a caress; and the way in which spoke the letter *t* betrayed a despotic heart. She unconsciously expanded the meaning of words, and led one's spirit away into a supernatural world. How often have I permitted a discussion to go on which I might have ended; how often have I allowed myself to be unjustly blamed, merely to hear that music of the human voice, to breathe the air that came from her lips so full of her soul, to clasp that spoken light with as much ardor as I could have thrown into pressing the Countess to my heart! What a song, as of some joyful swallow, when she could laugh; but what a ring, as of a swan calling to its fellow-swans, when she spoke of her sorrows!

The Countess' inattention to me allowed me to study her. My eyes feasted as they gazed at the lovely speaker; they embraced her form, kissed her feet, played with the ringlets of her hair. And all the time I was a prey to the terror which only those can understand who have, in the course of their lives, known the immeasurable joys of a genuine passion. I was afraid lest she should detect my gaze fixed on the spot between her shoulders which I had kissed so ardently. My fear whetted the temptation, and I yielded to it. I looked, my eye rent the stuff of her dress, and I saw a mole that marked the top of the pretty line between her shoulders, a speck lying on milk; this, ever since the ball, had blazed out of the darkness in which the sleep of youths seems to float when their imagination is ardent and their life chaste.

I can sketch for you the principal features which would everywhere have attracted attention to the Countess; but the most exact drawing, the warmest glow of color, would express nothing of it. Her face is one of those of which no one could give a true portrait but the impossible artist whose hand can paint the glow of inward fires, and render the luminous essence which science denies, which language has no word for, but which a lover sees. Her mass of fine, fair hair often gave her headaches, caused no doubt by a sudden rush of blood to the head. Her rounded forehead, prominent like that of La Gioconda, seemed to be full of unspoken ideas, of suppressed feelings—flowers drowned in bitter waters. Her eyes were greenish, with spots of hazel, and always pale in color; but when her children were concerned, of if she was betrayed into any vehement emotion of joy or grief, rare in the life of a resigned wife, her eye could flash with a subtle flame, which seemed to have derived its fire from the deepest springs of life, and which would, no doubt, dry them up; a lightning gleam that has wrung tears from me when she shed on me her terrible disdain, and that she found adequate to abash the boldest gaze.

A Greek nose that Phidias might have chiseled, joined by a double curve to lips of exquisite shape, gave strength to her oval face; and her complexion, like a camellia-petal, was charmingly tinted with tender rose in the cheeks. She was not thin, but this did not detract from the grace of her figure, nor from the roundness that made every outline beautiful, though fully developed. You will at once understand the character of this perfection when I tell you that at the junction with the upper arm of the dazzling bosom that had bewitched me, there could be no roll nor wrinkle. Her throat, where her head was set on, showed none of those hollows that make some women's necks look like tree-trunks; the muscles showed no cords, and every line was curved with a grace as distracting to the eyes as to the painter's brush. A delicate down died away on her cheeks and on the back of her neck, catching the light with a silky sheen. Her ears were small and shapely—the ears of a slave and of a mother, she used to say. Later, when I dwelt in her heart, she would say, "Here comes Monsieur de Mortsauf," and be quite right, when I could as yet hear nothing—I, whose hearing is remarkably keen. Her arms were beautiful; her hands, with their turned-up finger-tips, were long, and the nails set into the flesh as in antique statues.

I should offend you by attributing greater beauty to a flat figure than to a full one, but that you are an exception. A round figure is a sign of strength; but women who are built so are imperious, willful, and voluptuous rather than tender. Women who are flatly formed are, on the contrary, self-sacrificing, full of refinement, and inclined to melancholy; they are more thoroughly women. A flat figure is soft and supple;

a full one is rigid and jealous. Now you know the kind of shape she had. She had the foot of a lady, a foot that walks little, is easily tired, and is engaging to look upon when it peeps from under the petticoat.

Though she was the mother of two children, I have never met with any woman more genuinely maidenly. Her expression was so girlish, and at the same time amazed and dreamy, that it brought the eye back to gaze, as a painter invites it back to a face in which his genius has embodied a world of feelings. Her visible qualities, indeed, can only be expressed by comparisons. Do you remember the wild, austere fragrance of a heath we plucked on our way home from the Villa Diodati, a flower you admired so much for its coloring of pink and black—then you will understand how this woman could be elegant though so far from the world, natural in her expressions, refining all that came to belong to her—pink and black. Her frame had the green tenderness we admire in leaves but just opened; her mind had the intense concentration of a savage's; she was a child in feeling sobered by grief, the mistress of the house, and an unwedded soul.

She was charming without artifice in her way of sitting down, of rising, of being silent, or of throwing out a remark. Habitually reserved, and vigilant as the sentinel on whom the safety of all depends, ever on the watch for disaster, she sometimes smiled in a way that betrayed a laughing spirit buried under the demeanor required by her mode of life. Her womanly vanity had become a mystery; she inspired romance instead of the gallant attentions which most women love; she revealed her genuine self, her living fire, her blue dreams, as the sky shows between the parting clouds. This involuntary self-betrayal made a man thoughtful, unless, indeed, he were conscious of an unshed tear, dried by the fire of his passion.

The rareness of her movements, and yet more of her looks— for she never looked at anybody but her children—gave incredible solemnity to all she did and said, when she did or said a thing with that manner which a woman can assume if she is compromising her dignity by an avowal.

Madame de Mortsauf was, on that day, wearing a cambric gown with fine pink stripes, a collar with a broad hem, a black sash and black shoes. Her hair was simply twisted into a knot and held by a tortoise-shell comb.

There is the promised sketch. But the constant emanation of her spirit on all who were about her, that nourishing element diffused in waves as the sun diffuses its light, her essential nature, her attitude in serene hours, her resignation in a storm, all the chances of life which develop character, depend, like atmospheric changes, on unexpected and transient circumstances which have no resemblance to each other excepting in the background against which they are seen. This will inevitably be depicted as part of the incidents of this narrative—a true domestic epic, as great in the sight of the wise as tragedies are in the eyes of the crowd; a tale which will interest you, both by the part I played in it and by its resemblance to that of many a woman's destiny.

Everything at Clochegourde was characterized by English neatness. The drawing-room in which the Countess was sitting was paneled throughout and painted in two shades of stone color. On the chimney-shelf stood a clock in a mahogany case surmounted by a tazza, and flanked by two large white-and-gold china jars in which stood two Cape heaths. On the console was a lamp; in front of the fireplace a backgammon board. Thick cotton ropes looped back the plain white calico curtains without any trimmings. Holland covers, bound with green galoon, were over all the chairs, and the worsted work stretched on the Countess' frame sufficiently revealed the reason for so carefully hiding the furniture. This simplicity was really dignified. No room, of all I have seen since, has ever filled me with such a rush of pregnant impressions as I then felt crowding on me in that drawing-room at Clochegourde—a room as still and remote as its mistress' life, and telling of the monastic regularity of her occupations. Most of my ideas, even my most daring flights in science or in politics, have had their birth there, as perfumes emanate from flowers; and here grew the unknown plant which shed its fertilizing power over me; here glowed the solar heat which developed all that was good and dried up all that was bad in me.

From the window the view extended over the valley from the hill where Pont-de-Ruan lies scattered, to the château of Azay, and the eye could follow the curves of the opposite downs varied by the turrets of Frapesle, the church, village, and manor-house of Saché towering above the meadow-land. The scene, in harmony with a peaceful existence, unvaried by any emotions but those of family life, breathed peace into the soul. If I had seen her for the first time here, between the Comte de Mortsauf and her children, instead of discovering her in the splendor of her ball dress, I could not have stolen that delirious kiss, for which at this moment I felt some remorse, believing that it might wreck the future prospects of my passion! No, in the gloomy temper begotten of my sad life, I should have knelt before her, have kissed her little shoes, have dropped some tears on them, and, without trepidation, fear or regret, have thrown myself into the Indre.

But, having breathed the jessamine freshness of her skin and tasted the milk in that cup of love, my soul was filled with longing and hope for human joys: I would live, I would wait for the hour of fulfillment as a savage looks out for the moment of revenge. I longed to swing from the branches, to rush among the vines, to wallow in the Indre; my companions should be the silence of the night, the languor of living, the heat of the sun, that I might eat at my leisure the delicious apple I had bitten into. If she had asked me for the singing-flower, or the riches buried by Morgan the destroyer, I would have found them for her only to obtain the real riches, the speechless blossom that I longed for.

When I roused myself from the dream into which I had been thrown by contemplating my idol, during which a servant had come in to speak to her, I heard her talking of the Count. Then only did it strike me that a woman belonged to her husband. The thought made my brain reel. I felt a fierce but dreary curiosity to see the possessor of this treasure. Two feelings were uppermost—hatred and fear; hatred, which recognized no obstacle and measured every difficulty without dread; fear, vague indeed but genuine, of the coming struggle, of its result, and, above all, of Her. A prey to indescribable presentiments, I dreaded the handshaking which is so undignified; I had visions of those elastic difficulties against which the firmest will is battered and blunted; I feared the power of inertia, which in our day deprives social life of the moments of climax that passionate souls crave for.

"Here comes Monsieur de Mortsauf," said she.

I started to my feet like a frightened horse. Though this impulse did not escape the notice of either Monsieur de Chessel or the Countess, I was spared any speechless comment, for a diversion was effected by a little girl, of about six years old as I supposed, who came in saying—

"Here is my father."

"Well, Madeleine?" said her mother.

The child gave her hand to Monsieur de Chessel when he held out his, and looked at me fixedly after making an astonished little curtsey.

"Are you satisfied with her health?" said Monsieur de Chessel to the Countess.

"She is better," replied the mother, stroking the little girl's hair as she sat huddled in her lap.

A question from Monsieur de Chessel taught me the fact that Madeleine was nine years old; I showed some surprise at my mistake, and my astonishment brought a cloud to the mother's brow. My friend shot me one of those looks by which men of the world give us a second education. This was, no doubt, a mother's wound which might not be opened or touched. A frail creature, with colorless eyes and a skin as white as porcelain lighted from within, Madeleine would probably not have lived in the air of a town. Country air, and the care with which her mother brooded over her, had kept the flame alive in a body as delicate as a plant grown in a hot-house in defiance of the severity of a northern climate. Though she was not at all like her mother, she seemed to have her mother's spirit, and that sustained her. Her thin, black hair, sunken eyes, hollow cheeks, lean arms, and narrow chest told of a struggle between life and death, an unceasing duel in which the Countess had hitherto been victorious. The child made an effort to be gay, no doubt to spare her mother suffering; for now and again, when she was unobserved, she languished like a weeping-willow. You might have taken her for a gypsy child suffering from hunger, who had begged her way across country, exhausted but brave, and dressed for her public.

"Where did you leave Jacques?" asked her mother, kissing her on the white line that parted her hair into two bands like a raven's wings.

"He is coming with my father."

The Count at this moment came in, leading his little boy by the hand. Jacques, the very image of his sister, showed the same signs of weakliness. Seeing these two fragile children by the side of such a magnificently handsome mother, it was impossible not to understand the causes of the grief which gave pathos to the Countess' brow and made her silent as to the thoughts which are confided to God alone, but which stamp terrible meaning on the forehead. Monsieur de Mortsauf, as he bowed to me, gave me a glance not so much of inquiry as of the awkward uneasiness of a man whose distrust arises from his want of practical observation and analysis.

After mentioning my name, and what had brought me

thither, his wife gave him her seat and left the room. The children, whose eyes centred in their mother's as if they derived their light from her, wanted to go with her; she said, "Stay here, my darlings," and laid her finger on her lips.

They obeyed, but they looked sad.

Oh! To hear that word "darling," what task might one not have undertaken? Like the children, I felt chilled when she was no longer there.

My name changed the Count's impulses with regard to me. From being cold and supercilious, he became, if not affectionate, at least politely pressing, showed me every mark of consideration, and seemed happy to see me. Long ago my father had devoted himself to play a noble but inconspicuous part for our sovereigns, full of danger, but possibly useful. When all was lost, and Napoleon had climbed to the highest pinnacle, like many secret conspirators, he had taken refuge in the peace of a provincial life and quiet home, bowing before accusations as cruel as they were unmerited—the inevitable reward of gamblers who stake all for all or nothing, and collapse after having been the pivot of the political machine. I, knowing nothing of the fortunes, the antecedents, or the prospects of my own family, was equally ignorant of the details of this forgotten history which Monsieur de Mortsauf remembered. However, if the antiquity of my name, in his eyes the most precious hallmark a man could possess, might justify a reception which made me blush, I did not know the real reason until later. For the moment the sudden change put me at my ease. When the two children saw that the conversation was fairly started among us three, Madeleine slipped her head from under her father's hand, looked at the open door, and glided out like an eel, followed by Jacques. They joined their mother, for I heard them talking and trotting about in the distance, like the hum of bees around the hive that is their home.

I studied the Comte de Mortsauf, trying to guess at his

character, but I was so far interested by some leading features to go no further than a superficial examination of his countenance. Though he was no more than five-and-forty, he looked nearly sixty, so rapidly had he aged in the general wreck which closed the seventeenth century. The fringe of hair, like a monk's, which framed his bald head, ended over his ears in grizzled locks on his temples. His face had a remote resemblance to that of a white wolf with a blood-stained muzzle, for his nose was hot and red, like that of a man whose constitution is undermined, whose digestion is weak, and his blood vitiated by early disease. His flat forehead, too wide for a face that ended in a point, was furrowed across at unequal distances, the result of an open-air life, and not of intellectual labors, of constant ill-fortune, and not of the effort to defy it. His cheek-bones, high and sunburnt, while the rest of his face was sallow, showed that his frame was so strongly built as to promise a long life.

His bright, tawny, hard eye fell on you like winter sunshine, luminous without heat, restless without thought, distrustful without purpose. His mouth was coarse and domineering, his chin long and flat.

He was tall and thin, with the air of a gentleman who relies on a conventional standard of worth, who feels himself superior to his neighbor by right, inferior in fact. The easy-going habits of a country life made him neglectful of his person; his clothes were those of a country proprietor, regarded alike by the peasants and by his neighbors as merely representing a landed estate. His brown, sinewy hands showed that he never wore gloves, unless for riding or on Sunday to go to church. His shoes were clumsy.

Although ten years of exile, and ten of agricultural life, had thus affected his appearance, he still bore traces of noble birth. The most rancorous Liberal—a word not then coined —would at once have discerned in him the chivalrous loyalty, the unfading convictions of a constant reader of the "Quotidienne," and having admired him as a religious man, devoted to his party, frank as to his political antipathies, incapable of being personally serviceable to his side, very capable of ruining it, and ignorant of the state of affairs in France. The Count was, in fact, one of those upright men who yield not a jot, and obstinately bar all progress, valuable to die weapon in hand at the post assigned to them, but stingy enough to give their life rather than their money.

During dinner I detected in the hollows of his faded cheeks, and in the glances he stole at his children, the traces of certain importunate thoughts which came to die on the surface. Who that saw him could fail to understand him? Who would not have accused him of having transmitted to his children their lack of vitality! But even if he blamed himself, he allowed no one else the right of condemning him. He was as bitter as an authority consciously at fault, but without sufficient magnanimity or charm to make up for the quota of suffering he had thrown into the scale; and that his private life must be full of harshness could be seen in his hard features and ever-watchful eyes.

Thus, when his wife came back, with the two children clinging to her, I apprehended disaster, as when walking over the vaults of a cellar the foot has a sort of sense of the depths below. Looking at these four persons together, looking at them, as I did, each in turn, studying their faces and their attitude toward each other, thoughts of melancholy fell upon my heart as fine gray rain throws a mist over a fair landscape after a bright sunrise.

When the immediate subject of conversation was exhausted, the Count again spoke of me, overlooking Monsieur de Chessel, and telling his wife various facts relating to my family, which were perfectly unknown to me. He asked me how old I was. When I told him, the Countess repeated my start of surprise at hearing the age of her little girl. She thought me perhaps about fourteen. This, as I afterward learned, was a second tie that bound her to me so closely. I read it in her soul. Her motherly instinct was aroused, enlightened by a late sunbeam which gave her a hope. On seeing me at past twenty so fragile and yet so wiry, a voice whispered to her perhaps, "They will live!" She looked at me inquisitively, and I felt at the moment that much ice was melted between us. She seemed to have a thousand questions to ask, but reserved them all.

"If you are ill from overwork," said she, "the air of our valley will restore you."

"Modern education is fatal to children," the Count said. "We cram them with mathematics, we beat them with hammers of science, and wear them out before their time. You must rest here," he went on. "You are crushed under the avalanche of ideas that has been hurled down on you. What an age must we look forward to after all this teaching brought down to the meanest capacity, unless we can forefend the evil by placing education once more in the hands of religious bodies."

This speech was indeed the forerunner of what he said one day at an election when refusing to vote for a man whose talents might have done good service to the royalist cause: "I never trust a clever man," said he to the registrar of votes.

He now proposed to take us round the gardens, and arose.

"Monsieur——" said the Countess.

"Well, my dear," he replied, turning round with a rough haughtiness that showed how much he wished to be master in his own house, and how little he was so at this time.

"Monsieur walked from Tours this morning; Monsieur de Chessel did not know it, and took him for a walk in Frapesle."

"You were very rash," said he to me, "though at your age——," and he wagged his head in token of regret.

The conversation was then resumed. I very soon found out how perverse his royalism was, and what caution was necessary to swim in his waters without collisions. The servant, now arrayed in livery, announced dinner. Monsieur de Chessel gave his arm to Madame de Mortsauf, and the Count gaily put his hand in mine to go to the dining-room, which was at the opposite end to the drawing-room, on the same floor.

This room, floored with white tiles made in the country, and wainscoted waist high, was hung with a satin paper divided into large panels framed with borders of fruit and flowers; the window curtains were of cotton stuff, bound with red; the sideboards were old Boule inlay, and the woodwork of the chairs, upholstered with needle-work, was of carved oak. The table, though abundantly spread, was not luxurious; there was old family plate of various dates and patterns, Dresden china—not yet in fashion again—octagonal water bottles, agate-handled knives, and bottle ands of Chinese lacquer. But there were flowers in varnished tubs, with notched and gilt rims. I was delighted with these old-fashioned things, and I thought the réveillon paper, with its flowered border, superb.

The glee that filled all my sails hindered me from discerning the insuperable obstacles placed between her and me by this imperturbable life of solitude in the country. I sat by her, at her right, I poured out her wine and water. Yes! Unhoped-for joy! I could touch her gown, I ate her bread. Only three hours had gone by, and my life was mingling with hers! And we were bound together, too, by that terrible kiss, a sort of secret which filled us alike with shame.

I was defiantly base; I devoted myself to pleasing the Count, who met all my civilities half-way; I would have fondled the dog, have been subservient to the children's least whim; I would have brought them hoops or marbles, have been their horse to drive; I was only vexed that they had not already taken possession of me as a thing of their own. Love has its intuition as genius has, and I dimly perceived that his violence and surliness and hostility would be the ruin of my hopes. This dinner was to me a time of exquisite raptures. Finding myself under her roof, I forgot her real coldness and the indifference that lay beneath the Count's politeness. In love, as in life, there is a period of full growth where it is self-sufficient. I made some blundering answers, in keeping with the secret tumult of my passions; but no one could guess this, much less she who knew nothing of love. The rest of the evening was as a dream.

This beautiful dream came to an end when, by the light of the moon, in the hot fragrant night, I again crossed the Indre amid the white visions that hung over the fields and shore and hills, hearing the thin, monotonous call on one note, melancholy and incessant, at equal intervals, uttered by some tree-frog, of which I know not the scientific name, but which, since that fateful day, I never hear but with most exquisite and extreme delight.

Here, again, though rather late, I discerned, as elsewhere, the stony insensibility against which all my feelings had hitherto been blunted; I wondered whether it would be always thus; I believed myself to be under some fatal influence; the gloomy incidents of my past life struggled with the purely personal joys I had just experienced.

Before re-entering Frapesle, I looked back at Clochegourde and saw below a boat, a punt such as in Touraine is called a *toue*, moored to an ash tree and rocking in the stream. This boat belonged to Monsieur de Mortsauf, who used it for fishing.

"Well," said Monsieur de Chessel, when there was no danger of our being overheard, "I need not ask you if you have found the lady of the beautiful shoulders. You may be congratulated on the welcome you received from Monsieur de Mortsauf. The deuce! Why, you have taken the citadel at a blow."

This speech, followed up by the remarks I before mentioned, revived my downcast spirit. I had not spoken a word since leaving Clochegourde, and my host ascribed my silence to happiness.

"How so?" said I, with a touch of irony, which might have seemed to be the outcome of restrained passion.

"He never in his life received any one so civilly."

"I may confess that I was myself astounded at his politeness," said I, feeling what bitterness lay behind his words.

Though I was too much inexperienced in the ways of the world to understand the cause of Monsieur de Chessel's animus, I was struck by the tone which betrayed it. My host was so unlucky as to be named Durand, and he made himself ridiculous by renouncing his father's name—that of a noted manufacturer who had made an immense fortune during the revolution, and whose wife was the sole heiress of the Chessel family, an old connection of lawyers risen from the citizen class under Henry IV., like most of the Paris magistracy.

Monsieur de Chessel, ambitious of the highest flight, wished to kill the primitive Durand to attain to the realms he dreamed of. He first called himself Durand de Chessel, then D. de Chessel, then he was Monsieur de Chessel. After the restoration he endowed an entail with the title of Count under letters-patent granted by Louis XVIII. His children culled the fruits of his audacity without knowing its magnitude. A speech made by a certain satirical prince long clung to his heels: "Monsieur de Chessel generally has something of the Durand about him," said his highness. And this witticism was long a joy in Touraine.

Parvenues are like monkeys, and not less dexterous. Seen from above we admire their agility in climbing; but when they have reached the top, nothing is to be seen but their more shameful side. The wrong side of my entertainer was made of meanness puffed up with envy. He and a peerage are to this day points that cannot meet. To be pretentious and justify it is the insolence of strength; but a man who is beneath the pretentions he owns to is in a constantly ridiculous position, which affords a feast to petty minds. Now, Monsieur de Chessel has never walked in the straight path of a strong man; he has twice been elected deputy, twice rejected of the electors; one day director-general, the next nothing at all, not even préfet; and his successes and defeats have spoiled his temper and given him the acrid greed of an ambitious failure. Though a fine fellow, intelligent, and capable of high achievement, the spirit of envy perhaps—which gives zest to existence in Touraine, where the natives waste their brains in jealous spite—was fatal to him in the higher social spheres, where faces that frown at others' fortune are rarely popular, or sulky lips unready to pay compliments but apt at sarcasm. If he had wished for less, he might perhaps have gained more; but he, unfortunately, was always proud enough to insist on walking upright.

At the time of my visit, Monsieur de Chessel was in the dawn of his ambition, royalism smiled on him. He affected grand airs, perhaps, but to me he was the perfection of kindness. I liked him, too, for a very simple reason: under his roof I found peace for the first time in my life. The interest he took in me—little enough I dare say—seemed to me, the hapless outcast of my family, a model of paternal affection. The attentions of hospitality formed such a contrast with the indifference that had hitherto crushed me, that I showed childlike gratitude for being allowed to live unfettered and almost petted. The owners of Frapesle are indeed so intimately part of the dawn of my happiness that they dwell in my mind with the memories I love to live in. At a later time, in the very matter of the King's letters-patent, I had the satisfaction of doing my host some little service.

Monsieur de Chessel spent his fortune with an amount of

display that aggrieved some of his neighbors; he could buy fine horses and smart carriages; his wife dressed handsomely; he entertained splendidly; his servants were more numerous than the manners of the country demand; he affected the princely. The estate of Frapesle is vast.

So, as compared with his neighbor, and in the face of all this magnificence, the Comte de Mortsauf, reduced to the family coach, which in Touraine is a cross between a mail-cart and a post-chaise, compelled, too, by his lack of fortune, to make Clochegourde pay, was a tourangeau, a mere gentleman farmer, until the day when royal favor restored his family to unhoped-for dignity. The welcome he had extended to me, the younger son of an impoverished family, whose coat-of-arms dates from the Crusades, had been calculated to throw contempt on the wealth, the woods, the farms and meadows of his neighbor, a man of no birth.

Monsieur de Chessel had quite understood the Count. Indeed, their intercourse had always been polite, but without the daily exchange, the friendly intimacy which might have existed between Clochegourde and Frapesle, two domains divided only by the river, and whose mistresses could signal to each other from their windows.

Jealousy, however, was not the only reason for the Comte de Mortsauf's solitary life. His early education had been that given to most boys of good family—an insufficient and superficial smattering, on which were grafted the lessons of the world, court manners, and the exercise of high court functions, or some position of dignity. Monsieur de Mortsauf had emigrated just when this second education should have begun, and so missed it. He was one of those who believed in the early restoration of the monarchy in France; in this conviction he had spent the years of exile in lamentable idleness. Then, when Condé's army was broken up, after the Count's courage had marked him as one of its most devoted soldiers, he still counted on returning ere long with the white standard, and never attempted, like many of the *émigrés*, to lead an industrious life. Perhaps he could not bear to renounce his name in order to earn his bread in the sweat of the toil he despised.

His hopes, always held over till the morrow, and a sense of honor, too, kept him from engaging in the service of a foreign power.

Suffering undermined his strength. Long expeditions on foot without sufficient food, and hopes for ever deceived, injured his health and discouraged his spirit. By degrees his poverty became extreme. Though to some men misfortune is a tonic, there are others to whom it is destruction, and the Count was one of these. When I think of this unhappy gentleman of Touraine, wandering and sleeping on the highroads in Hungary, sharing a quarter of a sheep with Prince Esterhazy's shepherds—from whom the traveler could beg a loaf which the gentleman would not have accepted from their master, and which he many a time refused at the hands of the foes of France—I could never harbor a bitter feeling against the *émigré*, not even when I saw him ridiculous in his day of triumph.

Monsieur de Mortsauf's white hair had spoken to me of terrible sufferings, and I sympathize with all exiles too strongly to condemn them. The Count's cheerfulness—Frenchman and tourangeau as he was—quite broke down; he became gloomy, fell ill, and was nursed out of charity in some German asylum. His malady was inflammation of the mesentery, which often proves fatal, and which, if cured, brings in its train a capricious temper and almost always hypochondria. His amours, buried in the most secret depths of his soul, where I alone ever unearthed them, were of a debasing character, and not only marred his life at the time, but ruined it for the future.

After twelve years' misery, he came back to France, whither Napoleon's decree enabled him to return. When, as he crossed the Rhine on foot, he saw the steeple of Strasbourg one fine summer evening, he fainted away. "'France! France!' I cried. 'This is France!' as a child cries out 'Mother!' when it is hurt," he told me.

Born to riches, he was now poor; born to lead a regiment or govern the state, he had no authority, no prospects; born healthy and robust, he came home sick and worn out. Bereft of education in a country where men and things had been growing, without interest of any kind, he found himself destitute even of physical and moral strength. His want of fortune made his name a burden to him. His unshaken convictions, his former attachment to Condé, his woes, his memories, his ruined health, had given him a touchy susceptibility, which was likely to find small mercy in France, the land of banter. Half-dead, he got as far as le Maine, where, by some accident, due perhaps to the civil war, the revolutionary government had forgotten to sell a farm of considerable extent, which the farmer in possession had clung to, declaring that it was his own.

When the Lenoncourt family, living at Givry, a château not far from this farm, heard that the Comte de Mortsauf had come back, the Duc de Lenoncourt went to offer him shelter at Givry till he should have time to arrange his residence. The Lenoncourts were splendidly generous to the Count, who recovered his strength through several months' stay with them, making every effort to disguise his sufferings during this first interval of peace. The Lenoncourts had lost their enormous possessions. So far as name was concerned, the Comte de Mortsauf was a suitable match for their daughter; and Mademoiselle de Lenoncourt, far from being averse to marrying a man of five-and-thirty, old and ailing for his age, seemed quite content. Her marriage would allow her to live with her aunt, the Duchesse de Verneuil (sister to the Prince de Blamont-Chauvry), who was a second mother to the girl.

As the intimate friend of the Duchesse de Bourbon, Madame

de Verneuil was one of a saintly circle, whose soul was Monsieur de Saint-Martin, born in Touraine, and known as *le Philosophe inconnu* (the unrecognized philosopher). The disciples of this philosopher practiced the virtues inculcated by the lofty speculations of mystical Illuminism. This doctrine gives a key to the supernal worlds, accounts for life by a series of transmigrations through which man makes his way to sublime destinies, releases duty from its degradation by the law, views the woes of life with the placid fortitude of the Quaker, and enjoins contempt of pain, by infusing a mysterious maternal regard for the angel within us which we must bear up to heaven. It is stoicism looking for future life. Earnest prayer and pure love are the elements of this creed, which, born in the catholicism of the Roman Church, reverts to the bosom of primitive Christianity.

Mademoiselle de Lenoncourt remained attached, however, to the apostolic church, to which her aunt was equally faithful. Cruelly tried by the storms of the revolution, the Duchesse de Verneuil had, toward the close of her life, assumed a hue of impassioned piety which overflowed into the soul of her beloved niece with "the light of heavenly love and the oil of spiritual joy," to use the words of Saint-Martin. This man of peace and virtuous learning was several times the Countess' guest at Clochegourde after her aunt's death; to her he had been a constant visitor. When staying at Clochegourde, Saint-Martin could superintend the printing of his latest works by Letourney of Tours.

Madame de Verneuil, with the inspiration of wisdom that comes to old women who have experienced the storms of life, gave Clochegourde to the young wife that she might have a home of her own. With the good grace of old people—which, when they are gracious, is perfection—she surrendered the whole house to her niece, reserving only one room, over that she had formerly used, which was taken by the Countess. Her almost sudden death cast a shroud over the joys of the united household, and left a permanent tinge of sadness on Clochegourde as well as on the young wife's superstitious soul. The early days of her married life in Touraine were to the Countess the only period, not indeed of happiness, but of light-heartedness in all her life.

After the miseries of his life in exile, Monsieur de Mortsauf, thankful to foresee a sheltered existence in the future, went through a sort of healing of the spirit; he inhaled in this valley the intoxicating fragrance of blossoming hope. Being obliged to consider ways and means, he threw himself into agricultural enterprise, and at first found some delight in it; but Jacques' birth came like a lightning stroke, blighting the present and the future; the physician pronounced that the child could not live. The Count carefully concealed this sentence of doom from his wife; then he himself consulted a doctor, and had none but crushing answers, confirmed as to their purport by Madeleine's birth.

These two events, and a sort of inward conviction as to the inevitable end, added to the Count's ill-health. His name extinct; his young wife, pure and blameless but unhappy in her marriage, doomed to the anxieties of motherhood without knowing its joys—all this *humus* of his past life, filled with the germs of fresh sufferings, fell on his heart and crowned his misery.

The Countess read the past in the present, and foresaw the future. Though there is nothing so difficult as to make a man happy who feels where he has failed, the Countess attempted the task worthy of an angel. In one day she became a stoic. After descending into the abyss whence she could still see the heavens, she devoted herself, for one man, to the mission which a sister of charity undertakes for the sake of all; and to reconcile him with himself, she forgave him what he could not forgive himself. The Count grew avaricious, she accepted the consequent privations; he dreaded being imposed upon, as men do whose knowledge of the world has filled them with repulsions, and she resigned herself to solitude and to his distrust of men without a murmur; she used all a woman's wiles to make him wish for what was right, and he thus credited himself with ideas and enjoyed in his home the pleasures of superiority which he could not have known elsewhere.

Finally, having inured herself to the path of married life, she determined never to leave her home at Clochegourde; for she perceived in her husband a hysterical nature whose eccentricities, in a neighborhood so full of envy and gossip, might be interpreted to the injury of their children. Thus nobody had a suspicion of Monsieur de Mortsauf's incapacity and aberrations; she had clothed the ruin with a thick hanging of ivy. The Count's uncertain temper, not so much discontented as malcontent, found in his wife a soft and soothing bed on which it might repose, its secret sufferings alleviated by cooling dews.

This sketch is a mere outline of the facts repeated by Monsieur de Chessel under the promptings of private spite. His experience of the world had enabled him to unravel some of the mysteries lurking at Clochegourde. But though Madame de Mortsauf's sublime attitude might deceive the world, it could not cheat the alert wits of love.

When I found myself alone in my little bedroom, an intuition of the truth made me start up in bed. I could not endure to be at Frapesle when I might be gazing at the windows of her room. I dressed myself, stole downstairs, and got out of the house by a side-door in a tower where there was a spiral stair. The fresh night air composed my spirit. I crossed the Indre by the Moulin-Rouge bridge, and presently got into the heaven-sent little boat opposite Clochegourde, where a light shone in the end window toward Azay.

Here I fell back on my old dreams, but peaceful now, and soothed by the warbling of the songster of lovers' nights and the single note of the reed-warbler. Ideas stole through my brain like ghosts, sweeping away the clouds which till now had darkened the future. My mind and senses alike were under the spell. With what passion did my longing go forth to her! How many times did I repeat, like a madman, "Will she be mine?"

If, during the last few days, the universe had expanded before me, now, in one night, it gained a centre. All my will, all my ambitions were bound up in her; I longed to be all I might for her sake and to fill and heal her aching heart. How lovely was that night spent below her window, in the midst of murmurous waters, plashing over the mill-wheels, and broken by the sound of the clock at Saché as it told the hours. In that night, so full of radiance, when that starry flower illumined my life, I plighted my soul to her with the faith of the hapless Castilian knight whom we laugh at in Cervantes—the faith of the beginnings of love.

At the first streak of dawn in the sky, the first piping bird, I fled to the park of Frapesle; no early country yokel saw me, no one suspected my escapade, and I slept till the bell rang for breakfast.

Notwithstanding the heat, when breakfast was over I went down to the meadow to see the Indre and its islets once more, the valley and its downs of which I professed myself an ardent admirer; but, with a swiftness of foot which might defy that of a runaway horse, I went back to my boat, my willows, and my Clochegourde. All was still and quivering, as the country is at noon. The motionless foliage was darkly defined against the blue sky; such insects as live in sunshine—green dragon-flies and iridescent flies—hovered round the ash trees and over the reeds; the herds chewed the cud in the shade, the red earth glowed in the vineyards, and snakes wriggled over the banks. What a change in the landscape that I had left so cool and coy before going to sleep!

On a sudden I leaped out of the punt, and went up the road to come down behind Clochegourde, for I fancied I had seen the Count come out. I was not mistaken; he was skirting a hedge, going no doubt toward a gate opening on to the Azay road by the side of the river.

"How are you this morning, Monsieur le Comte?"

He looked at me with a pleased expression. He did not often hear himself thus addressed.

"Quite well," said he. "You must be very fond of the country to walk out in this heat?"

"Was I not sent here to live in the open air?"

"Well, then, will you come and see them reaping my rye?"

"With pleasure," said I. "But I am, I must confess to you, deplorably ignorant. I do not know rye from wheat, nor a poplar from an aspen; I know nothing of field-work, nor of the ways of tilling the land."

"Well, then, come along," said he gleefully, turning back by the hedge. "Come by the little upper gate."

He walked along inside the hedge, and I outside.

"You will never learn anything from Monsieur de Chessel," said he; "he is much too fine a gentleman to trouble himself beyond looking through his steward's accounts."

So he showed me his yards and outbuildings, his flower-garden, orchards, and kitchen-gardens. Finally, he led me along the avenue of acacias and ailanthus on the river-bank, where, at the further end, I saw Madame de Mortsauf and the two children.

A woman looks charming under the play of the frittered, quivering tracery of leaves. Somewhat surprised, no doubt, by my early visit, she did not move, knowing that we should go to her. The Count bid me admire the view of the valley, which, from thence, wore quite a different aspect from any I had seen from the heights. You might have thought yourself in a corner of Switzerland. The meadow-land, channeled by the brooks that tumble into the Indre, stretches far into the distance, and is lost in mist. On the side toward Montvazon spreads a wide extent of verdure; everywhere else the eye is checked by hills, clumps of trees, and rocks.

We hastened our steps to greet Madame de Mortsauf, who suddenly dropped the book in which Madeleine was reading, and took Jacques on her knee, in a fit of spasmodic coughing.

"Why, what is the matter?" asked the Count, turning pale.

"He has a relaxed throat," said the mother, who did not seem to see me; "it will be nothing."

She was supporting his head and his back, and from her eyes shot two rays that infused life into the poor feeble boy.

"You are extraordinarily rash," said the Count sharply; "you expose him to a chill from the river and let him sit on a stone bench!"

"But, father, the bench is burning," cried Madeleine.

"They were stifling up above," said the Countess.

"Women will always be in the right!" said he, turning to me.

To avoid encouraging or offending him by a look I gazed at Jacques, who complained of a pain in his throat, and his mother carried him away. As she went, she could hear her husband say—

"When a mother has such sickly children, she ought to know how to take care of them."

Hideously unjust, but his self-conceit prompted him to justify himself at his wife's expense.

The Countess flew on, up slopes and steps; she disappeared through the glazed door.

Monsieur de Mortsauf had seated himself on the bench, his head bent, lost in thought; my position was intolerable; he neither looked at me nor spoke. Good-by to the walk during which I meant to make such way in his good graces. I cannot remember ever in my life to have spent a more horrible quarter of an hour. I was bathed in perspiration as I considered—

"Shall I leave him? Shall I stay?"

How many gloomy thoughts must have filled his brain to make him forget to go and inquire how Jacques was! Suddenly he arose and came up to me. We turned together to look at the smiling scene.

"We will put off our walk until another day, Monsieur le Comte," I said gently.

"Nay, let us go," said he. "I am, unfortunately, used to see such attacks—and I would give my life without a regret to save the child's."

"Jacques is better now, my dear; he is asleep," said the golden voice. Madame de Mortsauf appeared at the end of the walk; she had come back without rancor or bitterness, and she returned my bow. "I am pleased to see that you like Clochegourde," she said to me.

"Would you like me to go on horseback to fetch Monsieur Deslandes, my dear?" said he, with an evident desire to win forgiveness for his injustice.

"Do not be anxious," replied she. "Jacques did not sleep last night, that is all. The child is very nervous; he had a bad dream, and I spent the time telling him stories to send him to sleep again. His cough is entirely nervous. I have soothed it with a gum lozenge, and he has fallen asleep."

"Poor dear!" said he, taking her hand in both his, and looking at her with moistened eyes. "I knew nothing of it."

"Why worry you about trifles? Go and look at your rye. You know that if you are not on the spot the farmers will let gleaners who do not belong to the place clear the fields before the sheaves are carried."

"I am going to take my first lesson in farming, madame," said I.

"You have come to a good master," replied she, looking at the Count, whose lips were pursed into the prim smile of satisfaction commonly known as *la bouche en cœur* (kiss-lips).

Not until two months later did I know that she had spent

that night in dreadful anxiety, fearing that her son had the croup. And I was in the punt, softly lulled by dreams of love, fancying that from her window she might see me adoring the light of the taper which shone on her brow furrowed by mortal fears.

As we reached the gate, the Count said in a voice full of emotion, "Madame de Mortsauf is an angel!"

The words staggered me. I knew the family but slightly as yet, and the natural remorse that comes over a youthful soul in such circumstances cried out to me—

"What right have you to disturb this perfect peace?"

The Count, enchanted to have for his audience a youth over whom he could so cheaply triumph, began talking of the future prospects of France under the return of the Bourbons. We chatted discursively, and I was greatly surprised at the strangely childish things he said. He was ignorant of facts as well proven as geometry; he was suspicious of well-informed persons; he had no belief in superiority; he laughed at progress, not perhaps without reason; and I found in him a vast number of sensitive chords compelling me to take so much care not to wound him that a long conversation was a labor to the mind. When I had thus laid a finger on his failings, I felt my way with as much pliancy as the Countess showed in coaxing them. At a later stage of my life I should undoubtedly have fretted him; but I was as timid as a child, and thinking that I myself knew nothing, or that men of experience knew everything, I was amazed at the wonders worked at Clochegourde by this patient husbandman. I heard his plans with admiration. Finally—a piece of involuntary flattery which won me the good gentleman's affections—I envied him this pretty estate so beautifully situated, as an earthly paradise far superior to Frapesle, the demesne of de Chessel.

"Frapesle," said I, "is a massive piece of plate, but Clochegourde is a casket of precious gems."

A speech that he constantly repeated, quoting me as the author.

"Well," said he, "before we came here it was a wilderness."

I was all ears when he talked of his crops and nursery plantations. New to a country life, I overwhelmed him with questions as to the price of things and the processes of agriculture, and he seemed delighted to have to tell me so much.

"What on earth do they teach you?" he asked in surprise.

And on that very first day, on going in, he whispered to his wife—

"Monsieur Félix is a charming young fellow."

In the afternoon I wrote to my mother to tell her I should remain at Frapesle, and begged her to send me clothes and linen.

Knowing nothing of the great revolution that was going on, and of the influence it was to exert over my destinies, I supposed that I should return to Paris to finish my studies, and the law schools would not reopen till early in November; so I had two months and a half before me.

During the first days of my stay I tried in vain to attach myself to the Count, and it was a time of painful shocks. I detected in this man a causeless irritability and a swiftness to act in cases that were hopeless which frightened me. Now and then there were sudden resuscitations of the brave gentleman who had fought so well under Condé, parabolic flashes of a will which, in a day of critical moment, might tear through policy like a bursting shell, and which in some opportunity for resolution and courage may make an Elbée, a Bonchamp, a Charette of a man condemned to live on his acres. The mere mention of certain possibilities would make his nose quiver and his brow clear, while his eyes flashed lightnings that at once died out. I feared lest Monsieur de Mortsauf, if he should read the language of my eyes, might kill me on the spot.

At this period of my life I was only tender; will, which affects a man so strangely, was but just dawning in me. My vehement longing had given me a swiftly responsive sensitiveness that was like a thrill of fear. I did not tremble at the prospect of a struggle, but I did not want to die till I had known the happiness of reciprocated love. My difficulties and my desires grew in parallel lines.

How can I describe my feelings? I was a prey to heart-rending perplexities. I hoped for a chance, I watched for it; I made friends with the children, and won them to love me; I tried to identify myself with the interests of the household.

By degrees the Count was less on his guard in my presence; then I learned to know his sudden changes of temper, his fits of utter, causeless dejection, his gusts of rebelliousness, his bitter and harsh complaining, his impulses of controlled madness, his childish whining, his groans as of a man in despair, his unexpected rages. Moral nature differs from physical nature, inasmuch as nothing in it is final. The intensity of effect is in proportion to the character acted on, or to the ideas that may be associated with an action. My continuing at Clochegourde, my whole future life depended on this fantastic will.

I could never express to you the anguish that weighed on my soul—as ready at that time to expand as to shrink—when on going in I said to myself, "How will he receive me?" What anxious fears crushed my heart when I descried a storm lowering on that snow-crowned brow! I was perpetually on the alert. Thus I was a slave to this man's tyranny, and my own torments enabled me to understand those of Madame de Mortsauf.

We began to exchange glances of intelligence, and my tears would sometimes rise when she repressed hers. Thus the Countess and I tested each other through sorrow. I made many discoveries in the course of the first six weeks—forty days of real annoyance, of silent joys, of hopes now engulfed and now rising to the top.

One evening I found her piously meditative as she looked at a sunset, which crimsoned the heights with so voluptuous a blush, the valley spread below it like a bed, that it was impossible not to understand the voice of this eternal Song of Songs by which nature bids her creatures love. Was the girl dreaming of illusions now flown? Was the woman feeling the pangs of some secret comparison? I fancied I saw in her languid attitude a favorable opening for a first avowal. I said to her—

"Some days are so hard to live through."

"You have read my mind," replied she. "But how?"

"We have so many points of contact," said I. "Are we not both of the privileged few, keen to suffer and to enjoy—in whom every sensitive fibre thrills in unison to produce an echoing chord of feeling, and whose nervous system dwells in constant harmony with the first principle of things? Such beings, placed in a discordant medium, suffer torture, just as their enjoyment rises to an ecstacy when they meet with ideas, sensations, or persons that they find sympathetic.

"And for us there is a third condition, of which the woes are known only to souls suffering from the same malady, and endowed with brotherly intelligence. We are capable of having impressions that are neither pleasure nor pain. Then an expressive instrument, gifted with life, is stirred in a void within us, is impassioned without an object, gives forth sounds without melody, utters words that die in the silence—a dreadful contradiction in souls that rebel against the uselessness of a vacuum; a terrible sport in which all our power is spent without nutrition, like blood from some internal wound. Our emotion flows in torrents, leaving us unutterably weak, in a speechless dejection for which the confessional has no ear.

Have I not expressed the sufferings we both are familiar with?"

She shivered, and, still gazing at the sunset, she replied—

"How do you, who are so young, know these things? Were you once a woman?"

"Ah!" said I, with some agitation, "my childhood was like one long illness?"

"I hear Madeleine coughing," said she, hastily leaving me.

The Countess had seen me constant in my attentions to her, without taking offense, for two reasons. In the first place, she was as pure as a child and her thoughts never wandered to evil. And then I amused the Count; I was food for this lion without claws or mane. For I had hit on a pretext for my visits which was plausible to all. I could not play backgammon; Monsieur de Mortsauf offered to teach me, and I accepted.

At the moment when this bargain was made, the Countess could not help giving me a pitying look, as much as to say, "Well, you are rushing into the wolf's jaws!"

If I had failed to understand this at first, by the third day I knew to what I had committed myself. My patience, which as a result of my child-life is inexhaustible, was matured during this time of discipline. To the Count it was a real joy to be cruelly sarcastic when I failed to practice some rule or principle he had explained to me; if I paused to reflect he complained of my slow play; if I played quickly, he hated to be hurried; if I left blots, while taking advantage of it, he said I was too hasty. It was the despotism of a schoolmaster, the bullying of the cane, of which I can only give you a notion by comparing myself to Epictetus made a slave to a malicious child.

When we played for money, his constant winnings gave him mean and degrading joy; then a word from his wife made up to me for everything, and brought him back to a sense of decency and politeness. But ere long I fell into the torments of a fiery furnace I had not foreseen : at this rate my pocket-money was melting.

Though the Count always remained between his wife and me till I took my leave, sometimes at a late hour, I always hoped to find a moment when I might steal into her heart ; but in order to attain that hour, watched for with the painful patience of a sportsman, I saw that I must persevere in these weariful games, through which I endured mental misery and which were winning away all my money !

Many a time had we sat in silence, watching an effect of the sun on the meadows, of the clouds in a gray sky, the blue misty hills, or the quivering moonbeams on the gem-like play of the river, without uttering a word beyond—

" What a beautiful night ! "

" Madame, the night is a woman."

" And what peace ! "

" Yes ; it is impossible to be altogether unhappy here.'

At this reply she returned to her worsted-work. I had in fact understood the yearnings of her inmost self stirred by an affection that insisted on its rights.

Without money my evenings were at an end. I wrote to my mother to send me some ; my mother scolded me, and would give me none for a week. To whom could I apply! And it was a matter of life or death to me !

Thus at the very beginning of my first great happiness I again felt the sufferings which had always pursued me ; in Paris, at school, I had evaded them by melancholy abstinence, my woes were only negative ; at Frapesle they were active ; I now knew that longing to steal, those dreamed-of crimes and horrible frenzies which blast the soul, and which we are bound to stifle or lose all self-respect. My remembrance of the miserable reflections, the anguish inflicted on me by my mother's parsimony, have given me that holy indulgence for young men which those must feel who, without having fallen, have stood on the edge of the gulf and sounded the abyss. Though my honesty, watered with cold sweats, stood firm at those moments when the waters of life part and show the stony depths of its bed, whenever human justice draws her terrible sword on a man's neck, I say to myself, "Penal laws were made by those who never knew want."

In this dire extremity I found in Monsieur de Chessel's library a treatise on backgammon, and this I studied; then my host was good enough to give me a few lessons. Under milder tuition I made some progress and could apply the rules and calculations which I learned by heart. In a few days I was able to beat my master. But when I won he waxed furious; his eyes glared like a tiger's, his face twitched, his brows worked as I never saw any other's work. His fractiousness was like that of a spoilt child. Sometimes he would fling the dice across the room, rage and stamp, bite the dice-box, and abuse me. But this violence had to be stopped. As soon as I could play a good game, I disposed of the battle as I pleased. I arranged it so that we should come out nearly even at the end, allowing him to win at the beginning of the evening, and restoring the balance in the latter games.

The end of the world would have amazed the Count less than his pupil's sudden proficiency; but, in fact, he never perceived it. The regular result of our play was a novelty that bewildered his mind.

"My poor brain is tired, no doubt," he would say. "You always win at the finish, because by that time I have exhausted my powers."

The Countess, who knew the game, detected my purpose from the first, and saw in it an evidence of immense affection. These details can only be appreciated by those to whom the extreme difficulty of backgammon is known. How much this trifle betrayed! But love, like God as depicted by Bossuet, regards the poor man's cup of water, the struggle of the soldier who dies inglorious, as far above the most profitable victories.

The Countess gave me one of those looks of silent gratitude that overpower a youthful heart: she bestowed on me such a glance as she reserved for her children. From that thrice-blessed evening she always looked at me when she spoke to me.

I could never find words for my state of mind when I left. My soul had absorbed my body. I weighed nothing, I did not walk—I floated. I felt within me still that look that had bathed me in glory, just as her "Good-night, monsieur," had echoed in my soul like the harmonies of the "O filii, O filiæ!" of the Easter benediction. I was born to new life. I was something to her, then!

I slept in wrappings of purple. Flames danced before my closed eyes, chasing each other in the dark like the pretty bright sparks that run over charred paper. And in my dreams her voice seemed something tangible—an atmosphere that lapped me in light and fragrance, a melody that lulled my spirit.

Next day her welcome conveyed the full expression of the feelings she bestowed on me, and thenceforth I knew every secret of her tones.

That day was to be one of the most noteworthy of my life. After dinner we went for a walk on the downs and up to a common where nothing would grow; the soil was strong and dry, with no vegetable mold. There were, however, a few oaks, and some bushes covered with sloes; but instead of grass, the ground was carpeted with curled brown lichen, bright in the rays of the setting sun, and slippery under foot. I held Madeleine by the hand to keep her from falling, and Madame de Mortsauf gave Jacques her arm. The Count, who led the way, suddenly struck the earth with his stick, and, turning round, exclaimed in a terrible tone—

"Such has my life been! Oh, before I knew you," he added, with an apologetic glance at his wife. But it was too late, the Countess had turned pale. What woman would not have staggered under such a blow?

"What delightful perfumes reach us here and what wonderful effects of light!" cried I. "I should like to own this common; I might perhaps find riches if I dug into it; but the most certain advantage would be living near you. But who would not pay highly for a view, so soothing to the eye, of that winding river in which the soul may bathe among ash trees and birch. That shows how tastes differ! To you this spot of land is a common; to me it is a paradise."

She thanked me with a look.

"Rhodomontade!" said he in a bitter tone. Then, interrupting himself, he said, "Do you hear the bells of Azay? I can positively hear the bells."

Madame de Mortsauf glanced at me with an expression of alarm, Madeleine clutched my hand.

"Shall we go home and play a hit?" said I. "The rattle of the dice will hinder you from hearing the bells."

We returned to Clochegourde, talking at intervals. When we went into the drawing-room we sat in indefinable indecision. The Count had sunk into an arm-chair, lost in thought, and undisturbed by his wife, who knew the symptoms of his malady and could foresee an attack. I was not less silent. She did not bid me leave, perhaps because she thought that a game of backgammon would amuse the Count and scare away this dreadful nervous irritation, for its outbreaks half-killed her.

Nothing was more difficult than to persuade the Count to play his game of backgammon, though he always longed for it. Like a mincing coquette, he had to be entreated and urged, so as not to seem under any obligation, perhaps because he felt that he was. If, at the end of some interesting conversation, I forgot to go through my *salamelek*, he was sulky, sharp, and offensive, and showed his annoyance by contradicting everything that was said. Then, warned by his fractiousness, I would propose a game, and he would play the coquette.

"It was too late," he would say, "and, beside, I did not really care for it." In short, no end of airs and graces, like a woman whose real wishes you cannot at last be sure of. I was humble, and besought him to give me practice in a science so easily forgotten for lack of exercise.

On this occasion I had to affect the highest spirits to persuade him to play. He complained of giddiness that hindered his calculations, his brain was crushed in a vice, he had a singing in his ears, he was suffocating, and sighed and groaned. At last he consented to come to the table. Madame de Mortsauf then left us to put the children to bed and to read prayers for the household. All went well during her absence; I contrived that Monsieur de Mortsauf should win, and his success restored his good humor. The sudden transition from a state of depression, in which he had given utterance to the most gloomy anticipations for himself, to this joviality like that of a drunken man, and to crazy, irrational mirth, distressed and terrified me. I had never seen him so frankly and unmistakably beside himself. Our intimacy had borne fruit; he was no longer on his guard with me. Day by day he tried to involve me in his tyranny, and find in me fresh food for his humors—for it really would seem that mental disorders are living things, with appetites and instincts, and a craving to extend the limits of their dominion as a landowner seeks to enlarge his borders.

The Countess came down again and drew near the backgammon table for a better light on her work, but she sat down to her frame with ill-disguised apprehension. An unlucky move, which I could not avoid, changed the Count's face; from cheerful it became gloomy, from purple it turned yellow, and his eyes wandered. Then came another blow which I could neither foresee nor make good. Monsieur de Mortsauf threw a fatally bad number which ruined him. He started

HE STARTED UP, THREW THE TABLE OVER ME AND THE
LAMP ON THE GROUND.

up, threw the table over me and the lamp on the ground, struck his fist on the console, and leaped—for I cannot say he walked—up and down the room. The rush of abuse, oaths, and ejaculations that he poured out was enough to make one think that he was possessed, according to mediæval belief. Imagine my position.

"Go out into the garden," said she, pressing my hand.

I went without the Count's noticing that I was gone.

From the terrace, whither I slowly made my way, I could hear his loud tones, and groans coming from his bedroom, adjoining the dining-room. Above the tempest I could also hear the voice of an angel, audible now and then like the song of the nightingale when the storm is passing over. I wandered up and down under the acacias on that exquisite night late in August, waiting for the Countess. She would come; her manner had promised it. For some days an explanation had been in the air between us, and must inevitably come at the first word that should unseal the overfull well in our hearts. What bashfulness retarded the hour of our perfect understanding? Perhaps she loved, as I did, the thrill, almost like the stress of fear, which quenches emotion at those moments when we hold down the gushing overflow of life, when we are as shy of revealing our inmost soul as a maiden bride of unveiling to the husband she loves. The accumulation of our thoughts had magnified this first and necessary confession on both sides.

An hour stole away. I was sitting on the brick parapet when the sound of her footstep, mingling with the rustle of her light dress, fluttered the evening air. It was one of the sensations at which the heart stands still.

"Monsieur de Mortsauf is asleep," said she. "When he has one of these attacks I give him a cup of tea made of poppy-heads, and the crisis is rare enough for the simple remedy always to take effect. Monsieur," she went on, with a change of tone to the most persuasive key, "an unfortunate accident has put you in possession of secrets which have hitherto been carefully kept; promise me to bury in your heart every memory of this scene. Do this for my sake, I beg of you. I do not ask you to swear it; the simple *Yes* of a man of honor will amply satisfy me."

"Need I even say *Yes?*" I asked. "Have we failed to understand each other?"

"Do not form an unjust opinion of Monsieur de Mortsauf from seeing the result of much suffering endured in exile," she went on. "He will have entirely forgotten by to-morrow all he said to you, and you will find him quite kind and affectionate."

"Nay, madame," said I, "you need not justify the Count. I will do exactly what you will. I would this instant throw myself into the Indre if I could thus make a new man of Monsieur de Mortsauf, and give you a life of happiness. The only thing I cannot do is to alter my opinion, nothing is more essentially a part of me. I would give my life for you; I cannot sacrifice my conscience; I may refuse to listen to it, but can I hinder its speaking? Now, in my opinion, Monsieur de Mortsauf is——"

"I quite understand you," she said, interrupting me to mitigate the idea of insanity by softening the expression. "The Count is as nervous as a lady with the megrims; but it occurs only at long intervals, at most once a year, when the heat is greatest. How much evil the emigration brought in its train! How many noble lives were wrecked! He, I am sure, would have been a distinguished officer and an honor to his country——"

"I know it," I replied, interrupting in my turn, to show her that it was vain to try to deceive me.

She paused and laid a hand on my brow, saying with great earnestness:

"Who has thus thrown you into our midst? Has God intended me to find a help in you, a living friendship to lean upon?" she went on, firmly grasping my hand. "For you are kind and generous——"

She looked up to heaven as if to invoke some visible evidence that should confirm her secret hopes; then she bent her eyes on me. Magnetized by that gaze which shed her soul into mine, I failed in tact by every rule of worldly guidance; but to some souls is not such precipitancy a magnanimous haste to meet danger, an eagerness to prevent disaster and dread of a misfortune that may never come; is it not more often the abrupt question of heart to heart, a blow struck to find out whether they ring in unison?

Many thoughts flashed through me like light, and counseled me to wash out the stain that soiled my innocency even at the moment when I hoped for full initiation.

"Before going any further," said I, in a voice quavering from my heart-beats, audible in the deep silence, "allow me to purify one memory of the past——"

"Be silent," said she hastily, and laying a finger on my lips for an instant. She looked at me loftily, like a woman who stands too high for slander to reach her, and said in a broken voice, "I know to what you allude—the first and last and only insult ever offered me! Never speak of that ball. Though as a Christian I have forgiven you, the woman still smarts under it."

"Do not be less merciful than God," said I, my eyelashes retaining the tears that rose to my eyes.

"I have a right to be more severe; I am weaker," replied she.

"But hear me," I cried, with a sort of childish indignation, "even if it be for the first and last and only time in your life."

"Well," said she, "speak then! Otherwise you will fancy that I am afraid to hear you."

I felt that this hour was unique in our lives, and I told her, in a way to command belief, "that every woman at that ball had been as indifferent to me as every other I had hitherto seen; but that when I saw her—I who had spent my life in study, whose spirit was so far from bold—I had been swept away by a sort of frenzy which could only be condemned by those who had never known it; that the heart of man had never been so overflowing with such desire as no living being can resist, and which conquers all things, even death——"

"And scorn?" said she, interrupting me.

"What, you scorned me!" said I.

"Talk no more of these things," said she.

"Nay, let us talk of them," replied I, in the excitement of superhuman anguish. "It concerns my whole being, my unknown life; it is a secret you must hear, or else I must die of despair! And does it not concern you, too—you who, without knowing it, are the lady in whose hand shines the crown held out to the conqueror in the lists?"

I told her the story of my childhood and youth, not as I have related it to you, calmly judged from a distance, but in the words of a young man whose wounds are still bleeding. My voice rang like the axe of the woodman in a forest. The dead years fell crashing down before it, and the long misery that had crowned them with leafless boughs. In fevered words I described to her a thousand odious details that I have spared you. I displayed the treasury of my splendid hopes, the virgin gold of my desires, a burning heart kept hot under the Alps of ice piled up through a perpetual winter. And then, when, crushed by the burden of my griefs uttered with the fire of an Isaiah, I waited for a word from the woman who had heard me with a downcast head, she lightened the darkness with a look, and vivified the worlds earthly and divine by one single sentence.

"Our childhood was the same," said she, showing me a face bright with the halo of martyrdom.

After a pause, during which our souls were wedded by the same consoling thought, "Then I was not the only one to suffer!" The Countess told me, in the tones she kept for her children, how luckless she had been as a girl when the boys were dead. She explained the difference, made by her condition as a girl always at her mother's skirt, between her miseries and those of a boy flung into the world of school. My isolation had been a paradise in comparison with the grinding millstone under which her spirit was perennially bruised, until the day when her true mother, her devoted aunt, had saved her by rescuing her from the torture of which she described the ever-new terrors. It was a course of those indescribable goading pricks that are intolerable to a nervous nature which can face a direct thrust, but dies daily under the sword of Damocles—a generous impulse quashed by a stern command; a kiss coldly accepted; silence first enjoined and then found fault with; tears repressed that lay heavy on her heart; in short, all the petty tyranny of convent discipline hidden from the eyes of the world behind a semblance of proud and sentimental motherhood. Her mother was vain of her and boasted of her; but she paid dearly afterward for the praise bestowed only for the glory of her teacher. When, by dint of docility and sweetness, she fancied she had softened her mother's heart and opened her own, the tyrant armed herself with her confessions. A spy would have been less cowardly and treacherous.

All her girlish pleasures and festivals had cost her dear, for she was scolded for having enjoyed them as much as for a fault. The lessons of her admirable education had never been given with love, but always with cruel irony. She owed her mother no grudge, she only blamed herself for loving her less than she feared her. Perhaps, the angel thought, this severity had really been necessary. Had it not prepared her for her present life?

She paused.

As I listened to her, I felt as though the harp of Job, from which I had struck some wild chords, was now touched by

Christian fingers, and responded with the chanted liturgy of the Virgin at the foot of the cross.

"We dwelt in the same sphere," I exclaimed emphatically, "before meeting here, you coming from the East and I from the West."

She shook her head with desperate agitation: "The East is for you and the West is for me," said she. "You will live happy, I shall die of grief! Men make the conditions of their life themselves; my lot is cast once for all. No power can break the ponderous chain to which a wife is bound by a ring of gold, the emblem of her purity."

Feeling now that we were twins of the same nurture, she could not conceive of semi-confidences between sister souls that had drunk of the same spring. After the natural sigh of a guileless heart opening for the first time, she told me the story of the early days of her married life, her first disillusionment, all the renewal of her sorrows. She, like me, had gone through those trivial experiences which are so great to spirits whose limpid nature is shaken through and through by the slightest shock, as a stone flung into a lake stirs the depths as well as the surface.

When she married she had some savings, the little treasure which represents the happy hours, the thousand trifles a young wife may wish for; one day of dire need she had generously given the whole sum to her husband, not telling him that these were not gold-pieces, but remembrances; he had never taken any account of it; he did not feel himself her debtor. Nor had she seen in return for her treasure, sunk in the sleeping waters of oblivion, the moistened eye which pays every debt, and is to a generous soul like a perpetual gem whose rays sparkle in the darkest day.

And she had gone on from sorrow to sorrow. Monsieur de Mortsauf would forget to give her money for housekeeping; he woke up as from a dream when she asked for it, after overcoming a woman's natural shyness; never once had he spared her this bitter experience! Then what terrors had beset her at the moment when this worn-out man had first shown symptoms of his malady! The first outbreak of his frenzied rage had completely crushed her. What miserable meditations must she have known before she understood that her husband—the impressive figure that presides over a woman's whole life—was a nonentity! What anguish had come on her after the birth of her two children! What a shock on seeing the scarcely living infants! What courage she must have had to say to herself, "I will breathe life into them; they shall be born anew day by day!" And then the despair of finding an obstacle in the heart and hand whence a wife looks for help!

She had seen this expanse of woes stretching before her, a thorny wilderness, after every surmounted difficulty. From the top of each rock she had discovered new deserts to cross, till the day when she really knew her husband, knew her children's constitution, and the land she was to dwell in; till the day when, like the boy taken by Napoleon from the tender care of home, she had inured her feet to tramp through mire and snow, inured her forehead to flying bullets, and broken herself entirely to the passive obedience of a soldier. All these things, which I abridge for you, she related in their gloomy details, with all their adjuncts of cruel incidents, of conjugal defeats, and fruitless efforts.

"In short," she said in conclusion, "only a residence here of months would give you a notion of all the troubles the improvements at Clochegourde cost me, all the weary coaxing to persuade him to do the thing that is most useful for his interests. What childish malice possesses him whenever anything I may have advised is not an immediate success! How delighted he is to proclaim himself in the right! What patience I need when I hear continual complaints while I am killing myself to clear each hour of weeds, to perfume the air he breathes, to strew sand and flowers on the paths he has beset with stones! My reward is this dreadful burden—'I am dying; life is a curse to me!'

"If he is so fortunate as to find visitors at home, all is forgotten; he is gracious and polite. Why can he not be the same to his family? I cannot account for this want of loyalty in a man who is sometimes chivalrous. He is capable of going off without a word, all the way to Paris, to get me a dress, as he did the other day for that ball. Miserly as he is in his housekeeping, he would be lavish for me if I would allow it. It ought to be just the other way; I want nothing, and the house expenses are heavy. In my anxiety to make him happy, and forgetting that I might be a mother, I perhaps gave him the habit of regarding me as his victim, whereas with a little flattery I might still manage him like a child if I would stoop to play so mean a part! But the interests of the household make it necessary that I should be as calm and austere as a statue of justice; and yet I, too, have a tender and effusive soul."

"But why," said I, "do you not avail yourself of your influence to be the mistress and guide him?"

"If I alone were concerned, I could never defy the stolid silence with which for hours he will oppose sound arguments, nor could I answer his illogical remarks—the reasoning of a child. I have no courage against weakness or childishness; they may hit me, and I shall make no resistance. I might meet force with force, but I have no power against those I pity. If I were required to compel Madeleine to do something that would save her life, we should die together. Pity relaxes all my fibres and weakens my sinews. And the violent shocks of the past ten years have undermined me; my nervous force, so often attacked, is sometimes deliquescent, nothing can restore it; the strength that weathered those storms is sometimes wanting. Yes, sometimes I am conquered.

"For want of rest and of sea-bathing, which would give tone to my whole system, I shall be worn out. Monsieur de Mortsauf will kill me if he keeps on, and he will die of my death."

"Why do you not leave Clochegourde for a few months? Why should you and the children not go to the sea?"

"In the first place, Monsieur de Mortsauf would feel himself lost if I left him. Though he will not recognize the situation, he is aware of his state. The man and the invalid are at war in him, two different natures, whose antagonism accounts for many eccentricities. And, indeed, he has every reason to dread it; if I were absent, everything here would go wrong. You have seen, no doubt, that I am a mother perpetually on the watch to guard her brood against the hawk that hovers over them; a desperate task, increased by the cares required by Monsieur de Mortsauf, whose perpetual cry is, 'Where is madame?' But this is nothing. I am at the same time Jacques' tutor and Madeleine's governess. This again is nothing. I am steward and bookkeeper. You will some day know the full meaning of my words when I say that the management of an estate is here the most exhausting toil. We have but a small income in money, and our farms are worked on a system of half-profits which requires incessant superintendence. We ourselves must sell our corn, our beasts, and every kind of crop. Our competitors are our own farmers, who agree with the purchasers over their wine at the tavern, and fix a price after being before us in the market.

"I should tire you out if I were to tell you all the thousand difficulties of our husbandry. With all my vigilance, I cannot keep our farmers from manuring their lands from our middens; I can neither go to make sure that our bailiffs do not agree with them to cheat us when the crops are divided, nor can I know the best time to sell. And if you think how little memory Monsieur de Mortsauf can boast of, and what trouble it costs me to induce him to attend to business, you will understand what a load I have to carry, and the impossibility of setting it down even for a moment. If I went away, we should be ruined. No one would listen to his orders; indeed, they are generally contradictory; then nobody is attached to him; he finds too much fault and is too despotic; and, like all weak natures, he is overready to listen to his inferiors, and so fails to inspire the affection that binds families together. If I left the house, not a servant would stay a week.

"So you see I am as much rooted to Clochegourde as one of the leaden finials is to the roof. I have kept nothing from you, monsieur. The neighbors know nothing of the secrets of Clochegourde; you now know them all. Say nothing of the place but what is kind and pleasant, and you will earn my esteem—my gratitude," she added in a softened tone. "On these conditions you can always come to Clochegourde —you will find friends here."

"But I have never known what it is to suffer," exclaimed I. "You alone——"

"Nay," said she, with that resigned woman's smile that might melt granite, "do not be dismayed by my confidences. They show you life as it is, and not as your fancy had led you to hope. We all have our faults and our good points. If I had married a spendthrift, he would have ruined me. If I had been the wife of some ardent and dissipated youth, he would have been a favorite with women; perhaps he would have been unfaithful, and I should have died of jealousy. I am jealous!" she exclaimed in an excited tone that rang like the thunderclap of a passing storm.

"Well, Monsieur de Mortsauf loves me as much as it is in him to love; all the affection of which his heart is capable is poured out at my feet, as the Magdalen poured out her precious balm at the feet of the Saviour. Believe me when I tell you that a life of love is an exception to every earthly law; every flower fades, every great joy has a bitter morrow—when it has a morrow. Real life is a life of sorrow; this nettle is its fit image; it has sprouted in the shade of the terrace, and grows green on its stem without any sunshine. Here, as in northern latitudes, there are smiles in the sky, rare, to be sure, but making amends for many griefs. After all, if a woman is exclusively a mother, is she not tied by sacrifices rather than by joys? I can draw down on myself the storms I see ready to break on the servants or on my children, and as I thus conduct them I feel some mysterious and secret strength. The resignation of one day prepares me for the next.

"And God does not leave me hopeless. Though I was at one time in despair over my children's health, I now see that as they grow up they grow stronger. And, after all, our house is improved, our fortune is amended. Who knows whether Monsieur de Mortsauf's old age may not bring me happiness.

"Believe me, the human being who can appear in the presence of the Great Judge, leading any comforted soul that had been ready to curse life, will have transformed his sorrows into delight. If my suffering has secured the happiness of my family, is it really suffering?"

"Yes," replied I. "Still, it was necessary suffering, as mine has been, to make me appreciate the fruit that has ripened here among stones. And now perhaps we may eat of it together, perhaps we may admire its wonders!—the flood of affection it can shed on the soul, the sap which can revive the fading leaves. Then life is no longer a burden; we have cast it from us. Great God! can you not understand?" I went on, in the mystical strain to which religious training had accustomed us both. "See what roads we have trodden to meet at last! What loadstone guided us across the ocean of bitter waters to the fresh springs flowing at the foot of the mountains, over sparkling sands, between green and flowery banks? Have we not, like the Kings of the East, followed the same star? And we stand by the manger where lies an awakening Babe—a divine Child who will shoot his arrows at the head of the leafless trees, who will wake the world to new life for us by his glad cries, who will lend savor to life by continual delights, and give slumbers by night and contentment by day. Are we not more than brother and sister? What heaven has joined, put not asunder.

"The sorrow of which you speak is the grain scattered freely abroad by the hand of the sower, to bring forth a harvest already golden under the most glorious sun. Behold and see! Shall we not go forth together and gather it ear by ear? What fervor is in me that I dare to speak to you thus. Answer me, or I will never cross the Indre again."

"You have spared me the name of love," said she, interrupting me in a severe tone; "but you have described a feeling of which I know nothing—which to me is prohibited. You are but a boy, and again I forgive you; but it is for the last time. Understand, monsieur, my whole heart is drunk, so to speak, with motherhood. I love Monsieur de Mortsauf, not as a social duty, nor as an investment to earn eternal bliss, but from an irresistible feeling, clinging to him by every fibre of my heart. Was I forced into this marriage? I chose it out of sympathy with misfortune. Was it not the part of woman to heal the bruises of time, to comfort those who had stood in the breach and come back wounded?

"How can I tell you? I felt a sort of selfish pleasure in seeing that you could amuse him. Is not that purely motherly? Has not my long story shown you plainly that I have three children who must never find me wanting, on whom I must shed a healing dew and all the sunshine of my soul without allowing the smallest particle to be adulterated? Do not turn a mother's milk.

"So, though the wife in me is invulnerable, never speak to me thus again. If you fail to respect this simple prohibition, I warn you, the door of this house will be closed against you for ever. I believed in pure friendship, in a voluntary brotherhood more stable than any natural relationship. I was mistaken! I looked for a friend who would not judge me, a friend who would listen to me in those hours of weakness when a voice of reproof is murderous, a saintly friend with whom I should have nothing to fear. Youth is magnanimous, incapable of falsehood, self-sacrificing, and disinterested; as I saw your constancy, I believed, I confess, in some help from heaven; I believed I had met a spirit that would be to me alone what the priest is to all, a heart into which I might pour out my sorrows when they are too many, and utter my cries when they insist on being heard and would choke me if I suppressed them. In that way my life, which is so precious to these children, might be prolonged till Jacques is a man. But this, perhaps, is too selfish. Can the tale of Petrarch's Laura be repeated? I deceived myself, this is not the will of God. I must die at my post like a soldier, without a friend. My confessor is stern, austere—and my aunt is dead."

Two large tears, sparking in the moonlight, dropped from her eyes and rolled down her cheeks to her chin; but I held out my hand in time to catch them and drank them with pious avidity, excited by her words, that rang with those ten years of secret weeping, of expanded feeling, of incessant care, of perpetual alarms—the loftiest heroism of your sex. She gazed at me with a look of mild amazement mingled with wonder.

"This," said I, "is the first, holy communion of love. Yes, I have entered into your sorrows, I am one with your soul, as we become one with Christ by drinking His sacred blood. To love even without hope is happiness. What woman on earth could give me any joy so great as that of having imbibed your tears! I accept the bargain which must, no doubt, bring me suffering. I am yours without reserve, and will be just whatever you wish me to be."

She checked me by a gesture, and said—

"I consent to the compact if you will never strain the ties that bind us."

"Yes," said I. "But the less you grant me, the more sure must I be that I really possess it."

"So you begin by distrusting me," she replied, with melancholy doubtfulness.

"No, by one pure delight. For listen, I want a name for you which no one ever calls you by; all my own, like the affection that we give each other."

"It is much to ask," said she. "However, I am less ungenerous than you think me. Monsieur de Mortsauf calls me Blanche. One person only, the one I loved best, my adorable aunt, used to call me Henriette. I will be Henriette again for you."

I took her hand and kissed it, and she yielded it with the full confidence which makes woman our superior—a confidence that masters us. She leaned against the brick parapet and looked out over the river.

"Are you not rash, dear friend," said she, "to rush with one leap to the goal of your course? You have drained at the first draught a cup offered you in all sincerity. But a true feeling knows no half-measures; it is all or nothing. Monsieur de Mortsauf," she went on after a moment's silence, "is above everything loyal and proud. You might perhaps be tempted for my sake to overlook what he said; if he has forgotten it, I will remind him of it to-morrow. Stay away from Clochegourde for a few days; he will respect you all the more. On Sunday next, as we come out of church, he will make the first advances. I know him. He will make up for past offenses, and will like you the better for having treated him as a man responsible for his words and deeds."

"Five days without seeing you, hearing your voice!"

"Never put such fervor into your speech to me," said she.

We twice paced the terrace in silence. Then, in a tone of command, which showed that she had entered into possession of my soul, she said—

"It is late; good-night."

I wished to kiss her hand; she hesitated; then she gave it me, saying in a voice of entreaty—

"Never take it unless I give it you; leave me completely free, or else I shall be at your bidding, and that must not be."

"Good-by," said I.

I went out of the little gate at the bottom of the garden, which she opened for me. Just as she was shutting it she opened it again, and held out her hand, saying—

"You have been indeed kind this evening. You have brought comfort into all my future life. Take it, my friend, take it."

I kissed it again and again, and when I looked up I saw that there were tears in her eyes.

She went up to the terrace and looked after me across the meadow. As I went along the road to Frapesle, I could still see her white dress in the moonlight; then, a few minutes later, a light was shining in her window.

"Oh, my Henriette!" thought I, "the purest love that ever burnt on earth shall be yours."

I got home to Frapesle, looking back at every step. My spirit was full of indescribable, ineffable gladness. A glorious path at last lay open to the self-devotion that swells every youthful heart, and that in me had so long lain inert. I was consecrated, ordained, like a priest who at one step starts on a totally new life. A simple "*Yes, madame,*" had pledged me to preserve in my heart and for myself alone an irresistible passion, and never to trespass beyond friendship to tempt this woman little by little to love. Every noble feeling awoke within me with a tumult of voices.

Before finding myself cabined in a bedroom, I felt that I must pause in rapture under the blue vault spangled with stars, to hear again in my mind's ear those tones as of a wounded dove, the simple accents of her ingenuous confidence, and inhale with the air the emanations of her soul which she must be sending out to me. How noble she appeared to me—the woman who so utterly forgot herself in her religious care for weak or suffering or wounded creatures, her devotedness apart from legal chains. She stood serene at the stake of saintly martyrdom! I was gazing at her face as it appeared to me in the darkness, when suddenly I fancied that I discerned in her words a mystical significance which made her seem quite sublime. Perhaps she meant that I was to be to her what she was to her little world; perhaps she intended to derive strength and consolation from me by thus raising me to her sphere, to her level—or higher? The stars, so some bold theorists tell us, thus interchange motion and light. This thought at once lifted me to ethereal realms. I was once more in the heaven of my early dreams, and I accounted for the anguish of my childhood by the infinite beatitude in which I now floated.

Ye souls of genius extinguished by tears, misprized hearts, Clarissa Harlowes, saintly and unsung, outcast children, guiltless exiles—all ye who entered life through its desert places, who have everywhere found cold faces, closed hearts, deaf ears—do not bewail yourselves! You alone can know the immensity of joy in the moment when a heart opens to you, an ear listens, a look answers you. One day wipes out all the evil days. Past sorrows, broodings, despair, and melancholy —past, but not forgotten—are so many bonds by which the soul clings to its sister soul. The woman, beautified by our suppressed desires, inherits our wasted sighs and loves; she refunds our deluded affections with interest; she supplies a reason for antecedent griefs, for they are the equivalent insisted on by fate for the eternal joy she bestows on the day when souls are wed. The angels only know the new name by which this sacred love may be called; just as you, sweet martyrs, alone can know what Madame de Mortsauf had suddenly become to me—hapless and alone.

This scene had taken place one Tuesday; I waited till

the following Sunday before recrossing the Indre in my walks.

During these five days great events occurred at Clochegourde. The Count was promoted to the grade of major-general, and the Cross of Saint-Louis was conferred on him with a pension of four thousand francs. The Duc de Lenoncourt-Givry was made a peer of France, two of his forest domains were restored to him, he had an appointment at court, and his wife was reinstated in her property, which had not been sold, having formed part of the imperial crown lands. Thus the Comtesse de Mortsauf had become one of the richest heiresses in the province. Her mother had come to Clochegourde to pay her a hundred thousand francs she had saved out of the revenues from Givry; this money, settled on her at her marriage, she had never received; but the Count, in spite of his necessity, had never alluded to this. In all that concerned the outer circumstances of life, this man's conduct was marked by disinterested pride.

By adding this sum to what he had saved, the Count could now purchase two adjoining estates, that would bring in about nine thousand francs a year. His son was to inherit his maternal grandfather's peerage; and it occurred to the Count to entail on Jacques the landed property of both families without prejudice to Madeleine, who, with the Duc de Lenoncourt's interest, would, no doubt, marry well.

All these schemes and this good fortune shed some balm on the exile's wounds.

The Duchesse de Lenoncourt at Clochegourde was an event in the district. I sorrowfully reflected what a great lady she was, and I then discerned in her daughter that spirit of caste which her noble soul had hitherto hidden from my eyes. What was I—poor, and with no hope for the future but in my courage and my brains? I never thought of the consequences of the restoration either to myself or to others.

On Sunday, from the side chapel, where I attended mass

with Monsieur and Madame de Chessel and the Abbé Quélus, I sent hungry looks to the chapel on the opposite side, where the Duchess and her daughter were, the Count, and the children. The straw bonnet that hid my idol's face never moved, and this ignoring of my presence seemed to be a stronger tie than all that had passed. The noble Henriette de Lenoncourt, who was now my beloved Henriette, was absorbed in prayer; faith gave an indescribable sentiment of prostrate dependence to her attitude, the feeling of a sacred statue, which penetrated my soul.

As is customary in village churches, vespers were chanted some little time after high mass. As we left the church, Madame de Chessel very naturally suggested to her neighbors that they should spend the two hours' interval at Frapesle instead of crossing the Indre and the valley twice in the heat. The invitation was accepted. Monsieur de Chessel gave the Duchess his arm, Madame de Chessel took the Count's, and I offered mine to the Countess. For the first time I felt that light wrist resting by my side. As we made our way back from the church to Frapesle through the woods of Saché, where the dappled lights, falling through the leaves, made pretty patterns like China silk, I went through surges of pride and thrills of feeling that gave me violent palpitations.

"What ails you?" said she, after we had gone a few steps in silence, which I dared not break; "your heart beats too fast."

"I have heard of good fortune for you," said I, "and, like all who love much, I feel some vague fears. Will not your greatness mar your friendship?"

"Mine?" cried she. "For shame! If you ever have such an idea I shall not despise you, but simply forget you for ever."

I looked at her in a state of intoxication, which must surely have been infectious.

"We get the benefit of an edict which we neither prompted

nor asked for, and we shall neither be beggars nor grasping," she went on. "Beside, as you know, neither I nor Monsieur de Mortsauf can ever leave Clochegourde. By my advice he has declined the active command he had a right to at the Maison Rouge. It is enough that my father should have an appointment. And our compulsory modesty," she went on, with a bitter smile, "has been to our boy's advantage already. The King, on whom my father is in attendance, has very graciously promised to reserve for Jacques the favors we have declined.

"Jacques' education, which must now be thought of, is the subject of very grave discussion. He will be the representative of the two houses of Mortsauf and Lenoncourt. I have no ambition but for him, so this is an added anxiety. Not only must Jacques be kept alive, but he must also be made worthy of his name, and the two necessities are antagonistic. Hitherto I have been able to teach him, graduating his tasks to his strength; but where am I to find a tutor who would suit me in this respect? And then, by-and-by, to what friend can I look to preserve him in that dreadful Paris, where everything is a snare to the soul and a peril to the body?

"My friend," she went on, in an agitated voice, "who that looks at your brow and eye can fail to see in you one of the birds that dwell on the heights. Take your flight, soar up, and one day become the guardian of our beloved child. Go to Paris; and if your brother and your father will not help you, our family, especially my mother, who has a genius for business, will have great influence. Take the benefit of it, and then you will never lack support or encouragement in any career you may choose. Throw your superabundant energy into ambition——"

"I understand," said I, interrupting her. "My ambition is to be my mistress! I do not need that to make me wholly yours. No; I do not choose to be rewarded for my good behavior here by favors there. I will go; I will grow up alone, unaided. I will accept what you can give me; from any one else I will take nothing."

"That is childish," she murmured, but she could not disguise a smile of satisfaction.

"Beside," I went on, "I have pledged myself. In considering our position, I have resolved to bind myself to you by ties which can never be loosened."

She shivered, and stood still to look in my face.

"What do you mean?" she asked, letting the other couples who were in front of us go forward, and keeping the children by her side.

"Well," replied I, "tell me plainly how you would wish me to love you."

"Love me as my aunt loved me; I have given you her rights by permitting you to call me by the name she had chosen from my names."

"Love you without hope, with entire devotion? Yes, I will do for you what men do for God. Have you not asked it of me? I will go into a seminary; I will come out a priest, and I will educate Jacques. Your Jacques shall be my second self: my political notions, my thoughts, my energy, and patience—I will give them all to him. Thus I may remain near you, and no suspicion can fall on my love, set in religion like a silver image in a crystal. You need not fear any of those perfervid outbreaks which come over a man, which once already proved too much for me. I will be burned in the fire, and love you with purified ardor."

She turned pale, and answered eagerly, without any hesitancy—

"Félix, do not fetter yourself with cords, which some day may be an obstacle in the way of our happiness. I should die of grief if I were the cause of such suicide. Child, is the despair of love a religious vocation? Wait to test life before you judge of life. I desire it—I insist. Marry neither the church nor a woman; do not marry at all; I forbid it. Remain free. You are now one-and-twenty; you scarcely know what the future may have in store.

"Good heavens!" she added, "am I mistaken in you? But I believed that in two months one might really know some natures."

"What, then, is it that you hope for?" I asked with lightning in my eyes.

"My friend, accept my assistance, educate yourself, make a fortune, and you shall know. Well, then," she added, as if she were betraying her secret, "always hold fast to Madeleine's hand, which is at this moment in yours."

She had bent toward me to whisper these words, which showed how seriously she had thought of my future prospects.

"Madeleine?" cried I. "Never!"

These two words left us silent again and greatly agitated. Our minds were tossed by such upheavals as leave indelible traces.

Just before us was a wooden gate into the park of Frapesle —I think I can see it now, with its tumble-down side-posts overgrown with climbing plants, moss, weeds, and brambles. Suddenly an idea—that of the Count's death—flashed like an arrow through my brain, and I said—

"I understand."

"That is fortunate," she replied, in a tone which made me see that I had suspected her of a thought that could never have occurred to her.

Her pure-mindedness wrung from me a tear of admiration, made bitter indeed by the selfishness of my passion. Then, with a revulsion of feeling, I thought that she did not love me enough to wish for freedom. So long as love shrinks from crime, it seems to have a limit, and love ought to be infinite. I felt a terrible spasm at my heart.

"She does not love me," thought I.

That she might not read my soul, I bent down and kissed Madeleine's hair.

"I am afraid of your mother," I said to the Countess, to reopen the conversation.

"So am I," she replied, with a childish gesture. "Do not forget to address her as Madame la Duchesse, and speak to her in the third person. Young people of the present day have forgotten those polite formalities; revive them; do that much for me. Beside, it is always in good taste to be respectful to a woman, whatever her age may be, and to accept social distinctions without hesitancy. Is not the homage you pay to recognized superiority a guarantee for what is due to yourself? In society everything holds together. The Cardinal de Rovere and Raphael d'Urbino were in their time two equally respected powers.

"You have drunk the milk of the revolution in your schools, and your political ideas may show the taint; but as you get on in life, you will discover that ill-defined notions of liberty are inadequate to create the happiness of nations. I, before considering, as a Lenoncourt, what an aristocracy is or ought to be, listen to my peasant commonsense, which shows me that society exists only by the hierarchy. You are at a stage in your life when you must make a wise choice. Stick to your party, especially," she added, with a laugh, " when it is on the winning side."

I was deeply touched by these words, in which wise policy lurked below the warmth of her affection, a union which gives women such powers of fascination. They all know how to lend the aspect of sentiment to the shrewdest reasoning.

Henriette, in her anxiety to justify the Count's actions, had, as it seemed, anticipated the reflections which must arise in my mind when, for the first time, I saw the results of being a courtier. Monsieur de Mortsauf, a king in his domain, surrounded with his historic halo, had assumed magnificent proportions in my eyes, and I own that I was greatly astonished at the distance he himself set between the Duchess and himself by his subservient manner. A slave even has his pride; he will only obey the supreme despot; I felt myself humbled at seeing the abject attitude of the man who made me tremble by overshadowing my love. This impulse of feeling revealed to me all the torment of a woman whose generous soul is joined to that of a man whose meanness she has to cover decently every day. Respect is a barrier which protects great and small alike; each on his own part can look the other steadily in the face.

I was deferent to the Duchess by reason of my youth; but where others saw only the Duchess, I saw my Henriette's mother, and there was a solemnity in my respect.

We went into the front court of Frapesle, and there found all the party. The Comte de Mortsauf introduced me to the lady with much graciousness, and she examined me with a cold, reserved manner. Madame de Lenoncourt was then a woman of fifty-six, extremely well-preserved, and with lordly manners. Seeing her hard, blue eyes, her wrinkled temples, her thin, ascetic face, her stately upright figure, her constant quiescence, her dull pallor—in her daughter brilliant whiteness—I recognized her as of the same race as my own mother, as surely as a mineralogist recognizes Swedish iron. Her speech was that of the old court circles; she pronounced *oit* as *ait*, spoke of *frait* for *froid*, and of *porteux* for *porteurs*. I was neither servile nor prim, and I behaved so nicely that, as we went to vespers, the Countess said in my ear, "You are perfect."

The Count came up to me, took my hand, and said, "We have not quarreled, Félix? If I was a little hasty, you will forgive your old comrade. We shall probably stay to dine here, and we hope to see you at Clochegourde on Thursday, the day before the Duchess leaves us. I am going to Tours on business. Do not neglect Clochegourde, my mother-in-law is an acquaintance I advise you to cultivate; her drawing-room will pitch the keynote for the Faubourg Saint-Germain. She has the tradition of the finest society, she is immensely well informed, and knows the armorial bearings of every gentleman in Europe from the highest to the lowest."

The Count's good taste, aided perhaps by the counsels of his good genius, told well in the new circumstances in which he was placed by the triumph of his party. He was neither arrogant nor offensively polite; he showed no affectation, and the Duchess no patronizing airs. Monsieur and Madame de Chessel gratefully accepted the invitation to dinner on the following Thursday.

The Duchess rather liked me, and her way of looking at me made me understand that she was studying me as a man of whom her daughter had spoken. On our return from church she inquired about my family, and asked whether the Vandenesse, who was already embarked in diplomacy, were a relation of mine.

"He is my brother," said I.

Then she became almost affectionate. She informed me that my grand-aunt, the old Marquise de Listomère, had been a Grandlieu. Her manner was polite, as Monsieur de Mortsauf's had been on the day when he saw me for the first time. Her eyes lost that haughty expression by which the princes of the earth make you feel the distance that divides you from them.

I knew hardly anything of my family; the Duchess told me that my great-uncle, an old abbé whom I did not know even by name, was a member of the privy council; that my brother had received promotion; and, finally, that, by a clause in the charter, of which I had heard nothing, my father was restored to his title of Marquis.

"I am but a chattel, a serf to Clochegourde," said I to the Countess in an undertone.

The fairy wand of the restoration had worked with a rapidity quite astounding to children brought up under Imperial rule. To me these changes meant nothing. Madame de Mortsauf's lightest word or merest gesture were the only events to which I attached any importance. I knew nothing of politics, nor of the ways of the world. I had no ambition but to love Henriette better than Petrarch loved Laura. This indifference made the Duchess look upon me as a boy.

A great deal of company came to Frapesle, and we were thirty at dinner. How enchanting for a young man to see the woman he loves the most beautiful person present and the object of passionate admiration, while he knows the light of those chastely modest eyes is for him alone, and is familiar enough with every tone of her voice to find in her speech, superficially trivial or ironical, proofs of an ever-present thought of him, even while his heart is full of burning jealousy of the amusements of her world!

The Count, delighted with the attentions paid him, was almost young again; his wife hoped it might work some change in him; I was gay with Madeleine, who, like all children in whom the body is too frail for the wrestling soul, made me laugh by her amazing remarks, full of sarcastic but never malignant wit, which spared no one. It was a lovely day. One word, one hope, born that morning had brightened all nature, and, seeing me so glad, Henriette was glad too.

"This happiness falling across my gray and cloudy life has done me good," she told me next day.

Of course I spent the morrow at Clochegourde; I had been exiled for five days, and thirsted for life. The Count had set out for Tours at five in the morning.

A serious matter of dispute had come up between the mother and daughter. The Duchess insisted that the Countess should come to Paris, where she would find her a place at court, and where the Count, by retracting his refusal, might fill a high position. Henriette, who was regarded as a happy wife, would not unveil her griefs to anybody, not even to her mother, nor betray her husband's incapacity. It was to prevent her mother from penetrating the secret of her home life that she had sent Monsieur de Mortsauf to Tours, where he was to fight out some questions with the lawyers. I alone, as she had said, knew the secrets of Clochegourde.

Having learned by experience how effective the pure air and blue sky of this valley were in soothing the irritable moods and acute sufferings of sickness, and how favorable the life at Clochegourde was to her children's health, she gave these reasons for her refusal, though strongly opposed by the Duchess—a domineering woman who felt humiliated rather than grieved by her daughter's far from brilliant marriage. Henriette could see that her mother cared little enough about Jacques and Madeleine, a terrible discovery!

Like all mothers who have been accustomed to treat a married daughter with the same despotism as they exerted over her as a girl, the Duchess adopted measures which allowed of no reply; now she affected insinuating kindness to extract consent to her views, and now assumed a bitter iciness to gain by fear what she could not achieve by sweetness; then, seeing all her efforts wasted, she showed the same acrid irony as I had known in my own mother. In the course of ten days Henriette went through all the heart-rendings a young wife must go through to establish her independence. You, who for your happiness have the best of mothers, can never understand these things. To form any idea of this struggle between a dry, cold, calculating, ambitious woman and her daughter overflowing with the fresh, genial sweetness that never runs dry, you must imagine the lily, with which I have compared the Countess, crushed in the wheels of a machine of polished steel. This mother had never had anything in common with her daughter; she could not suspect any of the real difficulties which compelled her to forego every advantage from the restoration, and to live her *solitary* life. This word, which she used to convey her suspicions, opened a gulf between the women which nothing could ever after bridge over.

Though families duly bury their terrible quarrels, look into their life ; you will find in almost every house some wide incurable wounds blighting natural feeling ; or some genuine and pathetic passion which affinity of character makes eternal, and which gives an added shock to the hand of death, leaving a dark and ineradicable bruise ; or, again, simmering hatred, slowly petrifying the heart, and freezing up all tears at the moment of eternal parting.

Tortured yesterday, tortured to-day, stricken by every one, even by the two suffering little ones, who were guiltless alike of the ills they endured and of those they caused, how could this sad soul help loving the one person who never gave a blow, but who would fain have hedged her round with a triple barrier of thorns, so as to shelter her from storms, from every touch, from every pain?

Though these squabbles distressed me, I was sometimes glad as I felt that she took refuge in my heart, for Henriette confided to me her new griefs. I could appreciate her fortitude in suffering, and the energy of patience she could maintain. Every day I understood more perfectly the meaning of her words, "Love me as my aunt loved me."

"Have you really no ambition?" said the Duchess to me at dinner, in a severe tone.

"Madame," replied I, with a very serious mien, "I feel myself strong enough to conquer the world ; but I am only one-and-twenty, and I stand alone."

She looked at her daughter with surprise ; she had believed that, in order to keep me at her side, the Countess had snuffed out all my ambition.

The time while the Duchess de Lenoncourt stayed at Clochegourde was one of general discomfort. The Countess besought me to be strictly formal ; she was frightened at a word spoken low ; to please her I was obliged to saddle myself with dissimulation.

The great Thursday came ; it was a festival of tiresome

formality, one of those days which lovers hate, when they are used to the facilities of every-day life, accustomed to find their place ready for them, and the mistress of the house wholly theirs. Love has a horror of everything but itself.

The Duchess returned to enjoy the pomps of the court, and all fell into order at Clochegourde.

My little skirmish with the Count had resulted in my being more firmly rooted in the house than before; I could come in at any time without giving rise to the slightest remark, and my previous life led me to spread myself like a climbing plant in the beautiful soul which opened to me the enchanted world of sympathetic feeling. From hour to hour, from minute to minute, our brotherly union, based on perfect confidence, became more intimate; we were confirmed in our relative positions: the Countess wrapped me in her cherishing affection in the white purity of motherly love; while my passion, seraphic in her presence, when I was absent from her grew fierce and thirsty like red-hot iron. Thus I loved her with a twofold love which by turns pierced me with the myriad darts of desire, and then lost them in the sky, where they vanished in the unfathomable ether.

If you ask me why, young as I was and full of vehement craving, I was satisfied to rest in the illusory hopes of a platonic affection, I must confess that I was not yet man enough to torment this woman, who lived in perpetual dread of some disaster to her children, constantly expecting some outbreak, some stormy change of mood in her husband; crushed by him when she was not distressed by some ailment in Jacques or Madeleine, and sitting by the bed of one or the other whenever her husband gave her a little peace. The sound of a too impassioned word shook her being, a desire startled her; for her I had to be love enshrined, strength in tenderness; everything, in short, that she was for others.

And, then, I may say to you, who are so truly woman, the

situation had its enchanting quietism, moments of heavenly sweetness, and of the satisfaction that follows on tacit renunciation. Her conscientiousness was infectious, her self-immolation for no earthly reward was impressive by its tenacity; the living but secret piety which held her other virtues together affected all about her like spiritual incense. Beside, I was young; young enough to concentrate my whole nature in the kiss she so rarely allowed me to press on her hand, giving me only the back of it, never the palm—that being to her, perhaps, the border-line of sensuality. Though two souls never fused and loved with greater ardor, never was the flesh more bravely or victoriously held in subjection.

Later in life I understood the causes of my complete happiness. At that age no self-interest distracted my heart, no ambition crossed the current of a feeling which, like an unstemmed torrent, fed its flow with everything it carried before it. Yes, as we grow older, the woman is what we love in a woman; whereas we love everything in the first woman we love—her children are our children, her house, her interests, are our own; her grief is our greatest grief; we love her dress and her belongings; it vexes us more to see her corn spilt than it would to lose our own money; we feel ready to quarrel with a stranger who should meddle with the trifles on the mantel. This sanctified love makes us live in another, while afterward, alas! we absorb that other life into our own, and require the woman to enrich our impoverished spirit with her youthful feeling.

I was ere long one of the family, and found here for the first time the infinite soothing which is to an aching heart what a bath is to the tired limbs; the soul is refreshed on every side, anointed in its inmost folds. You cannot understand this: you are a woman, and this is the happiness you give without ever receiving in kind. Only a man can know the delicate enjoyment of being the privileged friend of the mistress of another home, the secret pivot of her affections.

The dogs cease to bark at you; the servants, like the dogs, recognize the hidden passport you bear; the children, who have no insincerities, who know that their share will never be smaller, but that you bring joy to the light of their life— the children have a spirit of divination. To you they become kittenish, with the delightful tyranny that they keep for those they adore and who adore them; they are shrewdly knowing, and your guileless accomplices; they steal up on tiptoe, smile in your face, and silently leave you. Everything welcomes you, loves you, and smiles upon you. A true passion is like a beautiful flower, which it is all the more delightful to find when the soil that produces it is barren and wild.

But if I had the delights of being thus naturalized in a family where I made relationships after my own heart, I also paid the penalties. Hitherto Monsieur de Mortsauf had controlled himself in my presence; I had only seen the general outline of his faults, but I now discerned their application in its fullest extent, and I saw how nobly charitable the Countess had been in her description of her daily warfare. I felt all the angles of his intolerable temper; I heard his ceaseless outcries about mere trifles, his complaints of ailments of which no sign was visible, his innate discontent, which blighted her life, and the incessant craving to rule, which would have made him devour fresh victims every year. When we walked out in the evening, he chose the way we went; but, wherever it might be, he was always bored by it; when he got home he blamed others for his fatigue—it was his wife who had done it, by taking him against his will the way she wanted to go; he forgot that he had led us, and complained of being ruled by her in every trifle, of never being allowed to decide or think for himself, of being a mere cypher in the house. If his hard words fell on silent patience he got angry, feeling the limit to his power; he would inquire sharply whether religion did not require wives to submit to their husbands, and whether it was decent to make a father contemptible before his children.

He always ended by touching some sensitive chord in his wife; and when he had struck it, he seemed to find particular pleasure in this domineering pettiness.

Sometimes he affected gloomy taciturnity and morbid dejection, which frightened his wife and led her to lavish on him the most touching care. Like spoiled children, who exert their power without a thought of their mother's alarms, he allowed himself to be petted like Jacques or Madeleine; of whom he was very jealous. At last, indeed, I discovered that in the smallest, as in the most important matters, the Count behaved to his servants, his children, and his wife as he had to me over the backgammon.

On the day when I first understood, root and branch, those miseries which, like forest creepers, stifled and crushed the movement and the very breathing of this family, which cast a tangle of fine but infinitely numerous threads about the working of the household, hindering every advance of fortune by hampering the most necessary steps, I was seized with admiring awe, which subjugated my love and crushed it down into my heart. What was I, good God! The tears I had swallowed filled me with a sort of rapturous intoxication; it was a joy to me to identify myself with this wife's endurance. Till then I had submitted to the Count's tyranny as a smuggler pays his fines; thenceforth I voluntarily received the despot's blows to be as close as possible to Henriette. The Countess understood, and allowed me to take my place at her side, rewarding me by granting me to share her penance, as of old the repentant apostate, eager to fly heavenward with his brethren, won permission to die in the arena.

"But for you this life would be too much for me," she said one night when the Count had been more annoying, more acrid, and more whimsical than usual, as flies are in great heat.

He had gone to bed. Henriette and I sat during part of the evening under the acacias basking in the beams of sunset, the children playing near us. Our words, mere infrequent exclamations, expressed the sympathetic feelings in which we had taken refuge from our common sufferings. When words failed us, silence served us faithfully; our souls entered into each other, so to speak, without hindrance, but without the invitation of a kiss; each enjoying the charm of pensive torpor, they floated together on the ripples of the same dream, dipped together in the river, and came forth like two nymphs as closely one as even jealousy could wish, but free from every earthly tie. We plunged into a bottomless abyss, and came back to the surface, our hands empty, but asking each other by a look, "Out of so many days, shall we ever have one single day for our own?"

When rapture culls for us these blossoms without root, why is it that the flesh rebels? In spite of the enervating poetry of the evening which tinged the brickwork of the parapet with sober and soothing tones of orange; in spite of the religious atmosphere, which softened the shouts of the children, leaving us at peace, longing ran in sparks of fire through my veins like the signal for a blaze of rockets. At the end of three months I was beginning to be dissatisfied with the lot appointed to me; and I was softly fondling Henriette's hand, trying thus to expend a little of the fever that was scorching me.

Henriette was at once Madame de Mortsauf again; a few tears rose to my eyes, she saw them, and gave me a melting look, laying her hand on my lips.

"Understand," said she, "that this costs me tears too. The friendship that asks so great a favor is dangerous."

I broke out in a passion of reproach, I spoke of all I suffered, and of the small alleviation I craved to help me to endure it. I dared tell her that at my age, though the senses were spiritualized, the spirit had a sex; that I could die—but not without having spoken.

She reduced me to silence with a flashing look of pride, in

which I seemed to read the cacique's reply, "Am I then on a bed of roses?" Perhaps, too, I was mistaken. Ever since the day when, at the gate of Frapesle, I had wrongly ascribed to her the idea which would build our happiness on a tomb, I had been ashamed to stain her soul by uttering a wish tainted with mere criminal passion.

Then she spoke, and in honeyed words told me that she could never be wholly mine, that I ought to know that. I understood, as she spoke the words, that if I submitted, I should have dug a gulf between us. I bent my head. She went on, saying that she had an inmost conviction that she might love a brother without offense to God or man; that there is some comfort in thus taking such an affection as a living image of Divine love, which, according to the good Saint-Martin, is the life of the world. If I could not be to her some such person as her old director, less than a lover but more than a brother, we must meet no more. She could but die, offering up to God this added anguish, though she could not endure it without tears and torment.

"I have given you more than I ought," she said in conclusion, "since there is nothing more that you can take, and I am already punished."

I could but soothe her, promise never, never to cause her a moment's pain, and vow to love her at twenty as old men love their youngest born.

Next morning I came early to the house. She had no flowers to put in the vases in her gray drawing-room. I tramped across the fields and through the vineyards, hunting for flowers to make her two nosegays; and as I gathered them one by one, cutting them with long stems and admiring them, it struck that there was a harmony in their hues and foliage, a poetry that found its way to the understanding by fascinating the eye, just as musical phrases arouse a thousand associations in loved and loving hearts. If color is organic light, must it not have its meaning, as vibrations of the air have? Helped by Jacques and Madeleine, all three of us happy in contriving a surprise for our dear one, I sat down on the lower steps of the terrace flight, where we spread out our flowers and set to work to compose two nosegays, by which I intended to symbolize a sentiment.

Picture to yourself a fountain of flowers, gushing up, as it were, from the vase and falling in fringed waves, and from the heart of it my aspirations rose as silver-cupped lilies and white roses. Among this cool mass twinkled blue cornflowers, forget-me-not, bugloss—every blue flower whose hues, borrowed from the sky, blend so well with white; for are they not two types of innocence—that which knows nothing and that which knows all—the mind of a child and the mind of a martyr? Love has its blazonry, and the Countess read my meaning. She gave me one of those piercing looks that are like the cry of a wounded man touched on the tender spot; she was at once shy and delighted. What a reward I found in that look! What encouragement in the thought that I could please her and refresh her heart!

So I invented Father Castel's theory as applied to love and rediscovered for her a lore lost to Europe, where flowers of language take the place of the messages conveyed in the East by color and fragrance. And it was charming to express my meaning through these daughters of the sun, the sisters of the blossoms that open under the radiance of love. I soon had an understanding with the products of the rural flora, just as a man I met at a later time had with bees.

Twice a week, during the remainder of my stay at Frapesle, I carried out the long business of this poetical structure, for which I needed every variety of grass, and I studied them all with care, less as a botanist than as an artist, and with regard to their sentiment rather than their form. To find a flower where it grew I often walked immense distances along the river-bank, through the dells, to the top of cliffs, across the sandhills and commons, gathering ideas from among clumps of heath. In these walks I discovered for myself pleasures unknown to the student who lives in meditation, to the husbandman engaged on some special culture, to the artisan tied to the town, to the merchant nailed to his counting-house, but known to some foresters, to some woodsmen, to some dreamers.

Nature has certain effects of boundless meaning, rising to the level of the greatest intellectual ideas. Thus, a blossoming heath covered with diamonds of dew that hang on every leaf sparkling in the sun, a thing of infinite beauty for one single eye that may happen to see it. Or a forest nook, shut in by tumbled boulders, broken by willows, carpeted with moss, dotted with juniper shrubs—it scares you by its wild, hurtled, fearful aspect, and the cry of the hawk comes up to you. Or a scorching sandy common with no vegetation; a stony, precipitous plateau, the horizon reminding you of the desert—but there I found an exquisite and lonely flower, a pulsatilla waving its violet silk pennon in honor of its golden stamens; a pathetic image of my fair idol, alone in her valley! Or, again, broad pools over which nature flings patches of greenery, a sort of transition between animal and vegetable being, and in a few days life is there—floating plants and insects, like a world in the upper air. Or, again, a cottage with its cabbage garden, its vineyard, its fences, overhanging a bog, and surrounded by a few meagre fields of rye—emblematic of many a humble life. Or a long forest avenue, like the nave of a cathedral where the pillars are trees, their branches meeting like the groins of a vault, and at the end a distant glade seen through the foliage, dappled with light and shade, or glowing in the ruddy beams of sunset like the painted glass window of a chancel, filled with birds for choristers. Then, as you come out of the grove, a chalky fallow where full-fed snakes wriggle over the hot, crackling moss and vanish into their holes after raising their graceful, proud heads. And over these pictures cast floods of sunshine, rippling like a nourishing tide, or piles of gray cloud in bars like the furrows on an old man's brow, or the cool tones of a faintly yellow sky banded with pale light—and listen! You will hear vague harmonies in the depth of bewildering silence.

During the months of September and October I never collected a nosegay which took me less than three hours of seeking, I was so lost in admiration—with the mild indolence of a poet—of these transient allegories which represented to me the strongest contrasts of human life, majestic scenes in which my memory now digs for treasure. To this day I often wed to such grand spectacles my remembrance of the soul that then pervaded nature. I still see in them my queen, whose white dress floated through the copse and danced over the lawns, and whose spirit came up to me like a promise of fruition from every flower-cup full of amorous stamens.

No declaration, no proof of unbounded passion was ever more contagious than were these symphonies of flowers, wherein my cheated desires gave me such inspiration as Beethoven could express in notes; with vehement reaction on himself, transcendent heavenward flights. When she saw them Henriette was no longer Madame de Mortsauf. She came back to them again and again; she fed on them; she found in them all the thoughts I had woven into them, when, to accept the offering, she looked up from her work-frame and said, "Dear! how lovely that is!"

You can imagine this enchanting communication through the arrangement of a nosegay, as you would understand Saadi from a fragment of his poetry. Have you ever smelt in the meadows, in the month of May, the fragrance which fills all creatures with the heady joy of procreation; which, if you are in a boat, makes you dip your hands in the water; which makes you loosen your hair to the breeze, and renews your thoughts like the fresh greenery on the trees of the forest? A small grass, the vernal anthoxanthum, is one of the chief elements in this mysterious combination. No one can wear it with impunity. If you put a few sprays of it in a nosegay, with its shining variegated blades like a finely striped green-and-white dress, unaccountable pulses will stir within you, opening the rosebuds in your heart that modesty keeps closed. Imagine, then, round the wide edge of the china jar a border composed entirely of the white tufts peculiar to a sedum that grows in the vineyards of Touraine, a faint image of the wished-for forms, bowed like a submissive slave-girl. From this base rise the tendrils of bindweed with its white funnels, bunches of pink rest-harrow mingled with young shoots of oak gorgeously tinted and lustrous; these all stand forward, humbly drooping like weeping willow, timid and suppliant like prayers. Above, you see the slender blossoming sprays, for ever tremulous, of quaking grass and its stream of yellowish anthers; the snowy tufts of feathergrass from brook and meadow, the green hair of the barren brome, the frail agrostis —pale, purple hopes that crown our earliest dreams, and that stand out against the gray-green background in the light that plays on all these flowering grasses. Above these, again, there are a few China roses, mingling with the light tracery of carrot leaves with plumes of cottongrass, marabout tufts of meadow-sweet, umbels of wild parsley, the pale hair of travelers' joy, now in seed; the tiny crosslets of milky-white candytuft and milfoil, the loose sprays of rose-and-black fumitory, tendrils of the vine, twisted branches of the honeysuckle—in short, every form these artless creatures can show that is wildest and most ragged—flamboyant and trident; spear-shaped, dentate leaves, and stems as knotted as desire writhing in the depths of the soul. And from the heart of this overflowing torrent of love, a grand red double poppy stands up with bursting buds, flaunting its burning flame above starry jessamine and above the ceaseless shower of pollen, a cloud dancing in the air and reflecting the sunshine in its glittering motes. Would not any woman, who is alive to the seductive perfume that lurks in the anthoxanthum, understand this mass of abject ideas, this tender whiteness broken by uncontrollable impulses, and this red fire of love imploring joys denied it in the hundred struggles of an undying, unwearied, and eternal passion? Set this appeal in the sunshine of a window so as to do justice to all its subtle details, its delicate contrasts and arabesque elegance, that its mistress may see perhaps an open blossom moist with a tear— she will be very near yielding; an angel, or the voice of her children, alone will check her on the edge of the abyss.

What do we offer up to God? Incense, light and song, the purest expression at our command. Well, then, was not all that we offer to God dedicated to love in this poem of glowing flowers, ever murmuring sadly to the heart while encouraging hidden raptures, unconfessed hopes, and illusions which flash and are gone like shooting stars on a hot night?

These neutral pleasures were a comfort to us, helping us to cheat nature, exasperated by long study of the beloved face and by glances which find enjoyment in piercing to the very core of the form they gaze on. To me—I dare not say to her—these utterances were like the rifts through which the water spurts in a solid dyke, and which often prevent a catastrophe by affording a necessary outlet. Abstinence brings overwhelming exhaustion that finds succor in the few crumbs dropping from the sky, which, from Dan to the Sahara, sheds manna on the pilgrim. And I have found Henriette before one of those nosegays, her hands hanging loosely, a prey to those stormy contemplations when the feelings swell the bosom, give light to the brow, surge up in waves that toss and foam and leave us enervated by exhaustion.

I have never since gathered nosegays for any one!

When we had invented this language for our own use, we felt the sort of satisfaction that a slave finds in deceiving his master.

All the rest of the month, when I hurried up the garden, I

often saw her face at the window, and when I went into the drawing-room she was sitting at her frame. If I did not arrive punctually at the time we had agreed upon, without ever fixing an hour, I sometimes saw her white figure on the terrace, and when I found her there she would say—

"I came to meet you to-day. Must we not pet the youngest child?"

The dreadful games of backgammon with the Count had come to an end. His recent purchases required him to be constantly busy, inspecting, verifying, measuring, and planning; he had orders to give, field-work that required the master's eye, and matters to be settled between him and his wife. The Countess and I frequently walked out to join him on his new land, taking the two children, who all the way would run after butterflies, stag-beetles, and crickets; and gather nosegays too—or, to be exact, sheaves of flowers.

To walk with the woman he loves, to have her hand on his arm, to pick her road for her! These infinite joys are enough for a man's lifetime. Their talk is then so confiding! We went alone, we came back with the general—a little mocking name we gave the Count when he was in a good humor. This difference in our order of march tinged our happiness by a contrast of which the secret is known only to hearts which meet under difficulties. On our way home, this felicity—a look, a pressure of the hand—was checkered by uneasiness. Our speech, freely uttered as we went, had mysterious meanings as we came back, when one of us, after a pause, found a reply to some insidious inquiry, or a discussion we had begun was carried on in the enigmatic phraseology to which our language lends itself, and which women invent so cleverly. Who has not known the pleasure of such an understanding, in an unknown sphere, as it were, where spirits move apart from the crowd and meet superior to all ordinary laws? Once a mad hope rose in me, to be immediately crushed when, in reply to the Count who asked what we were talking about, Henriette said something with a double meaning, which he took quite simply. This innocent jest amused Madeleine, but it brought a blush to her mother's cheek; and, by a stern look, she told me that she was capable of withdrawing her soul as she had once withdrawn her hand, intending to be always a blameless wife. But a purely spiritual union has such charms that we did the same again on the morrow.

Thus the hours, days, and weeks flew on, full of ever-new felicity. We had come to the season of the vintage, in Touraine always a high festival. By the end of September the sun is less fierce than during harvest, making it safe to linger in the open air without fear of sunstroke or fatigue. It is easier, too, to gather grapes than to reap corn. The fruit is fully ripe. The crops are carried, bread is cheaper, and increased abundance makes life brighter. Then the fears that always hang over the result of the year's toil, in which so much money and so much sweat are expended, are relieved by filled granaries and cellars waiting to be filled. The vintage comes as a jovial dessert to the harvest feast, and the sky always smiles on it in Touraine, where the autumn is a beautiful season.

In that hospitable province the vintagers are fed by the owner; and as these meals are the only occasions throughout the year when these poor laborers have substantial and well-cooked food, they look forward to them as, in patriarchal households, the children count on anniversary festivals. They crowd to the estates where the masters are known to be open-handed. So every house is full of people and provisions. The winepresses are always at work. The world seems alive with the merry gang of coopers at work, the carts crowded with laughing girls and men, who, getting better wages than at any other time of year, sing on every opportunity. Again, as another cause of enjoyment, all ranks mingle—women and children, masters and servants, every one takes part in the sacred gathering. These various circumstances may account for the joviality, traditional from age to age, which breaks forth in these last fine days of the year, and of which the remembrance inspired Rabelais of yore to give a Bacchic form to his great work.

Jacques and Madeleine, who had always been ailing, had never before taken part in the vintage, nor had I, and they found childlike delight in seeing me a sharer in their pleasure. Their mother had promised to come with us. We had been to Villaines, where the country baskets are made, and had ordered very nice ones; we four were to gather the fruit off a few rows left for us; but we all promised not to eat too many grapes. The *Gros Co* of the Touraine vineyards is so delicious eaten fresh, that the finest table grapes are scorned in comparison. Jacques made me solemnly promise that I would go to see no other vineyards, but devote myself exclusively to the *Clos* of Clochegourde. Never had these two little creatures, usually so wan and pale, been so bright, and rosy, and excited, and busy as they were that morning. They chattered for the sake of chattering, went and came and trotted about for no visible reason but that, like other children, they had too much vitality to work off; Monsieur and Madame de Mortsauf had never seen them so well. And I was a child with them, more a child than they were perhaps, for I too hoped for my harvest.

The weather was glorious; we went up to the vineyards and spent half the day there. How we vied with each other in seeking the finest bunches, in seeing which could fill a basket first! They ran to and fro from the vines to their mother, every bunch was shown to her as it was gathered. And she laughed the hearty laugh of youth when, following the little girl with my basketful, I said, in a mocking spirit of playfulness, like Madeleine, "And look at mine, too, mamma."

"Dear child," she said to me, "do not get too hot." Then,

stroking my hair and my neck, she gave me a little slap on the cheek, adding, "Thou art in a bath!"

This is the only time I ever received from her that verbal caress, the lover's *tu*. I stood looking at the pretty hedgerows full of red berries, of sloes, and blackberries, I listened to the children shouting; I gazed at the girls pulling the grapes, at the cart full of vats, at the men with baskets on their backs—I stamped every detail on my memory, down to the young almond tree by which she was standing, bright, flushed, and laughing, under her parasol.

Then I set to work to gather the fruit with a steady, wordless perseverance, and a slow, measured step that left my spirit free. I tasted the ineffable pleasure of a physical employment such as carries life along, regulating the rush of passion which, but for this mechanical movement, was very near a conflagration. I learned how much wisdom comes of labor, and I understood monastic rule.

For the first time in many days, the Count was neither sullen nor vicious. His boy so well, the future Duc de Lenoncourt-Mortsauf, rosy and fair, and smeared with grape-juice, gladdened his heart. This being the last day of the vintage, the general had promised his people a dance in the evening in the field by Clochegourde, in honor of the return of the Bourbons; thus the festival was to be complete for everybody. On our way home, the Countess took my arm; she leaned on me so as to let my heart feel all the weight of her hand, like a mother who longs to impart her gladness, and said in my ear—

"You bring us good fortune."

And to me, knowing of her sleepless nights, her constant alarms, and her past life, through which she had indeed been supported by the hand of God, but in which all had been barren and weariful, these words, spoken in her deep, soft voice, brought such joys as no woman in the world could ever give me again.

"The monotonous misery of my days is broken and life is bright with hope," she added after a pause. "Oh, do not desert me! Do not betray my innocent superstitions! Be my eldest, the providence of the little ones."

This is no romance, Natalie; none can discern the infinite depth of such feelings who have not in early life sounded the great lakes on whose shores we live. If to many souls the passions have been as lava-torrents flowing between parched banks, are there not others in which a passion subdued by insurmountable obstacles has filled the crater of the volcano with limpid waters?

We had one more such festival. Madame de Mortsauf wished that her children should learn something of practical life, and know by what hard labor money must be earned; she had, therefore, given each certain revenues depending on the chances of produce. Jacques was owner of the walnut crop, Madeleine of the chestnuts. A few days after we went forth to the chestnut and walnut harvests. Thrashing Madeleine's chestnut trees; hearing the nuts fall, their spiny husks making them rebound from the dry velvety moss of the unfertile soil on which chestnuts grow; seeing the solemn gravity of the little girl as she looked at the piles, calculating their value, which meant for her such pleasures as she could give herself without control; then the congratulations of Manette, the children's maid, the only person who ever filled the Countess' place with them; the lesson to be derived from this little business, of toil requisite to reap the humblest harvest, so often imperiled by variation of climate—all these things made up a little drama, the children's ingenuous delight forming a charming contrast with the sober hues of early autumn.

Madeleine had a loft of her own where I saw the brown crop safely stowed, sharing in her delight. I am thrilled to this day as I remember the clatter of each basketful of chestnuts rolling out over the yellow chaff that formed the flooring. The Count bought some for the house; the farm bailiffs, the laborers, every one in the neighborhood found buyers from "Mignonne," a kindly name which the peasants in those parts are ready to give even to a stranger, but which seemed especially appropriate to Madeleine.

Jacques was not so lucky for his walnut harvest. It rained several days; but I comforted him by advising him to keep his nuts for a time and sell them later. Monsieur de Chessel had told me that the walnut crop had failed in le Brehémont, in the district around Amboise, and in the country about Vouvray. Nut oil is very largely used in Touraine. Jacques would make at least forty sous on each tree, and there were two hundred trees, so the sum would be considerable. He meant to buy himself a saddle and bridle for a pony. His wish led to a general discussion, and his father led him to consider the uncertainty of such returns, and the need for making a reserve fund for the years when the trees should be bare of fruit, so as to secure an average income.

I read the Countess' heart in her silence; she was delighted to see Jacques listening to his father, and the father winning back some of the reverence he had forfeited, and all thanks to the subterfuge she had arranged. I told you when describing this woman that no earthly language can ever do justice to her character and genius. While these little scenes are enacted the spirit revels in them with joy, but does not analyze them; but how clearly they afterward stand out against the gloomy background of a life of vicissitude! They shine like diamonds, set amid thoughts of baser alloy and regrets that melt into reminiscences of vanished happiness! Why should the names of the two estates Monsieur and Madame de Mortsauf had lately purchased, and which gave them so much to do—la Cassine and la Rhétorière—touch me far more than the greatest names in the Holy Land or in Greece? "*Qui aime, le dire*" (Let those who love tell), says La Fontaine. Those names have the talismanic power of the starry words used in sorcery, they are magical to me; they call up sleeping images which stand forth and speak to me; they carry me back to that happy valley; they create a sky and landscape. But has not conjuration always been possible in the realm of the spiritual world? So you need not wonder to find me writing to you of such familiar scenes. The smallest details of that simple and almost homely life were so many ties, slight as they must seem, which bound me closely to the Countess.

The children's future prospects troubled Madame de Mortsauf almost as much as their feeble health. I soon saw the truth of what she had told me with regard to her unconfessed importance in the business of the property, which I gradually understood as I studied such facts about the country as a statesman ought to know. After ten years' struggles Madame de Mortsauf had at last reformed the management of the lands. She had *quartered* them—*mis en quatre*—a term used in those parts for the rotation of crops, a method of sowing wheat on the same field only once in four years, so that the land yields some crop every year instead of lying fallow. To overcome the pig-headed resistance of the peasantry, it had been necessary to cancel the old leases, to divide the property into four large holdings, and farm on half-profits, the system peculiar to Touraine and the adjacent provinces. The landowner provides the dwelling and outbuildings, and supplies seed to working farmers, with whom he agrees to share the cost of husbandry and the profits. The division is undertaken by a *métivier* (a farm bailiff), who is authorized to take the half due to the proprietor; and this system, a costly one, is complicated by the way of keeping accounts, which leads to constant changes in the estimate of the shares.

The Countess had persuaded Monsieur de Mortsauf to keep a fifth farm, consisting of the enclosed lands round Clochegourde, in his own hands, partly to give him occupation, but also to demonstrate to the sharefarmers by the evidence of facts the superiority of the new methods. Being able here to manage the crops, she had by degrees, with womanly tenacity, had two of the farmhouses rebuilt on the plan of the farms in Artois and Flanders. Her scheme was self-evident. She intended, when the leases on half-profits should expire, to make these two farms into first-class holdings and let them for rent in money to active and intelligent tenants, so as to simplify the returns to Clochegourde. Dreading lest she should die the first, she was anxious to leave to the Count an income easily collected, and to the children a property which no misadventure could make ruinous.

By this time the fruit trees planted ten years since were in full bearing. The hedges which guaranteed the boundaries against any dispute in the future had all grown up. The poplars and elms were flourishing. With the recent additions, and by introducing the new system of culture, the estate of Clochegourde, divided into four large holdings, might be made to yield sixteen thousand francs a year in hard cash, at a rent of four thousand francs for each farm; exclusive of the vineyards, the two hundred acres of coppice adjoining and the home farm. The lanes from these farms were all to come into an avenue leading straight from Clochegourde to the Chinon road. The distance to Tours by this road was no more than five leagues; farmers would certainly not be lacking, especially at a time when everybody was talking of the Count's improvements and his success, and the increased return from his land.

She proposed to spend about fifteen thousand francs on each of the newly purchased properties, to convert the houses on them into fine homesteads so as to let them to advantage after farming them for a year or two, while placing there as steward a man named Martineau, the most trustworthy of the bailiffs, who would presently be out of place; for the leases of the four half-profit farms were about to fall in, and the moment was coming for uniting them into two holdings and letting them for a rent in money.

These very simple plans, complicated only by the necessary

outlay of more than thirty thousand francs, were at this time the subject of long discussions between her and the Count— terrible arguments, in which she was emboldened only by the thought of the children's interests. The mere thought, "If I were to die to-morrow, what would become of them?" made her sick at heart. Only gentle and peaceable souls, to whom rage is impossible, and who long to see the peace they feel within them reign around them, can ever understand what an effort such a contest needs, what rushes of blood oppress the heart before the struggle is faced, what exhaustion follows after a battle in which nothing has been won. Just now, when her children were less wan, less starveling, and more full of life, for the fruitful season had had its effect on them; just now, when she could watch their play with moistened eyes, and a sense of satisfaction that renewed her strength by reviving her spirits, the poor woman was a victim to the insulting thrusts and cutting innuendoes of determined antagonism. The Count, startled by these changes, denied their utility and their possibility with rigid oppugnancy. To all conclusive reasoning he answered with the argument of a child who should doubt the heat of the sun in summer. The Countess won at last; the triumph of commonsense over folly salved her wounds, and she forgot them.

On that day she walked to la Cassine and la Rhétorière, to give orders for the buildings. The Count went on in front alone, the children came between, and we followed slowly behind, for she was talking in the sweet, low voice which made her speech sound like tiny ripples of the sea murmuring on fine sand.

She was "sure of success," she said. A rival service was about to start on the road between Chinon and Tours under the management of an active man, a cousin of Manette's, and he wanted to rent a large farmstead on the high-road. He had a large family; the eldest son would drive the coach, the second would attend to the heavy carrying business, while the father, settled at la Rabelaye, a farm half-way on the road, would attend to the horses and cultivate the ground to advantage with the manure from the stables. She had already found a tenant for the second farm, la Baude, lying close to Clochegourde; one of the four half-profit farmers, an honest, intelligent, and active man, who understood the advantages of the new system, had offered to take it on lease. As to la Cassine and la Rhétorière, the soil was the best in all the country-side; when once the houses were ready and the fields fairly started, they would only have to be advertised at Tours. Thus, in two years, the estate would bring in about twenty-four thousand francs a year; la Gravelotte, the farm in le Maine recovered by Monsieur de Mortsauf, had just been let for nine years, at seven thousand francs a year; the Count's pension as major-general was four thousand francs; if all this could not be said to constitute a fortune, at any rate it meant perfect ease; and later, perhaps, further improvements might allow of her going some day to Paris to attend to Jacques' education—two years hence, when the heir presumptive's health should be stronger.

How tremulously did she speak the word *Paris!* And I was at the bottom of this plan; she wanted to be as little apart as possible from her friend.

At these words I caught fire; I told her she little knew me; that, without saying anything to her, I had planned to finish my own education by studying night and day so as to become Jacques' tutor; for that I could never endure to think of any other young man at home in her house.

On this she grew very serious.

"No, Félix," said she. "This is not to be, any more than your becoming a priest. Though you have by that speech touched my motherly heart to the quick, the woman cares for you too well to allow you to become a victim to your fidelity. The reward of such devotion would be that you would be irremediably looked down upon, and I could do nothing to prevent it. No, no! Never let me injure you in any way. You, the Vicomte de Vandenesse, a tutor? You, whose proud motto is '*Ne se Vend*' (For no guerdon). If you were Richelieu himself, your life would be marred for ever. It would be the greatest grief to your family. My friend, you do not know all the insolence such a woman as my mother can throw into a patronizing glance, all the humiliation into one word, all the scorn into a bow!"

"And, so long as you love me, what do I care for the world?"

She affected not to hear, and went on—

"Though my father is most kind and willing to give me anything I may ask, he would not forgive you for having put yourself into a false position and would refuse to help you on in the world. I would not see you tutor to the Dauphin! Take society as you find it, make no blunders in life. My friend, this offer, prompted by——"

"By love," I put in.

"No, by charity," said she, restraining her tears; "this crazy proposition throws a light on your character; your heart will be your enemy. I insist henceforth on my right to tell you certain truths; give my woman's eyes the care of seeing for you sometimes.

"Yes, buried here in Clochegourde, I mean to look on silent but delighted at your advancement. As to a tutor, be easy on that score; we will find some good old abbé, some learned and venerable jesuit, and my father will gladly pay the sum needed for the education of the boy who is to bear his name. Jacques is my pride! And he is eleven years old," she added after a pause. "But he, like you, looks younger. I thought you were thirteen when I first saw you."

By this time we had reached la Cassine; Jacques and Madeleine and I followed her about as children follow their mother; but we were in the way. I left her for a moment and went into the orchard, where the elder Martineau, the gamekeeper, with his son the bailiff, were marking trees to be cut down; they discussed the matter as eagerly as if it were their own concern. I saw by this how much the Countess was beloved. I expressed myself to this effect to a day laborer who, with one foot on his spade and his elbow on the handle, was listening to the two men learned in pomology.

"Oh yes, sir," said he, "she is a good woman, and not proud, like those apes at Azay, who would leave us to die like dogs rather than give a sou extra on a yard of ditching. The day when she leaves the place, the Virgin will cry over it, and we too. She knows what is due to her, but she knows what hard times we have and considers us."

With what delight I gave all my spare cash to that man!

A few days after this a pony was bought for Jacques; his father, a capital horseman, wished to inure him very gradually to the fatiguing exercise of riding. The boy had a neat little outfit that he had bought with the price of his walnuts. The morning when he had his first lesson, riding with his father and followed by Madeleine's shouts of glee as she danced on the lawn round which Jacques was trotting, was to the Countess her first high festival as a mother. Jacques' pretty collar had been worked by her hands; he had a little sky-blue cloth coat, with a varnished leather belt around the waist, white tucked trousers, and a Scotch cap over his thick, fair curls; he really was charming to look upon. All the servants of the household came out to share the family joy, and the little heir smiled as he passed his mother, without a sign of fear.

This first act of manliness in the child who had so often been at death's door, the hope of a happier future of which this ride seemed the promise, making him look so bright, so handsome, so healthy—what a delightful reward! Then the father's joy, looking young again, and smiling for the first time in many weeks, the satisfaction that shone in the eyes of the assembled servants, the glee of the old Lenoncourt huntsman, who had come over from Tours, and who, seeing how well the child held his bridle, called out, "Bravo, Monsieur le Vicomte!"—all this was too much for Madame de Mortsauf and she melted into tears. She, who was so calm in distress, was too weak to control her joy as she admired her boy riding round and round on the path where she had so often mourned him by anticipation as she carried him to and fro in the sun.

She leaned on my arm without reserve, and said, as she turned her eyes on me—

"I feel as if I had never been unhappy. Stay with us to-day."

The lesson ended, Jacques flew into his mother's arms, and she clutched him to her bosom with the vehemence that comes of excessive delight, kissing and fondling him again and again. Madeleine and I went off to make two splendid nosegays to dress the dinner-table in honor of the young horseman.

When we returned to the drawing-room, the Countess said to me—

"The fifteenth of October is indeed a high day! Jacques has had his first riding lesson and I have set the last stitch in my piece of work."

"Well, then, Blanche," said the Count, laughing, "I will pay you for it."

He offered her his arm and led her into the inner courtyard, where she found a carriage, a present from her father, for which the Count had bought a pair of horses in England; they had arrived with those sent to the Duc de Lenoncourt. The old huntsman had arranged all this in the courtyard during the riding lesson. We got into the carriage and went off to see the line cleared for the avenue that was to lead directly into the Chinon road, and that was cut straight through the new property acquired by the Count. On our return the Countess said to me, with deep melancholy—

"I am too happy; happiness is to me like an illness, it overpowers me and I fear lest it should vanish like a dream."

I was too desperately in love not to be jealous, and I had nothing to give her! In my fury I tried to think of some way of dying for her.

She asked me what thoughts had clouded my eyes, and I told her frankly; she was more touched than by any gifts and poured balm on my spirit when, taking me out on the terrace steps, she whispered to me—

"Love me as my aunt loved me—is not that to give your life for me? And if I take it so, is it not to lay me under an obligation every hour of the day?"

"It was high-time I should finish my piece of work," she went on, as we returned to the drawing-room, and I kissed her hand as a renewal of my allegiance. "You perhaps do not know, Félix, why I set myself that long task. Men find a remedy against their troubles in the occupations of life; the bustle of business diverts their minds; but we women have no support in ourselves to help us to endure. In order to be able to smile at my children and my husband when I was possessed by gloomy ideas, I felt the need of keeping my grief in check by physical exertion. I thus avoided the collapse that follows any great effort of resolve, as well as the lightning strokes of excitement. The action of lifting my arm in measured time lulled my brain and acted on my spirit when the storm was raging, giving it the rest of ebb and flow and regulating its emotions. I told my secrets to the stitches, do you see? Well, as I worked the last chain, I was thinking too much of you! Yes, my friend, far too much. What you put into your nosegays I imparted to my patterns."

The dinner was a cheerful one. Jacques, like all children to whom we show kindness, jumped upon me and threw his arms around my neck when he saw the flowers I had picked him by way of a crown. His mother pretended to be angry at this infidelity to her, and the dear child gave her the newly made posy she affected to covet, you know how ingenuously and sweetly.

In the evening we played backgammon, I against Monsieur and Madame de Mortsauf, and the Count was charming. Finally, at nightfall, they walked with me as far as the turning to Frapesle, in one of those placid evenings when the harmony of nature gives added depth to our feelings in proportion as it soothes their vividness.

It had been a day by itself to this hapless woman, a spark of light that often shone caressingly on her memory in days of difficulty.

For, indeed, before long the riding lessons became a subject of contention. The Countess, not unreasonably, was afraid of the Count's hard speeches to his little son. Jacques was already growing thinner, and dark rings came around his blue eyes; to save his mother, he would suffer in silence. I suggested a remedy by advising him to tell his father he was tired when the Count was angry, but this was an insufficient palliative, so the old huntsman was to teach him instead of his father, who would not give up his pupil without many struggles. Outcries and discussions began again; the Count found a text for his perpetual fault-finding in the ingratitude of wives, and twenty times a day he threw the carriage, the horses, and the liveries in her teeth.

Finally, one of those disasters occurred which are a stalking-horse for such tempers and such maladies of the brain; the expense of the works at la Cassine and la Rhétorière, where the walls and floors were found to be rotten, amounted to half as much again as the estimate. A clumsy fellow at work there came to report this to Monsieur de Mortsauf, instead of telling the Countess privately. This became the subject of a quarrel, begun mildly, but gradually increasing in bitterness; and the Count's hypochondria, which for some days had been in abeyance, now claimed arrears from the unfortunate Henriette.

That morning I set out from Frapesle, after breakfast, at half-past ten, to make my nosegays at Clochegourde with Madeleine. The little girl brought out the two vases, setting them on the balustrade of the terrace, and I wandered from the gardens to the fields, seeking the lovely but rare flowers of autumn. As I returned from my last expedition, I no longer saw my little lieutenant in her pink sash and frilled cape, and I heard a commotion in the house.

"The general," said Madeleine, in tears, and with her the name was one of aversion for her father, "the general is scolding our mother; do go and help her."

I flew up the steps and went into the drawing-room, where neither the Count nor his wife saw or noticed me. Hearing the madman's noisy outcries, I first shut all the doors, and then came back, for I had seen that Henriette was as white as her gown.

"Never marry, Félix," exclaimed the Count excitedly. "A wife has the devil for her counselor; the best of them would invent evil if it did not exist. They are all brute beasts."

Then I had to listen to arguments without beginning and without end. Monsieur de Mortsauf, recurring to his original refusal, now repeated the sottish remarks of the peasants who objected to the new system. He declared that if he had taken the management of Clochegourde, they would have been twice as rich by now. He worded his blasphemies with insulting violence; he swore, he rushed from pillar to post, he moved and banged all the furniture, and in the middle of a sentence he would stop and declare that his marrow was on fire, or his brain running away in a stream, like his money. His wife was ruining him! Wretched man, of the thirty-odd thousand francs a year he possessed, she had brought him more than twenty thousand. The fortune of the Duke and

Duchess, bringing in fifty thousand francs a year, was entailed on Jacques.

The Countess smiled haughtily, and gazed out at the sky.

"Yes!" he cried; "you, Blanche, are my tormentor. You are killing me! You want to be rid of me! You are a monster of hypocrisy! And she laughs! Do you know why she can laugh, Félix?"

I said nothing, and hung my head.

"This woman," he went on, answering his own question, "denies me all happiness—she is no more mine than yours, and calls herself my wife! She bears my name, but she fulfills none of the duties which laws, human and divine, require of her; she lies to God and man. She exhausts me with long walks that I may leave her in peace; I disgust her; she hates me, she does all she can to live the life of a girl. And she is driving me mad by imposing privations on me—for everything goes to my poor head. She is burning me at a slow fire and believes herself a saint—that woman takes the sacrament every month!"

The Countess was by this time weeping bitterly, humiliated by the disgrace of this man, to whom she could only say by way of remonstrance: "Monsieur! Monsieur! Monsieur!"

Although the Count's words made me blush for him as much as for Henriette, they moved me deeply, for they found a response in the instinct of chastity and delicacy which is, so to speak, the very material of a first love.

"She lives a maiden at my expense!" cried the Count, and again his wife exclaimed—

"Monsieur!"

"What do you mean," he went on, "by your pertinacious *monsieur?* Am I not your master? Must I teach you to know it?"

He went toward her, thrusting out his white, wolf-like face, that was really hideous, for his yellow eyes had an expression that made him look like a ravenous animal coming out of a wood. Henriette slid off her chair on to the floor to avoid the blow which was not struck, for she lost consciousness as she fell, completely broken.

The Count was like an assassin who feels the blood-jet of his victim; he stood amazed. I raised the poor woman in my arms, and the Count allowed me to lift her as if he felt himself unworthy to carry her; but he went first and opened the door of the bedroom next the drawing-room, a sacred spot I had never entered. I set the Countess on her feet, and supported her with my arm round her body, while Monsieur de Mortsauf took off the upper coverlet, the eiderdown quilt, and the bedclothes; then, together, we laid her down just as she was. As she recovered consciousness, Henriette signed to us to undo her waistband; Monsieur de Mortsauf found a pair of scissors, and cut through everything. I held some salts to her nose, and she presently opened her eyes. The Count went away, ashamed rather than grieved.

Two hours went by in perfect silence, Henriette holding my hand and pressing it without being able to speak. Now and again she looked up to make me understand that she longed only for peace without a sound; then there was a moment's truce, when she raised herself on her elbow and murmured in my ear—

"Unhappy man! If you could but know——"

She laid her head on the pillow again. The remembrance of past sufferings, added to her present anguish, brought on again the nervous spasms, which I had soothed only by the magnetism of love—its effects were hitherto unknown to me, but I had used it instinctively. I now supported her with gentle and tender firmness, and she gave me such looks as brought tears to my eyes.

When the convulsive attack was over, I smoothed her disordered hair—the first and only time I ever touched it—then again I held her hand, and sat a long time looking at the room—a brown-and-gray room, with a bed simply hung with

I RAISED THE POOR WOMAN IN MY ARMS.

cotton chintz, a table covered with an old-fashioned toilet set, a poor sofa with a stitched mattress. What poetry I found here! What indifference to personal luxury! Her only luxury was exquisite neatness. The noble cell of a married nun, stamped with holy resignation, where the only adornments were a crucifix by her bed, and over it the portrait of her aunt; then, on each side of the holy-water shell, sketches of her two children, done in pencil by herself, and locks of their hair when they were babies. What a hermitage for a woman whose appearance in the world of fashion would have cast the loveliest into the shade!

Such was the retreat where tears were so constantly shed by this daughter of an illustrious race, at this moment swamped in bitterness, and rejecting the love that might have brought her consolation. A hidden and irremediable misfortune! The victim in tears for the torturer, the torturer in tears for his victim.

When the children and the maid came in, I left her. The Count was waiting for me; he already regarded me as a mediator between his wife and himself; and he grasped my hands, exclaiming, "Stay with us; stay with us, Félix!"

"Unluckily," said I, "Monsieur de Chessel has company; it would not do for his guests to wonder at the reason for my absence; but I will return after dinner."

He came out with me and walked to the lower gate without saying a word; then he accompanied me all the way to Frapesle, unconscious of what he was doing. When there, I said to him—

"In heaven's name, Monsieur le Comte, leave the management of your house to her if she wishes it, and do not torment her."

"I have not long to live," he replied seriously; "she will not suffer long on my account; I feel that my head will burst."

He turned away in a fit of involuntary egoism.

After dinner I went back to inquire for Madame de Mortsauf, and found her better already. If these were for her the joys of marriage, if such scenes were to be frequently repeated, how could she live? What slow, unpunished murder! I had seen this evening the indescribable torture by which the Count racked his wife. Before what tribunal could such a case be brought?

These considerations bewildered me; I could say nothing to Henriette, but I spent the night in writing to her. Of three or four letters that I wrote, I have nothing left but this fragment, which did not satisfy me; but though it seems to me to express nothing, or to say too much about myself when I ought only to have thought of her, it will show you the state of my mind.

To Madame de Mortsauf.

"How many things I had to say to you this evening that I had thought of on the way and forgot when I saw you! Yes, as soon as I see you, dearest Henriette, I feel my words out of harmony with the reflections from your soul that add to your beauty. And, then, by your side, I feel such infinite happiness that the immediate experience effaces every memory of what has gone before. I am born anew each time to a larger life, like a traveler who, as he climbs a crag, discovers a new horizon. In every conversation with you I add some new treasure to my vast treasury. This, I believe, is the secret of long and indefatigable attachments. So I can only speak of you to yourself when I am away from you. In your presence I am too much dazzled to see you, too happy to analyze my happiness, too full of you to be myself, made too eloquent by you to speak to you, too eager to seize the present to be able to remember the past. Understand this constant intoxication, and you will forgive its aberrations. When I am with you I can only feel.

"Nevertheless, I will dare to tell you, dear Henriette, that never in all the joy you have given me, have I felt any rapture to compare with the delights that filled my soul yesterday when, after the dreadful storm, in which, with superhuman courage, you did battle with evil, you came back to me alone in the twilight of your room, whither the unfortunate scene had led me. I alone was there to know the light that can shine in a woman when she returns from the portal of death to the gates of life, and the dawn of a new birth tinges her brow. How harmonious was your voice! How trivial words seemed —even yours—as the vague recollection of past suffering made itself heard in your adored tones, mingled with the divine consolations, by which you at last reassured me as you thus uttered your first thoughts! I knew that you shone with every choicest human gift, but yesterday I found a new Henriette, who would be mine if God should grant it. I had a glimpse yesterday of an inscrutable being, free from the bonds of the flesh, which hinder us from exhaling the fire of the soul. You were lovely in your dejection, majestic in your weakness.

"I found something yesterday more beautiful than your beauty, something sweeter than your voice, a light more glorious than the light of your eyes, a fragrance for which there is no name—yesterday your soul was visible and tangible. Oh! it was torment to me that I could not open my heart and take you into it to revive you. In short, I yesterday got over the respectful fear I have felt for you, for did not your weakness draw us nearer to each other? I learned the joy of breathing as I breathed with you, when the spasm left you free to inhale our air. What prayers flew up to heaven in one moment! Since I did not die of rushing through the space I crossed to beseech God to leave you to me yet awhile, it is not possible to die of joy or of grief.

"That moment has left, buried in my soul, memories which can never rise to the surface without bringing tears to my eyes; every joy will make the furrow longer, every grief will make it deeper. Yes, the fears that racked my soul yesterday will remain a standard of comparison for all my sorrows to come, as the happiness you have given me, dear perpetual first-thought of my life, will prevail over every joy that the hand of God may ever vouchsafe me. You have made me understand Divine love, that trustful love, which, secure in its strength and permanency, knows neither suspicion nor jealousy."

The deepest melancholy gnawed at my heart; the sight of this home was heart-breaking to a youth so fresh and new to social emotions—the sight, at the threshold of the world, of a bottomless gulf, a dead sea. This hideous concentration of woes suggested infinite reflections, and at my very first steps in social life I had found a standard so immense that any other scenes could but look small when measured by it. My melancholy left Monsieur and Madame de Chessel to suppose that my love affair was luckless, so that I was happy in not injuring my noble Henriette by my passion.

On the following day, on going into the drawing-room, I found her alone. She looked at me for a moment, holding out her hand; she said, "Will the friend always persist in being too tender?" The tears rose to her eyes; she got up, and added in a tone of desperate entreaty, "Never write to me again in such a strain."

Monsieur de Mortsauf was most friendly. The Countess had recovered her courage and her serene brow; but her pallor showed traces of yesterday's trouble which, though subdued, was not extinct.

In the evening, as we took a walk, the autumn leaves rustling under our feet, she said—

"Pain is infinite, joy has its limits," a speech which revealed the extent of her sufferings by comparison with her transient happiness.

"Do not calumniate life," said I. "You know nothing of love; there are delights which flame up to the heavens."

"Hush," said she, "I do not want to know them. A Greenlander would die in Italy! I am calm and happy in your society, I can tell you all my thoughts; do not destroy my confidence. Why should you not have the virtue of a priest and the charms of a free man?"

"You could make me swallow a cup of hemlock," I replied, laying her hand on my heart, which was beating rapidly.

"Again!" she said, withdrawing her hand as if she felt some sudden pain. "Do you want to deprive me of the melancholy joy of feeling my bleeding wounds stanched by a friend's hand? Do not add to my miseries; you do not yet know them all, and the most secret are the hardest of all to swallow. If you were a woman, you would understand the distress and bitterness into which her proud spirit is plunged when she is the object of attentions which make up for nothing, and are supposed to make up for everything. For a few days now I shall be courted and petted; he will want to be forgiven for having put himself in the wrong. I could now gain assent to the most unreasonable desires. And I am humiliated by this servility, by caresses which will cease as soon as he thinks I have forgotten everything. Is it not a terrible condition of life to owe the kindness of one's tyrant only to his errors——"

"To his crimes," I eagerly put in.

"Beside," she went on, with a sad smile, "I do not know how to make use of this temporary advantage. At this moment I am in the position of a knight who would never strike a fallen foe. To see the man I ought to honor on the ground, to raise him only to receive fresh blows, to suffer more from his fall than he himself does, and consider myself dishonored by taking advantage of a transient success, even for a useful end, to waste my strength, and exhaust all the resources of my spirit in these ignominious struggles, to rule only at the moment when I am mortally wounded?—— Death is better!

"If I had no children, I should let myself be carried down

the stream; but if it were not for my covert courage, what would become of them? I must live for them, however terrible life may be. You talk to me of love! Why, my friend, only think of the hell I should fall into if I gave that man—ruthless, as all weak men are—the right to despise me? I could not endure a suspicion! The purity of my life is my strength. Virtue, my dear child, has holy waters in which we may bathe, and emerge born again to the love of God!"

"Listen, dear Henriette, I have only a week more to stay here, and I want——"

"What, you are leaving us?" said she, interrupting me.

"Well, I must know what my father has decided on for me. It is nearly three months——"

"I have not counted the days," she cried, with the vehemence of agitation. Then she controlled herself, and added, "Let us take a walk; we will go to Frapesle."

She called the Count and the children, and sent for a shawl; then, when all were ready, she, so deliberate and so calm, had a fit of activity worthy of a Parisian, and we set out for Frapesle in a body, to pay a visit which the Countess did not owe.

She made an effort to talk to Madame de Chessel, who, fortunately, was prolix in her replies. The Count and Monsieur de Chessel discussed business. I was afraid lest Monsieur de Mortsauf should boast of his carriage and horses, but he did not fail in good taste.

His neighbor inquired as to the work he was doing at la Cassine and la Rhétorière. As I heard the question, I glanced at the Count, fancying he would avoid talking of a subject so full of painful memories and so bitter for him; but he demonstrated the importance of improving the methods of agriculture in the district, of building good farmhouses on healthy, well-drained spots; in short, he audaciously appropriated his wife's ideas. I gazed at the Countess and reddened. This want of delicacy in a man who, under certain circumstances, had so much, this oblivion of that direful scene, this adoption of ideas against which he had rebeled so violently, this belief in himself, petrified me.

When Monsieur de Chessel asked him—

"And do you think you will recover the outlay?"

"And more!" he exclaimed positively.

Such vagaries can only be explained by the word insanity. Henriette, heavenly soul, was beaming. Was not the Count showing himself to be a man of sense, a good manager, an admirable farmer? She stroked Jacques' hair in rapture, delighted for herself and delighted for her boy. What an odious comedy, what a sardonic farce!

At a later time, when the curtain of social life was raised for me, how many Mortsaufs I saw, minus the flashes of chivalry and the religious faith of this man. What strange and cynical power is that which constantly mates the madman with an angel, the man of genuine and poetic feelings with a mean woman, a little man with a tall wife, a hideous dwarf with a superb and beautiful creature; which gives the lovely Juana a Captain Diard—whose adventures at Bordeaux you already know; pairs Madame de Beauséant with a d'Ajuda, Madame d'Aiglemont with her husband, the Marquis d'Espard with his wife! I have, I confess, long sought the solution of this riddle. I have investigated many mysteries, I have discovered the reasons for many natural laws, the interpretation of a few sacred hieroglyphics, but of this I know nothing; I am still studying it as if it were some India puzzle figure, of which the Brahmins have kept the symbolical purpose secret. Here the Spirit of Evil is too flagrantly the master, and I dare not accuse God. Irremediable disaster! who takes pleasure in plotting you? Can it be that Henriette and her unrecognized philosopher were right? Does their mysticism contain the general purport of the human race?

The last days I spent in this district were those of leafless autumn, darkened with clouds which sometimes hid the sky of Touraine, habitually clear and mild at that fine season of the year. On the day before I left, Madame de Mortsauf took me out on the terrace before dinner.

"My dear Félix," said she, after taking a turn in silence under the bare trees, "you are going into the world, and I shall follow you there in thought. Those who have suffered much have lived long. Never suppose that lonely spirits know nothing of the world; they see and judge it. If I am to live in my friend's life, I do not wish to be uneasy, either in his heart or in his conscience. In the heat of the fray it is sometimes very difficult to remember all the rules, so let me give you some motherly advice, as to a son.

"On the day when you leave, dear child, I will give you a long letter in which you will read my thoughts as a woman on the world, on men, on the way to meet difficulties in that great seething of interests. Promise me not to read it till you are in Paris. This entreaty is the expression of one of the sentimental fancies which are the secret of a woman's heart; I do not think it is possible to understand it, but perhaps we should be sorry if it were understood. Leave me these little paths where a woman loves to wander alone."

"I promise," said I, kissing her hands.

"Ah!" said she, "but I have another pledge to ask of you; but you must promise beforehand to take it."

"Oh, certainly!" I said, thinking it was some vow of fidelity.

"It has nothing to do with me," she went on, with a bitter smile. "Félix, never gamble in any house whatever; I make no exception."

"I will never play," I promised.

"That is well," said she. "I have found you a better use to make of the time you would spend at cards. You will see that while others are certain to lose sooner or later, you will always win."

"How?"

"The letter will tell you," she replied gaily, in a way to

deprive her injunctions of the serious character which are given to those of our grandmothers.

The Countess talked to me for about an hour and proved the depth of her affection by betraying how closely she had studied me during these three months. She had entered into the secret corners of my heart, trying to infuse her own into it; her voice was modulated and convincing, showing as much by the tone as by her words how many links already bound us to each other.

"If only you could know," she said in conclusion, "with what anxiety I shall follow you on your way, with what joy if you go straight, with what tears if you bruise yourself against corners! Believe me, my affection is a thing apart; it is at once involuntary and deliberately chosen. Oh! I long to see you happy, powerful, respected—you who will be to me as a living dream."

She made me weep. She was at once mild and terrible. Her feelings were too frankly expressed, and too pure to give the smallest hope to a man thirsting for happiness. In return for my flesh, left torn and bleeding in her heart, she shed on mine the unfailing and unblemished light of the divine love that can only satisfy the soul. She bore me up to heights whither the shining wings of the passion that had led me to kiss her shoulders could never carry me; to follow her flight a man would have needed to wear the white pinions of a seraph.

"On every occasion," said I, "I will think, 'What would my Henriette say?'"

"Yes, I want to be both the Star and the Sanctuary," said she, alluding to my childhood's dreams, and trying to realize them, so as to cheat my desires.

"You will be my religion, my light, my all," I cried in a voice of rapture.

"No," said she. "I can never be the giver of your pleasures."

She sighed, and gave me a smile of secret sorrow, the smile of a slave in an instant of revolt.

From that day forth she was not merely a woman I loved—she was all I loved best. She dwelt in my heart not as a woman who insists on a place there, whose image is stamped there by devotion or excess of pleasure; no, she had my whole heart, and was indispensable to the action of its muscles; she became what Beatrice was to the Florentine poet, or the spotless Laura to the Venetian—the mother of great thoughts, the unknown cause of saving determinations, my support for the future, the light that shines in darkness like a lily among sombre shrubs. Yes, she dictated the firm resolve that cut off what was to be burned, that reinstated what was in danger; she endowed me with the fortitude of a Coligny to conquer the conquerors, to rise after defeat, to wear out the stoutest foe.

Next morning, after breakfasting at Frapesle, and taking leave of the hosts who had been so kind to the selfishness of my passion, I went to Clochegourde. Monsieur and Madame de Mortsauf had agreed to drive with me as far as Tours, whence I was to set out for Paris that night. On the way the Countess was affectionately silent; at first she said she had a headache; then she colored at the falsehood, and suddenly mitigated it by saying that she could not but regret to see me depart. The Count invited me to stay with them if, in the absence of the Chessels, I should ever wish to see the valley of the Indre once more. We parted heroically, with no visible tears; but, like many a sickly child, Jacques had a little emotional spasm which made him cry a little; while Madeleine, a woman already, clasped her mother's hand.

"Dear little man!" said the Countess, kissing Jacques passionately.

When I was left alone at Tours, after dinner I was seized by one of those inexplicable rages which only youth ever goes through. I hired a horse, and in an hour and a quarter had ridden back the whole distance from Tours to Pont de Ruan. There, ashamed of letting my madness be seen, I ran down the road on foot, and stole under the terrace on tiptoe, like a spy. The Countess was not there; I fancied she might be ill. I had still the key of the little gate, and I went in. She was at that very moment coming down the steps with her two children, slowly and sadly, to revel in the tender melancholy of the landscape under the setting sun.

"Why, mother, here is Félix," said Madeleine.

"Yes, I myself," I whispered low. "I asked myself why I was at Tours when I could easily see you once more. Why not gratify a wish which, a week hence, will be beyond fulfillment?"

"Then he is not going away," cried Jacques, skipping and jumping.

"Be quiet, do," said Madeleine; "you will bring out the general.

"This is not right," said the Countess. "What madness!"

The words, spoken through tears in her voice, were indeed a payment of what I may call usurious calculations in love!

"I had forgotten to return you this key," I said, with a smile.

"Then are you never coming back again?" said she.

"Can we ever be apart?" I asked, with a look before which her eyelids fell to veil the mute reply.

I went away after a few minutes spent in the exquisite blankness of souls strung to the pitch at which excitement ends and frenzied ecstasy begins. I went away, riding slowly, and constantly looking back. When I gazed at the valley for the last time from the top of the down, I was struck by the contrast between its aspect now and when I first came to it: was it not then as green, as glowing, as my hopes and desires had sprung and glowed. Now, initiated into the dark and melancholy mysteries of a home, sharing the pangs of a Christian Niobe, as sad as she, my spirit overshadowed, I saw in the landscape, at this moment, the hues of my ideas. The fields were cleared of their crops, the poplar leaves were falling, and those that remained were rust-color; the vine-canes were burned, the woods wore solemn tints of the russet which kings of yore adopted for their dress, disguising the purple of power under the brown hues of care. And, still in harmony with my thoughts, the valley under the dying yellow rays of the warm sun presented to me a responsive and living image of my soul.

To part from the woman we love is a very simple or a very dreadful thing, depending on one's nature; I suddenly felt myself in an unknown land of which I could not speak the language; I could find nothing to cling to, as I saw only things to which my soul was no longer attached. Then my love unfolded to its fullest extent, and my dear Henriette rose to her full dignity in the desert wherein I lived only by memories of her. It was an image so piously worshiped that I resolved to remain unspotted in the presence of my secret divinity, and in fancy I robed myself in the white garb of a Levite, imitating Petrarch, who never appeared in the presence of Laura but in white from head to foot.

With what impatience did I look forward to the first night when I should be under my father's roof, and might read the letter, which I kept feeling during my journey, as a miser feels a sum in bank-notes that he is obliged to carry about with him. During the night I kissed the paper on which Henriette had expressed her will, where I should find the mysterious effluvium of her touch, whence the tones of her voice would fall on my absorbed mental ear. I have never read her letters but as I read that first one, in bed, and in the deepest silence. I do not know how otherwise we can read the letters written by a woman we love; and yet there are men who mingle the reading of such letters with the business of daily life, taking them up and putting them down with odious coolness.

Here, then, Natalie, is the exquisite voice which suddenly sounded in the stillness of the night; here is the sublime figure which rose before me, pointing out the right road from the cross-ways where I now stood:

"It is happiness, my friend, to be obliged to collect the scattered fragments of my experience to transmit it to you and arm you against the perils of the world in which you must guide yourself with skill. I have felt the permitted joys of motherly affection while thinking of you for a few nights. While writing this, a sentence at a time, throwing myself forward into the life you are about to lead, I went now and again to my window. Seeing the turrets of Frapesle in the moonlight, I could say to myself, 'He is asleep, while I am awake for his sake,' a delightful emotion reminding me of the first happy days of my life when I watched Jacques asleep in his cradle, waiting for him to wake to feed him from my bosom. Did you not come to me as a child-man whose soul needed comforting by such precepts as you could not find to nourish it in those dreadful schools where you endured so much, and as we women have the privilege of affording you?

"These trifles will influence your success; they prepare and consolidate it. Will it not be a form of spiritual motherhood thus to create the system to which, as a man, you must refer the various acts of life, a motherhood well understood by the son? Dear Félix, permit me, even if I should make some mistakes, to give our friendship the seal of disinterestedness that will sanctify it; for in giving you up to the world, am I not foregoing every claim on you? But I love you well enough to sacrifice my own joys to your splendid future.

"For nearly four months you have led me to reflect strangely on the laws and habits that govern our time. The conversations I have held with my aunt, of which the purport must be given to you who have taken her place; the events of Monsieur de Mortsauf's life as he has related them to me; my father's dicta, familiar as he was with the court; the greatest and the smallest facts have risen up in my mind for the benefit of the adopted son whom I see now about to plunge, almost alone, into the throng of men; about to find himself without an adviser in a country where many perish by a heedless misuse of their best qualities, and some succeed by a clever use of their bad ones.

"Above all, reflect on the brief utterance of my opinion on society considered as a whole—for to you a few words are enough. Whether social communities had a divine origin, or are the invention of man, I know not, nor do I know which way they are going; one thing seems certain, and that is: that they exist. As soon as you accept a social life instead of isolation, you are bound to adhere to its constitutional conditions, and to-morrow a sort of contract will be signed between it and you.

"Does society, as now constituted, get more benefit out of a man than it gives? I believe so; but if a man finds in it more burden than profit, or if he purchases too dearly the advantages he derives from it, these are questions for the legislator and not for the individual. You ought, in my opinion, to obey the general law in all things, without disputing it, whether it hurts or advances your interest. Simple as this principle may appear to you, it is not always easy of application; it is like the sap which must permeate the smallest capillary vessels to give life to a tree, to preserve its verdure, develop its bloom, and elaborate its fruit to a magnificence that excites general admiration. My dear, these laws are not all written in a book; customs also create laws; the most important are the least known; there are neither professors, nor treatises, nor any school of that law which guides your actions, your conversation, your external life, and the way in which you must appear in the world and meet fortune.

If you sin against these unwritten laws, you must remain at the bottom of the social community instead of dominating it. Even though this letter should be full of echoes of your own thoughts, suffer me to set before you my woman's policy.

"To formulate society by a theory of personal happiness, grasped at the cost of everybody else, is a disastrous doctrine which, strictly worked out, would lead a man to believe that everything he secretly appropriates, without any offense discernible by the law, by society, or by an individual, is fairly his booty or his due. If this were the charter, then a clever thief would be blameless; a wife faithless to her duties, but undetected, would be happy and good; kill a man, and so long as justice can find no proofs, if you have thus won a crown, like Macbeth, you have done well; your own interest becomes the supreme law; the only question is to navigate, without witnesses or evidence, among the obstacles which law and custom have placed between you and your satisfaction. To a man who takes this view of society, my friend, the problem of making a fortune is reduced to playing a game where the stakes are a million or the galleys, a position in politics or disgrace. And, indeed, the green cloth is not wide enough for all the players; a sort of genius is ever necessary to calculate a *coup*.

"I say nothing of religious beliefs or feelings; we are concerned merely with the wheels of a machine of iron or of gold, and of the immediate results which men look for.

"Dear child of my heart, if you share my horror of this criminal theory, society will resolve itself in your eyes, as in every healthy mind, into a theory of duty. Yes, men owe service to each other under a thousand different forms. In my opinion, the duke and peer has far greater duties to the artisan or the pauper than the artisan or the pauper has to the duke. The obligations laid on us are greater in proportion to the benefits we derive from society, in accordance with the axiom—as true in commerce as in politics—that the burden of care is always in proportion to the profits accruing. Each one pays his debt in his own way. When our poor farmer at la Rhétorière comes home to bed, tired out with his labor, do you think he has not done his duty? He has undoubtedly fulfilled it better than many a man in a high position. Hence, in contemplating the world in which you desire a place suitable to your intelligence and your faculties, you must start with this maxim as fundamental principle— Never allow yourself to do anything against your own conscience or against the public conscience. Though my insistency may seem to you superfluous, I beseech you—yes, your Henriette beseeches you—to weigh the full sense of these two words. Simple as they may seem, they mean, my dear, that uprightness, honor, loyalty, and good breeding are the surest and quickest roads to fortune. In this selfish world there will be plenty of people to tell you that a man cannot get on by his feelings; that moral considerations, too tenaciously upheld, hamper his progress; you will see ill-bred men, boorish or incapable of taking stock of the future, who will crush a smaller man, be guilty of some rudeness to an old woman, or refuse to endure a few minutes' boredom from an old man, saying they can be of no use; but later you will find these men caught by the thorns they have neglected to break, and missing fortune by a trifle; while another, who has early trained himself to this theory of duty, will meet with no obstacles. He may reach the top more slowly, but his position will be assured, and he will stand firm when others are tottering to a fall.

"When I add that the application of this principle demands, in the first place, a knowledge of manners, you will fancy, perhaps, that my jurisprudence smacks of the court and of the teaching I brought from the house of the Lenoncourts. My dear friend, I attach the greatest importance to this training, trivial as it may seem. The manners of the best company are quite as indispensable as the varied and extensive knowledge you already possess; they have often taken its place! Some men, ignorant in fact, but gifted with mother-wit, and used to argue soundly from their ideas, have attained to greatness which has evaded the grasp of others, their superiors. I have watched you carefully, Félix, to see whether your education with other youths in various schools had spoilt anything in you. I discerned, with great joy, that you may easily assimilate what you lack—little enough, God knows! In many persons, though brought up in good traditions, manners are merely superficial; for perfect politeness and noble manners come from the heart and a lofty sense of personal dignity. This is why, in spite of their training, some men of birth are of very bad style, while others of humbler rank have a natural good taste and need but a few lessons to acquire the best manners without clumsy imitation. Take the word of a poor woman who will never quit her valley—A noble tone, a gracious simplicity stamped on speech, action, and demeanor—nay, even on the details of a house—constitute a sort of personal poetry, and give an irresistible charm; judge, then, of their effect when they come from the heart.

"Politeness, dear child, consists in forgetting yourself for others; with many people it is no more than a company grimace that fails as soon as self-interest is rubbed too hard and peeps through; then a great man is ignoble. But true politeness—and on this I insist in you, Félix—implies a Christian grace; it is the very flower of charity, and consists in really forgetting self. In memory of Henriette, do not be a fountain without water, have the spirit as well as the form. Do not be afraid of finding yourself too often the dupe of this social virtue; sooner or later you will gather the harvest of so much seed cast apparently to the winds.

"My father remarked, long ago, that one of the most offensive things in superficial politeness is the misuse of promises. When you are asked to do something that is out of your power, refuse point-blank and give no false hopes. On the other hand, give at once whatever you mean to grant; you will thus be credited with the grace of refusing as well as the grace of conferring a benefit—twofold honesty which really elevates the character. I am not sure that we do not earn more ill-will by a hope deceived than good-will by a favor bestowed.

"Above all, my friend—for such little things are all within my province, and I may emphasize the things I feel that I know—be neither confidential, nor commonplace, nor over-eager—three rocks ahead. Too much confiding in others diminishes their respect, the commonplace is despised, enthusiasm makes us a prey to adventurers. In the first place, dear child, do not have more than two or three friends in the whole course of your life, and your confidence is their right; if you give it to many, you betray them to each other. If you find yourself more intimate with some men than with others, be reserved about yourself, as reserved as though they some day were to be your rivals, your opponents, or your enemies; the chances of life require this. Preserve an attitude neither cold nor perfervid, try to hit the medium line, on which a man may take his stand without compromising himself. Believe me, a man of heart is as far from Philinte's feeble amiability as from Alceste's harsh austerity. The genius of the comic poet shines in the suggestion of a happy medium apprehended by a high-minded spectator; and certainly every one will have a leaning to the absurdities of virtue rather than to the sovereign contempt that hides under the good-nature of egoism, but they will probably preserve themselves from either. As to commonplace civility, though it may make some simpletons pronounce you to be a charming man, those who are accustomed to gauge and value human intellects will estimate your capacity, and you will soon be neglected, for the commonplace is the resource of all weak men. Now, weak men are looked down upon by a world which regards its several members merely as organs—and perhaps it is right:

nature crushes out every ineffectual creature. Indeed, the kindly influence of women is perhaps the outcome of the pleasure they take in struggling with a blind power, and asserting the triumph of the heart's perceptions over the brute strength of matter. But society, a stepmother rather than a mother, adores the children who flatter her vanity.

"As for zeal, that first sublime error of youth which finds real enjoyment in expending its strength, and so begins by being its own dupe before it is duped by others, keep it for the sentiments you share, keep it for woman and for God. Never offer such treasures in the world's mart, nor in the speculations of politics; they will only give you paste for them. You surely must believe the adviser who enjoins noble conduct on you in every particular, when she implores you not to waste yourself in vain; for, unfortunately, men will esteem you in proportion to your usefulness, taking no account of your real worth. To use a figure of speech which will abide in your poetic mind: A cypher, though it be never so large, traced in gold or written in chalk, will never be anything but a cypher. A man of our day said—'Never show zeal!' Zeal verges on trickery, it leads to misunderstandings; you would never find a fervor to match your own in any one above you; kings, like women, think that everything is due to them. Sad as this principle may seem, it is true; but it need not blight the soul. Place your purest feelings in some inaccessible spot where their flowers may be passionately admired, where the artist may lovingly dream over the masterpiece.

"Duties, my friend, are not feelings. To do what you ought is not to do what you please. A man must be ready to die in cold blood for his country, but may give his life for a woman with joy.

"One of the most important rules in the science of manners is almost absolute silence concerning yourself. Allow yourself, for the amusement of it, some day to talk about yourself to some mere acquaintances; tell them of your ailments, your pleasures, or your business, you will see indifference supervene on affected interest; then, when they are utterly bored, if the mistress of the house does not politely check you, every one will find a clever excuse to withdraw. But if you want to collect about you every man's sympathies, to be regarded as an agreeable and witty man, always pleasant, talk to them of themselves, find an opportunity for bringing them to the front—even by asking questions apparently irrelevant to the individual. Heads will bow, lips will smile at you, and, when you have left, every one will sing your praises. Your conscience and the voice of your heart will warn you of the limit where the cowardice of flattery begins, where the grace of conversation ends.

"One word more about talking in public. My friend, youth is always inclined to a certain hastiness of judgment which does it honor, but which serves it ill. Hence the silence which used to be impressed on the young, who went through an apprenticeship to their betters, during which they studied life; for, of old, the nobility had their apprentices as artists had, pages attached to the masters who maintained them. In these days young people have a sort of hot-house training, sour at that, which leads them to judge severely of actions, thoughts, and books; they cut rashly, and with a new knife. Do not indulge in this bad habit. Your condemnation would be such censure as would hurt many of those about you, and they would all perhaps be less ready to forgive a secret wound than an offense given in public. Young men are not indulgent, because they do not know life and its difficulties. An old critic is kind and mild; a young critic is merciless, for he knows nothing; the other knows all. And then there is at the back of every human action a labyrinth of determining causes, of which God has reserved to Himself the right of final judgment. Be severe only to yourself.

"Your fortune lies before you, but nobody in this world

can make a fortune unaided. My father's house is open to you; visit there frequently; the connections you will form there will be of use to you in a thousand ways. But do not yield an inch of ground to my mother; she crushes those who bend, but admires the spirit of those who resist her. She is like iron which, when hammered, can be welded with iron, but by its mere contact breaks everything less hard than itself. But cultivate my mother's acquaintance; if she likes you, she will introduce you to houses where you will pick up the inevitable knowledge of the world, the art of listening, speaking, replying, coming in, and going away; the tone of speech, the indescribable something, which is not superiority any more than the coat is genius, but without which the greatest talents are never acceptable. I know you well enough to be sure that I am not deluding myself when I picture you beforehand just what I wish you to be—simple in manner, gentle in tone, proud without conceit, deferent to old people, obliging without servility, and, above all, discreet. Use your wit, but not merely to amuse your company, for you must remember that if your superiority irritates a commonplace man, he will be silent; but he will afterward speak of you as 'most amusing,' a word of scorn. Your superiority must always be leonine. Indeed, do not try to please men. In your intercourse with them I would recommend a coolness verging on such a degree of impertinence as cannot offend them; every man respects those who look down on him, and such contempt will win you the favor of women who value you in proportion to your indifference to men. Never be familiar with persons in discredit, not even if they do not merit their reputation, for the world exacts an account alike of our friendships and our aversions; on this point let your judgment be slowly and fully matured, but irrevocable.

"If men to whom you will have nothing to say justify your aversion, your esteem will be valued; and thus you will inspire that unspoken respect which raises a man above his fellows. Thus you will be armed with youth to attract, grace to charm, and prudence to preserve your conquests. And all I have said may be summed up in the old motto '*Noblesse oblige.*'

"Now apply these principles to the policy of business. You will hear many men declare that craft is the element of success, that the way to push through the crowd is by dividing it to make room. My friend, these principles held good in the dark ages, when princes had to use rival forces to destroy each other; but in these days everything is open to the day and such a system would serve you very ill. You will always meet men face to face; either an honest gentleman or a treacherous foe, a man whose weapons are calumny, slander, and dishonesty. Well, understand that against him you have no better ally than himself; he is his own enemy; you can fight him with the weapons of loyalty; sooner or later he will be despised. As to the first, your own frankness will conciliate his esteem; and when your interests are reconciled—for everything can be arranged—he will be of service to you. Do not be afraid of making enemies; woe to him who has none in the world you will move in! But try never to give a handle to ridicule or discredit. I say *try*, for in Paris a man is not always free to act; he is liable to inevitable circumstances; you cannot escape mud from the gutter, nor a falling tile. There are gutters in the moral world, and those who fall try to splash nobler men with the mud in which they are drowning. But you can always command respect by showing yourself invariably relentless in your final decision.

"In this conflict of ambitions, and amid these tangled difficulties, always go straight to the point; resolutely attack the question, and never fight more than one point with all your strength. You know how Monsieur de Mortsauf hated Napoleon; he persistently cursed him, he watched him as the police watch a criminal, every evening he called out on him for the Duc d'Enghien's death—the only disaster, the only death that ever wrung tears from him; well, he admired him as the boldest of leaders, and often expatiated on his tactics. Cannot a similar strategy be applied in the war of interests? It would economize time, as Napoleon's economized men and space. Think this over, for a woman is often mistaken about such things, judging only by feeling and instinct.

"On one point I may confidently insist: all trickery and craft is certain to be detected, and does harm in the end, whereas every crisis seems to me less perilous when a man takes his stand on plain-dealing. If I may quote myself as an example, I may tell you that at Clochegourde, forced by Monsieur de Mortsauf's temper to be on my guard against any litigation, and to have every question settled at once by arbitration, lest it should become a sort of illness to him which he would enjoy giving himself up to, I have always settled matters myself by going straight to the point and saying to my opponent, 'Untie the knot or cut it.'

"You will often find yourself of use to others, doing them some service, and getting small thanks; but do not imitate those who complain, and declare that they have met with nothing but ingratitude. Is not that putting one's self on a pedestal? And is it not rather silly to confess one's scant knowledge of the world? And do you do good as a usurer lends money? Will you not do it for its own sake? *Noblesse oblige!* At the same time, do not render men such service as compels them to be ungrateful, for then they will become your implacable enemies; there is a despair of obligation as there is a despair of ruin, which gives incalculable strength. On the other hand, accept as little as you can. Do not become the vassal of any living soul; depend on yourself alone.

"I can only advise, dear friend, as to the minor matters of life. In the political world everything has a different aspect, the rules that guide your personal conduct must bow to higher interests. But if you should reach the sphere in which great men have their being, you, like God, will be sole judge of your decisions. You will be more than a man, you will be the embodiment of the law; you will be more than an individual, you will represent the nation incarnate. But though you will judge, you will also be judged. In later times you will be called to appear before the Ages, and you know history well enough to appreciate what the feelings and deeds are which lead to true greatness.

"I now come to the serious point—your conduct to women. In the drawing-rooms where you will visit make it a law to yourself never to squander yourself by indulging in the trivialities of flirtation. One of the men of the last century, who was in every way most successful, made it a practice never to devote himself but to one lady in an evening, and to select those who seemed forlorn. That man, my dear boy, was supreme in his day. He had shrewdly calculated that in due time he would be persistently praised by everybody. Most young men lose their most precious possession, the time, namely, which is needful for making the connections which are half of social life. While they are intrinsically attractive they would have little to do to attach others to their interests; but that springtime is brief—make the most of it. Cultivate the society of influential women. Influential women are old women; they will inform you as to the alliances and secrets of every family, and show you the cross-roads that may take you quickly to the goal. They will be really fond of you; patronage is their last passion when they are not bigots; they will be of invaluable service, they will speak well of you, and make other people want to know you.

"Avoid young women! Do not think that there is the least personal animus in this advice. The woman of fifty will do everything for you; the woman of twenty, nothing; she will demand your whole life; the elder woman will only ask for a moment, a little attention. Jest with young women, take them very lightly, they are incapable of a serious thought. Young women, my dear, are selfish, petty, incapable of true friendship; they only love themselves and would sacrifice you for a success. Beside, they will require your full devotion, and your position will need the devotion of others—two irreconcilable propositions. No young woman will understand your interests; they will always be thinking of themselves, not of you, and do you more harm by their vanity than good by their attachment; they will unhesitatingly appropriate your time; they will mar your fortune and ruin you with the best grace in the world. If you complain, the silliest of them all can argue that her glove is worth the universe, that nothing can be more glorious than her service. They will all tell you that they can give you happiness and so make you forget your high destiny. The happiness they give is variable; your future greatness is certain.

"You do not know with what perfidious art they go about to gratify their caprices, to make a transient liking appear as a passion begun on earth to be eternal in heaven. When they throw you over, they will tell you that the words, 'I love you no longer,' justify their desertion, as the words, 'I love you,' justified their love—love that is irresponsible. My dear, the doctrine is absurd. Believe me, true love is eternal, infinite, always the same; equable and pure without vehement outbreaks; it is found under white hairs when the heart is still young. Nothing of the kind is to be found in women of fashion; they only act their part.

"This one will interest you by her sorrows, and seem the sweetest and least exacting of her sex; but when she has made herself necessary she will gradually domineer over you and make you do her bidding; you will wish to be a diplomatist, to go and come, to study men, interests, and foreign lands. No, you must stay in Paris or at her country-house, she will ingeniously tie you to her apron-string, and the more devoted you are the less grateful will she be. That one will try to engage you by her submissiveness; she would be your page and follow you romantically to the ends of the earth; she would compromise herself for your sake—and hang like a stone around your neck. Thus one day you will be drowned, but she will come to the top.

"The least crafty of their sex have endless snares; the stupidest triumph by exciting no suspicions; the least dangerous of them all would be an audacious flirt who would fall in love with you, hardly knowing why, who would desert you without reason and take you up again out of vanity. But they will all do you a mischief sooner or later. Every young woman who goes into the world and lives on pleasure and the triumphs of vanity is half-corrupt and will corrupt you.

"That is not the chaste, meditative being in whose heart you may reign for ever. Nay, the woman who loves you will dwell in solitude, her highest festivals will be your looks, and she will feed on your words. Then let that woman be all the world to you, for you are all in all to her; love her truly, give her no pain, no rival, do not torture her jealousy. To be loved, my dear, and understood is the highest happiness—I only wish that you may know it; but do not compromise the first bloom of your soul; be very sure of the heart to which you give your affections. That woman must never be herself, never think of herself, but of you alone; she will never contradict you, she will not listen to her own interests; she will scent danger for you when you do not suspect it and forget her own; if she suffers, she will endure without complaining; she will have no personal vanity, but she will respect what you love in her. Return such love with even greater love. Love begets love.

"And if you should be so happy as to find, what your poor friend here can never have, an affection equally inspired and equally felt, however perfect that love may be, remember still that in a valley there lives for you a mother whose heart is so deeply minded by the feeling with which you fill it that you can never reach the bottom of it.

"Yes, you can never know the extent of the affection I bear you: for it to show its full extent you would have had to be bereft of your noble intellect; you cannot think how far my devotion would have carried me then. Do you doubt me when I bid you avoid young women, who are all more or less superficial, sarcastic, vain, frivolous, and wasteful, and attach yourself to important dowagers, full of sense, as my aunt was, who will do you good service, who will defend you against secret calumny by quashing it, who will speak of you in terms you cannot use in speaking of yourself? After all, am I not generous when I bid you reserve your worship for the purehearted angel to come? If the words *Noblesse oblige* include a great part of my first injunctions, my advice as to your dealings with women may also be summed up in this chivalrous motto, '*Les servir toutes, n'en aimer qu'une*' (Serve all, love but one).

"Your learning is vast; your heart, preserved by suffering, is still unspotted, all is fair and good in you: then WILL! Your whole future lies in this one word, the watchword of great men. You will obey your Henriette, my child, will you not, and allow her still to tell you what she thinks of you and your doings in the world? I have a 'mind's eye' which can foresee the future for you, as for my children; then let me make use of the faculty for your benefit; it is a mysterious gift which has brought peace into my life; and which, far from waning, grows stronger in solitude and silence.

"In return, I ask you to give me a great joy; I want to see you growing great among men without having to frown over one of your successes; I want you very soon to raise your fortune to a level with your name, and to be able to tell me that I have contributed something more than a wish to your advancement. This secret coöperation is the only pleasure I can allow myself. I can wait.

"I do not say farewell. We are divided, you cannot press my hand to your lips; but you must surely have understood the place you fill in the heart of your

"HENRIETTE."

As I finished reading this letter, I seemed to feel a motherly heart throbbing beneath my fingers at the moment when I was still frozen by my mother's stern reception. I could guess why the Countess had forbidden me to read this letter so long as I was in Touraine; she had feared, no doubt, to see me fall with my head at her feet and to feel them wetted by my tears.

At last I made the acquaintance of my brother Charles, who had hitherto been a stranger to me; but he showed such arrogance in our most trifling intercourse as held us too far apart for us to care for each other as brothers. All kindly feeling is based on equality of mind and there was no point of contact between us. He lectured me solemnly on various trivial details which the mind or the heart knows by instinct; he always seemed distrustful of me; if my love had not been to me as a corner-stone, he might have made me awkward and stupid by seeming to think that I knew nothing. He, nevertheless, introduced me into society, where my rusticity was to be a foil to his accomplishment. But for the woes of my childhood, I might have taken his patronizing vanity for brotherly affection; but mental isolation produces the same effects as earthly solitude: the silence allows us to discern the faintest echo, and the habit of relying on one's self develops a sensitiveness so delicate that it vibrates to the lightest touch of the affections that concern us.

Before knowing Madame de Mortsauf a stern look hurt me, the tone of a rough word went to my heart; I groaned over it, though I knew nothing of the gentler life of caresses. Whereas, on my return from Clochegourde, I could draw comparisons which gave completeness to my premature knowledge. Observation based on mere suffering is incomplete. Happiness, has its lights too. But I allowed myself to be crushed under Charles' superiority as my elder, all the more readily because I was not his dupe.

I went alone to the Duchesse de Lenoncourt's house and heard no mention made of Henriette; no one but the good old Duke, who was simplicity itself, ever spoke of her; but, from the reception he gave me, I guessed that his daughter had secretly recommended me.

Hardly had I begun to get over the loutish surprise which a first sight of the great world produces in every tyro, when, just as I was getting a glimpse of the resources it has for ambitious men, and thinking of the joy of practicing Henriette's axioms, while recognizing their entire truth, the events of the twentieth of March supervened. My brother accompanied the court to Ghent, and I, by the Countess' advice— for I kept up a correspondence with her, frequent on my side only—I also went thither with the Duc de Lenoncourt. His habitual benevolence became a sincere desire to help me when he found that I was devoted head, heart, and hands to the Bourbons; he presented me to his majesty.

The courtiers of disaster are few. Youth has artless enthusiasms and disinterested fidelity; the King was a judge of men; what would have passed unnoticed at the Tuileries were conspicuous at Ghent, and I was so happy as to find favor with Louis XVIII.

A letter from Madame de Mortsauf to her father, brought with some dispatches by an emissary of the Vendéens, contained a scrap for me, informing me that Jacques was ill. Monsieur de Mortsauf, in despair alike at his son's frail health, and at a second emigration of the sovereign, in which he had no part, had added a few lines that enabled me to imagine my dear lady's situation. Fretted by him, no doubt, for spending all her time by Jacques' bedside, getting no rest day or night, scorning such vexations but incapable of controlling herself when she was expending herself wholly in nursing her child, Henriette must be needing the support of a friendship that had made life less burdensome to her, if it were only by amusing Monsieur de Mortsauf. Several times already I had had the Count out for a walk when he was threatening to worry her—an innocent trick of which the success had earned me some of those looks expressing passionate gratitude, and in which love reads a promise. Though I was eager to follow in the footsteps of my brother Charles, recently sent to the congress at Vienna; though, at the risk of my life even, I longed to justify Henriette's predictions and free myself from being his vassal, my ambition, my desire for independence, my interests, which bid me remain with the King, all paled before Madame de Mortsauf's heart-stricken image. I decided on leaving the court at Ghent, and on going to serve my true sovereign.

God rewarded me. The messenger sent out by the Vendéens could not return to France; the King wanted a man who would devote himself to be the bearer of his instructions. The Duc de Lenoncourt knew that his majesty would not overlook the man who should undertake this perilous task; without consulting me, he obtained it for me, and I accepted it, only too glad to be able to return to Clochegourde while serving the good cause.

Thus, after having an audience of the King, at one-and-twenty, I returned to France, where, either in Paris or in la Vendée, I was to be so happy as to do his majesty's bidding. By the end of May, being the object of pursuit to the Bonapartists who were on my track, I was obliged to fly; affecting to make my way homeward, I went on foot from place to place, from wood to wood, across Upper Vendée, the Bocage, and Poitou, changing my route as circumstances required.

I thus reached Saumur; from Saumur I went to Chinon, and from Chinon, in a single night, I arrived in the woods of Neuil, where I met the Count, on horseback, on a common;

he took me up behind him and carried me home, without our meeting a soul who could recognize me.

"Jacques is better," was his first speech.

I explained to him my position as a diplomatic infantryman, hunted like a wild animal, and the gentleman rose up in him, in arms to dispute with Chessel the risk of harboring me.

When I saw Clochegourde I felt as if the past eight months were but a dream. The Count said to his wife as we entered, "Guess who is come with me! Félix."

"Is it possible?" she asked, her arms hanging limp, and looking quite amazed.

I came in; we stood, both immovable, she riveted to her seat, I on the threshold, gazing at each other with the fixed avidity of two lovers who want to make up in one look for lost time. But she, ashamed of her surprise, which laid her heart bare, arose, and I went forward.

"I have prayed much for you," said she, holding out her hand for me to kiss.

She asked for news of her father; then, understanding my fatigue, she went to arrange a room for me, while the Count had some food brought, for I was dying of hunger. My room was over hers, that which had been her aunt's; she left me to be taken to it by the Count, after setting foot on the bottom step of the stairs, considering no doubt whether she should show me the way herself; I turned around, she colored, wished me a sound nap, and hastily withdrew. When I came down to dinner I heard of the defeat at Waterloo, of Napoleon's flight, the march of the allies on Paris and the probable return of the Bourbons. To the Count these events were everything; to us they were nothing.

Do you know what the greatest news was after I had greeted the children, for I will say nothing of my alarm on seeing how pale and thin the Countess was? I knew the dismay I might produce by a gesture of surprise, and expressed nothing but pleasure at seeing her. The great news for us was, "You will have some ice."

She had often been annoyed last year because she had no water cold enough for me; for, drinking nothing else, I liked it iced. God knows what it had cost her in importunities to have an ice-house built. You, better than any one, know that love is satisfied with a word, a look, a tone of voice, an attention apparently most trifling; its highest privilege is to be its own evidence. Well, this word, with her look and her pleasure, revealed to me the extent of her sentiments, as I had formerly shown her mine by my conduct over the backgammon.

But there was no end to the artless proofs of her tenderness. By the seventh day after my arrival she was quite herself again; she was sparkling with health, glee, and youth; I found my beloved lily more beautiful, more fully developed, just as I found all my heart's treasures increased. Is it not a narrow soul only, or a vulgar heart, which finds that absence diminishes feeling, effaces the impression of the soul, and deteriorates the beauty of the person beloved? To an ardent imagination, to those beings in whom enthusiasm flows in their blood, dying it with a fresher purple, and in whom passion takes on the form of constancy, has not absence such an effect as the torments which fortified the faith of early Christians and made God visible to them? Are there not, in a heart full of love, certain undying hopes which give a higher value to the image we desire by showing it in glimpses tinged by the glow of dreams? Can we not feel such promptings as lend the beauty of an ideal to those adored features by informing them with thought? The past, remembered bit by bit, is magnified; the future is furnished with hopes. Between two hearts overcharged with such electric tension, the first interview is then like a beneficent storm which revives the earth and fertilizes it, while shedding on it the flashing gleams of the lightning. How much exquisite pleasure I tasted in finding that in us these thoughts, these experiences were reciprocal! With what rapture did I watch the growth of happiness in Henriette!

A woman who resuscitates under the eyes of the man she loves gives a greater proof of feeling perhaps than one who dies, killed by a suspicion, or withered on the stem for lack of nutrition. Which of the two is the more pathetic I cannot tell. Madame de Mortsauf's revival was as natural as the effect of the month of May on the meadows, or of sunshine and shower on drooping plants. Like our vale of love, Henriette had gone through her winter; like it, she was born anew with the spring.

Before dinner we went down to our beloved terrace. There, as she stroked the head of her poor child, weaker now than I had ever seen him, while he walked by her side in silence as though he were sickening for some disease, she told me of the nights she had spent by his sick-bed. For those three months, she said, she had lived exclusively in herself; she had dwelt, as it were, in a gloomy palace, dreading to enter the rooms where lights were blazing, where banquets were given that were forbidden to her; she had stood at the open door with one eye on her child and the other on a vague face, with one ear listening to sorrow and the other hearing a voice. She spoke in poems, suggested by solitude, such as no poet has ever written; and all quite simply, without knowing that there might be the slightest trace of love or taint of voluptuous thought, or of Oriental sweetness like a rose of Frangistan. When the Count joined us she went on in the same tone, as a wife proud of herself, who can look her husband boldly in the face and kiss her son's brow without a blush.

She had prayed much, holding her clasped hands over Jacques for whole nights, *willing* that he should not die.

"I went up to the gates of the sanctuary," she said, "to ask his life of God."

And she had seen visions; she repeated them to me; but when she presently said in her angel's voice these wonderful words, "When I slept, my heart kept watch!" "That is to say, you were almost crazy," said the Count, interrupting her.

She was silenced, as if this was the first blow she had ever had, as if she had forgotten that for thirteen years this man had never failed to aim an arrow at her heart. Like a glorious bird, she was stayed in her flight by this clumsy bullet; she fell into a mood of dull dejection.

"Dear me, monsieur," said she, after a pause, "will nothing I say ever find favor before the bar of your wit? Will you never have pity on my weakness, nor any sympathy with my womanly fancies?"

She paused. This angel already repented of having murmured, and sounded the past and the future alike at a glance. Could she be understood, had she not provoked some virulent retort? The blue veins throbbed strongly in her temples; she shed no tears, but her green eyes lost their color; then she looked down to the ground to avoid seeing in mine the exaggeration of her suffering, her own feelings guessed by me, her soul cherished in mine, and, above all, the sympathy, crimsoned by young love, that was ready, like a faithful dog, to fly at any one who should offend his mistress without measuring the force or the dignity of the foe. At such a moment the airs of superiority assumed by the Count were a thing to see; he fancied he had triumphed over his wife and battered her with a hailstorm of words, reiterating the same idea again and again, like the blows of an axe repeating the same sound.

"So he is the same as ever?" I asked when the Count left us, called away by the stableman who came to fetch him.

"Always!" replied Jacques.

"Always most kind, my boy," said she to Jacques, trying to screen Monsieur de Mortsauf from the criticism of his children. "You see the present, you know nothing of the past; you cannot judge of your father without some injustice; and even if you were so unhappy as to see your father in the wrong, the honor of the family would require you to bury such secrets in the deepest silence."

"How are the improvements going on at la Cassine and la Rhétorière?" I inquired, to turn her mind from these bitter reflections.

"Beyond my hopes," she replied. "The buildings being finished, we found two capital farmers who took one at a rental of four thousand five hundred francs, we paying the taxes, and the other at five thousand; the leases for fifteen years. We have already planted three thousand young trees on the two new farms. Manette's cousin is delighted with la Rabelaye; Martineau has la Baude. The return on the four farms is chiefly in hay and wood, and they do not fatten the soil, as some dishonest farmers do, with the manure intended for the arable land. So our efforts are crowned with complete success. Clochegourde, apart from what we call the home farm, from our woods and the vineyards, brings in nineteen thousand francs, and the plantations will in time yield us an annuity. I am struggling now to get the home farm placed in the hands of our keeper, Martineau, whose place could be filled by his son. He offers a rental of three thousand francs if Monsieur de Mortsauf will only build him a house at la Commanderie. We could then clear the approach to Clochegourde, finish the proposed avenue to the Chinon road, and have nothing in our own hands but the wood and the vineyards. If the King returns, we shall have our pension again, and we shall accept it after a few days' contest with our wife's common sense! Thus Jacques' fortune will be perfectly secure. When we have achieved this result I shall leave it to monsieur to save for Madeleine, and the King will endow her, too, as is customary. My conscience is at peace, my task is nearly done. And you?" she asked.

I explained my mission and showed her how wise and

fruitful her advice had been. Had she been gifted with second sight to see events so accurately?

"Did I not say so in my letter?" replied she. "But it is only for you that I can exercise that strange faculty, of which I have spoken to no one but Monsieur de la Berge, my director; he explains it by divine intervention. Often, after any deep meditation to which my fears for the children have given rise, my eyes used to close to the things of this world and awake to another realm. When I saw Jacques and Madeleine as luminous figures, they were well for some little time; when I saw them wrapped in mist, they soon after fell ill. As for you, not only do I always see you radiant, but I hear a soft voice telling me what you ought to do—without words, by spiritual communication. By what law is it that I can use this marvelous faculty only for my children's behoof and yours?" she went on, becoming thoughtful. "Is it that God means to be a father to them?" she added, after a pause.

"Allow me to believe that I obey you alone," I earnestly answered.

She gave me one of those whole-hearted, gracious smiles which so intoxicated my soul that I should not in such a moment have felt a death-blow.

"As soon as the King reaches Paris, go there, leave Clochegourde," she said. " Degrading as it is to sue for place and favor, it is, on the other hand, ridiculous not to be at hand to accept them. There will be great changes. The King will need capable and trustworthy men; do not fail him. You will find yourself in office while still young, and you will benefit by it; for statesmen, as for actors, there is a certain routine of business which no genius can divine; it must be taught. My father learned that from the Duc de Choiseul. Think of me," she added, after a pause; "let me enjoy the pleasures of superiority in a soul that is all my own. Are you not my son?"

"Your son?" I said sullenly.

"Nothing but my son," said she, mimicking me. "And is not that a good enough place to hold in my heart?"

The bell rang for dinner, she took my arm, leaning on it with evident pleasure.

"You have grown," she said, as we went up the steps. When we reached the top she shook my arm as if my fixed gaze held her too eagerly; though her eyes were downcast she knew full well that I looked at her alone, and she said in her tone of affected impatience, so gracious and so insinuating—

"Come, let us look at our favorite valley."

She turned, holding her white silk parasol over our heads, and clasping Jacques closely to her side; the movement of her head, by which she directed my attention to the Indre, to the punt, and the fields, showed me that since my visit and our walks together she had made herself familiar with those misty distances and hazy curves. Nature was the cloak that had sheltered her thoughts; she knew now what the nightingale sobs over at night, and what the marsh-bird repeats in its plaintive, droning note.

At eight o'clock that evening I was present at a scene which touched me deeply, and which I had never before witnessed, because I had always remained to play with Monsieur de Mortsauf while she went into the dining-room before putting the children to bed. A bell rang twice and all the house-servants appeared.

"You are our guest; will you submit to convent rule?" she asked, leading me away by the hand with the look of innocent gaiety that is characteristic of all truly pious women.

The Count followed us. Masters, children, and servants, all knelt bareheaded in their accustomed places. It was Madeleine's turn to say prayers; the dear child did it in her thin, young voice, its artless tones clearly audible in the harmonious country silence, and giving each phrase the holy purity of innocence, that angelic grace. It was the most touching prayer I ever heard. Nature whispered a response to the child's words in the myriad low rustlings of the evening hour, an accompaniment as of an organ softly played at the time of vespers.

Madeleine was on her mother's right hand, Jacques on the left. The pretty curly heads, and, rising between them, the mother's plaits of hair; above them, again, Monsieur de Mortsauf's perfectly white hair and ivory yellow skull, formed a picture of which the coloring seemed to repeat to the mind the idea suggested by the melody of prayer; and to fulfill the conditions of unity which stamp the sublime, the devout little assembly was wrapped in the subdued light of sunset, while the room was touched with the red beams. The poetical or the superstitious soul could thus imagine that the fires of heaven were shed on the faithful worshipers kneeling there before God without distinction of rank, all equals, as the church requires. My thoughts reverted to patriarchal times, and my fancy gave added dignity to the scene, itself so grand in its simplicity. The children bade their father good-night, the servants bowed, the Countess went away, each child holding a hand, and I went back to the drawing-room with the Count.

"You will have found salvation there and perdition here," said he, pointing to the backgammon board.

The Countess joined us in about half an hour, and brought her work-frame to the table.

"This is for you," said she, unrolling the canvas; "but the work has hung fire these three months past. Between that red carnation and that rose, my poor boy was very ill."

"Come, come," said Monsieur de Mortsauf; "do not talk about it. *Size-cinq*, master king's messenger."

When I went to my room, I sat motionless to hear her moving about below. Though she was calm and pure, I was tormented by crazy ideas and intolerable cravings.

"Why could she not be mine?" thought I. "Perhaps she, like me, is tossed on the whirlwind of the senses?"

At one o'clock I crept down the stairs, treading without a sound, and outside her door I lay down; with my ear to the crack I heard her soft and even breathing, like a child's. When I was quite chilled I went up again and to bed, where I slept quietly till morning.

To what predestination, to what taint of nature can I ascribe the pleasure I find in going to the edge of a precipice, in sounding the abyss of evil, in peering into its depths, shuddering at the chill, and drawing back in anguish. That hour at night spent on the threshold of her door, where I wept with frenzy, without her ever knowing on the morrow that she had trodden on my tears and my kisses—wept over her virtue, ruined and respected by turns, cursed and then worshiped—that hour, a madness in the eyes of many persons, was an inspiration of the same nameless feeling that carries on a soldier. Men have told me that in such a mood they have risked their life, rushing in front of a battery, to see whether they would escape the grapeshot, and whether they would not enjoy thus trying to leap the gulf of probabilities, like Jean Bart smoking while he sat on a powder barrel.

On the following day I went out and gathered two nosegays; the Count admired them—the Count, who cared for nothing of the kind, and for whom Champenetz's jest seemed to have been invented: "He builds dungeons in the air!"

I spent several days at Clochegourde, paying short calls only at Frapesle, where I dined, however, three times. The French army took up its quarters at Tours. Though I was evidently life and health to Madame de Mortsauf, she entreated me to get to Châteauroux and return as fast as possible to Paris through Issoudun and Orleans. I tried to rebel; she insisted, saying that her familiar had counseled her; I obeyed. Our parting this time was watered with tears; she was afraid of the captivations of the world I was about to live in. Should I not have to enter seriously into the whirl of interests, of passions, of pleasures, which make Paris an ocean fraught with perils no less to chaste affections than to a clear conscience? I promised her that I would write her every evening the events and the thoughts of the day. At this promise she laid her weary head on my shoulder, and said—

"Omit nothing; everything will interest me."

She gave me letters to the Duke and Duchess, on whom I called the day after my arrival.

"You are in luck," said the Duke. "Dine here and come with me to the palace this evening; your fortune is made. The King mentioned your name this morning, adding, 'He is young, able, and faithful.' And the King regretted not knowing whether you were dead or alive, and whither the course of events had led you after you had so well fulfilled your mission."

That evening I was a master of appeals to the council of state, and was appointed to certain secret employment for the King—a confidential post which was to be permanent so long as he should reign, not splendid in appearance, but with no risk of overthrow, and which placed me at the heart of government, and was, in fact, the very foundation of all my prosperity.

Madame de Mortsauf had seen clearly, and I owed everything to her: power and wealth, happiness and knowledge; she guided and purified my heart, and gave my purpose that unity without which the powers of youth are vainly fritted away. At a later date I had a colleague. Each of us was on service for six months at a time. We could at need take each other's place; we had a room in the palace, a carriage at our command, and a handsome allowance for expenses when called upon to travel.

It was a strange position! We were the secret disciples of a monarch to whose policy his enemies have since done signal justice; we heard his judgment on all matters internal and foreign; we had no acknowledged influence, but were occasionally consulted, as Laforêt was consulted by Molière, and we heard the hesitancy of long experience corrected by the conscience of youth.

Our prospects were indeed settled in a way to satisfy our ambition. Beside my pay as master of appeals, paid out of the revenue of the council of state, the King gave me a thousand francs a month out of the privy purse, and not unfrequently made me a present. Though the King knew full well that a young man of three-and-twenty could not long withstand the amount of work he piled upon me, my colleague, now a peer of France, was not appointed till the month of August, 1817. A choice was so difficult, our functions demanded such various qualities, that the King was long in coming to a decision. He did me the honor to ask me which of the young men among whom he was prepared to choose would best suit me as a companion. One of the number was a former comrade of mine at the Lepître boarding-house, and I did not name him.

The King asked me why, not understanding why I should pass him over.

"Your majesty," said I, "has mentioned men of equal loyalty, but of different degrees of ability. I have named the man I consider the most capable, feeling certain that we shall always agree."

My judgment coincided with the King's, who was always grateful for the sacrifice I had made. On this occasion he said to me, "You will be the first of the two." And he gave my colleague to understand this; still, in return for this service, my deputy became my friend.

The consideration with which I was treated by the Duc de Lenoncourt was the standard for that shown me by the rest of the world. The mere words—"The King is greatly interested in this young man; he has a future before him; the King likes him"—would have sufficed in lieu of talents; but they also added to the kindness shown to a young official the indescribable tribute that is paid only to power.

Either at the Duc de Lenoncourt's or at my sister's house—married at about this time to our cousin the Marquis de Listomère, the son of the old aunt I had been wont to visit in the Ile Saint-Louis—I gradually made the acquaintance of the most influential persons of the Faubourg Saint-Germain.

Henriette ere long threw me into the heart of the circle known as the "Petit-Château" (little castle), by the good offices of the Princesse de Blamont-Chauvry, whose grand-niece she was by marriage. She wrote of me in such glowing terms that the Princess at once invited me to call on her. I was assiduous and was so happy as to please her; she became not my patroness, but a friend whose feelings were almost maternal. The old Princess set her heart on making me intimate with her daughter Madame d'Espard, with the Duchesse de Langeais, the Vicomtesse de Beauséant, and the Duchesse de Maufrigneuse—women who, by turns, held the sceptre of fashion and who were all the more gracious to me because I made no claims upon them, and was always ready to be of service to them.

My brother Charles, far from ignoring me, thenceforth relied on my support; but my rapid success was the cause of some secret jealousy, which at a later period gave me much annoyance. My father and mother, amazed by such unexpected good fortune, felt their vanity flattered and at last recognized me as their son; but as the sentiment was to some extent artificial, not to say acted, this revulsion had not much effect on my ulcerated heart. Beside, affection that is tainted with selfishness excites little sympathy; the heart abhors every form of calculation and profit.

I wrote regularly to my dear Henriette, who answered me in a letter or two each month. Thus her spirit hovered over me, her thoughts traversed space and kept a pure atmosphere about me. No woman could attract me. The King knew of my reserve; in such matters he was of the school of Louis XV., and used to laugh and call me "Mademoiselle de Vandenesse," but the propriety of my conduct was very much approved by him. I am quite sure that the patience which had become a habit during my childhood, and yet more at Clochegourde, did much to win me the King's good graces; he was always most kind to me. He no doubt indulged a fancy for reading my letters, for he was not long under any mistake as to my blameless life. One day when the Duke was in attendance I was writing from the King's dictation, and he, seeing the Duke come in, looked mischievously at us both.

"Well, that confounded fellow Mortsauf still persists in living on?" said he, in his fine ringing voice, to which he could at will give a tone of biting sarcasm.

"Yes, still," replied the Duke.

"But the Countess de Mortsauf is an angel whom I should very much like to see here," the King went on. "However, I can do nothing; but perhaps my secretary," and he turned to me, "may be more fortunate. You have six months' leave. I shall engage as your colleague the young man of whom we were speaking yesterday. Enjoy yourself at Clochegourde, Master Cato!" and he smiled as he was wheeled out of the room in his chair.

I flew like a swallow to Touraine. For the first time I was about to show myself to the woman I loved, not only as rather less of a simpleton, but in the paraphernalia of a young man of fashion whose manners had been formed in the politest circles, whose education had been finished by the most charming women, who had at last won the reward of his sufferings, and who had made good use of the experience of the fairest angel to whom heaven ever intrusted the care of a child.

When I had stayed at Clochegourde at the time of my mission in la Vendée, I had been in shooting dress; I wore a jacket with tarnished white metal buttons, finely striped trousers, leather gaiters, and shoes. My long tramp and the thickets had served me so ill that the Count was obliged to lend me some linen. This time, two years' residence in Paris, the duty of attending the King, the habits of wealth, my now complete development, and a youthful countenance which beamed with indescribable light, derived from the serenity of a soul magnetically united to the pure soul at Clochegourde that went forth to me—all had transfigured me; I was sure of myself without being conceited; I was deeply satisfied at finding myself, young as I was, at the top of the tree; I had the proud consciousness of being the secret mainstay of the most adorable woman on earth, and her unconfessed hope.

I felt perhaps some stirrings of vanity when the postillion's whip cracked in the newly-made avenue from the Chinon road to Clochegourde, and a gate, I had never seen, opened in an enclosing wall that had been recently built. I had not written to announce my arrival to the Countess, wishing to take her by surprise; but this was a twofold blunder: in the first place, she suffered the shock of a pleasure long wished for, but regarded as impossible, and she also proved to me that elaborate surprises are always in bad taste.

When Henriette beheld a young man where she had remembered a boy, her eyes fell with a tragical droop; she allowed me to take her hand and kiss it without showing any of the heartfelt pleasure which I had been wont to perceive in her sensitive thrill; and when she raised her face to look at me again, I saw that she was pale.

"So you do not forget old friends!" said Monsieur de Mortsauf, who had neither altered nor grown older.

The two children sprang into my arms; I saw in the doorway the grave face of the Abbé de Dominis, Jacques' tutor.

"No," said I to the Count, "and henceforth I shall have six months of every year to devote always to you. Why, what is the matter?" I said to the Countess, putting my arm around her waist to support her, in the presence of all her family.

"Oh! leave me!" she exclaimed with a start; "it is nothing."

I read her soul, and answered her secret thought; I said to her, "Do you no longer acknowledge me for your faithful slave?"

She took my arm, turned away from the Count, the children, the abbé, and all the servants who had hurried out, and led me round the lawn, still within sight of them all. When we had gone so far that she thought she could not be heard—

"Felix, my friend," she said, "forgive the alarms of a woman who has but one clue by which to guide herself in an underground labyrinth, and fears to find it broken. Tell me once more that I am more than ever your Henriette, that you will not desert me, that nothing can dislodge me, that you will always be my faithful friend. I have had a sudden vision of the future—and you were not there as usual, with a radiant face and your eloquent eyes fixed on mine; you had your back to me."

"Henriette, dear idol, whom I worship more than I do God; lily, flower of my life, how can you, who are my conscience, fail to know that I am so entirely part of your heart, that my soul is here when my body is in Paris? Need I tell you that I have traveled hither in seventeen hours; that every turn of the wheel bore with it a world of thought and longing, which broke out like a tempest the moment I saw you——"

"Tell me, tell me! I am sure of myself. I can listen to you without sinning. God does not desire my death; He sends you to me as He gives the breath of life to His creatures, as He sheds rain from the clouds on a barren land. Speak, tell me, do you love me with a holy love?"

"With a holy love."

"And for ever?"

"For ever."

"As a Virgin Mary, to be left shrouded in her draperies under her spotless crown?"

"As a visible Virgin."

"As a sister?"

"As a sister too dearly loved."

"As a mother?"

"As a mother I secretly long for."

"Chivalrously, without hope?"

"Chivalrously, but hoping."

"In short, as if you were still but twenty, and had your shabby, blue evening-coat?"

"Oh, far better! I love you like that, but I also love you as——" She looked at me in keen alarm. "As you loved your aunt."

"Ah! I am happy; you have relieved my fears," said she, going to the others, who were puzzled by our private colloquy.

"Be still a child here! for you are but a child. If your best policy is to be a man to the King, understand that here it is to be a boy. As a boy you will be loved. I shall always resist the powers of the man, but what can I deny a child? Nothing; he can ask nothing that I would not grant. We have told all our secrets," she added, looking at the Count with a saucy smile, in which I saw her a girl again in all her simple nature. "I am now going in to dress."

Never for three years had I known her voice so thoroughly happy. It was the first time I heard those swallow-like notes, that childlike tone of which I have spoken.

I had brought a sportsman's outfit for Jacques and a workbox for Madeleine—which her mother always used; in short, I had made up for the shabbiness to which I had hitherto been condemned by my mother's parsimony. The delight of the two children as they displayed their presents to each other seemed to annoy the Count, who was always aggrieved if he was not the centre of attentions. I gave Madeleine a look of intelligence and followed the Count, who wanted to talk about himself. He led me to the terrace; but we paused on the steps at each solemn fact he impressed upon me.

"My poor, dear Félix," said he, "you find them all happy and in good health. It is I who give shadow to the picture. I have absorbed their maladies, and I can bless God for having inflicted them on me. I used not to know what ailed me; but I know now—I have a disease of the pylorus; I can digest nothing."

"By what good luck have you become as learned as a professor of the College of Physicians?" said I, smiling. "Is your doctor so indiscreet as to tell you this?"

"Heaven preserve me from consulting doctors!" he exclaimed, with the look of repugnance that most imaginary invalids show at the thought of medical treatment.

Then I had to listen to a crazy harangue, in the course of which he was ridiculously confidential, complaining of his wife, his servants, his children, and his life, taking evident delight in repeating his remarks of every day to a friend who, not knowing them, might be startled by them and who was obliged by politeness to seem interested. He must have been satisfied, for I listened with deep attention, trying to formulate this inconceivable character, and to guess what new torments he was inflicting on his wife, though she had not said so.

Henriette herself put an end to the monologue by coming out on the steps. The Count saw her, shook his head, and added—

"You, Félix, listen to me; but no one here has any pity for me."

And he went away as though aware that he would be in the way during my conversation with Henriette, or perhaps as a chivalrous attention to her, knowing that he would give her pleasure by leaving us together. His character was full of really inexplicable contradictions, for he was jealous, as all weak persons are; but his confidence in his wife's saintliness knew no bounds; perhaps it was the irritation to his vanity caused by the superiority of her lofty virtue that gave rise to his constant antagonism to the Countess' wishes, whom he loved to defy as children defy their mother and their masters. Jacques was at his lessons, Madeleine was dressing; thus I had an hour to walk alone with the Countess on the terrace.

"Well, dear angel," I asked, "so the chain is heavier than ever, the sands more scorching, the thorns more thickly set?"

"Be silent," said she, guessing what thoughts had been suggested to me by the Count's conversation. "You are here and all is forgotten! I am not, I have not been unhappy."

She danced a few light steps as if to flutter her white dress, to let the breezes play with her frills of snowy tulle, her loose sleeves, her bright ribbons, her cape, and the airy curls of her hair dressed *à la Sévigné;* I saw her for the first time really girlish and young, naturally gay, and as ready for sport as a child. I experienced both the tears of happiness and the delight a man feels in giving pleasure.

"Sweet flower of humanity," cried I, "that my fancy caresses and my spirit kisses! Oh my lily! still intact and erect on its stem, still white, proud, fragrant, and alone!"

"That is enough, monsieur," she said, with a smile. "Talk to me about yourself, and tell me everything."

And then, under the moving canopy of quivering leaves, we had a long conversation, full of endless parentheses, each subject dropped and taken up again, in which I initiated her into my whole life and all my occupations. I described my rooms in Paris, for she wanted to know everything, and I—joy then not fully appreciated!—I had nothing to conceal. As she thus read all my soul, and learned all the details of my life full of overwhelming toil, as she discerned the importance of my functions, in which, but for the strictest honesty, it would be so easy to cheat and grow rich, and which I exercised with such fidelity that the King, as I told her, nicknamed me Mademoiselle de Vandenesse, she clasped my hand and kissed it, leaving on it a tear of joy. This sudden inversion of our parts, this splendid praise, the swiftly expressed feeling, even more swiftly understood. "You are indeed the master I could have obeyed, the fulfillment of my dream!"—all the avowal expressed in this action, whose very humility was dignity, betraying love in a sphere far above the senses; this whirl of heavenly emotions fell on my heart and crushed me. I felt so small! I wished I could die at her feet.

"Oh!" I exclaimed, "you women will always outdo us in every way. How could you doubt me?—for you did doubt me just now, Henriette."

"Not in the present," she replied, looking at me with the ineffable sweetness that softened the light in her eyes for me alone. "But seeing you so handsome, I said to myself: Our plans for Madeleine will be marred by some woman who will guess what treasures lie below, who will worship you, rob us of our Félix, and destroy everything for us."

"Still Madeleine!" said I, with an expression of surprise which only half-distressed her. "Is it to Madeleine that I remain faithful?"

We then sat in silence, very provokingly interrupted by Monsieur de Mortsauf. My heart was full, but I had to keep up a conversation beset with difficulties, in which my truthful replies as to the policy then carried out by the King offended the Count's views, while he insisted on my explaining his majesty's intentions. Notwithstanding my questions as to his horses, the state of agriculture, whether he was satisfied with his five farms, if he meant to fell the trees in the old avenue, he constantly came back to politics with the petulance of an old maid and the pertinacity of a child; for minds of this type always eagerly turn to the side where light shines, they blunder up to it again and again, buzzing round but getting no nearer, exhausting one's spirit as bluebottle flies weary the ear by humming against the window-pane.

Henriette said nothing. I, to put an end to a dialogue which the warmth of youth might have heated to a flame, replied in assenting monosyllables, thus avoiding a useless discussion; but Monsieur de Mortsauf was far too clear-sighted not to discern the offensive side of my politeness. Presently he turned restive, vexed at being constantly agreed with; his eyebrows and the wrinkles in his forehead twitched, his tawny eyes flashed, his bloodshot nose turned redder than ever, as on that day when, for the first time, I witnessed one of his fits of frenzy. Henriette gave me a beseeching look to convey to me that she could not exert on my behalf the firmness she employed in justifying or defending the children.

I then answered the Count, taking him seriously, and managing him with the greatest skill.

"Poor dear! poor dear!" she said, murmuring the words again and again; they fell on my ear like a breath of air. Then, when she thought she could interfere with some success, she exclaimed, interrupting us—

"Do you know, gentlemen, that you are desperately unamusing?"

Recalled by this remark to the chivalrous deference due to a woman, the Count ceased discussing politics; it was now his turn to be bored as we talked of trifles, and he left us free to walk together, saying that perpetually pacing up and down on the same spot made him giddy.

My gloomy conjectures were accurate. The fair scenery, the mild atmosphere, the clear sky, the exquisite poetry of this valley, which for fifteen years had soothed the acutest vagaries of this sick brain, had now lost their power. At an age when in most men the rough edges wear down and the angles rub smooth, this old gentleman's temper was more aggressive than ever. For some months now he had been contradictory for contradiction's sake, without reason, without justifying his opinions; he asked the wherefore of everything, fussed over a delay or a message, interfered incessantly in domestic matters, and demanded an account of the smallest details of the household, till he wore out his wife and his servants, leaving them no freedom of action. Formerly he had not given way to his temper without some plausible reason, now his fractiousness was incessant. The care of his money and the anxieties of husbandry, with the stir of a busy life, had perhaps diverted his atrabilious humor by giving his anxious spirit something to work on, and employing his active mind; perhaps it was want of occupation that now left his disorder to react upon itself; having nothing outside him to fret it, it took the form of fixed ideas; the physical individual had become the victim of the moral individual.

He was now his own doctor. He compared medical works, and believed he had all the complaints of which he read the descriptions; then he took the most elaborate precautions to guard his health; always something new, impossible to foresee, more impossible to satisfy. At one time he would have no noise; and when the Countess had succeeded in establishing total silence he would suddenly complain of living in a tomb, and say that there was a medium between making no noise and the muteness of La Trappe. Sometimes he affected absolute indifference to all earthly things; then the whole house breathed again : the children could play, the work of the household was carried on without any fault-finding; suddenly, in the midst of it all, he would cry out piteously, "You want to kill me! My dear, if it concerned the children, you would know by instinct what annoyed them!" he would say to his wife, adding to the injustice of the words by the hard, cold tone in which he spoke them. Then he was for ever dressing and undressing, studying the least variations of temperature, and never doing anything without consulting the barometer. In spite of his wife's motherly care, he never found any food to his liking, for he declared that his stomach was always out of order, and that painful digestion hindered his sleeping; at the same time, he ate, drank, digested and slept in a way that the most learned physician might have admired. His endless caprices wore out the household; like all servants, they were the slaves of routine, and incapable of accommodating themselves to the exigencies of constantly varying orders. The Count would desire that all the windows were to be left open, as fresh air was indispensable to his health; a few days later the air was too damp, or too hot, he could not endure it; he scolded, he quarreled over it, and, to be in the right, would deny his previous order. This lack of memory, or of honesty, of course gave him the victory in every discussion when his wife tried to prove that he contradicted himself.

A residence at Clochegourde was so unendurable that the Abbé de Dominis, an exceedingly learned man, had fallen back on the solution of certain problems and intrenched himself in affected absence of mind. The Countess no longer hoped to be able to keep the secret of his fits of mad fury within the family circle, as of old. The servants had already witnessed many scenes when the prematurely old man's unreasoning rage passed all bounds; they were so much attached to the Countess that nothing was ever repeated, but she lived in daily terror of some outburst in public of a frenzy which no respect of persons could now control. At a later time I heard terrible details of the Count's behavior to his wife; instead of being a help to her he overwhelmed her with gloomy predictions, making her responsible for future ills because she refused to follow the insane medical treatment he wished to inflict on the children. If the Countess went out walking with Jacques and Madeleine, her husband would prophesy of coming storms in spite of a clear sky; then, if by chance his prediction was justified by the event, his conceit was so much gratified as to be indifferent to the harm done to his children. If one of them fell ill, the Count exercised his wit in finding a cause for the attack in the system of nursing adopted by his wife, which he would dispute in its minutest details, always ending with these brutal words, "If your children are ill again, it is all your own doing!"

He carried this system into the smallest points of domestic

management, in which he always saw the worst side of things, and made himself "the devil's advocate," to quote his old coachman's expression. The Countess had arranged that Jacques and Madeleine should have their meals at a different hour from their parents, and had thus preserved them from the dreadful effects of the Count's malady, meeting every storm as it broke. The children rarely saw their father.

By an illusion peculiar to selfish people, the Count had no suspicion of the mischief he caused. In his confidential conversation with me he had, indeed, blamed himself for too great leniency to his family. Thus he wielded the knout, felling and destroying everything about him as a monkey might have done, and after wounding his victim denied that he had ever touched her. I understood now what had drawn the lines, as fine as razor-cuts, across the Countess' brow; I had noticed them as soon as I saw her. There is a sort of modesty in noble souls that keeps them from uttering their sorrows; they hide their griefs from those they love, out of pride and a feeling of luxurious charity. And in spite of my urgency, I did not at once extract this confession from Henriette. She feared to distress me; she let things out, bit by bit, with sudden blushes; but I was not slow to guess the aggravated bitterness that her husband's want of occupation had infused into the domestic miseries of Clochegourde.

"Henriette," said I a few days later, showing her that I had sounded the depths of her new griefs, "did you not make a mistake when you planned your estate so completely as to leave the Count nothing to employ him?"

"Nay, dear," she said with a smile, "my position is so critical as to need all my attention; believe me, I have studied every alternative—they are all exhausted. It is true, worries increase every day. As Monsieur de Mortsauf and I are always together, I cannot diminish them by distributing them to several points; everything must bring the same suffering on me. I had thoughts of amusing Monsieur de Mortsauf by advising him to introduce the culture of silk-worms at Clochegourde; there are some mulberry trees here already, survivors from that industry, once known in Touraine; but I understood that he would be none the less tyrannical at home, that all the thousand troubles of the undertaking would fall upon me.

"You see, my observing friend," she went on, "while a man is young his bad qualities are controlled by the outer world, impeded in their rise by the other passions, checked by respect of persons; but later, in retirement, as a man grows old, little faults come forth, all the more terrible because they have so long been kept under. Human weakness is essentially cowardly; it grants neither peace nor truce; what has once been surrendered yesterday it insists on to-day, to-morrow, and for ever after; it takes possession of all that is conceded and demands more. Strength is merciful; it yields to conviction; it is just and peaceable, while the passions that are born of weakness are pitiless. They are never satisfied but when they can behave like children, who like stolen fruit better than what they may eat at table. Monsieur de Mortsauf takes a real pleasure in stealing a march on me; he who would never deceive anybody loves to deceive me so long as the trick remains unknown."

One morning, about a month after my arrival, as we came out from breakfast, the Countess took my arm, hurried out by a railed gate that opened into the orchard, and dragged me away to the vineyard.

"Oh! he will kill me!" she cried. "And yet I must live, if only for the children's sake! Can I not have a single day's respite? Must I always be stumbling over brambles, expecting every moment to fall, compelled every moment to summon all my strength to keep my balance! No living creature can endure such an expenditure of energy. If only I knew the ground I should be called upon to struggle over, if my endurance were a fixed quantity, my spirit would bend to it; but no, the attack comes every day in a new form and finds me defenseless; my trouble is not single, but manifold. Félix, Félix, you could never imagine the odious aspect his tyranny has assumed, or the odious measures suggested to him by his medical books. Ah! my friend——" she leaned her head on my shoulder without finishing her sentence. "What is to become of me; what can I do?" she went on, fighting with the ideas she had not uttered. "How can I contend with him? He will kill me. No, I will kill myself —only that is a crime! Can I fly? There are the children! Demand a separation? But how, after fifteen years of married life, am I to tell my father that I cannot live with Monsieur de Mortsauf when, if my father or my mother were to come here, he would be calm, well-conducted, polite, and witty. And, beside, has a married woman a father and a mother? She belongs, body and soul, to her husband. I used to live in peace; if not happy, I found some strength in my chaste isolation. I confess it, if I am bereft of that negative comfort, I, too, shall go mad! My objection is founded on reasons not personal to myself. Is it not wicked to bring poor little creatures into the world, who are doomed from birth to constant suffering? At the same time, this question of conduct is so serious that I cannot solve it unaided: I am judge and party to the suit. I will go to Tours to-morrow and consult the Abbé Birotteau, my new director — for my dear and worthy Abbé de la Berge is dead," she said in a parenthesis. "Though he was stern, I shall always miss his apostolic firmness; his successor is an angel of mildness who is too easily touched to reprimand me. However, what courage can fail to find refreshment in religion? What reason but will gain strength from the voice of the Holy Ghost?

"Dear God!" she exclaimed, drying her tears and looking up to heaven, "for what am I thus punished? But we must believe—yes, Félix," she said, laying her hand on my arm, "let us believe that we must pass through a red-hot crucible before we can mount holy and perfect to the higher spheres. Ought I to be silent? Does God forbid my crying out to a friend's heart. Do I love him too well?" She clasped me to her as though she feared to lose me. "Who will answer my doubts? My conscience does not reproach me. The stars above shine down on men; why, then, should not the soul, that living star, shed its fires over and round a friend when only pure thoughts go out to him?"

I listened in silence to this terrible outcry, holding her clammy hand in my own, which was moister still; I grasped it with a force to which my Henriette responded with equal pressure.

"You are there, are you?" exclaimed the Count, coming toward us bareheaded.

Since my return he had insisted on always being the third whenever we met, either because he counted on some amusement, or because he suspected the Countess of telling me of all her sorrows and bewailing herself to me; or, again, because, perhaps, he was morbidly jealous of a pleasure he did not share.

"How he follows me about!" said she in a tone of despair. "We will go to look at the *clos* (field), and then we shall avoid him. Stoop low behind the hedges and we shall escape." We screened ourselves behind a thick hedge, and reaching the vineyard at a run, found ourselves far enough from the Count under an alley of almond trees.

"Dear Henriette," said I, holding her arm pressed against my heart, and standing still to contemplate her in her sorrow, "you could once steer me wisely through the perilous ways of the great world. Allow me now to give you some instructions to help you to end the single-handed duel in which you must infallibly be defeated, for you and he are not fighting with equal weapons. Cease, struggle no longer against a madman——"

"Hush!" she exclaimed, keeping back the tears that filled her eyes.

"Listen to me, my dearest. After an hour of his talk, which I endure for your sake, my mind is often bewildered and my head aches; the Count makes me doubt my very senses; the same things repeated are stamped in my brain in spite of myself. A strongly marked monomania is not infectious; when madness takes the form of affecting a man's views and hides itself behind perpetual discussions, it may act terribly on those who live with it. Your patience is sublime, but is it not stultifying? For your own sake, for your children's, change your system with the Count. Your exquisite submissiveness has increased his egoism; you treat him as a mother treats the child she spoils. But now, if you wish to live—and you do," I added, looking her in the face, "exert all the influence you have over him. He loves and he fears you—you know it; make him fear you more; meet his diffused willfulness with a narrow, set will. Increase your power, just as he has managed to increase the concessions you have granted; imprison his infirmities in a narrow moral sphere, as a maniac is imprisoned in a cell."

"Dear boy," said she, smiling bitterly, "none but a heartless woman could play such a part. I am a mother; I should make a feeble executioner. I can suffer—yes; but to make others suffer!—Never," she said, "not even to attain some great or conspicuous advantage. Should I not have to falsify my feelings, disguise my voice, set my face, restrain every gesture? Do not require such lies of me. I can stand between Monsieur de Mortsauf and his children; I can take his blows so that they may fall on no one else; that is the utmost I can do to reconcile so many antagonistic interests."

"Let me worship you! Saint, thrice saintly!" I exclaimed, kneeling on one knee, kissing her dress, and wiping on it the tears that rose to my eyes. "But if he should kill you!" said I.

She shuddered, turned pale, and raising her moisture-laden eyes to heaven—

"God's will be done," she replied.

"Do you know what the King said to your father when speaking of you: 'That old wretch of a Mortsauf still lives on?'"

"What is a jest on the King's lips is a crime here," she replied.

In spite of our precautions, the Count had tracked us; bathed in sweat, he came up with us under a walnut tree, where the Countess had paused to speak these grave words. As soon as I saw him, I began to discuss the vintage. Had he any unjust suspicions? I know not, but he stood looking at us without saying a word, or heeding the damp chill that falls from a walnut tree.

After a few minutes, during which he spoke in broken sentences of little or no meaning, with pauses of very great significance, the Count said he had a sick headache; he complained of it mildly, not claiming our pity nor describing his indisposition in exaggerated terms. We paid no heed to him. When we went in he felt still worse, talked of going to bed, and did so without ceremony, with a simplicity that was very unusual. We took advantage of the armistice granted to us by his fit of hypochondria and went down to our beloved terrace, taking Madeleine with us.

"Let us go out on the river," said the Countess after a few turns, "we will go to see the fish caught by the gamekeeper for to-day's supply."

We went out of the little gate, found the punt, got into it, and slowly pushed up stream. Like three children, delighted with trifles, we looked at the flowers on the banks, at the blue and green dragon-flies, and the Countess wondered that she could enjoy such tranquil pleasures in the midst of so much acute grief. But does not the calm influence of nature moving on, indifferent to our struggles, exert a consoling charm? The swirl of passion, with its suppressed longings, harmonizes with that of the river; the flowers, unforced by the hand of man, express his most secret dreams; the delicious see-saw of a boat vaguely repeats the thoughts that float in the brain.

We felt the lulling influence of this twofold poetry. Our words, strung to the diapason of nature, were full of mysterious grace, and our eyes shone with brighter beams, as they caught the light so lavishly shed by the sun on the scorching shore. The river was like a road on which we flew. In short, disengaged from the mechanical movement exerted in walking, the mind took possession of creation. And was not the excited glee of the little girl in her freedom—so pretty in her movements, so puzzling in her remarks—the living expression of two souls set free, and indulging in the ideal creation of the being dreamed of by Plato, and known to all whose youth has been filled with happy love?

To give you an idea of that hour, not in its indescribable details, but as a whole, I may say that we loved each other in every creature, in every object that we saw about us; we felt outside us the happiness each longed for; it sank so deeply into our hearts that the Countess drew off her gloves and let her beautiful hands play in the water, as if to cool some secret fires. Her eyes spoke; but her lips, parted like a rose to the air, would have closed on a desire. You know the harmony of deep notes in perfect concord with a high treble; it always reminds me of the harmony of our two souls that day, never more to be repeated.

"Where do your men fish," I asked, "if you can only fish from your own banks?"

"Near the bridge at Ruan," said she. "The river is ours now from the bridge at Ruan down to Clochegourde. Monsieur de Mortsauf has just bought forty acres of meadow with the savings of the last two years and the arrears of his pension. Does that surprise you?"

"I? I only wish that the whole valley was yours!" I exclaimed, and she answered with a smile.

We were presently above Pont de Ruan, at a spot where the Indre widens and where the men were fishing.

"Well, Martineau?" said she.

"Oh, Madame la Comtesse, luck is against us. We have been out three hours, working up from the mill, and we have caught nothing."

We landed to help draw the net once more, standing, all three of us, in the shade of a poplar, with silvery bark, of a kind common on the Danube and the Loire, which in springtime sheds a silky white fluff, the wrapper of its catkins. The Countess had resumed her serene dignity; she repented of having confessed her pangs to me, and of crying out like Job instead of weeping like a Magdalen—a Magdalen bereft of lovers, of feasts and dissipations, but not without perfume and beauty.

The net was drawn at her feet, full of fish—tench, barbel, pike, perch, and an enormous carp leaped upon the grass.

"They were sent on purpose!" said the keeper.

The laborers stared open-eyed with admiration of the woman standing like a fairy who had touched the net with her wand.

At this moment a groom appeared, riding at a gallop across the fields, and filling her with qualms of horror. Jacques was not with us; and a mother's first instinct, as Virgil has so poetically expressed it, is to clasp her children to her bosom on the slightest alarm.

"Jacques!" she cried. "Where is Jacques? What has happened to my boy?"

She did not love me; if she had loved me, for my sufferings too, she would not have uttered this cry as of a lioness in despair.

"Madame la Comtesse, Monsieur le Comte is much worse."

She drew a breath of relief, and ran off with me, followed by Madeleine.

"Come after me slowly," said she, "that the dear child may not overheat herself. You see, Monsieur de Mortsauf's walk in this heat had put him into a perspiration, and standing in the shade of the walnut trees may bring misfortune on us."

The words revealed her purity of mind. The Count's death a misfortune!

She hurried on to Clochegourde, went in by a break in the wall and crossed the vineyard. I returned as slowly as she could wish. Henriette's words had enlightened me, but as the lightning-flash which destroys the garnered harvest. During that hour on the river I had fancied that she cared most for me; I now felt bitterly that her words were perfectly sincere. The lover who is not all in all is nothing. So I was alone in my love with the longing of a passion that knows all its wants, that feeds on anticipation, on hoped-for kindness, and is satisfied with the joys of imagination, because it confounds with them those it looks for in the future. If Henriette loved me, she still knew nothing of the joys or the storms of love. She lived on the feeling itself, as a saint is the spouse of God.

I was the object with which her thoughts were bound up, the sensations she misunderstood, as a swarm of bees clings to some blossoming bough; but I was not the element of life to her, only an adventitious fact. A king unthroned, I walked on, wondering who should restore me to my kingdom. In my crazy jealousy I blamed myself for never having greatly dared, for not having tightened the bonds of an affection— which now seemed to me refined out of all reality—by the chains of self-evident right conferred by possession.

The Count's indisposition, caused probably by a chill under the walnut tree, in a few hours had become serious. I went off to Tours to fetch a physician of note, Monsieur Origet, whom I could not bring back till the evening; but he spent the night and the next day at Clochegourde. Though he had sent the groom to fetch a large number of leeches, he thought immediate bleeding necessary and had no lancet with him. I rushed off to Azay, in dreadful weather; I roused Monsieur Deslandes the surgeon, and made him come off with the rapidity of a bird. Ten minutes later the Count would have succumbed; bleeding saved him.

In spite of this first triumph the doctor pronounced him in a dangerously high fever, one of those attacks which come on people who have ailed nothing for over twenty years. The Countess was overwhelmed; she believed herself to be the cause of this disastrous illness. Unable to thank me for what I did she was content to give me an occasional smile, with an expression that was equivalent to the kiss she had pressed on my hand; I wished I could read in it the remorse of an illicit passion; but it was an act of contrition, painful to see in so pure a soul, and the expression of admiring affection for him whom she considered noble, while she accused herself alone of an imaginary crime. She loved indeed as Laura de Noves loved Petrarch, and not as Francesca da Rimini loved Paolo —a crushing discovery for a man who had dreamed of the union of these two types of love. The Countess was reclining, her frame exhausted, her arms lying limp, in a dirty armchair in Count Mortsauf's room—a place that reminded me of a wild boar's den.

Next evening, before leaving, the doctor told the Countess, who had watched all night, that she must send for a nurse; the illness would be long.

"A nurse!" she exclaimed. "No, no. We will nurse him," she added, looking at me. "We owe it to ourselves to save him."

At these words, the doctor glanced at us with an observing eye full of astonishment. The expression of her words was enough to lead him to suspect some crime that had failed in the execution. He promised to come twice a week, suggested the treatment to be pursued by Monsieur Deslandes, and described the alarming symptoms which might necessitate his being fetched from Tours.

To secure the Countess at least one night's rest out of two, I proposed that she should allow me to sit up with the Count in turns with her; and thus, not without difficulty, I persuaded her to go to bed the third night. When all was still in the house, during a minute when the Count was dozing, I heard a sigh of anguish from Henriette's room. My anxiety was so keen that I went to see her; she was on her knees before her *prie-Dieu* (kneeling bench) in tears and accusing herself: "Ah, God! if this is the price of a murmur," she cried, "I will never complain again."

"You have left him!" she exclaimed as she saw me.

"I heard you wailing and moaning, and I was alarmed about you."

"About me? Oh, I am quite well," she said.

She wanted to be sure that Monsieur de Mortsauf was really asleep. We went down together, and by the light of a lamp we looked at him. He was weakened by loss of blood rather than sleeping; his restless hands were trying to pull the counterpane up.

"They say that is a trick of the dying," said she. "Oh, if he were to die of this illness brought on by us, I would never marry again; I swear it!" she went on, solemnly holding out her hand over the Count's head.

"I have done all that I can to save him," I answered.

"You! Oh, you are most good!" said she. "It is I— I am the guilty one."

She bent down over the puckered brow, wiped away the moisture with her hair, and gave it a sacred kiss. But I noted, not without secret satisfaction, that she bestowed this caress as an expiation.

"Blanche—some drink," said the Count in a feeble voice.

"You see, he only recognizes me," she said as she brought him a glass. And by her tone and her affectionate attentions to him she tried to heap insult on the feelings that bound us, immolating them to the sick man.

"Henriette," said I, "go and take some rest, I entreat you."

"Henriette no more!" she said, interrupting me with imperious haste.

"Go to bed, or you will be ill. Your children—he himself would desire you to spare yourself. There are times when selfishness is a sublime virtue."

"Yes," said she.

And she went, urging me to watch her husband, by gestures that might have seemed to indicate approaching delirium if the grace of childhood had not mingled with the passionate entreaty of repentance.

This scene, frightful as compared with the usual state of this placid soul, alarmed me; I feared the extravagance of her conscience. When the doctor next came, I explained to him the scruples, as of a sacred ermine, that were tormenting my spotless Henriette. This confidence, though very guarded, dispelled Monsieur Origet's suspicions, and he soothed the terrors of that sweet soul by assuring her that, from whatever cause, the Count must have had this violent attack, and that the chill he had taken under the walnut tree had been beneficial rather than injurious by bringing it on. Thus the Countess felt no remorse.

For fifty-two days the Count hovered between life and death. Henriette and I sat up with him in turn, each for twenty-six nights. Monsieur de Mortsauf undoubtedly owed his recovery to our care, and the scrupulous exactitude with which we carried out Monsieur Origet's instructions. Like all philosophical doctors, whose shrewd observation justifies them in doubting a noble action, even when it is merely the secret fulfillment of a duty, this man, while noticing the rivalry of heroism between the Countess and me, could not help watching us with inquisitive eyes, so fearful was he of being cheated of his admiration.

"In such a case as this," said he on the occasion of his third visit, "death finds a ready auxiliary in the mind when it is so seriously affected as that of the Count. The doctor, the nurse, those who are about the patient, hold his life in their hands; for a single word, a mere gesture of apprehension, may be as fatal as poison."

As he spoke thus Origet studied my face and my expression; but he read in my eyes the sincerity of an honest soul. For, indeed, throughout this cruel illness, my mind was never once invaded by the very slightest of those involuntary evil ideas which sometimes sear the most innocent conscience.

For those who contemplate nature as a whole, everything tends to union by assimilation. The spiritual world must be governed by an analogous principle. In a pure realm all is pure. In Henriette's presence there was a fragrance as of heaven itself; it seems as though any not irreproachable thought must alienate me from her for ever. Hence she was not only my happiness, she was also my virtue. Finding us always unfailingly attentive and careful, the doctor put an indescribable tone of pious pathos into his words and manner, as if he were thinking—"These are the real sufferers; they hide their wounds and forgot them."

By an effect of contrast which, as this worthy man assured us, is common enough in such wrecks of manhood, Monsieur de Mortsauf was patient and tractable, never complained, and showed the most wonderful docility—he who in health could not do the least thing without a thousand comments. The secret of this submission to medicinal treatment, formerly so scouted, was a covert dread of death, another contrast in a man of unblemished courage. And this fear may, perhaps, account for various singular features in the altered temper he owed to his misfortunes.

Shall I confess to you, Natalie, and will you believe me?

Those fifty days, and the month that came after, were the golden days of my life. In the infinite expanse of the soul is not love what, in a broad valley, the river is to which flow all the rains, the brooks and torrents, into which are borne the trees and flowers, the gravel of its banks, and the fragments of the higher rocks; it is fed alike by storms and by the slow tribute of rippling springs. Yes, when we love, everything feeds love.

The first great danger past, the Countess and I became accustomed to sickness. In spite of the confusion caused by the constant care needed by the Count, his room, which we had found in such disorder, was made neat and pretty. Ere long we lived there like two beings dropped on a desert island; for not only do troubles isolate us, but they silence the petty conventionality of the world. And then for the sick man's benefit we were forced into contact such as no other event could have brought about. How often did our hands meet, heretofore so shy, in doing her husband some service. Was it not my part to support and help Henriette? Carried away by a duty that may be compared with that of a soldier at an outpost, she would often forget to eat; then I would bring her food, sometimes on her knee—a hasty meal necessitating a hundred little services. It was a childish scene on the brink of a yawning grave. She would hastily order me to prepare what might save the Count some discomfort, and employ me on a variety of trivial tasks.

In the early days, when the imminence of danger stifled the subtle distinctions of ordinary life, as on the field of battle, she inevitably neglected the reserve which every woman, even the most simple-minded, maintains in her speech, looks, and behavior when she is surrounded by the world or by her family, but which is incompatible with the undress of intimacy. Would she not come to call me at the chirp of awakening birds in a morning wrapper that sometimes allowed me a glimpse of the dazzling charms, which, in my wild hopes, I regarded as my own? Though always dignified and lofty, could she not also be familiar? And, indeed, during the first few days, that danger so completely eliminated every passionate meaning from the privacy of our intimate intercourse, that she thought of no harm; and afterward, when reflection came, she felt perhaps that any change of demeanor would imply an insult as much to herself as to me. We found ourselves insensibly familiarized, half-wed, as it were. She showed herself nobly confiding, as sure of me as of herself. Thus I grew more deeply into her heart.

The Countess was my Henriette once more, Henriette constrained to love me yet more, as I strove to be her second self. Ere long, I never had to wait for her hand, which she would give me irresistibly at the least beseeching glance; and I could study with delight the outliness of her fine figure without her shrinking from my gaze, during the long hours while we sat listening to the patient's slumbers. The slender joys we allowed ourselves, the appealing looks, the words spoken in a whisper not to awake the Count, the hopes and fears repeated again and again, in short the myriad details of this fusion of two hearts so long sundered, stood out distinctly against the sad gloom of the real scene before us. We read each other's souls through and through in the course of this long test, to which the strongest affections sometimes succumb, unable to withstand the familiarity of every hour, and dropping away after testing the unyielding cohesion which makes life so heavy or so light a burden.

You know what mischief comes of a master's long illness, what disorder in his business; there is never time for anything; the stoppage put to his life hampers the movement of the house and family. Though everything always fell on Madame de Mortsauf, the Count was of use on the estate; he went to talk to the farmers, he called on the business agents, he drew the rents; if she was the soul, still he was the body. I now appointed myself steward that she might nurse the

Count without fear of ruin out of doors. She accepted everything without apologies, without thanks. This partition of household cares was another happy community of interests, and the orders I gave in her name. In her room in the evening we often discussed the children's prospects. These conversations lent a still further semblance of reality to our make-believe married life. How gladly would Henriette lend herself to my playing the master's part, putting me in his place at table, sending me to speak to the gamekeeper; and all with simple innocence, but not without the secret pleasure which the most virtuous woman on earth must feel at finding a middle course combining strict observation of every law with the satisfaction of her unconfessed wishes. The Count, nullified by illness, was no longer a weight on his wife or on the house; and now the Countess was herself, she had a right to attend to me and make me the object of endless cares. What joy I felt on discovering in her a purpose of which she, perhaps, was but vaguely conscious, though it was exquisitely expressed—of revealing to me all the worth of her person and her character, of making me feel the change that came over her when she felt herself understood! This blossom, constantly curled up in the cold atmosphere of her home, unfolded before my eyes and for me alone; she had as much delight in opening as I had in looking on with the inquisitive eye of love.

On the mornings when I slept late, after sitting up all night, Henriette was up before any one. She preserved the most perfect silence; Jacques and Madeleine, without needing to be told, went away to play. She would devise endless wiles to lay my table herself, and she would serve my breakfast with such a sparkle of glee in every movement, with such a wild swallow-like precision, with such a color in her cheeks, such quaverings in her voice, such a lynx-like keenness of eye! Can such expansions of the soul be described? She was often overpowered by fatigue; but if by chance at one of these moments I needed anything she found fresh strength for me, as for her children; she started up active, busy, and glad. She loved to shed her tenderness like sunbeams through the air. Yes, Natalie, some women here below enjoy the privileges of angelic spirits, and, like them, diffuse the light which Saint-Martin, the unknown philosopher, tells us is intelligent, melodious, and fragrant.

Henriette, secure in my reticence, rejoiced in lifting the heavy curtain which hid the future from us by showing herself to me as two women: the woman in bonds who had fascinated me in spite of her asperities; the woman freed, whose sweetness was to seal my love to eternity. What a difference! Madame de Mortsauf was a love-bird transported into cold Europe, sadly drooping on its perch, mute and dying in the cage where it is kept by some naturalist; Henriette was the bird singing its Oriental raptures in a grove on the banks of the Ganges, and flying like a living gem from bough to bough amid the rosy flowers of an ever-blooming Volkameria.

Her beauty was renewed, her spirit revived. These constant fireworks of gladness were a secret between our two souls; for to the Countess the eye of the Abbé de Dominis, who represented the world, was more alarming than her husband's. She, like me, took pleasure in giving her words ingenious turns; she hid her glee under a jest and veiled the evidences of her affection under the specious flag of gratitude.

"We have put your friendship to the severest tests, Félix," she would say at dinner. "We may surely grant him such liberties as we allow to Jacques, Monsieur l'Abbé?"

The austere abbé replied with the kindly smile of a pious man who reads hearts and finds them pure; indeed, he always treated the Countess with the respect mingled with adoration that we feel for angels.

Twice in those fifty days the Countess went perhaps across the border-line that limited our affection; but those two occasions were shrouded in a veil that was not lifted till our day of supreme avowals. One morning, in the early days of the Count's illness, just when she was repenting of having treated me so severely by denying me the harmless privileges of a chastened affection, I sat waiting for her to take my place. I was overtired, and fell asleep, my head resting against the wall. I awoke with a start, feeling my forehead touched by something mysteriously cool, that gave me a sensation as if a rose had lain on it. I saw the Countess some steps away from me, saying—

"Here I am!"

I went away, but, as I wished her good-morning, I took her hand and felt that it was moist and trembling.

"Are you ailing?" I asked.

"Why do you ask?" she inquired. I looked at her, coloring with confusion.

"I had been dreaming," I answered.

One evening, during the last visits paid by Origet, who had pronounced the Count certainly convalescent, I was in the garden with Jacques and Madeleine; we were all three lying on the steps absorbed in a game of jackstraws that we had contrived with splinters of straw and hooks made of pins. Monsieur de Mortsauf was asleep. The doctor, while waiting for his horse to be put to, was talking in a low voice to the Countess in the drawing-room. Monsieur Origet presently left without my noticing his departure. After seeing him off, Henriette leaned against the window, whence she looked down on us for a long time, though we did not know it. It was one of those hot evenings when the sky turns to copper color, when the country sends out a thousand confused voices to the echoes. A last gleam of sunshine lingered on the roofs, the flowers of the garden scented the air, the bells of the cattle being brought home to the byres came from afar. And we, in sympathy with the stillness of this calm hour, stifled our laughter for fear of waking the Count.

Suddenly, above the flutter of a gown, I heard the guttural gasp of a strongly suppressed sob; I rushed into the drawing-room, I found the Countess sitting in the window recess, her handkerchief to her face; she knew my step, and, by an imperious gesture, desired me to leave her alone. I went up to her, heartsick with alarm, and wanted to force away her handkerchief; her face was drowned in tears. She fled to her own room, and did not come out till it was time for prayers. For the first time in those fifty days I led her to the terrace, and asked her the cause of her agitation; but she affected the most flippant cheerfulness, justifying it by Origet's good news.

"Henriette, Henriette," said I, "you knew that when I found you crying. Between us a lie is preposterous. Why would you not allow me to wipe away your tears? Can they have been for me?"

"I was thinking," she answered, "that to me this illness has been a respite from misery. Now that there is nothing more to fear for Monsieur de Mortsauf I must fear for myself."

She was right. The Count's returning health was marked by his grotesque moods; he began to declare that neither his wife, nor I, nor the doctor knew how to treat him; we were all ignorant of his complaint and of his constitution, of his sufferings, and of the suitable remedies. Origet, infatuated by heaven knows what quackery, thought it was a degeneracy of the secretions, while he ought only to have studied the disorder of the pylorus!

One day, looking at us mischievously, like a man who has spied out or guessed something, he said to his wife, with a smile—

"Well, my dear, and if I had died—you would have regretted me, no doubt, but, confess, you would have been resigned."

"I should have worn court mourning, red and black," she said, laughing, to silence him.

It was especially with regard to his food, which the doctor had carefully limited, forbidding that the patient's craving should be satisfied, that we had the most violent scenes and outcries, with which nothing could be compared in the past, for the Count's temper was all the more atrocious for having been to sleep, so to speak. Fortified by the physician's orders and the faithfulness of the servants, and confirmed by me, for I saw in this contest a way of teaching her to govern her husband, the Countess was resolute in her resistance; she listened with a calm countenance to his frenzy and scolding; by thinking of him as a child—as he was—she accustomed herself to hear his abusive words. Thus at last I was so happy as to see her assert her authority over this disordered mind. The Count called out, but he obeyed; and he obeyed all the more after the greatest outcry.

In spite of the evidence of the results, Henriette would often shed tears at the sight of this feeble and haggard old man, his forehead yellower than a falling leaf, his eyes dim, his hands tremulous; she would blame herself for her sternness and could seldom resist the delight she saw in the Count's eyes when, as she doled out his meals, she exceeded the doctor's restrictions. She was all the sweeter and milder to him for having been so to me; still, there were shades of difference which filled my heart with boundless joy. She was not indefatigable; she knew when to call the servants to wait on the Count if his whims were too many in rapid succession, and he began to complain of her misunderstanding him.

The Countess purposed an act of thanksgiving to God for Monsieur de Mortsauf's recovery; she commanded a special mass and bade me offer her my arm to escort her to church. I did her bidding; but during the service I went to call on Monsieur and Madame de Chessel. On my return she tried to scold me.

"Henriette," said I, "I am incapable of deceit. I can throw myself into the water to rescue my enemy when he is drowning, I can lend him my cloak to warm him—in short, I can forgive, but I cannot forget."

She said nothing, but pressed my arm to her heart.

"You are an angel; you were, no doubt, sincere in your thanksgiving," I went on. "The mother of the Prince of the Peace was snatched from the hands of a mob who wanted to kill her, and when the Queen asked her, 'What did you do?'—'I prayed for them,' she said. Women are all like that; I am a man, and necessarily imperfect."

"Do not slander yourself," said she, shaking my arm sharply. "Perhaps you are better than I am."

"Yes," I replied, "for I would give eternity for a single day of happiness, while to you!——"

"Me!" she cried, with a haughty glance.

I was silent, and my eyes fell under the lightning of her eyes.

"Me!" she went on. "Of what *me* are you speaking? There are in me many *mes*. Those children," and she pointed to Jacques and Madeleine, "are part of me. Félix," she said in a heart-rending tone, "do you think me selfish? Do you think that I could sacrifice eternity to recompense him who is sacrificing this life for me? The thought is a shocking one; it is contrary to every sentiment of religion. Can a woman who falls so low rise again? Can her happiness absolve her? You will drive me soon to decide the question! Yes, I am betraying at last a secret of my conscience; the idea has often crossed my mind, I have expiated it by bitter penance; it was the cause of the tears you wanted me to account for the other day——"

"Are you not attributing too great importance to certain things on which ordinary women set a high value and which you ought to——"

"Oh," cried she, interrupting me, "do you value them less?"

Such an argument put an end to all reasoning.

"Well," she went on, "I will tell you! Yes, I could be so mean as to desert the poor old man whose life is in my hands. But, dear friend, those two poor, feeble little creatures you see before us, Jacques and Madeleine—would not they be left with their father? And do you think, I ask you, do you believe that they could survive three months under that man's insensate tyranny? If by failing in my duty, I alone"—she smiled loftily. "But should I not be killing my two children? Their doom would be certain. Great God!" she exclaimed, "how can we talk of such things? Go and marry, and leave me to die."

She spoke in a tone of such concentrated bitterness that she stifled the outburst of my passion.

"You cried out up there, under the walnut tree. I have just cried out here, under these alders. That is all. Henceforth I am silent."

"Your generosity overwhelms me," said she, looking up to heaven.

We had by this time reached the terrace and found the Count seated there in a chair, in the sunshine. The sight of that sunken face, hardly animated by a faint smile, extinguished the flames that had flared up from the ashes. I leaned against the parapet, contemplating the picture before me: the infirm man with his two still delicate children; his wife, pale with watching and grown thin from excess of work, from the alarms, and perhaps from the joys, of these two dreadful months, though at this moment she was deeply flushed from the emotions of the scene she had gone through. At the sight of this suffering family, shrouded under the tremulous foliage through which fell the gray light of a dull autumn day, I felt the ties relax which hold body and soul together. I experienced for the first time that moral revulsion which, it is said, the stoutest fighters feel in the fury of the fray, a sort of chilling madness that makes a coward of the bravest, a bigot of a disbeliever, which induces total indifference to everything, even to the most vital sentiments—to honor, to love; for doubt robs us of all knowledge of ourselves, and disgusts us with life. Poor nervous creatures, who, by your high-strung organization, are delivered over defenseless to I know not what fatality, who shall be your peers and judges? I understood how the bold youth who had erewhile put out a hand to grasp the marshal's bâton, who had been no less skilled in diplomacy than intrepid as a captain, had become the unconscious murderer I saw before me! Could my own desires, at this moment wreathed with roses, bring me, too, to such an end? Appalled alike by the cause and the effect, asking, like the impious, where in all this was providence, I could not restrain two tears that fell down my cheeks.

"What is the matter, dear, good Félix?" asked Madeleine in her childish voice.

Then Henriette dispelled those black vapors and gloom by an anxious look, which shone on my soul like the sun.

At this moment the old groom from Tours brought me a letter, at the sight of which I could not help uttering a cry of surprise, and Madame de Mortsauf trembled at my dismay. I saw the seal of the cabinet. The King ordered me back. I held the letter out to her; she read it in a flash.

"He is going away!" said the Count.

"What will become of me?" she said to me, for the first time contemplating her desert without sunshine.

We paused in a stupefied frame of mind which oppressed us all equally, for we had never before so acutely felt that we were all indispensable to each other. The Countess, as she talked even of the most indifferent matters, spoke in an altered voice, as though the instrument had lost several strings and those that remained were loosened. Her movements were apathetic, her looks had lost their light. I begged her to confide her thoughts to me.

"Have I any thoughts?" said she.

She led me away to her room, made me sit down on the

sofa, hunted in the drawer of her dressing-table, and, then, kneeling down in front of me, she said—

"Here is all the hair I have lost these twelve months past; take it—it is yours by right; you will some day know how and why."

I gently bent over her, she did not shrink to avoid my lips, and I pressed them to her brow solemnly, with no guilty excitement, no inviting passion. Did she mean to sacrifice everything? Or had she, like me, only come to look over the precipice? If love had prompted her to abandon herself, she could not have been so profoundly calm, have given me that religious look, or have said in her clear voice—

"You have quite forgiven me?"

I set out in the evening, she accompanied me on the road to Frapesle, and we stood under the walnut tree; I pointed it out to her, telling her how I had first seen it, four years ago.

"The valley was so lovely!" I exclaimed.

"And now?" she said eagerly.

"Now you are under the tree," said I; "and the valley is our own."

She bent her head, and there we parted. She got into the carriage again with Madeleine and I into mine, alone.

On my return to Paris, I was fortunately taken up by a press of work which forcibly diverted my mind, and obliged me to live apart from the world, which forgot me. I corresponded with Madame de Mortsauf, to whom I sent my journal every week, and who replied twice a month. It was an obscure and busy life, resembling the overgrown, flowery nooks, quite unknown, which I had admired in the depths of the woods when composing fresh poems of flowers during the last fortnight.

All ye who love, bind yourselves by these delightful duties; impose a rule on yourselves to be carried out, as the church does on Christians every day.

The rigorous observances created by the Roman Catholic religion are a grand idea; they trace deeper and deeper grooves of duty in the soul by the repetition of acts which encourage hope and fear. The feelings always flow, a living stream, in these channels which keep the current within bounds and purify it, perpetually refreshing the heart and fertilizing life by the abounding treasures of hidden faith, a divine spring multiplying the single thought of a single love.

My passion, a relic of the Middle Ages, recalling the days of chivalry, became known, I know not how; perhaps the King and the Duc de Lenoncourt spoke of it. From this uppermost sphere, the story, at once romantic and simple, of a young man piously devoted to a beautiful woman who had no public, who was so noble in her solitude, and faithful without the support of duty, no doubt became known in the Faubourg Saint-Germain. I fouud myself the object of inconvenient attention in drawing-rooms, for an inconspicuous life has advantages which, once tasted, make the parade of a life in public unendurable. Just as eyes that are accustomed to see none but subdued colors are hurt by broad daylight, so there are minds averse to violent contrasts. I was then one of these; you may be surprised now to hear it; but have patience, the eccentricities of the Vandenesse you know will be accounted for.

I found women amiably disposed toward me and the world kind.

After the Duc de Berry's marriage the court became splendid once more, the French fêtes were revived. The foreign occupation was a thing of the past, prosperity returned, amusements were possible. Personages of illustrious rank or considerable wealth poured in from every part of Europe to the capital of intelligence, where all the advantages and the vices of other countries were magnified and intensified by French ingenuity.

Five months after leaving Clochegourde, my good angel

wrote me a letter in despair, telling me that her boy had had a serious illness, from which he had recovered indeed, but which had left her in dread for the future; the doctor had spoken of care being needed for his lungs—a terrible verdict that casts a black shadow on every hour of a mother's life. Hardly had Henriette drawn a breath of relief as Jacques was convalescent, before his sister made her anxious. Madeleine, the pretty flower that had done such credit to her mother's care, went through an illness which, though not serious, was a cause of anxiety in so fragile a constitution.

Crushed already by the fatigues of Jacques' long sickness, the Countess had no courage to meet this fresh blow, and the sight of these two beloved beings made her insensible to the increasing torment of her husband's temper. Storms, each blacker than the last, and bringing with it more stones, uprooted by their cruel surges the hopes that were most deeply rooted in her heart. Weary of strife she had submitted altogether to the Count's tyranny, for he had regained all his lost ground.

"When all my strength was devoted to enfolding my children," she wrote me, "could I use it to defy Monsieur de Mortsauf, could I defend myself against his aggressions when I was fighting with death? As I make my onward way, alone and feeble, between the two young, melancholy creatures at my side, I feel an invincible disgust of life. What blow can hurt me, or what affection can I respond to when I see Jacques motionless on the terrace, life no longer beaming in anything but his beautiful eyes, made larger by emaciation, as hollow as an old man's, and where—fatal prognostic—his forward intelligence is contrasted with his bodily weakness? When I see at my side my pretty Madeleine so lively, so fond, so brightly colored, now as pale as the dead; her very hair and eyes seem to me more pallid, she looks at me with languishing eyes as if she was bidding me farewell. No food tempts her, or, if she has a fancy for anything, she alarms me by her strange appetites; the innocent child, though one with my heart, blushes as she confesses to them.

"Do what I will, I cannot amuse my children; they smile at me, but the smile is forced from them by my playfulness and is not spontaneous; they cry because they cannot respond to my fondness. Illness has left them completely run down, even their affection. So you may imagine how dismal Clochegourde is. Monsieur de Mortsauf reigns unopposed.

"Oh my glory, my dear friend!" she wrote me again, "you must love me well indeed if you can love me still— can love me, so apathetic as I am, so unresponsive, so petrified by grief."

At this juncture, when I felt myself more deeply appealed to than ever, when I lived only in her soul, on which I strove to shed the luminous breath of morning and the hope of purpled evenings, I met, in the rooms of the Elysée Bourbon, one of those superb English ladies who are almost queens. Immensely wealthy, the daughter of a race unstained by any mésalliance since the time of the Conquest, married to an old man, one of the most distinguished members of the British peerage—all these advantages were no more than accessories adding to her beauty, her manners, her wit, a faceted lustre that dazzled before it charmed you. She was the idol of the day, and reigned all the more despotically over Paris society because she had the qualities indispensable to success, the iron hand in a velvet glove spoken of by Bernadotte.

You know the curious individuality of the English—the impassable and arrogant channel, the icy St. George's straits that they set between themselves and those who have not been introduced to them. The human race might be an ant-heap on which they tread; they recognize none of their species but those whom they accept; they do not understand the language even of the rest; those have lips that move and eyes that see; but neither voice nor looks can reach so high; to them the herd are as though they were not. Thus the

English are an image of their island where the law rules everything; where in each sphere everything is uniform; where the practice of virtue seems to be the inevitable working of wheels that move at fixed hours.

These fortifications of polished steel built up round an Englishwoman, caged by golden wires into her home, where her feeding trough and drinking cup, her perches and her food are all perfection, lend her irresistible attractions. Never did a nation more elaborately scheme for the hypocrisy of a married woman by placing her always midway between social life and death. For her there is no compromise between shame and honor; the fall is utter, or there is no slip; it is all or nothing—the *To be or not to be* of Hamlet. This alternative, combined with the habits of disdain to which manners accustom her, makes an Englishwoman a creature apart in the world. She is but a poor creature, virtuous perforce, and ready to abandon herself, condemned to perpetual falsehood buried in her soul; but she is enchanting in form, because the race has thrown everything into form. Hence the beauties peculiar to the women of that country: the exaltation of an affection in which life is compulsorily summed up, their extravagant care of their person, the refinement of their love—so elegantly expressed in the famous scene in Romeo and Juliet, in which Shakespeare has with one touch depicted the Englishwoman.

To you, who envy them so many things, what can I say that you do not know about these fair sirens, apparently impenetrable but so quickly known, who believe that love is enough for love, and who taint their pleasures with satiety by never varying them, whose soul has but one note, whose voice but one word—an ocean of love, in which, if a man has not bathed, he will for ever remain ignorant of one form of poetic sensuality, just as a man who has never seen the sea must always lack certain chords to his lyre?

You know the purport of these words. My acquaintance

with Lady Dudley was notorious. At an age when the senses exert their greatest power over our decisions, and in a man whose fires had been so violently suppressed, the image of the saint who was enduring her long martyrdom at Clochegourde shone so brightly that he could resist every fascination. This fidelity was the distinction that won me Lady Arabella's attention. My obstinacy increased her passion. What she longed for, like many Englishwomen, was something conspicuous and extraordinary. She craved for spice, for pepper on which to feed her heart, as English epicures insist on pungent condiments to revive their palate. The lethargy produced in these women's lives by unfailing perfection in everything about them, and methodical regularity of habits, reacts in a worship of the romantic and difficult. I was incapable of gauging this character. The more I retired into cold disdain, the more eager was Lady Dudley. This contest, of which she boasted, excited some curiosity in certain drawing-rooms, and this was the first fruits of satisfaction which made her feel it incumbent on her to triumph. Ah! I should have been saved if only some friend had repeated the odious speech she had uttered concerning Madame de Mortsauf and me—

"I am sick," she said, "of this turtle-dove sighing!"

Though I have no wish to justify my crime, I must point out to you, Natalie, that a man has less chances of resisting a woman than you women have of evading our pursuit. Our manners forbid to our sex those tactics of stern repression which in you are baits to tempt the lover, and which indeed propriety requires of you. In us, on the contrary, some jurisprudence of masculine coxcombry treats reserve as ridiculous; we leave you the monopoly of modesty to secure to you the privilege of conferring favors; but reverse the parts, and a man is crushed by satire. Protected as I was by my passion, I was not at an age to be insensible to the threefold attractions of pride, devotion, and beauty. When Lady Arabella laid at my feet the homage paid to her at a ball of which she was the queen, when she watched my eye to read whether I admired her dress, and thrilled with pleasure when she pleased me, I was agitated by her agitation. She stood on ground, too, whence I could not fly: it was impossible for me to refuse certain invitations in the diplomatic circle; her rank opened every house to her; and with the ingenuity which women can display to obtain the thing they wish for, she contrived at table that the mistress of the house should seat me next to her.

Then she would murmur in my ear—

"If I were loved as Madame de Mortsauf is, I would sacrifice everything to you." She proposed the humblest conditions with a smile, she promised uncompromising reticence, or besought me to allow her only to love me. She spoke these words to me one day, satisfying alike the capitulation of a timid conscience and the unbridled cravings of youth—

"Your friend for ever, and your mistress when you please!"

Finally she resolved to make my sense of honor the means to my ruin; she bribed my manservant; and one evening, after a party where she had shone with such beauty that she was sure of having captivated me, I found her in my rooms. This scandal was heard of in England, where the aristocracy was in as much consternation as heaven at the fall of its highest angel. Lady Dudley came down from her clouds in the British empyrean, kept nothing but her own fortune, and tried by self-sacrifice to eclipse the woman whose virtue had led to this celebrated scandal. Lady Arabella, like the devil on the pinnacle of the temple, took pleasure in showing me the richest kingdoms of her ardent world.

Read my confession, I beseech you, with indulgence. It deals with one of the most interesting problems of human life, with a crisis through which the greater portion of mankind must pass, and which I long to account for, if it were only to light a beacon on the reef. This beautiful English lady, so slender, so fragile; this milk-white woman, so crushed, so breakable, so meek, with her refined brow crowned with such soft tan-brown hair; this creature, whose brilliancy seems but a transient phosphorescence, has a frame of iron. No horse, however fiery, can defy her sinewy wrist, her hand that seems so weak, and that nothing can tire. She has the foot of the roe, a small, wiry, muscular foot of indescribable beauty of form. Her strength fears no rivalry; no man can keep up with her on horseback; she would win a steeplechase riding a centaur; she shoots stags, and does it without checking her horse. Her frame knows not perspiration; it radiates a glow in the air, and lives in water, or it would perish.

Her passion is quite African; her demands are a tornado like the sand-spouts of the desert—the desert whose burning vastness is to be seen in her eyes, the desert all azure and love, with its unchanging sky and its cool, star-lit nights.

What a contrast to Clochegourde! The East and the West; one attracting to herself the smallest atoms of moisture to nourish her; the other exhaling her soul, enveloping all who were faithful to her in a luminous atmosphere. This one eager and slight; the other calm and solid.

Tell me, have you ever duly considered the general bearing of English habits? Are they not the apotheosis of matter, a definite, premeditated, and skillfully adapted epicureanism? Whatever she may do or say, England is materialist—unconsciously perhaps. She has religious and moral pretensions from which the divine spirituality, the soul of catholicism, is absent; its fruitful grace can never be replaced by any hypocrisy, however well acted. She possesses in the highest degree the science of life, which adds a grace to the smallest details of materialism: which makes your slipper the most exquisite slipper in the world; which gives your linen an indescribable fragrance; which lines and perfumes your drawers with cedar; which pours out at a fixed hour a delicious cup of tea, scientifically infused; which banishes dust, and nails down carpets from the very doorstep to the inmost nook of the house;

which washes the cellar walls, polishes the door knocker, gives elasticity to the springs of a carriage; which turns all matter into a nutritious pulp, a comfortable, lustrous, and cleanly medium in the midst of which the soul expires in enjoyment and which produces a terrible monotony of ease; which results in a life uncrossed and devoid of initiative; which, in one word, makes a machine of you.

Thus I came suddenly, in the heart of this English luxury, on a woman perhaps unique of her sex, who entangled me in the meshes of that love born anew from its death, whose prodigality I met with severe austerity—that love which has overpowering charms and an electricity of its own, which often leads you to heaven through the ivory gates of its half-slumbers, or carries you up mounted behind its winged shoulders. A horribly graceless love that laughs at the corpses of those it has slain; love devoid of memory, a cruel love, like English politics, and to which almost every man succumbs.

You understand the problem now. Man is composed of matter and spirit. In him the animal nature culminates and the angel begins. Hence the conflict we all have felt between a future destiny of which we have presentiments and the memories of our original instincts from which we are not wholly detached—the love of the flesh and the love that is divine. One man amalgamates the two in one; another abstains. This one seeks the whole sex through, to satisfy his anterior appetites; that one idealizes it in a single woman, who to him epitomizes the universe. Some hover undecided between the raptures of matter and those of the spirit; others spiritualize the flesh and ask of it what it can never give. If, considering these general features of love, you take into account the repulsions and the affinities which, being the outcome of diversity of constitution, presently break the bonds between those who have not tested each other; if you add to this the errors resulting from the hopes of those who live more especially by the mind, by the heart, or by action—who think, or feel, or act—and whose vocation is cheated or misprized in an association of two human beings, each equally complex, you will be largely indulgent to some misfortunes to which society is pitiless.

Well, Lady Arabella satisfies the instincts, the organs, the appetites, the vices, and the virtues of the subtle matter of which we are compounded; she was the mistress of my body. Madame de Mortsauf was the wife of my soul. The love the mistress could satisfy has it limits; matter is finite, its properties have recognized forces, it is liable to inevitable saturation; I often felt an indescribable void in Paris with Lady Dudley. Infinity is the realm of the heart; love unbounded was at Clochegourde. I was passionately in love with Lady Arabella, and certainly, though the animal in her was supreme, she had also a superior intelligence; her ironical conversation embraced everything.

But I worshiped Henriette. If at night I wept with joy, in the morning I wept with remorse. There are some women shrewd enough to conceal their jealousy under angelic sweetness; these are women who, like Lady Dudley, are past thirty. Women then know how to feel and calculate both at once; they squeeze out the juice of the present and yet think of the future; they can stifle their often quite justifiable groans with the determination of a hunter who does not feel a wound as he rides in pursuit of the bugle call.

Without ever speaking of Madame de Mortsauf, Arabella tried to kill her in my soul, where she constantly found her, and her own passion flamed higher under the breath of this ineradicable love. To triumph, if possible, by comparisons to her own advantage, she would never be suspicious, nor provoking, nor curious, as most young women are; but, like a lioness that has carried her prey in her mouth and brought it to her den to devour, she took care that nothing should disturb her happiness and watched me like an unsubdued conquest. I wrote to Henriette under her very eyes, she never read a single line, she never made the least attempt to know the address on my letters. I was perfectly free. She seemed to have said to herself, "If I lose, I shall blame no one but myself."

And she trusted proudly to a love so devoted that she would have laid down her life without hesitation if I had asked it of her. In fact, she made me believe that if I should abandon her she would at once kill herself.

It was a thing to hear when she sang the praises of the Indian custom for widows to burn themselves on their husband's funeral pyre.

"Though in India the practice is a distinction reserved to the higher castes, and is consequently little appreciated by Europeans, who are incapable of perceiving the proud dignity of the privilege, you must confess," she would say to me, "that in the dead level of our modern manners the aristocracy cannot resume its place unless by exceptional feelings. How can I show the middle-class that the blood flowing in my veins is not the same as theirs, if not in dying in another way than they die? Women of no birth can have diamonds, silks, horses, even coats-of-arms, which ought to be ours alone, for a name can be purchased! But to love, unabashed, in opposition to the law, to die for the idol she has chosen, and make a shroud of the sheets off her bed to bring earth and heaven into subjection to a man and thus rob the Almighty of His right to make a god, never to be false to him, not even for virtue's sake—for to refuse him anything in the name of duty is to abandon one's self to something that is not he—whether it be another man or a mere idea, it is a betrayal! These are the heights to which vulgar women cannot rise; they know only two roads—the highway of virtue or the miry path of the courtesan."

She argued, you see, from pride; she flattered all my vanities by deifying them; she set me so high that she could only reach to my knees; all the fascinations of her mind found expression in her slave-like attitude and absolute submission. She would remain a whole day lounging at my feet in silence, gazing at me, waiting on my pleasure like a seraglio slave. What words can describe the first six months when I gave myself up to the enervating joys of an affection full of raptures varied by the knowledge of experience that was concealed under the vehemence of passion. Such joys, a revelation of the poetry of the senses, constitute the strong link that binds young men to women older than themselves; but this link is the convict's chain; it leaves an indelible scar, implanting a premature distaste for fresh and innocent love rich in blossom only, which cannot serve us with alcohol in curiously chased golden cups, enriched with precious stones, sparkling with inexhaustible fires.

When I tasted the enjoyments of which I had dreamed, knowing nothing of them, which I had expressed in my nosegays, and which the union of souls makes a thousand times more intense, I found no lack of paradoxes to justify myself in my own eyes for the readiness with which I slaked my thirst at this elegant cup. Often when I felt lost in immeasurable lassitude, my soul, freed from my body, flew far from earth, and I fancied that such pleasures were a means of annihilating matter and freeing the spirit for its sublimest flights. Not unfrequently Lady Dudley, like many another woman, took advantage of the excitement superinduced by excessive happiness to bind me by solemn vows; and she could even tempt me into blaspheming and denouncing the angel at Clochegourde.

Being a traitor, I became a cheat. I wrote to Madame de Mortsauf as though I were still the boy in the ill-made blue coat of whom she was so fond; but, I own, her gift of second-sight appalled me when I thought of the disaster any indiscretion might bring on the charming castle of my hopes. Often in the midst of my happiness a sudden pang froze me; I heard the name of Henriette spoken by a voice from on high, like the "Cain, where is Abel?" of the Scripture narrative.

My letters remained unanswered. I was in mortal anxiety and wanted to set out for Clochegourde. Arabella raised no obstacles, but she spoke as a matter of course of going with me to Touraine. Her fancy, spurred by difficulty, her presentiments, justified by more happiness than she had hoped for, had given birth in her to a real affection, which she now meant should be unique. Her womanly wit showed her that this journey might be made a means of detaching me completely from Madame de Mortsauf; and I, blinded by alarm and misled by genuine guilelessness, did not see the snare in which I was to be caught.

Lady Dudley proposed the fullest concessions, and anticipated every objection. She agreed to remain in the country near Tours, unknown, disguised, never to go out by daylight, and to choose for our meetings an hour of the night when no one could recognize us.

I started on horseback from Tours for Clochegourde. I had my reasons for this; I needed a horse for my nocturnal expeditions, and I had an Arab, sent to the Marchioness by Lady Hester Stanhope, which I had taken in exchange for the famous picture by Rembrandt now hanging in her drawing-room in London, after it had come into my hands in so singular a way.

I took the road I had gone on foot six years before, and paused under the walnut tree. From thence I saw Madame de Mortsauf, in a white dress, on the terrace. I flew toward her with the swiftness of lightning, and in a few minutes was below the wall, traversing the distance in a direct line, as if I was riding a steeplechase. She heard the prodigious leaps of the Swallow of the Desert; and when I pulled up sharp at the corner of the terrace, she said, "Ah! Here you are!"

These four words struck me dumb. Then she knew of my

adventure! Who had told her of it? Her mother, whose odious letter she subsequently showed me. The indifference of that weak voice, formerly so full of vitality—the dead, colorless tone confessed a mature sorrow and breathed, as it were, a perfume of flowers cut off beyond all recovery. The tempest of my infidelity, like the floods of the Loire that bury the land past redemption in sand, had passed over her soul and made a desert where rich meadows had been green. I led my horse in by the side-gate; he knelt down on the grass at my command; and the Countess, who had come forward with a slow step, exclaimed, "What a beautiful creature!"

She stood with her arms crossed that I might not take her hand, and I understood her intention.

"I will go and tell Monsieur de Mortsauf," said she, and turned away.

I remained standing, quite confounded, letting her go, watching her—noble, deliberate, and proud as ever; whiter than I had ever seen her, her brow stamped with the yellow seal of the bitterest melancholy, and hanging her head like a lily weighed down by too much rain.

"Henriette!" I cried, with the passion of a man who feels himself dying.

She did not turn round, she did not pause; she scorned to tell me that she had taken back that name, that she would no longer answer to it; she walked on. In that terrible valley where millions of men must be lying turned to dust, while their souls now animate the surface of the globe, I may find myself very small in the midst of the crowd closely packed under the luminous dignities who shall light it up with their glory; but even there I shall be less utterly crushed than I was as I gazed at that white figure going up, up—as an undeviating flood mounts the streets of a town—up to Clochegourde, her home, the glory and the martyrdom of this Christian Dido!

I cursed Arabella in one word that would have killed her

had she heard it—and she had given up everything for me, as we leave all for God! I stood lost in an ocean of thought, seeing endless pain on every side of me.

Then I saw them all coming down; Jacques running with the impetuosity of his age; Madeleine, a gazelle with pathetic eyes, followed with her mother. Monsieur de Mortsauf came toward me with open arms, clasped me to him, and kissed me on both cheeks, saying, "Félix, I have heard—I owed my life to you!"

Madame de Mortsauf stood with her back to us, under pretense of showing the horse to Madeleine, who was amazed.

"The devil!" cried the Count in a fury, "that is a woman all over! They are looking at your horse."

Madeleine turned and came to me. I kissed her hand, looking at the Countess, who reddened.

"Madeleine seems much better," said I.

"Poor little girl!" replied the Countess, kissing her forehead.

"Yes, for the moment they are all well," said the Count. "I alone, my dear Félix, am a wreck, like an old tower about to fall."

"The general still suffers from his black dragons, it would seem," said I, looking at Madame de Mortsauf.

"We all have our *blue devils*," she replied. "That, I think, is the English word!"

We went up to the house, all walking together, all feeling that something serious had happened. She had no wish to be alone with me; in short, I was a visitor.

"By the way, what about your horse?" said the Count, when we went out.

"You see," retorted the Countess, "I was wrong to think about it, and equally wrong not to think about it."

"Why, yes," said he; "there is a time for everything."

"I will go to him," said I, finding this cold reception unendurable. "I alone can unsaddle him and put him up properly. My groom is coming from Chinon by coach, and he will rub him down."

"Is the groom from England too?" said she.

"They are only made there," replied the Count, becoming cheerful as he saw his wife depressed.

His wife's coolness was an opportunity for tacit opposition; he loaded me with kindness. I learned what a burden a husband's friendship can be. Do not suppose that it is when the wife lavishes an affection of which he seems to be robbed, that her husband's attentions are overpowering to a noble soul! No. It is when that love has fled that they are odious and unendurable. A friendly understanding, which is the indispensable condition of such attachments, is then seen as a mere means; it then is a burden, and as horrible as all means are when no longer justified by the ends.

"My dear Félix," said the Count, taking my hands, and pressing them affectionately, "you must forgive Madame de Mortsauf. Women must be fractious, their weakness is their excuse; they cannot possibly have the equable temper which gives us strength of character. She has the greatest regard for you. I know it; but——"

While the Count was speaking, Madame de Mortsauf moved gradually away from us so as to leave us together.

"Félix," said he in an undertone, as he looked at his wife returning to the house with her two children, "I cannot think what has been going on in Madame de Mortsauf's mind, but within the last six weeks her temper has completely altered. She who used to be so gentle, so devoted, has become incredibly sulky."

Manette afterward told me that the Countess had fallen into a state of dejection which left her insensible to the Count's aggravations. Finding no tender spot into which to thrust his darts, the man had become as fidgety as a boy when the insect he is torturing ceases to wriggle. At this moment he needed a confidant, as an executioner needs a mate.

"Try to question Madame de Mortsauf," he went on after a pause. "A woman always has secrets from her husband, but to you she will perhaps confide the secret of her trouble. If it should cost me half my remaining days of life and half my fortune, I would sacrifice everything to make her happy. She is so indispensable to my existence. If in my old age I should miss that angel from my side, I should be the most miserable of men! I would hope to die easy. Tell her she will not have to put up with me for long. I, Félix, my poor friend—I am going fast; I know it. I hide the dreadful truth from all the world; why distress them before the time? Still the pylorus, my good friend. I have at last mastered the causes of the malady: my sensitive feelings are surely killing me. In fact, all our emotions converge on the gastric centre——"

"So that people of strong feeling die of indigestion," said I with a smile.

"Do not laugh, Félix; nothing is truer. Too great a grief overexcites the great sympathetic nerve. This excessive sensibility keeps up a constant irritation of the mucous membrane of the stomach. If this condition continues it leads to disturbance of the digestive functions, at first imperceptible; the secretions are vitiated, the appetite is morbid, and digestion becomes uncertain; ere long acute suffering supervenes, worse and more frequent every day. Finally the organic mischief reaches a climax; it is as though some poison were lurking in every bowl. The mucous membrane thickens, the valve of the pylorus hardens, and a scirrhus forms there of which the patient must die. Well, that is my case, my dear boy. The induration is progressing; nothing can stop it. Look at my straw-colored skin, my dry, bright eye, my excessive emaciation? I am withering up. What can you expect? I brought the germ of the complaint in me from exile: I went through so much at that time.

"And my marriage, which might have repaired the mischief done during the emigration, far from soothing my ulcerated soul, only reopened the wound. What have I found here? Eternal alarms on account of my children, domestic trials, a fortune to be patched up, economy which entailed a thousand privations I had to inflict on my wife, while I was the first to suffer from them.

"And, above all, to you alone can I confide the secret—this is my greatest trouble. Though Blanche is an angel, she does not understand me; she knows nothing of my sufferings, she only frets them. I forgive her. It is a terrible thing to say, my friend, but a less virtuous woman would have made me happier by little soothing ways which never occur to Blanche, for she is as great a simpleton as a baby! Add to this that the servants do nothing but plague me. They are perfect owls! I speak French, and they hear Greek.

"When our fortune was somewhat amended by hook and by crook, when I began to be less worried, the mischief was done; I had reached the stage of morbid appetite. Then I had that bad illness which Origet so entirely misunderstood. In short, at this moment I have not six months to live."

I listened to the Count in terror. On seeing the Countess, the glitter of her hard eyes and the straw-colored complexion of her brow had struck me. I now dragged the Count back to the house as I pretended to listen to his complaining, interspersed with medical dissertations, but I was thinking only of Henriette, and was bent on studying her.

I found the Countess in the drawing-room; she was listening to a lesson in mathematics that the Abbé de Dominis was giving to Jacques, while she showed Madeleine a stitch in tapestry. Formerly she would have found means, on the day of my arrival, to put off such occupations and devote herself to me; but my love was so deep and true that I buried in the depths of my heart the sorrow I felt at the contrast between the past and present; for I could see that terrible yellow tinge on her heavenly face, like the reflection of a divine light which Italian painters have given to the faces of their female saints. I felt in my soul the cold blast of death. When the blaze of her eyes fell on me, bereft now of the liquid moisture in which her looks had floated, I shuddered; and I then observed certain changes due to grief which I had not noticed out of doors. The fine lines which, when I had last seen her, were but faintly traced on her forehead, were now deep furrows; her temples, bluely veined, were dry and hollow; her eyes were sunk under reddened brows and had dark circles round them; she had the look of fruit on which bruises are beginning to show, and which has turned prematurely yellow from the ravages of a worm within.

And was it not I, whose sole ambition it had been to pour happiness in a full tide into her soul, who had shed bitterness into the spring whence her life derived strength and her courage refreshment?

I sat down by her, and said in a voice tearful with repentance—

"Is your health satisfactory?"

"Yes," she replied, looking straight into my eyes. "Here is my health," and she pointed lovingly to Madeleine and Jacques.

Madeleine, who had come out victorious from her struggle with nature, at fifteen was a woman; she had grown, the tint of a China rose bloomed in her dark cheeks; she had lost the light heedlessness of a child that looks everything in the face, and had begun to cast down her eyes. Her movements, like her mother's, were rare and sober; her figure slight, and the charms of her bust already filling out. A woman's vanity had smoothed her fine black hair, parted into bands on her Spanish-looking brow. She had a look of the pretty mediæval busts, so refined in outline, so slender in mould, that the eye that lingers on them fears lest it should break them; but health, the fruit that had ripened after so much care, had given her cheek the velvety texture of the peach, and a silky down on her neck which caught the light—as it did in her mother.

She would live! God had written it, sweet bud of the loveliest of human blossoms, on the long lashes of your eyelids, on the slope of your shoulders, which promised to be as beautiful as your mother's had been!

This nut-brown maiden, with the growth of a poplar, was a contrast indeed to Jacques, a fragile youth of seventeen, whose head looked too large, for his brow had expanded so rapidly as to give rise to alarms, whose fevered, weary eyes were in keeping with a deep sonorous voice. The throat gave out too great a volume of sound, just as the eye betrayed too much thought. Here Henriette's intellect, soul, and heart were consuming with eager fires a too frail body; for Jacques had the milk-white complexion touched with the burning flush that is seen in young English girls marked by that awful scourge, consumption, to be felled within a limited time—delusive health!

Following a gesture by which Henriette, after pointing to Madeleine, made me look at Jacques, tracing geometrical figures and algebraical sums on a blackboard before the abbé, I was startled at this glimpse of death hidden under roses and respected the unhappy mother's mistake.

"When I see them so well, joy silences all my griefs, as, indeed, they are silent and vanish when I see those two ill. My friend," said she, her eyes beaming with motherly pleasure, "if other affections desert us, those that find their reward here—duties fulfilled and crowned with success—make up for defeat endured elsewhere. Jacques, like you, will be a highly cultivated man, full of virtuous learning; like you, he will be an honor to his country—which he may help to govern perhaps, guided by you, who will hold so high a place—but I will try to make him faithful to his first affections. Madeleine, dear creature, has already an exquisite heart. She is as pure as the snow on the highest Alpine summit; she will have the devotedness and the sweet intelligence of woman; she is proud, she will be worthy of the Lenoncourts!

"The mother, once so distraught, is now very happy—happy in an infinite and unmixed happiness; yes, my life is full, my life is rich. As you see, God has given me joys that unfold from permitted affection, has infused bitterness into those to which I was being tempted by a dangerous attachment."

"Well done!" cried the abbé gleefully. "Monsieur le Vicomte knows as much as I do——"

Jacques, as he finished the demonstration, coughed a little.

"That is enough for to-day, my dear abbé," said the Countess in some agitation. "Above all, no chemistry lesson! Go out riding, Jacques," she added, kissing her son with the justifiable rapture of a mother's caress, her eyes fixed on me as if to insult my remembrances. "Go, dear, and be prudent."

"But you have not answered my question," said I, as she followed Jacques with a long look. "Do you suffer any pain?"

"Yes, sometimes in my chest. If I was only in Paris I could rise to the honors of gastritis, the fashionable complaint."

"My mother suffers a great deal and often," replied Madeleine.

"So my health really interests you?" said she to me.

Madeleine, astonished at the deep irony with which the words were spoken, looked at us by turns; my eyes were counting the pink flowers on the cushions of the gray and green furniture in the room.

"The situation is intolerable!" I said in her ear.

"Is it of my making?" she asked. "My dear boy," she said aloud, affecting the cruel cheerfulness with which women give lightness to revenge, "do you know nothing of modern history? Are not France and England always foes? Why,

Madeleine knows that; she knows that they are divided by a vast sea, a cold sea, a stormy sea."

The vases on the mantel had been replaced by candelabra, no doubt to deprive me of the pleasure of filling them with flowers; I found them at a later day in her room. When my servant arrived, I went out to give my orders; he had brought me a few things that I wished to carry up to my room.

"Félix," said the Countess, "make no mistake! My aunt's old room is Madeleine's now. Yours is over the Count's."

Guilty as I was, I had a heart, and all the speeches were poniard thrusts coldly directed to the tenderest spots, which they seemed chosen to hit. Mental suffering is not a fixed quantity; it is in proportion to the sensitiveness of the soul, and the Countess had bitterly gone through the whole scale of anguish; but for this very reason the best woman will always be cruel in proportion to what her kindness has been. I looked at her, but she kept her head down.

I went up to my new room, which was pretty—white and green. There I melted into tears. Henriette heard me; she came in, bringing me a bunch of flowers.

"Henriette," said I, "have you come to such a point that you cannot forgive the most excusable fault?"

"Never call me Henriette," she said. "She has ceased to exist, poor woman; but you will always find Madame de Mortsauf an attached friend who will listen to you and care for you. Félix, we will talk later. If you still have an affection for me let me get accustomed to see you, and as soon as words are a less heart-rending effort, as soon as I have recovered a little courage—then, and not till then. You see the valley?" and she pointed to the river. "It hurts me—but I love it still."

"Oh, perish England and all its women! I shall send in my resignation to the King. I will die here, forgiven!"

"No, no; love her—love that woman! Henriette is no more; this is no jest, as you will see!"

She left the room; the tone of her last speech showed how deeply she was wounded.

I hurried after her; I stopped her, saying—

"Then you no longer love me?"

"You have pained me more than all the others put together. To-day I am suffering less, and I love you less: but it is only in England that they say, 'Neither never nor for ever.' Here we only say, 'for ever.' Be good; do not add to my pain; and if you, too, are hurt, remember that I can still live on."

She withdrew her hand which I had taken; it was cold, inert, but clammy, and she was off like an arrow along the passage where this really tragical scene had taken place.

In the course of dinner the Count had a torture in store for me of which I had not dreamed.

"Then the Marchioness of Dudley is not in Paris?" he said.

I colored crimson and replied, "No."

"She is not at Tours," he went on.

"She is not divorced; she may go to England. Her husband would be delighted if she would return to him," I said excitedly.

"Has she any children?" asked Madame de Mortsauf in a husky voice.

"Two sons," said I.

"Where are they?"

"In England with their father."

"Now, Félix, be candid. Is she as lovely as people say?"

"Can you ask him such a question," cried the Countess. "Is not the woman a man loves always the most beautiful of her sex?"

"Yes, always," I replied with emphasis, and a flashing look that she could not meet.

"You are in luck," the Count went on. "Yes, you are a lucky rascal! Ah! when I was young my head would have been turned by such a conquest——"

"That is enough!" said Madame de Mortsauf, glancing from Madeleine to her father.

"I am not a boy," said the Count, who loved to think himself young again.

After dinner the Countess led the way down to the terrace, and when we there she exclaimed—

"What, there are women who can sacrifice their children for a man! Fortune and the world, yes—I understand that; eternity perhaps? But her children! To give up her children!"

"Yes, and such women would be glad to have more to sacrifice; they give everything——"

To the Countess the world seemed to be upside down; her ideas were in confusion. Startled by the magnitude of this idea, suspecting that happiness might justify this immolation, hearing within her the outcries of the rebellious flesh, she stood aghast, gazing at her spoilt life. Yes, she went through a minute of agonizing doubts. But she came out great and saintly, holding her head high.

"Love her truly, Félix; love that woman," she said with tears in her eyes. "She will be my happier sister. I forgive her the ill she has done me if she can give you what you could never have found here, what you could never find in me. You are right; I never told you that I could love you as you of the world love—and I never did love you so. Still, if she is not a true mother, how can she love?"

"Dear saint," said I, "I should have to be much less agitated than I now am to explain to you how victoriously you soar above her head; that she is a creature of earth, the daughter of a fallen race, while you are the daughter of heaven, the angel of my adoration; that you have my heart and she has only my body. She knows it; she is in despair over it, and she would change places with you even if the cruelest martyrdom were the price of the exchange.

"But all this is past remedy. Yours are my soul, my thoughts, my purest love, yours are my youth and my old age; hers are the desires and raptures of transient passion. You will fill my memory in all its extent; she will be utterly forgotten."

"Tell me, tell me—oh, tell me this, my dear!" She sat down on a bench and melted into tears. "Then virtue, Félix, a saintly life, motherly love, are not a mere blunder. Oh, pour that balm on my sorrows! Repeat those words which restore me to the bliss for which I hoped to strive in equal flight with you! Bless me with a sacred word, a look, and I can forgive you the misery I have endured these two months past."

"Henriette, there are mysteries in a man's life of which you know nothing. When I met you, I was at an age when sentiment can smother the cravings of our nature; still several scenes, of which the memory will warm me in the hour of death, must have shown you that I had almost outlived that stage, and it was your unfailing triumph that you could prolong its mute delights. Love without possession is upheld by the very exasperation of hope; but a moment comes when every feeling is pure suffering to us who are not in any respect like you. A power is ours which we cannot abdicate, or we are not men. The heart, bereft of the nourishment it needs, feeds on itself and sinks into exhaustion, which is not death but which leads to it. Nature cannot be persistently cheated, at the least accident it asserts itself with a vehemence akin to madness.

"No, I did not love, I thirsted in the desert!"

"In the desert!" she bitterly echoed, pointing to the valley. "And how he argues," she went on; "what subtle distinctions. Believers have not so much wit!"

"Henriette," said I, "do not let us quarrel for the sake

of a few overbold expressions. My soul has never wavered, but I was no longer master of my senses. That woman knows that you are the only one I love. She plays a secondary part in my life; she knows it, and is resigned. I have a right to desert her as we desert a courtesan."

"What then?"

"She says she shall kill herself," said I, thinking that this resolution would startle Henriette.

But as she heard me, she gave one of those scornful smiles that are even more expressive than the ideas they represent. "My dearest conscience," I went on, "if you gave me credit for my resistance and for the temptations that led to my ruin, you would understand this fated——"

"Yes, fated!" she exclaimed; "I believed in you too completely. I fancied you would never lack the virtue a priest can practice, and—Monsieur de Mortsauf!" she added, with satirical emphasis.

"It is all over," she went on, after a pause. "I owe much to you, my friend; you have extinguished the light of earthly life in me. The hardest part of the road is past; I am growing old, I am often ailing, almost invalided. I could never be the glittering fairy, showering favors on you. Be faithful to Lady Arabella. And Madeleine, whom I was bringing up so well for you, whose will she be? Poor Madeleine, poor Madeleine!" she repeated, like a sorrowful burthen. "If you could have heard her say, 'Mother, you are not nice to Félix.' Sweet creature!"

She looked at me in the mild rays of the setting sun that slanted through the foliage; and, filled with some mysterious pity for the ruin of us both, she looked back on our chastened past, giving herself up to reminiscences that were mutual. We took up the thread of our memories, our eyes went from the valley to the vineyard, from the windows of Clochegourde to Frapesle, filling our day-dream with the perfumes of our nosegays, the romance of our hopes. It was her last piece of self-indulgence, enjoyed with the guilelessness of a Christian soul. The scene, to us so full of meaning, had plunged us both into melancholy. She believed my words, and felt herself in the heaven where I had placed her.

"My friend," exclaimed she, "I submit to God, for His hand is in all this."

It was not till later that I understood all the deep meaning of this speech.

We slowly went back by the terraces. She took my arm and leaned on me, resigned, bleeding, but having bound up her wounds.

"This is human life," she said. "What had Monsieur de Mortsauf done to deserve his fate? All this proves the existence of another world. Woe to those who complain of walking in the narrow way."

She went on to estimate the value of life, to contemplate it so profoundly in its various aspects, that her calm balance showed me what disgust had come over her of everything here below. As we reached the top steps she took her hand from my arm, and said these last words—

"Since God has given us the faculty and love of happiness, must He not take care of those innocent souls that have not known anything but affliction on earth? Either this is so, or there is no God, and our life is but a cruel jest."

With these words she hastily went indoors, and I found her presently lying on the sofa, stricken as though she had heard the Voice which confounded Saint Paul.

"What is the matter?" I asked.

"I no longer know what virtue means," said she. "I have ceased to be conscious of my own."

We both remained petrified, listening to the echo of these words as to a stone flung into a chasm.

"If I have been mistaken in my life, it is she who is right—*she!*" added Madame de Mortsauf.

Thus her last indulgence had led to this last struggle.

When the Count came in, she, who never complained, said she felt ill; I implored her to define her pain, but she refused to say more and went to bed, leaving me a victim to remorse, one regret leading to another.

Madeleine went with her mother, and on the following day I heard from her that the Countess had had an attack of sickness, brought on, as she said, by the violent agitation she had gone through. And so I, who would have given my life for her, was killing her.

"My dear Count," said I to Monsieur de Mortsauf, who insisted on my playing backgammon, "I think the Countess is very seriously ill; there is yet time to save her. Send for Origet, and entreat her to follow his orders——"

"Origet! Who killed me!" cried he, interrupting me. "No, no. I will consult Charbonneau."

All through that week, especially during the first day or two, everything was torture to me, an incipient paralysis of the heart, wounded vanity, a wounded soul. Until one has been the centre of everything, of every look and sigh, the vital principle, the focus from which others derived their light, one cannot know how horrible a void can be. The same things were there, but the spirit that animated them was extinct, like a flame that is blown out. I understood now the frightful necessity lovers feel never to meet again when love is dead. Think what it is to be nobody where one has reigned supreme, to find the cold silence of death where the glad days of life had glowed. Such comparisons are crushing. I soon began even to regret the miserable ignorance of every joy that had blighted my youth. My despair was so overpowering, indeed, that the Countess was touched, I certainly believe.

One day, after dinner, when we were all walking by the river, I made a final effort to gain forgiveness. I begged Jacques to take his sister a little way in front; I left the

Count to himself, and taking Madame Mortsauf down to the punt:

"Henriette," I said, "one word of mercy, or I will throw myself into the Indre! I fell, it is true; but am I not like a dog in my devoted attachment? I come back as he does, like him full of shame; if he does wrong he is punished, but he adores the hand that strikes him; scourge me, but give me back your heart."

"Poor boy," said she. "Are you not as much as ever my son?"

She took my arm and slowly rejoined Jacques and Madeleine with whom she went homeward, leaving me to the Count, who began to talk politics apropos to his neighbors.

"Let us go in," I said, "you are bareheaded, and the evening dew may do you some harm."

"You can pity me—you, my dear Félix!" replied he, misapprehending my intentions. "My wife never will comfort me—on principle perhaps."

Never of old would she have left me alone with her husband; now I had to find excuses for being with her. She was with the children explaining the rules of backgammon to Jacques.

"There," said the Count, always jealous of the affection she gave to her two children; "there, it is for them that I am persistently neglected. Husbands, my dear Félix, go to the wall; the most virtuous woman on earth finds a way of satisfying her craving to steal the affection due to her husband."

She still caressed the children, making no reply.

"Jacques," said he, "come here."

Jacques made some difficulty.

"Your father wants you—go, my boy," said his mother, pushing him.

"They love me by order," said the old man, who sometimes perceived the position.

"Monsieur," said she, stroking Madeleine's smooth bands of hair again and again, "do not be unjust to us hapless wives; life is not always easy to bear, and perhaps a mother's children are her virtues!"

"My dear," said the Count, who was pleased to be logical, "what you say amounts to this: that, but for their children, women would have no virtue, but would leave their husbands in the lurch."

The Countess arose hastily and went out on to the steps with Madeleine.

"Such is marriage, my dear boy," said the Count. "Do you mean to imply by walking out of the room that I am talking nonsense?" he cried, taking Jacques' hand and following his wife, to whom he spoke with flashing looks of rage and fury.

"Not at all, monsieur, but you frightened me. Your remark wounded me terribly," she went on in a hollow voice, with the glance of a criminal at me. "If virtue does not consist in self-sacrifice for one's children and one's husband, what is virtue?"

"Self-sa-cri-fice!" echoed the Count, rapping out each syllable like a blow on his victim's heart. "What is it that you sacrifice to your children? What do you sacrifice to me? Whom? What? Answer—will you answer? What is going on then? What do you mean?"

"Monsieur," said she, "would you be content to be loved for God's sake, or to know that your wife was virtuous for virtue's sake?"

"Madame is right," said I, speaking in a tone of emotion that rang in the two hearts into which I cast my hopes for ever ruined, and which I stilled by the expression of the greatest grief of all, its hollow cry extinguishing the quarrel, as all is silence when a lion roars. "Yes, the noblest privilege conferred on us by reason is that we may dedicate our virtues to those beings whose happiness is of our making, and whom we make happy not out of self-interest or sense of duty, but from involuntary and inexhaustible affection."

A tear glistened in Henriette's eye.

"And, my dear Count, if by chance a woman were involuntarily subjugated by some feeling alien to those imposed on her by society, you must confess that the more irresistible that feeling the more virtuous would she be in stifling it—in *sacrificing herself* to her children and her husband.

"This theory, however, is not applicable to me, since I unfortunately am an example to the contrary; nor to you, whom it can never concern."

A burning but clammy hand was laid on mine, and rested there, in silence.

"You have a noble soul, Félix," said the Count, putting his arm not ungraciously round his wife's waist, and drawing her to him, as he said : "Forgive me, my dear—a poor invalid who longs to be loved more, no doubt, than he deserves."

"Some hearts are all generosity," said she, leaning her head on the Count's shoulder, and he took the speech for himself.

The mistake caused some strange revulsion in the Countess. She shuddered, her comb fell out, her hair fell down, and she turned pale; her husband, who was supporting her, gave a deep groan as he saw her faint away. He took her up as he might have taken his daughter, and carried her on to the sofa in the drawing-room, where we stood beside her. Henriette kept my hand in hers as if to say that we alone knew the secret of this scene, apparently so simple, but so terribly heart-rending for her.

"I was wrong," she said in a low voice, at a moment when the Count had gone to fetch a glass of orange-flower water. "A thousand times wrong in treating you so as to drive you to despair when I ought to have admitted you to mercy. My dear, you are adorably kind; I alone can know how kind.

Yes, I know, some forms of kindness are inspired by passion. Men have many ways of being kind—from disdain, from impulse, from self-interest, from indolence of temper; but you, my friend, have been simply, absolutely kind."

"If so," I said, "remember that all that is great in me comes from you. Do you not know that I am wholly what you have made me?"

"Such a speech is enough for a woman's happiness," she answered, just as the Count came in. "I am better," said she, rising. "I want some fresh air."

We all went down to the terrace, now scented by the acacias still in bloom. She had taken my right arm and pressed it to her heart, thus expressing her painful thoughts; but, to use her own words, it was a pain she loved. She wished, no doubt, to be alone with me; but her imagination, unpracticed in woman's wiles, suggested no reason for dismissing the children and her husband; so we talked of indifferent matters while she racked her brain trying to find a moment when she could at last pour out her heart into mine.

"It is a very long time since I took a drive," said she at length, seeing the evening so fine. "Will you give the orders, monsieur, that I may make a little round?"

She knew no explanation was possible before prayer-time, and feared that the Count would want a game of backgammon. She might indeed come out here again, on this sheltered terrace, after the Count was gone to bed; but perhaps she was afraid to linger under these boughs through which the light fell with such a voluptuous play, or to walk by the parapet whence our eyes could trace the course of the Indre through the meadows. Just as a cathedral, with its gloomy and silent vault suggests prayer, so does foliage spangled by moonlight, perfumed with piercing scents, and alive with the mysterious sounds of spring, stir every fibre and relax the will. The country, which calms an old man's passions, fires those of youthful hearts—and we knew it.

Two peals of a bell called us to prayers. The Countess started.

"My dear Henriette, what ails you?"

"Henriette is no more," said she. "Do not call her back to life again; she was exacting and capricious. Now you have a friend whose virtue is confirmed by the words which heaven must have dictated to you. We will speak of this later. Let us be punctual for prayers. It is my turn to read them to-day."

When the Countess used the words in which she besought God to preserve us against all the adversities of life, she gave them an emphasis which I was not alone in noticing; she seemed to have used her gift of second-sight to discern the dreadful agitation she was fated to go through in consequence of my clumsiness in forgetting my agreement with Arabella.

"We have time to play three hits while the horses are put in," said the Count, leading me off to the drawing-room. "Then you will drive with my wife. I shall go to bed."

Like all our games, this one was stormy. From her own room or Madeleine's the Countess could hear her husband's voice.

"You make a strange misuse of hospitality," she said to her husband when she came back to the room.

I looked at her in bewilderment; I could not get used to her sternness; in former times she would never have tried to shield me from the Count's tyranny; she had liked to see me sharing her penalties and enduring them patiently for love of her.

"I would give my life," said I in her ear, "to hear you murmur once more—*Poor dear, poor dear!*"

She looked down, recalling the occasion to which I alluded; her eyes turned on me with a sidelong glance, and expressed the joy of a woman who sees the most fugitive accents of her heart more highly prized than the deepest delights of any other love.

Then, as ever when she had done me such an injustice, I forgave her, feeling that she understood me. The Count was losing; he said he was tired, to break off the game, and we went to walk around the lawn while waiting for the carriage. No sooner had he left us than my face beamed so vividly with gladness that the Countess questioned me by a look of surprise and inquiry.

"Henriette still lives," I said; "I still am loved! You wound me with too evident intention to break my heart; I may yet be happy."

"There was but a shred of the woman left," she said, in terror, "and you at this moment have it in your grasp. God be praised! He gives me the strength to endure the martyrdom I have deserved. Yes, I still love; I was near falling; the Englishwoman throws a light into the gulf."

We got into the carriage, and the coachman waited for orders.

"Go by the avenue to the Chinon road, and come home by the Landes de Charlemagne and the Saché road."

"What is to-day?" I asked too eagerly.

"Saturday."

"Then do not drive that way, madame; on Saturday evenings the road is crowded with noisy bumpkins going to Tours, and we shall meet their carts."

"Do as I say," said the Countess to the coachman, with emphasis.

We knew each other too well, and every inflection of tone, endless as they were, to disguise the most trifling feeling. Henriette had understood everything.

"You did not think of the country bumpkins when you chose this evening," she remarked, with a faint tinge of irony. "Lady Dudley is at Tours. Tell no falsehoods; she is waiting for you near here. What day is it—bumpkins—carts!" she went on. "Did you ever make such remarks when we used to go out together?"

"They prove that I have forgotten all about Clochegourde," I replied, simply.

"She is waiting for you?"

"Yes."

"At what hour?"

"Between eleven and midnight."

"Where?"

"On the Landes."

"Do not deceive me. Not under the walnut tree?"

"On the Landes."

"We will be there," she said. "I shall see her."

On hearing these words I regarded my fate as definitely settled. I determined to marry Lady Dudley and so put an end to the dreadful conflict which really threatened to exhaust my nerves, and to destroy by such constant friction the delicate pleasures which are like the bloom on a fruit. My savage silence wounded the Countess, whose magnanimity was not yet fully known to me.

"Do not be provoked with me, dear," she said in her golden tones. "This is my penance. You will never find such love as lies here," and she placed her hand on her heart. "Did I not confess to you that the Marchioness of Dudley has saved me? The stain is hers; I do not envy her. Mine is the glorious love of the angels! Since you came I have traveled over a vast extent of country; I have pronounced judgment on life. Uplift the soul and you rend it; the higher you rise the less sympathy you find; instead of suffering in the valley you suffer in the air, like an eagle soaring up and bearing in his heart an arrow shot by some clumsy shepherd. I know now that heaven and earth are incompatible. Yes, and for those who can dwell in the celestial zone God alone is possible. Then our soul must be detached from all things earthly.

"We must love our friends as we love our children—for their sake, not for our own. We are ourselves the source of our woes and griefs. My heart will rise higher than the eagle soars; there is a love which will never fail me.

"As to living the life of this earth, it hinders us too much by making the selfishness of the senses predominate over the spirituality of the angel that is in us. The joys we get from passion are horribly stormy, and paid for by enervating fears that break the springs of the soul.

"I have stood on the shore of the sea where these tempests roar, I have seen them too near; they have caught me in their clouds; the wave did not always break at my feet, I have felt its rough embrace freezing my heart; I must retire to the heights, I should perish on the strand of that vast ocean. In you, as in all who have brought me sorrow, I see a guardian of my virtue. My life has been mingled with anguish, happily in proportion to my strength, and has been there preserved pure from evil passions, finding no beguiling repose, but always ready for God.

"Our attachment was the insane attempt, the hopeless effort, of two guileless children who tried to satisfy at once their own hearts, man, and God. Folly, Félix! Ah!" she asked, after a pause, "what does that woman call you?"

"Amédée," said I. "Félix is another creature, who can never be known to any one but you."

"Henriette dies hard," she replied, with a faint, pious smile. "But she will die," she went on, "in the first effort of the humble Christian, the proud mother, the woman whose virtues, tottering yesterday, are confirmed to-day.

"What can I say? Yes, yes, my life has been uniform in its greatest as in its least circumstances. The heart to which the first rootlets of affection ought to have attached themselves—my mother's heart—was closed to me, in spite of my persistently seeking a cranny into which I could steal. I was a girl, the last child after the death of three boys, and I vainly strove to fill their place in my parents' affections; I could not heal the wound inflicted on the family pride. When having gotten through that melancholy childhood I knew my adorable aunt, death soon snatched her from me. Monsieur de Mortsauf, to whom I devoted my life, struck me persistently without respite—without knowing it, poor man! His love is full of the artless selfishness of our children's love. He knows nothing of the pangs he causes me; he is always forgiven.

"My children, my darling children, flesh of my flesh in all their sufferings, soul of my soul in their characters, like me in nature, in their innocent joys—were not those children given to me to show how much strength and patience there is in mothers? Oh, yes, my children are my virtues! You know whether I have been scourged by them, through them, in spite of them. To be a mother was to me to purchase the right of perpetual suffering.

"When Hagar cried in the desert an angel made a font of pure water spring for that too well-beloved slave. But when the limpid brook to which you desired to lead me, do you remember? flowed round Clochegourde, for me it ran with bitter waters. Yes, you have brought incredible suffering on me. God will no doubt forgive one who has known affection only through suffering.

"Still, though the acutest anguish I have known has been brought upon me by you, perhaps I deserved it. God is not unjust. Yes, Félix, a kiss given by stealth is perhaps a crime; and perhaps I have paid thus dearly for the steps I have taken to get ahead of my husband and children when walking out in the evening, so as to be alone with memories and thoughts which were not given to them, since, while walking on in front, my soul was wedded to another! When the inmost self shrinks and shrivels, to fill only the spot offered to an embrace, that is perhaps a heinous crime! When a wife stoops that her husband's kiss may fall on her hair, so as to be entirely neutral, it is a crime! It is a crime to count on a future built up on death, a crime to dream of a future of motherhood without terrors, of beautiful children playing in the evening with a father worshiped by all, under the softened gaze of a happy mother. Ah, I have sinned, I have sinned greatly! I have even found pleasure in the penance inflicted by the church, which insufficiently atoned for these faults to which the priest was surely too indulgent. But God, no doubt, has set retribution in the very heart of the sin itself, by making him for whom it was committed the instrument of His vengeance! Giving you my hair—was not that a promise? Why did I love to wear white? I fancied myself more like your lily; did you not see me for the first time in a white dress? Alas! And I have loved my children the less, for every ardent affection is stolen from those that are due. So you see, Félix, all suffering has a meaning. Strike me, strike me harder than Monsieur de Mortsauf and my children could.

"That woman is an instrument of God's wrath; I can meet her without hatred. I will smile on her; I must love her or I am neither a Christian, a wife, nor a mother. If, as you say, I have helped to preserve your heart from the contact of what might have soiled it, the Englishwoman cannot hate me. A woman must love the mother of the man she loves; and I am your mother.

"What did I look for in your heart? The place left empty by Madame de Vandenesse. Oh, yes; for you have always complained of my coldness! Yes, I am indeed no more than your mother. Forgive me for all I said to you when you arrived, for a mother ought to rejoice to know that her son is so much loved."

She leaned her head on my bosom and repeated—

"Forgive, forgive!"

The accent of her voice was new to me. It was not her girlish voice with its gleeful intonation; nor her wifely voice with its imperative fall; nor the sighing of a grieving mother. It was a heart-rending voice, a new tone for new sorrows.

"As for you, Félix," she went on, with more animation, "you are the friend who can do no wrong. You have lost nothing in my heart; do not blame yourself, feel not the slightest remorse. Was it not the height of selfishness to ask you to sacrifice to an impossible future the most stupendous pleasure, since a woman can abandon her children for its sake, abdicate her rank, and renounce eternity! How often have I seen you my superior! You were lofty and noble, I was mean and sinful!

"Well, well, all is said. I can never be anything to you but a far-away light, high up, sparkling, cold, but unchanging. Only, Félix, do not let me be alone in loving the brother I have chosen. Love me too. A sister's love has no bitter morrow, no perverse moods. You need never be untrue to the indulgent soul that will live in your beautiful life, will never fail to weep over your sorrows, and be glad over your joys, that will love the women who make you happy, and be indignant if you are betrayed. I have never had a brother to love so. Be magnanimous enough to cast off all pride and solve all the difficulties of our attachment, hitherto so ill-defined and stormy, by this sweet and holy affection. I can still live on those terms. I will be the first to shake hands with Lady Dudley."

She shed no tears, alas, as she spoke these words full of bitter experience, while, by snatching away the last veil that hid her soul and her sufferings from me, they showed me by how many links she was bound to me and what strong chains I had broken through.

We were in such a delirium of agitation that we did not observe that it was raining in torrents.

"Will Madame la Comtesse take shelter here for a few minutes?" said the coachman, pointing to the principal inn of Ballan.

She nodded consent and we sat for about half an hour

under the archway of the entrance, to the great astonishment of the people of the inn, who wondered why Madame de Mortsauf was driving about the country at eleven o'clock at night.

Was she going to Tours? Or on her way back?

When the storm was over, and the rain had settled into what is called in Touraine a *brouée*, a heavy mist which did not hinder the moon from silvering the upper strata as they were swept swiftly past by the higher currents of wind, the coachman went out and turned homeward, to my great joy.

"Go the way I told you," said the Countess gently.

So we took the road to the Landes de Charlemagne, and there the rain began again. Half-way across the sandy common I heard Lady Arabella's pet dog barking. A horse suddenly dashed out from under a clump of oaks, crossed the road at a bound, leaped the ditch made by the owners to show the boundary of each plot where the soil was considered worth cultivating, and Lady Dudley pulled up on the common to see the carriage pass.

"What joy thus to wait for one's child when it is not a sin!" said Henriette.

The dog's barking had told Lady Dudley that I was in the carriage; she thought, no doubt, that I had come to fetch her in it, in consequence of the bad weather. When we reached the spot where the Marchioness was waiting, she flew along the road with the skill in horsemanship for which she is noted and which Henriette admired as a marvel. Arabella, by way of a pet name, called me only by the last syllable of Amédée, pronouncing it in the English fashion, and on her lips the cry had a charm worthy of a fairy. She knew that I alone should understand her when she called "My Dee."

"It is he, madame," answered the Countess, looking, in the clear moonlight, at the whimsical personage whose eager face was strangely framed in long locks out of curl.

You know how swiftly women take stock of each other.

The Englishwoman recognized her rival, and was arrogantly English; she comprehended us in one flash of English scorn, and vanished on the heath with the rapidity of an arrow.

"Back to Clochegourde—fast," cried the Countess, to whom this ruthless glance was like an axe at her heart.

The coachman went back by the Chinon road, which was better than that by Saché. When the carriage was on the skirts of the common again we heard the mad gallop of Arabella's horse and her dog's footsteps. They were all three hurrying round the woods on the other side of the heath.

"She is going away; you have lost her forever!" said Henriette.

"Well," replied I, "let her go. She will not cost me a regret."

"Oh, poor woman!" cried the Countess, with compassionate horror. "But where is she going?"

"To La Grenadière, a little house near Saint-Cyr," said I.

"And she is going alone," said Henriette, in a tone which told me that all women make common cause in love and never desert each other.

As we turned into the Clochegourde avenue, Arabella's dog barked gleefully and ran on in front of the carriage.

"She is here before us!" cried the Countess. Then, after a pause, she added: "I never saw a finer woman. What a hand! What a figure! Her complexion shames the lily and her eyes flash like diamonds. But she rides too well; she must love to exert her strength; I fancy she is energetic and violent; then, too, she seems to me too defiant of conventionality, a woman who recognizes no law is apt to listen only to her own caprice. Those who are so anxious to shine, to be always moving, have not the gift of constancy. To my notions love needs greater quietude; I picture it to myself as an immense lake where the sounding-line finds no bottom, where the tempests may indeed be wild, but rare, and restricted within impassable bounds—where two beings dwell on an island of flowers, far from the world whose luxury and display would repel them.

"But love must take the stamp of character. I am perhaps mistaken. If the elements of nature yield to the mould impressed by climate, why should it not be so with the feelings of individuals? Feelings, which as a whole obey a general law, no doubt differ in expression only. Each soul has its own modes. The Marchioness is a powerful woman who traverses distances and acts with the vigor of a man; jailers, wardens, and executioner must be killed to deliver her lover. Whereas certain women know no better than to love with all their soul; in danger they kneel down, pray, and die.

"Which of the two do you prefer? That is the whole question. Yes, the Marchioness loves you; she sacrifices so much for you! It is she, perhaps, who will love on when you have ceased to love her."

"Permit me, dear angel, to echo the question you asked the other day: How do you know these things?"

"Each form of suffering brings its lesson, and I have suffered in so many ways that my knowledge is vast."

My servant had heard the order given, and, expecting that we should return by the terraces, he held my horse in readiness, in the avenue. Arabella's dog had scented the horse, and his mistress, led by very legitimate curiosity, had followed it through the wood where she, no doubt, had been lurking.

"Go and make your peace," said Henriette, smiling, with no trace of melancholy. "Tell her how much she is mistaken as to my intentions. I wanted to show her all the value of the prize that has fallen to her; my heart has none but kindly feelings toward her—above all, neither anger nor scorn. Explain to her that I am her sister, and not her rival."

"I will not go!" cried I.

"Have you never experienced," said she, with the flashing pride of a martyr, "that certain forms of consideration may be an insult. Go—go!"

I went to join Lady Dudley and find out what humor she was in. "If only she might be angry and throw me over," thought I, "I would return to Clochegourde."

The dog led me to an oak tree from whence the Marchioness flew off, shouting to me, "Away, away!"

I had no choice but to follow her to Saint-Cyr, which we reached at midnight.

"The lady is in excellent health," said Arabella, as she dismounted.

Only those who have known her can conceive of the sarcasm implied in this observation drily flung at me in a tone that was meant to convey: "I should have died."

"I forbid you to cast any of your three-barbed witticisms at Madame de Mortsauf," I replied.

"And does it offend your grace when I remark on the perfect health enjoyed by one so dear to your precious heart? Frenchwomen, it is said, hate even their lovers' dogs; but in England we love everything that is dear to our sovereign lord, we hate what they hate, for we live in their very skin. Allow me then to be as fond of that lady as you are. Only, dear boy," said she, throwing her arms around me, all wet from the rain, "if you were faithless to me, I should neither stand up, nor lie down, nor ride in a carriage with men-servants; neither drive through the Landes de Charlemagne, nor over the heaths of any country in the world, nor be in my bed, nor under the roof of my fathers. *I* should be no more.

"I was born in Lancashire, where women can die of love. To have owned you, and give you up? I will give you up to no power in the world, not even to death, for I would go with you!"

She took me into her room, where comfort already made its presence felt.

"Love her, my dear," said I warmly, "for she loves you, and not ironically but sincerely."

"Sincerely, child?" she said, unfastening her riding-habit.

With a lover's vanity, I tried to make this arrogant creature understand the sublimity of Henriette's character. While the maid, who did not know a word of French, was dressing her hair, I tried to describe Madame de Mortsauf, sketching her life, and repeating the generous thoughts suggested to her by a crisis in which all women are petty and spiteful. Though Arabella affected to pay not the slightest attention, she did not lose a word.

"I am delighted," said she when we were alone, "to know of your taste for this style of Christian conversation; there is on my estate a curate who has not his match in composing sermons, our laborers can understand them, so well is his prose adapted to his audience. I will write to-morrow to my father to dispatch this worthy by steamer, and you shall find him in Paris. When once you have heard him you will never want to listen to any one else, all the more so because he, too, enjoys perfect health. His moralizing will give you none of those shocks that end in tears; it flows without turmoil, like a limpid brook, and secures delightful slumbers. Every evening, if you like, you can satisfy your craving for sermons while digesting your dinner.

"English moralizing, my dear boy, is as superior to that of Tours as our cutlery, our plate, and our horses are superior to your knives and your animals. Do me the favor of hearing my curate—promise me. I am but a woman, my dearest; I know how to love, how to die for you, if you like; but I have not studied at Eton, nor at Oxford, nor at Edinburgh; I am neither doctor nor reverend; I cannot moralize for you, I am quite unfit for it and should be to the last degree clumsy if I attempted it.

"I do not complain of your taste; you might have far more degraded tastes than this, and I would try to accommodate myself to them; for I intend that you should find with me everything you like best—the pleasures of love, the pleasures of the table, the pleasures of church-going—good claret and the Christian virtues. Would you like to see me in a hair-shirt this evening? That woman is happy indeed to be able to supply you with moralities! In what university do Frenchwomen take their degree? Poor me! I have nothing to give you but myself, I am only a slave——"

"Then why did you fly when I wanted to bring you two together?"

"Are you mad, my Dee? I would travel from Paris to Rome disguised as your footman, I would do the most preposterous things for you; but how could I stop to talk on the highroad to a woman who has not been introduced to me, and who was ready with a sermon under three heads? I can talk to peasants. I would ask a workman to share his loaf with me if I were hungry, I would give him a few guineas, and it would be all in order; but as to stopping a chaise—as highwaymen do in England—that is not included in my code of honor.

"My poor boy, all you know is how to love; and you do not know how to live? Beside, my angel, I am not yet made exactly in your image. I have no taste for moralities. However, to please you, I am capable of the greatest efforts. Come, say no more, I will set to work, I will try to preach. I will never allow myself to caress you without throwing in a text from the Bible."

She exerted all her power—used it, abused it, till she saw in my eyes the ardent look that always came into them when she began her enchantments. She triumphed completely, and I submissively agreed to set above the vain subtleties of the Catholic Church the magnanimity of the woman who wrecks herself, renounces all future hope and makes love her sole virtue.

"Does she love herself better than she loves you?" she asked. "Does she prefer to you something which is not you? How can a woman attach any importance to anything in herself beyond that with which you honor it? No woman, however great a moralist she may be, can be the equal of a man. Walk over us, kill us, never let us encumber your life. Our part is to die, yours to live great and supreme. In your hand is the poniard; we have only to love and forgive. Does the sun care about the midges that live in his beams, by his glow? They exist as long as they can, and when he disappears they die——"

"Or fly away," I put in.

"Or fly away," she replied, with an indifference that would have spurred any man determined to use the strange power she attributed to us. "Do you think it worthy of a woman to stuff a man with bread buttered with virtue to convince him that love and religion are incompatible? Am I then an infidel? A woman may yield or refuse; but to refuse and preach is to inflict a double penalty, which is against the law of every land. Now here you will have nothing but delicious sandwiches prepared by the hand of your humble servant Arabella, whose whole morality consists in inventing caresses such as no man has ever known, and which are suggested by the angels."

I know nothing so undoing as such banter in the hands of an Englishwoman; she throws into it the eloquent gravity, the pompous air of conviction under which the English cover the lofty imbecilities of their prejudiced views. French irony is like lace with which women dress out the pleasure they give and the disputes they invent; it is a trimming, and as graceful as their dress. But English "fun" is an acid so corrosive to those on whom it falls that it leaves them skeletons, picked and cleaned. A witty Englishwoman's tongue is like a tiger's, which strips off the flesh to the very bone, and all in play; mockery, that all-powerful weapon of the devil's, leaves a deadly poison in the wounds it reopens at will.

That night Arabella chose to exert her power like the Grand Turk, who, to show his skill, amuses himself with decapitating innocent persons.

"My angel," said she, when she had soothed me to the dozing condition in which everything is forgotten but a sense of happiness, "I have been moralizing too—I myself! I was wondering whether I am committing a crime in loving you, whether I was violating divine laws, and I decided that nothing could be more pious or more natural. Why should God create some beings more beautiful than others unless to show us that they are to be adored? The crime would not be to love you, for are you not an angel? That lady insults you by classing you with other men; the rules of morality do not apply to you; God has set you above them. Is not loving you rising to be nearer to Him? Can He be wroth with a poor woman for longing for things divine? Your large and radiant heart is so like the sky that I mistake it, as midges come to burn themselves in the lights at a festival! Are they to be punished for their mistake? Indeed, is it a mistake? Is it not too fervent a worship of light? They perish from too much piety—if, indeed, flinging one's self into the arms we love can be called perishing?

"I am weak enough to love you while that woman is strong enough to remain in her chapel! Do not frown on me. You think I condemn her? Nay, child! I delight in her morality, since it has led her to leave you free and so allowed me to win you and to keep you for ever—for you are mine for ever, are you not?"

"Yes."

"For ever and ever?"

"Yes."

"Then grant me a favor, my sultan. I alone have discerned all your value. She, you say, cultivates the land? I leave that to the farmers; I would rather cultivate your heart."

I have tried to recall all this chatter to give you a clear idea of this woman, to justify all I have said about her and to give you a clue to the catastrophe. But how am I to describe the accompaniment to the sweet words you know so well—conceits only to be compared to the most extravagant fictions of our dreams; inventions sometimes reminding me of my nosegays: grace united to strength, tenderness and languid softness contrasting with volcanic eruptions of passions; the most elaborate modulations of music applied to the harmony of our delight, the most insinuating words graced with charming ideas, everything most poetical that wit can add to the pleasures of sense. She aimed at destroying the impression left on my heart by Henriette's chaste reserve, by the flashes of her own impetuous passion. The Marchioness had seen the Countess quite as well as Madame de Mortsauf had seen her. They had judged each other clearly. The elaborate attack planned by Arabella showed how great her fears had been and her secret admiration for her rival.

In the morning I found her with eyes full of tears; she had not slept.

"What is the matter?" I asked.

"I am afraid my excess of love may militate against me," said she. "I give you all; she, cleverer than I, still has something for you to desire. If you prefer her, think no more of me; I will not bore you with my sufferings, my remorse, my sorrows—no, I will go to die far away from you, like a plant far from the life-giving sun."

She extracted from me such protestations as filled her with joy. What is to be said of a woman who weeps in the morning? A hard word then seems brutal. If she has not been denied over night, we must need tell lies in the morning, for the code of man makes such falsehood a duty.

"Well, then, I am happy," she said, wiping away her tears. "Go back to her; I do not wish to owe you to the vehemence of my love, but to your own free will. If you come back again I shall believe that you love me as much as I love you, which I had always thought impossible."

She managed to persuade me to return to Clochegourde.

How false the situation in which I should then find myself was not to be imagined by a man gorged with raptures. If I had refused to go to Clochegourde, Lady Arabella would have won the day at Henriette's expense. Arabella would then carry me off to Paris. Still, to go thither was to insult Madame de Mortsauf. In that case I should come back more certainly than ever to Arabella.

Has any woman forgiveness for such crimes of treason? Short of being an angel come down from heaven rather than a purified spirit about to attain to it, a loving woman would see her lover suffer any agony sooner than see him made happy by another. The more she loves, the more she will be hurt.

Thus regarded from both sides, my position, when I had once left Clochegourde to go to La Grenadière, was as fatal to my first true love as it was profitable to my chance passion. The Marchioness had foreseen it all with deep calculation. She confessed later that if Madame de Mortsauf had not met her on the heath she had intended to commit me by hanging about Clochegourde.

The instant I saw the Countess, whom I found pale and stricken, like a person who has endured intolerable insomnia, I exercised—not the tact—but the instinct which enables a still young and generous heart to appreciate the full bearing of actions that are criminal in the jurisprudence of noble souls though indifferent in the eyes of the vulgar. Suddenly, as a child that has gone down a steep while playing and plucking flowers sees, in terror, that he cannot go up it again, discerns no human ground but at an immeasurable distance, feels himself alone in the dark and hears savage howls, I perceived that a whole world lay between us. A loud cry went up in our souls, an echo, as it were, of the funereal *Consummatum est* which is pronounced in church on Good Friday, at the hour when the Saviour died—a dreadful scene which freezes those young souls in which religion is their first love. Every illusion Henriette had known had died under one blow; her heart had gone through its passion. She whom pleasure had never involved in its deadening coils—could she suspect the joys of happy lovers that she refused to look at me? for she would not shed on my gaze the light which for six years had irradiated my life. She knew, then, that the source of the beams that shone from our eyes lay in our souls, for which they were as a pathway, leading from one to the other, so that they might visit, become one, separate, and play—like two confiding girls who have no secrets from each other. I was bitterly conscious of the sin of bringing under this roof, where caresses were unknown, a face on which the wings of enjoyment had shed their sparkling dust.

If, the day before, I had left Lady Dudley to go home alone; if I had come back to Clochegourde, where Henriette perhaps expected me; perhaps—well, perhaps, Madame de Mortsauf would not have behaved so strictly as my sister. She gave all her civilities the solemnity of exaggerated emphasis; she played her part to excess so as not to forget it. During breakfast she paid me a thousand little attentions, humiliating attentions; she made much of me like a sick man to be pitied.

"You were out betime," said the Count; "you must have a fine appetite, you whose digestion is not ruined."

This speech, which failed to bring the smile of a wily sister to the Countess' lips, put the crowning touch to the impossibility of my position. I could not be at Clochegourde by day and at Saint-Cyr by night. Arabella had counted on my sense of delicacy and Madame de Mortsauf's magnanimity.

All through that long day I felt the difficulty of becoming the friend of a woman one has long desired. This transition, simple enough when years have led up to it, in youth is a distemper. I was ashamed, I cursed all pleasure, I wished that Madame de Mortsauf would demand my blood! I could not tear her rival to pieces before her eyes; she avoided mentioning her, and to speak ill of Arabella was a baseness which would have incurred the contempt of Henriette, herself noble and lofty to the inmost core. After five years of exquisite intimacy we did not know what to talk about; our words did not express our thoughts; we hid gnawing pangs, we to whom suffering had hitherto been a faithful interpreter. Henriette affected a cheerful air on my behalf and her own; but she was sad. Though she called herself my sister on every opportunity, and though she was a woman, she could find no subject to keep up the conversation and we sat for the most part in awkward silence. She added to my mental torment by affecting to think herself Lady Arabella's only victim.

"I am suffering more than you are," I said, at a moment when the sister spoke in a tone of very feminine irony.

"How can that be?" she returned, in the haughty voice a woman can put on when her feelings are underestimated.

"I have done all the wrong."

Then there was a moment when the Countess assumed a cold indifference that was too much for me. I determined to go.

That evening, on the terrace, I took leave of all the family together. They followed me to the lawn where my horse waited, pawing the ground. They stood out of the way. When I had taken the bridle, the Countess came up to me.

"Come, we will walk down the avenue alone," she said.

I gave her my arm, and we went out through the courtyards, walking slowly as if lingering over the sensation of moving together; we thus reached a clump of trees that screened a corner of the outer enclosure.

"Good-by, my friend," she exclaimed, stopping and throwing her arms around my neck with her head on my heart. "Good-by, we shall see each other no more. God has given me the melancholy power of looking into the future. Do you remember the panic that came over me that day when you came back so handsome, so youthful; and when I saw you turn to quit me, just as to-day you are leaving Clochegourde for La Grenadière? Well, last night I was once more enabled to look forward to our destinies. My friend, we are speaking to each other for the last time. I can hardly say a few words to you even now, for not all of me speaks; death has already stricken something within me. You will have robbed my children of their mother—take her place! You can! Jacques and Madeleine love you already as though you had made them suffer!"

"Die?" cried I in alarm, as I looked at the dry flame in her glittering eyes, of which I can only give an idea to those whose dear ones have never been attacked by the dreadful malady by comparing her eyes with balls of tarnished silver. "Die! Henriette, I command you to live. You often used to require vows of me—now I, to-day, require one of you: swear to me that you will consult Origet and do exactly what he tells you."

"Then would you contend against the loving mercy of God?" she asked, interrupting me with a cry of despair, indignant at being misunderstood.

"Then you do not love me enough to obey me blindly in everything, as that miserable lady does?"

"Yes, yes; whatever you wish," she replied, urged by a jealousy which made her overleap in that instant the distance she had till now preserved.

"I stay here," I said, kissing her eyes.

Startled by this capitulation she escaped from my embrace and went to lean against a tree. Then she turned homeward, walking very fast without turning her head; I followed her, she was praying and weeping. When we reached the lawn I took her hand and kissed it respectfully. This unlooked-for surrender touched her heart.

"Yours, come what may," I ejaculated. "I love you as your aunt loved you."

She started and wrung my hand with the most fervent affection.

"One look," said I, "only one of your old looks!" And feeling my whole soul enlightened by the flashing glance she gave me, I cried, "The woman who gives herself wholly gives me less of life and spirit than I have now received! Henriette, you are the best beloved—the only love."

"I will live," she returned, "but you, too, must get well."

That gaze had effaced the impression of Arabella's sarcasms. Thus was I the plaything of the two irreconcilable passions I have described to you, and of which I felt the alternating influence. I loved an angel and a demon: two women equally lovely; one graced with all the virtues we torture out of hatred of our own defects, the other with all the vices we deify out of selfishness. As I rode down the avenue, turning around again and again to see Madame de Mortsauf leaning against a tree, her children standing by her and waving their handkerchiefs, I detected in my soul an impulse of pride at knowing myself to be the arbiter of two such noble destinies, the glory, on such different grounds, of two superior women, and at having inspired such passions that either of them would die if I failed her.

This brief but fatuous dream was severely punished, believe me. Some demon prompted me to wait with Arabella till a fit of despair or the Count's death should throw Henriette into my arms, since Henriette still loved me; her severity, her tears, her remorse, and her Christian resignation were the eloquent symptoms of a feeling which could no more be effaced from her heart than from my own. As I slowly walked my horse along the pretty avenue, making these reflections, I was not five-and-twenty, I was fifty. Does not a young man, even more than a woman, leap in a moment from thirty to sixty?

Though I could drive away these evil thoughts with a breath they haunted me, I must confess. Their source, perhaps, was at the Tuileries behind the panels of the royal cabinet. Who could come unharmed under the tainting influence of Louis XVIII., who was wont to say that a man knows nothing of true passion till he is past maturity, since passion is never splendid and frenzied till there is some loss of power and each pleasure is like the gambler's last stake.

When I reached the end of the avenue I looked round once more, and in the twinkling of an eye I was back again, on seeing Henriette still standing there alone. I flew to bid her a last adieu, bathed in tears of expiation of which she knew not the secret. Sincere tears, shed, though I knew it not, on the sweet love that was for ever past, on the virgin emotions, the flowers of life that can never bloom again. Later in life a man can no longer give, he only receives; what he loves in his mistress is himself; whereas in youth he loves her in himself. Later, he inoculates the woman who loves him with his tastes, perhaps with his vices; whereas, in the early days, the woman he loves imparts her virtues, her refinement, invites him to what is beautiful by her smile and shows him what devotion means by her example.

Alas for the man who has not had his Henriette! Alas for him who has not met a Lady Dudley! If he marries, the second will fail to retain his wife, the first may perhaps be deserted by his mistress; happy is he who finds both in one woman; happy, Natalie, is the man you love!

On our return to Paris Arabella and I became more intimate; by small degrees we insensibly abrogated the laws of propriety to which I had subjected myself—laws whose observance often leads the world to overlook the false position to which Lady Dudley had committed herself. The world, which dearly loves to get behind the curtain of things, accepts them as soon as it knows the hidden secret. Lovers who are obliged to live in the world of fashion are always wrong to break down the barriers insisted on by the common law of drawing-rooms, wrong not to obey implicitly all the conventions demanded by good manners; more for their own sake than for that of others. Distances to be traversed, superficial respect to be maintained, comedies to be played out, mystery to be kept up—all the strategy of a happy love-affair fills up life, revives desire and preserves the heart from the lassitude of habit. But a first passion, like a young man, is by nature profligate and cuts down its timber recklessly, instead of economizing its resources.

Arabella scorned such commonplace ideas and submitted to them only to please me. Like the destroyer who marks his prey beforehand to secure it, she hoped to compromise me in the eyes of all Paris so as to attach me to her permanently. She displayed every coquettish art to keep me at the house, for she was not satisfied with the elegant scandal which, for lack of evidence, countenanced nothing more than whisperings behind a fan. Seeing her so anxious to commit an imprudence which must definitely certify her position, how could I do otherwise than believe in her love?

Once involved in the beguilements of an illicit union I fell a prey to despair, for I saw my life cut out in antagonism to received ideas and to Henriette's injunctions. I lived, then, in the sort of frenzy which comes over a consumptive man, when, conscious of his approaching end, he will not allow his breathing to be sounded. There was one corner of my heart I could not look into without anguish; a spirit of vengeance was constantly suggesting ideas on which I dared not dwell.

My letters to Henriette painted this mental disorder, and caused her infinite pain.

"At the cost of so much lost treasure she had hoped I should at least be happy," she wrote, in the only reply I ever received.

And I was not happy! Dear Natalie, happiness can only be positive; it cannot endure comparisons. My first ardor expended, I could not help comparing these two women, a contrast I had not yet been capable of studying. In fact, any great passion lies so heavily on our whole nature that, in the first instance, it levels all angles and fills up the ruts of habit which represent our good or evil qualities. But later, in lovers who are thoroughly accustomed to each other, the features of their moral physiognomy reappear; they judge each other calmly, and not unfrequently, in the course of this reaction of character on passion, antipathies are discovered which lead to the separations regarded by superficial minds as evidence of the inconstancy of the human heart.

This stage had begun for us. Less dazzled by her fascinations, and taking my pleasures retail, so to speak, I, half involuntarily perhaps, took stock of Lady Dudley to her disadvantage.

In the first place, I found her lacking in the mother-wit which distinguishes the Frenchwoman from all others and makes her the most delightful to love, as men have owned who have had opportunities for judging of the women of many lands. When a Frenchwoman loves she is metamorphosed; her much talked-of vanity is devoted to beautifying her love; she sacrifices her dangerous conceit and throws all her pretentiousness into the art of loving. She weds her lover's interests, his hatreds, his friendships; in one day she masters the experienced shrewdness of a man of business; she studies the law; she understands the machinery of credit and can seduce a banker's counting-house; reckless and prodigal, she will not make a single blunder or waste a single louis. She is at once mother, housekeeper, and physician; and to every fresh phase she gives a grace of delight that betrays infinite love in the most trifling details. She combines the special qualities which charm us in the women of various countries, giving unity to the compound by wit, the growth of France, which vivifies, sanctions, and justifies everything, lends variety, and redeems the monotony of a sentiment based on the present tense of a single verb.

The Frenchwoman loves once for all; without pause or

fatigue, at all hours, in public or alone; in public she finds a tone that argues to one ear only, her very silence speaks, and her eyes appeal to you without looking up; if speech and looks are alike prohibited she can use the sand under her feet to trace a thought in; alone she expresses her passion even in her sleep; in short, she bends the world to her love.

The Englishwoman, on the contrary, bends her love to the world. Accustomed by education to preserve the icy manners, the egotistic British mien of which I have told you, she opens and shuts her heart with the readiness of English-made machinery. She has an impenetrable mask which she takes on and off with phlegmatic coolness; as impassioned as an Italian when no eye can see, she turns coldly dignified as soon as the world looks on. Then the man she loves best on earth doubts his power as he meets the utterly passive countenance, the calm intonation, the perfect freedom of expression that an Englishwoman assumes as she comes out of her boudoir. At such a moment dissimulation becomes indifference; the Englishwoman has forgotten everything. Certainly, a woman who can throw off her love like a garment makes one think that she may change.

What storms toss the surges of the heart when they are stirred by wounded self-love, as we see a woman taking up her love, laying it down and returning to it, like a piece of needlework! Such women are too thoroughly mistresses of themselves to be wholly yours; they allow the world too much influence for your sovereignty to be undivided. In cases when a Frenchwoman comforts the sufferer by a look or betrays her annoyance at intrusion by some lively jest, the Englishwoman's silence is complete: it frets the soul and irritates the brain. These women are so accustomed to reign wherever they may be, that, to most of them, the omnipotence of fashion dominates even their pleasures.

Those who are excessive in prudery should be excessive in love; Englishwomen are so; they throw everything into form, but the love of form does not, in them, produce a feeling for art; they may say what they will, Protestantism and Catholicism account for the differences which give to a Frenchwoman's spirit so great a superiority over the reasoned, calculating love of Englishwomen. Protestantism is skeptical, it examines and kills belief; it is the death of art and of love. Where the world rules the people of the world must obey; but those who know what passion means flee away; to them it is intolerable.

You may understand, then, how much my self-respect was wounded by discovering that Lady Dudley would not live without the world, and that these British transitions were habitual with her. They were not a necessity imposed on her by the world; no, she naturally showed herself under two aspects adverse to each other; when she loved it was with intoxication; no woman of any nationality could be compared with her, she was as good as a whole seraglio; but then a curtain fell on this fairy display and shut out even the remembrance of it. She would respond neither to a look nor a smile; she was neither mistress nor slave; she behaved like an ambassadress compelled to be precise in her phrases and demeanor; she put me out of patience with her calmness, outraged my heart by her primness; she thus stored up her love till it was required, instead of raising it to the ideal by enthusiasm. In which of the two women was I to believe?

I felt by a myriad pin-pricks the infinite difference that divided Henriette from Arabella. When Madame de Mortsauf left me for a few minutes she seemed to charge the air with the care of speaking of her; as she went away the sweep of her gown appealed to my eyes, as its rippling rustle came to my ear when she came back; there was infinite tenderness in the way her eyelids unfolded when she looked down; her voice, her musical voice, was a continual caress; her speech bore witness to an ever-present thought; she was always the same. She did not divide her soul between two atmospheres, one burning and the other icy; in short, Madame de Mortsauf kept her wit and the bloom of her intelligence to express her feelings, she made herself fascinating to her children and to me by the ideas she uttered. Arabella's wit did not serve her to make life pleasant, she did not exert it for my benefit, it existed only by and for the world; it was purely satirical, she loved to rend and bite, not for the fun of it, but to gratify a craving. Madame de Mortsauf would have hidden her happiness from every eye; Lady Arabella wanted to show hers to all Paris, and yet with horrible dissimulation she maintained the proprieties even while riding with me in the Bois de Boulogne.

This mixture of ostentation and dignity, of love and coldness, was constantly chafing my soul that was at once virgin and impassioned, and as I was incapable of thus rushing from one mood to another my temper suffered; I was throbbing with love when she relapsed into conventional prudery. When I ventured to complain, not without the greatest deference, she turned her three-barbed tongue on me, mingling the rhodomontade of adoration with the English wit I have tried to describe. As soon as she found herself in antagonism to me she made a sport of wounding my heart and humiliating my mind, and moulded me like dough. To my remarks as to a medium to be observed in all things, she retorted by caricaturing my ideas and carrying them to extremes. If I reproached her for her conduct, she would ask me if I wanted her to embrace me under the eyes of all Paris—at the Italian opera—and she took the matter so seriously that I, knowing her mania for making herself talked about, quaked lest she should fulfill her words.

In spite of her real passion, I never felt in her anything sacred, reserved, and deep, as in Henriette; she was as insatiable as a sandy soil. Madame de Mortsauf was always composed; she felt my soul in an accent or a glance, while the Marchioness was never overpowered by a look, by a pressure of the hand, or a murmured word. Nay, more, the happiness of yesterday was as nothing on the morrow. No proof of love ever surprised her; she had such a craving for excitement, turmoil, and show that nothing, I imagine, came up to her ideal in these points; hence her frenzied excesses of passion; it was for her own sake, not for mine, that she indulged her extravagant fancies.

Madame de Mortsauf's letter, the beacon that still shone on my path, and showed how the most virtuous wife can obey her genius as a Frenchwoman by proving her perpetual vigilance, her unfailing comprehension of all my vicissitudes—that letter must have enlightened you as to the care with which Henriette kept watch over my material interests, my political connections, my moral conquests and her intimate interest in my life in all permitted ways.

On all these points Lady Dudley affected the reserve of a mere acquaintance. She never inquired as to my doings, nor my aversions or friendships with men. Lavish for herself, without being generous, she decidedly made too little distinction between interest and love; whereas, without having tested her, I knew that, to spare me a regret, Henriette would have found for me what she would never have sought for herself. In one of those catastrophes which may befall the highest and the wealthiest—history has many instances—I should have taken counsel of Henriette, but I would have been dragged to prison rather than say a word to Lady Dudley.

So far the contrast is based on feelings, but it was equally great with regard to externals. In France luxury is the expression of the man, the reproduction of his ideas, of his personal poetry; it represents the character, and, between lovers, gives value to the most trifling attentions by drawing out the ruling idea of the one we love; but English luxury, which had bewitched me by its selectness and refinement, was as mechanical as the rest. Lady Dudley infused nothing of herself into it; it was the work of her servants—bought, paid for. The thousand comforting attentions at Clochegourde were in Arabella's eyes the concern of the servants; each had his duty and special function. The choice of good footmen was her steward's business, just as if they were horses. This woman felt no attachment to those about her; the death of the best of them would not have affected her; another, equally well trained, was to be had for money. As to her fellows, I never saw a tear in her eye for the woes of others; indeed, there was a frank selfishness about her which it was impossible not to laugh at.

The crimson robe of a great lady covered this iron soul. The exquisite *almée* who, in the evening, lounged on her rugs and rang all the tinkling bells of amorous folly, could quickly reconcile a young man to the hard and unfeeling Englishwoman; indeed, it was only step by step that I discerned the volcanic rock on which I was wasting my labors, since it could never yield a harvest.

Madame de Mortsauf had read this nature at a glance in their brief meeting; I remembered her prophetic words. Henriette was right throughout: Arabella's love was becoming intolerable. I have since noticed that women who ride well are never tender; like the Amazons they have lost a breast, and their hearts are petrified in one spot, I know not which.

Just when I was beginning to feel the weight of this yoke, when weariness was stealing over me, body and soul, when I understood how great a sanctity true feeling can give to love, and when the memories of Clochegourde were too much for me as, in spite of the distance, I smelt the perfume of its roses, heard the song of its nightingales—at the moment when I first perceived the stony bed of the torrent under its diminished flood—I had a blow which still echoes in my life, for it is repeated every hour.

I was writing in the King's private room; he was to go out

at four o'clock; the Duc de Lenoncourt was in waiting. As he came into the room the King asked for news of the Countess. I looked up hastily with a too significant gesture, and the King, startled by my eagerness, gave me the look which commonly introduced the stern words he could speak on occasion.

"Sire, my poor daughter is dying," replied the Duke.

"Will your majesty condescend to grant me leave of absence?" said I, with tears in my eyes, and risking an outburst of wrath.

"Fly, *my lord!*" replied he, smiling at the irony he had infused into the words, and letting me off a reprimand in honor of his own wit.

The Duke, more a courtier than a father, asked for no leave, but got into the carriage with the King. I went off, without saying good-by to Lady Dudley, who by good luck was not at home, and for whom I left a note saying that I was called away on the King's service. At La Croix de Berny I met his majesty returning from Verrières. As he accepted a bouquet which he dropped at his feet, the King gave me a look full of the royal irony that is so crushingly piercing, and which was as much as to say: "If you mean to become a somebody in political life, come back. Do not amuse yourself with interviewing the dead!"

The Duke, from his carriage, waved me a melancholy signal with his hand.

The two gorgeous coaches, drawn by eight horses, the colonels in gold lace, the mounted escort, and the clouds of dust whirled swiftly past to cries of "Vive le roi!" (Long live the King!) And to me it was as though the court had trampled the body of Madame de Mortsauf under foot, with the indifference of nature herself to human disaster. Though he was an excellent good fellow, the Duke, I make no doubt, went off to play whist with MONSIEUR (the Dauphin) after the King had retired. As to the Duchess, it was she, and she alone, who long since had dealt her daughter the first death-blow by telling her about Lady Dudley.

My hasty journey was like a dream, but it was the dream of the ruined gambler; I was in despair at having had no news. Had her confessor carried severity to the point of forbidding my entering Clochegourde? I accused Madeleine, Jacques, the Abbé de Dominis, everybody, even to Monsieur de Mortsauf.

After passing Tours, as I turned off to the bridges of Saint-Sauveur, to go down the road that leads to Poncher between poplars—those poplars I had admired when I set out in search of my unknown fair—I met Monsieur Origet. He guessed that I was going to Clochegourde, I guessed that he was coming from it; we stopped our chaises and got out, I to ask news and he to give it.

"Well," I asked, "how is Madame de Mortsauf?"

"I doubt if you will find her alive," said he. "She is enduring a terrible death from inanition. When she sent for me, in the month of June last, no medical power could control the malady; she had all the symptoms which Monsieur de Mortsauf must have described to you, since he fancied he was suffering from them. The Countess was no longer at the stage of a transient attack due to an internal disorder which medicine can deal with, and which may lead to an improved condition, nor was she suffering from a beginning of acute illness which may be cured in time; her disease had already reached a point at which our art is useless; it is the incurable result of some sorrow, as a mortal wound is the result of a poniard thrust. The malady is produced by the torpor of an organ as indispensable to life as the action of the heart. Grief had done the work of the dagger. Be under no mistake. What Madame de Mortsauf is dying of is some unconfessed sorrow."

"Unconfessed?" said I. "Her children have not been ill?"

"No," said he, looking at me with meaning. "And since she has been so seriously ill, Monsieur de Mortsauf has left her in peace. I can be of no further use; Monsieur Deslandes from Azay can do everything. There is no remedy, and her sufferings are terrible. Rich, young, handsome—and she is dying aged and pinched by hunger, for she will die of starvation. For the last forty days the stomach is closed, as it were, and rejects every kind of food in whatever form it is given."

Monsieur Origet pressed the hand I offered him; he had almost asked for it by a respectful movement.

"Courage, monsieur," said he, raising his eyes to heaven.

The words expressed compassion for the sorrow he supposed me to share equally with him; he had no suspicion of the poisoned dart they bore, like an arrow piercing my heart. I hastily got into my carriage again, promising the postillion a handsome reward if he made good haste.

In spite of my impatience, I fancied I had made the journey in only a few minutes, so much was I absorbed by the bitter reflections that crowded on my soul. "She is dying of grief—and yet her children are well! then I am the cause of her death!" My threatening conscience underwent one of those examinations which echo through life, and sometimes beyond it. How feeble, how impotent is human justice! It punishes none but visible crimes. Why death and disgrace to the assassin who kills with a single blow, who generally comes upon you in your sleep and leaves you to sleep for ever, or who strikes you unexpectedly and spares you the agony of death? Why a happy life and the world's respect for the murderer who pours venom drop by drop into the soul and undermines the body to destroy it? How many assassins go unpunished! What deference for superior lives! What an acquittal for the homicide caused by moral persecution!

Some unknown and avenging hand suddenly lifted the painted curtain that veils society. I saw a number of such victims, as well known to you as to me. Madame de Beau-

séant, who had set out, dying, for Normandy a few days
before my departure ; the Duchesse de Langeais compromised !
Lady Brandon gone to Touraine to die in the humble dwelling where Lady Dudley had just spent a fortnight—killed—
by what terrible disaster you know. Our age is full of events
of the kind. Who does not know the story of the poor young
wife who poisoned herself, overcome by such jealousy as
perhaps was killing Madame de Mortsauf? Who has not
shuddered at the fate of the charming girl dying, like a flower
cankered by a gad-fly, after two years of married life, the
victim of her guileless ignorance, the victim of a wretch with
whom Ronquerolles, Montriveau, and de Marsay shake hands
because he helps them in their political schemes? Has not
Madame d'Aiglemont been on the very verge of the grave ?
Would she be alive now but for my brother's care ?

Science is the world's accomplice in these crimes, for which
there is no tribunal. No one, it would seem, ever dies of
grief, or despair, or love, or hidden poverty, or hopes fruit-
lessly cherished, perpetually uprooted and replanted ! The
new nomenclature has ingenious words that account for everything: gastritis, pericarditis, the thousand feminine ailments
of which the names are spoken in a whisper, are mere pass-
ports to the coffin on which hypocritical tears are shed, to be
soon wiped away by the lawyer.

Is there behind all this woe some law of which we know
nothing? Must the man who lives to a hundred ruthlessly
strew the ground with the dead and see everything destroyed
that he may live, just as the millionaire absorbs the efforts of
a thousand minor industries? Is there a strong and venomous
type of life which is fed on these sweet and gentle creatures?
Good God ! Was I then one of that race of tigers ? Remorse
clawed at my heart with burning fingers and tears ran down
my cheeks as I turned into the avenue to Clochegourde, on
a damp October morning that brought the dead leaves down
from the poplars planted under Henriette's directions—that

MADELEINE, JACQUES, AND THE ABBÉ DE DOMINIS ALL KNEELING AT THE FOOT OF A WOODEN CROSS.

avenue where I had seen her wave her handkerchief as though to call me back.

Was she still alive? Might I yet feel her two white hands laid on my prostrate head? In that moment I paid the price of every pleasure Arabella had given me, and I thought them dearly bought! I swore never to see her again and took an aversion for England. Though Lady Dudley is a distinct variety of the species, I involved every Englishwoman in the black cerecloth of my condemnation.

On entering the grounds I had another shock. I found Madeleine, Jacques, and the Abbé de Dominis all kneeling at the foot of a wooden cross that stood on the corner of a plot of ground which had been included in the park at the time when the gate was erected. Neither the Count nor the Countess had wished to remove it. I sprang out of the chaise, went up to them bathed in tears, my heart wrung at the sight of these two young things and the solemn priest beseeching God. The old huntsman was there, too, standing bareheaded a few paces away.

"Well, monsieur?" said I to the abbé as I kissed Madeleine and Jacques on the brow; but they gave me a cold glance and did not interrupt their prayers.

The abbé arose; I took his arm to lean on him, pleadingly asking him: "Is she still living?" He bent his head mildly and sadly.

"Speak, I entreat you, in the name of our Saviour's Passion! Why are you praying at the foot of this cross? Why are you here and not with her? Why are the children out in this cold morning? Tell me everything, that I may not blunder fatally in my ignorance."

"For some days past Madame la Comtesse will only see her children at fixed hours. Monsieur," he went on after a pause, "you may perhaps have to wait some hours before you can see Madame de Mortsauf: she is terribly altered! But it will be well to prepare her for the interview; you might cause her some increase of suffering—as to death, it would be a mercy!"

I pressed the holy man's hand; his look and voice touched a wound without reopening it.

"We are all praying for her here," he went on, "for she, so saintly, so resigned, so fit to die, has for the last few days had a secret horror of death; she looks at us who are full of life with eyes in which, for the first time, there is an expression of gloom and envy. Her delusions are, I think, not so much the result of a fear of dying as of a sort of inward intoxication—the faded flowers of her youth rotting as they wither. Yes, the angel of evil is struggling with heaven for that beautiful soul. Madame is going through her agony in the garden; her tears mingle with the white roses that crowned her head as a daughter of Jephtha, though married, and that have fallen one by one.

"Wait a little while; do not let her see you yet; you will bring in the glitter of the court, she will see in your face a reflection of worldly enjoyments, and you will add to her regrets. Have pity on a weakness which God Himself forgave to His Son made man. Though what merit indeed should we have in triumphing where there was no adversary? Allow us, her director and myself, two old men whose ruins cannot offend her sight, to prepare her for this unlooked-for interview and emotions which the Abbé Birotteau had desired her to forego. But there is in the things of this world an invisible warp of celestial causation which a religious eye can discern, and, since you have come here, you have perhaps been guided by one of the stars which shine in the moral sphere and lead to the tomb as they did to the manger."

And then he told me, with the unctuous eloquence that falls on the spirit like dew, that for the last six months the Countess' sufferings had increased every day, in spite of all Origet could do for her. The doctor had come to Clochegourde every evening for two months, striving to snatch this prey from death, for the Countess had said to him: "Save me!"

"But to cure the body the heart must be cured!" the old physician had one day exclaimed.

"As the malady increased the gentle creature's words became bitter," the Abbé de Dominis went on. "She cries out to earth to keep her, rather than to God to take her; then she repents of murmuring against the decrees of the Most High. These alternations rend her heart, and make the conflict terrible between body and soul. Often it is the body that conquers.

"'You have cost me dear!' she said one day to Madeleine and Jacques, sending them away from her bedside. But in the next breath, called back to God by seeing me, she spoke these angelic words to Mademoiselle Madeleine: 'The happiness of others becomes the joy of those who can no longer be happy.' And her accent was so pathetic that I felt my own eyes moisten. She falls, indeed, but each time she rises again nearer to heaven."

Struck by the successive messages sent to me by fate, all leading up, in this vast concert of woe, through mournful modulations, to the funereal theme, the great cry of dying love, I exclaimed—

"Then you do believe that this beautiful lily, cut off in its prime, will bloom again in heaven?"

"You left her as a flower," he replied, "but you will find her burnt, purified in the fire of sorrow, as pure as a diamond still lying hidden in rubbish. Yes, that brilliant spirit, that angelical star, will emerge glorified from the clouds about it, to pass into the realms of light."

Just as I pressed the hand of this apostolic man, my heart overpowered with gratitude, the Count's perfectly white head was seen outside the house, and he flew to meet me with a gesture of great surprise.

"She was right! Here he is. 'Félix, Félix, Félix!

Félix is come!' Madame de Mortsauf cried out. My dear fellow," he added, with looks distraught by terror, " death is here. Why did it not take an old lunatic like me, whom it had already laid hands on?"

I walked on to the house, summoning all my courage; but on the threshold of the long corridor through the house, from the lawn to the terrace steps, I was met by the Abbé Birotteau.

"Madame la Comtesse begs you will not go to her yet," said he.

Looking around me I saw the servants coming and going, all very busy, dizzy with grief, and evidently startled by the orders delivered to them through Manette.

"What is the matter?" said the Count, irritated by this bustle, not only from a dread of the terrible end, but as a consequence of his naturally petulant temper, which seemed to be worse than before.

"A sick woman's caprice," replied the abbé. "Madame la Comtesse does not choose to receive Monsieur le Vicomte in the state she is in. She talks of dressing. Why contradict her?"

Manette went to call Madeleine, and a few minutes later we saw her come out again from her mother's room. As we walked, all five of us—Jacques and his father, the two abbés and I—in perfect silence along the front to the lawn, we went beyond the house. I looked by turns at Montvazon and at Azay, contemplating the yellowing valley, in mourning as it seemed, and responding, as it ever did, to the feelings that agitated me.

I suddenly saw the dear "Mignonne" running to seek autumn flowers, gathering them to compose a nosegay, no doubt; and thinking of all that was conveyed by this reflection of my loving attentions, a strange, indescribable sensation came over me, I tottered, my eyes grew dim, and the two priests between whom I was walking carried me to the low parapet of a terrace where I sat for some time, broken, as it were, but without entirely losing consciousness.

"Poor Félix!" said the Count. "She said you were not to be written to; she knows how much you love her!"

Though prepared to suffer, I had found myself too weak to bear a contemplation which summed up all my happy memories. "There," thought I to myself, "there lies the heath, as dry as a skeleton, in the gray daylight, and in the midst of it there used to be one lonely flowering shrub which, in my walks of old, I could never admire without a shudder of ill-omen, for it was the emblem of this dreadful day!"

Everything was dejected about the little mansion, formerly so lively, so busy. Everything mourned, everything spoke of despair and neglect. The paths were but half-raked, work begun had been left unfinished, the laborers stood idle, gazing at the house. Though the vintage was being gathered, there was no noise, no chatter of tongues. The vineyards seemed deserted, so profound was the silence.

We walked on, grief repressing commonplace words, but listening to the Count, the only one of us who could talk. Having said the things which his mechanical affection for his wife dictated, from sheer habit and tendency of mind, he began finding fault with the Countess. His wife had never chosen to take any care of herself nor to listen when he gave her good counsel; he had discerned the first symptoms of her illness, for he had studied them in himself, he had physicked and cured himself with no aid but that of a strictly regulated diet and the avoidance of any strong emotion. He could perfectly well have cured the Countess, but a husband cannot take on himself such a responsibility, especially when he is so unhappy as to find his experience treated with contempt. In spite of all he could say, the Countess had called in Origet for her adviser—Origet, who had so mismanaged him and was killing his wife! If the cause of this disease was excess of troubles, he certainly had been in a condition to develop it, but what troubles could his wife have had? The Countess was quite happy, she had nothing to grieve or annoy her. Their fortune was assured, thanks to his care and his good management; he allowed Madame de Mortsauf to reign supreme at Clochegourde; their children—well brought up and in good health—caused them no further anxiety; what then could have brought on the malady?

And he mixed up the expression of his despair with the silliest accusations. Then, presently, recalled by some reminiscence to the admiration the noble creature deserved, tears started to his eyes so long since dried up.

Madeleine came to tell me that her mother was ready to see me. The Abbé Birotteau came with me. The grave little girl remained with her father, saying that her mother wished to see me alone, making it her excuse that the presence of several persons was too fatiguing. The solemnity of the moment gave me that strange sense of being hot within and cold on the surface that is so overwhelming on some great occasions in life. The Abbé Birotteau, one of the men whom God has marked for His own by clothing them in gentleness and simplicity and endowing them with patience and mercy, drew me aside.

"Monsieur," he said, "you must know that I have done all that was humanly possible to hinder this meeting between you. The salvation of that saint required it. I thought only of her, not of you. Now that you are going once more to see her, whose door ought to be held against you by angels, I must inform you that I intend to be present to protect her against you and perhaps against herself! Respect her feeble state. I ask you to be merciful, not as a priest, but as a humble friend of whom you knew not and who would fain save you from remorse.

"Our poor invalid is dying literally of hunger and thirst. Since the morning she has been suffering from the feverish irritability that precedes that dreadful end, and I cannot tell you how sorely she regrets leaving life. The outcries of her rebellious flesh are buried in my heart where they wound still tender echoes; but Monsieur de Dominis and I have assumed this religious duty so as to conceal the spectacle of her mental agony from the noble family which has lost its morning and its evening star. For her husband, her children, her servants, all ask, 'Where is *she?*' so greatly is she changed.

"When she sees you her laments will begin afresh. Put from you the thoughts of the man of the world, forget all the vanities of the heart, be to her the advocate of heaven and not of the world. Do not suffer that saint to die in a moment of doubt, her last accents words of despair!"

I made no reply. My silence filled the poor priest with consternation. I saw, I heard, I walked, and yet I was no longer on the earth. The one thought, "What can have happened? In what state shall I find her that everybody takes such elaborate precautions?" gave rise to apprehensions all the more torturing because they were undefined. That thought summed up every possible sorrow.

We reached the door of her room, and the anxious priest opened it. I then saw Henriette, dressed in white, reclining on her little sofa in front of the fireplace; on the mantel were two vases filled with flowers; there were more flowers on a table in front of the window. The abbé's face, amazed at this unexpectedly festal sight and at the change in the room so suddenly restored to its original order, showed me that the dying woman had banished all the odious apparatus that surrounds a bed of sickness. She had exerted the last strength of a dying fever to dress her disordered room for the worthy reception of him whom she loved at this moment above all else.

Her haggard face, under a voluminous lace wrapper, had the greenish pallor of magnolia flowers when they first open, and looked like the first outline for a portrait of a head we love sketched in chalk on yellow-white canvas; but, to understand how deeply the vulture's talons clutched at my heart, picture this sketch with the eyes finished and full of life— hollow eyes, glittering with unwonted light in a colorless face. She no longer had the calm supremacy which she had derived from constant victory over her griefs. Her brow, the only part of her face that had preserved its fine proportions, expressed the aggressive audacity of suppressed craving and threats. In spite of the waxen hues of her drawn face, internal fires flashed forth with an effluence that resembled the quivering atmosphere over the fields on a hot day. Her hollow temples, her sunken cheeks, showed the bony structure of the face, and her white lips wore a smile that vaguely resembled the grin of a skull. Her gown, crossed over her bosom, betrayed how thin she had grown. The expression of her face plainly showed that she knew how much she was changed, and that it had brought her to despair. She was no longer the sportive Henriette, nor the sublime and saintly Madame de Mortsauf; but the nameless thing that Bossuet speaks of, struggling against annihilation, urged by hunger and cheated appetites, to a self-centred battle of life and death.

I sat down by her side and took her hand to kiss it; it was burning and dry. She read my pained surprise in the very effort I made to conceal it. Her discolored lips were stretched over her ravenous teeth in an attempt at one of those forced smiles under which we disguise alike irony and vengeance, the anticipation of pleasure, ecstasy of soul, or the fury of disappointment.

"It is death, my poor Félix," she said; "and death does not charm you! Hideous death—death which every creature, even the boldest lover, holds in horror. Love ceases here! I knew it full well. Lady Dudley will never see you shocked by such a change. Oh! why have I so longed for you, Félix? And at last you are here—and I reward your devotion by the horrible spectacle which made the Comte de Rancé turn Trappist; I, who hoped to dwell in your remembrance beautiful, noble, like an immortal lily, I destroy all your illusions. True love makes no calculations.

"But do not fly: stay. Monsieur Origet thought me much better this morning; I shall live again—be renewed under your eyes. And then, when I shall have recovered my strength a little, when I can take some food, I shall grow handsome again. I am but five-and-thirty; I may have some years of beauty yet. Happiness renews youth, and I mean to be happy. I have made the most delightful plans. We will leave them all at Clochegourde and go to Italy together."

Tears rose to my eyes; I turned away to the table, as if to admire the flowers; the abbé hastily came up to me and leaned over the nosegay: "No tears," said he in a whisper.

"What, Henriette, have you ceased to love our dear valley?" said I, as an excuse for my sudden movement.

"No," she said, touching my forehead with her lips with coaxing softness; "but without you it is fatal to me—without thee (*sans toi*)," she corrected herself, touching my ear with her hot lips to breathe the two words like a sigh.

I was dismayed by this crazy caress, which gave weight to the terrible hints of the two priests. My first surprise passed off; but though I could now exercise my reason, my will was not strong enough to restrain the nervous excitement that tormented me during this scene. I listened without replying, or rather I replied by a fixed smile and nods of assent, merely not to contradict her, as a mother treats her child. After being startled by the change in her person, I perceived that the woman who had once been so dignified in her loftiness had now, in her attitude, her voice, her manners, her looks, and her ideas, the artless simplicity of a child, the ingenuous grace, the restless movements, the absolute indifference to everything that is not itself or the object of its desire, which, in a child, cry out for protection.

Is it always thus with the dying? Do they cast off every social disguise, as a child has not yet assumed them? Or was it that the Countess, on the brink of eternity, while rejecting every human emotion but love, expressed its sweet innocence after the manner of Chloe?

"You will bring me health as you used to do, Félix?" said she, "and my valley will be good to me again. How can I help eating anything you give me? You are such a good nurse! And, beside, you are so rich in health and strength that life is contagious from you.

"My dear, prove to me that I am not to die, and to die disappointed. They think that I suffer most from thirst. Oh, yes, I am very thirsty, my dear. It hurts me dreadfully to see the waters of the Indre; but my heart suffers a more burning thirst. I thirsted for you," she said in a smothered voice, taking my hands in her burning hands and drawing me toward her to speak the words in my ear. "My agony was that I could not see you. Did you not bid me live? I will live! I will ride—I, too, I will know everything—Paris, festivities, pleasures!"

Oh, Natalie! this dreadful outcry, which the materialism of the senses makes so cold at a distance, made our ears tingle —the old priest's and mine; the tones of that beautiful voice represented the struggles of a whole life, the anguish of a true love always balked. It was indescribable torture to me and grewsome to the abbé.

The Countess stood up with an impatient effort, like a child that wants a toy. When the confessor saw his penitent in this mood, the poor man fell on his knees, clasped his hands, and began to pray.

"Yes, I will live!" she cried, making me stand, too, and leaning on me; "live on realities and not on lies. My whole life has been one of lies; I have been counting them over these last days. Is it possible that I should die, I who have not lived! I who have never been to meet any one on a heath?" She paused, seemed to listen, and smelt something through the very walls.

"Félix, the vintagers are going to dinner, and I, the mistress, am starving," she said in a childish tone. "It is the same with love; they are happy!"

"*Kyrie eleison!*" said the poor abbé, who, with clasped hands and eyes raised to heaven, was repeating litanies.

She threw her arms around my neck, clasping me with vehemence as she said—

"You shall escape me no more! I mean to be loved, I will be as mad as Lady Dudley, I will learn English to say *My Dee* very prettily." She gave me a little nod, as she had been wont to do when leaving me, to assure me that she would return immediately. "We will dine together," said she. "I will go and tell Manette——" But she stopped, overcome by weakness, and I laid her, dressed as she was, on her bed.

"Once before you carried me just so," she said, opening her eyes.

She was very light, but very hot; as I held her I felt her whole body burning. Monsieur Deslandes came in, and was astonished to find the room dressed out; on seeing me he understood everything.

"We suffer much before we die, monsieur," said she in a husky voice.

He sat down, felt her pulse, rose hastily, spoke a few words to the priest in an undertone, and left the room; I followed him.

"What are you going to do?" I asked him.

"To spare her intolerable torments," said he. "Who could have conceived of so much vitality? We cannot understand how she is still living. This is the forty-second day that the Countess has neither eaten, drunk, nor slept."

Monsieur Deslandes sent for Manette. The abbé led me into the gardens.

"Let us leave the doctor free," said he. "With Manette's help he will wrap her in opium. Well, you have heard her," he said, "if indeed it is she who yields to these mad impulses——"

"No," said I, "it is she no more."

I was stupefied with grief. As I walked on, every detail of this brief scene gained importance. I hastily went out of the little gate of the lower terrace and seated myself in the punt, where I ensconced myself to be left alone with my thoughts. I tried to tear myself away from the power by which I lived; a torture like that by which the Tartars were wont to punish adultery by wedging a limb of the guilty person into a cleft rock, and giving him a knife wherewith to free himself if he did not wish to starve; a fearful penance through which my soul was passing, since I had to amputate its nobler half. My life, too, was a failure!

Despair suggested strange ideas. Now, I would die with her; again, I would cloister myself at La Meilleraye where the Trappists had just established a retreat. My clouded eyes no longer saw external objects. I gazed at the windows of the room where Henriette lay suffering, fancying I saw the light that burned there that night when I had dedicated myself to her. Ought I not to have obeyed the simple rule of life she had laid down for me, preserving myself hers in the toil of business? Had she not enjoined on me to become a great man, so as to preserve myself from the base and degrading passions to which I had given way like every other man? Was not chastity a sublime distinction which I had failed to keep. Love, as Arabella conceived of it, suddenly filled me with disgust.

Just as I raised my stricken head, wondering whence henceforth I was to derive light and hope, a slight rustle disturbed the air; I looked toward the terrace and saw Madeleine slowly walking there, alone. While I made my way up to the terrace, intending to ask the dear child the reason of the cold look she had given me at the foot of the cross, she had seated herself on the bench; as she saw me coming she arose, affecting not to have perceived me, so as not to be alone with me; her step was rapid and significant. She hated me. She was flying from her mother's murderer. Returning to the house up the flight of steps I saw Madeleine standing motionless, listening to my approach. Jacques was sitting on a step, and his attitude was expressive of the same insensibility as had struck me when we were walking together, leaving me possessed by such ideas as we bury in a corner of the soul to return to and examine later, at leisure. I have observed that all those who are doomed to die young are calmly indifferent to burials.

I wanted to question this melancholy soul. Had Madeleine kept her thoughts to herself, or had she communicated her hatred to Jacques?

"You know," said I, to open a conversation, "that you have in me a most devoted brother."

"Your friendship is worthless to me," said he. "I shall follow my mother," and he gave me a fierce look of suffering.

"Jacques!" I cried, "you too?"

He coughed and turned away; then when he came back he hastily showed me his bloodstained handkerchief.

"You understand?" he said.

Thus each had a secret. As I afterward saw, the brother and sister avoided each other. Henriette gone, everything at Clochegourde was falling into ruin.

"Madame is asleep," Manette came to tell us, happy to see the Countess reprieved from pain.

In such fearful moments, though everybody knows the inevitable end, true affection goes crazy and clings to the smallest joys. The minutes are ages which we would gladly make ages of ease. We wish that the sufferer might sleep in roses; we would take their pain if we could; we long that the last sigh should be unconsciously breathed.

"Monsieur Deslandes had the flowers removed; they were too much for madame's nerves," said Manette.

So it was the flowers that had made her delirious; she was not guilty. The loves of earthly creatures, the joys of fruitfulness, the yearnings of plants had intoxicated her with their fragrance, and had no doubt revived the thoughts of happy love that had slumbered within her from her youth.

"Come, Monsieur Félix," said Manette, "come and look at madame; she is as lovely as an angel."

I went back to the dying woman's room just as the setting sun was gilding the gabled roofs of the Château of Azay. All was still and clear. A softened light fell upon the bed where Henriette lay lapped in opium. At this moment the body was, so to speak, annihilated; the soul alone was seen in the face, as serene as a bright sky after a storm. Blanche and Henriette—the two beautiful aspects of the same woman—appeared before me, all the more beautiful because my memory, my mind, my imagination, helping nature, restored the perfection of each feature, to which the spirit triumphant lent fitful lights, coming and going and as she breathed.

The two priests sat at the foot of the bed. The Count stood thunderstruck, recognizing the banners of death floating above that adored head. I took a seat on the sofa she had been occupying. Then we four exchanged glances in which our admiration of her heavenly beauty mingled with tears of regret.

The gleam of intelligence announced the return of God to one of His loveliest tabernacles. The Abbé de Dominis and I communicated our mutual feelings by signs. Yes, the angels kept guard over Henriette! Yes, their swords flashed above that noble brow, where we now saw the august stamp of virtue which of old had made the soul visible, as it were, holding communion with the spirits of its own sphere. The lines of her face were purified, every feature grew grander and more majestic under the invisible censers of the seraphim that watched over her. The green hues of physical torment gave way to the perfect whiteness, the dead, cold pallor of approaching death.

Jacques and Madeleine came in; Madeleine gave us all a thrill by the adoring impulse which made her fall on her knees by the bed, clasp her hands and utter the inspired exclamation: "At last! This is my mother!" Jacques was smiling: he knew that he was following his mother whither she was going.

"She is reaching the haven!" said the Abbé Birotteau.

The Abbé de Dominis looked at me, as much as to say: "Did I not tell you that the star would rise effulgent?"

Madeleine kept her eyes riveted on her mother, breathing with her breath, echoing her faint sighs, the last thread that held her to life, we counting them with dread lest it should break at each effort. Like an angel at the gates of the sanctuary the young girl was at once eager and calm, strong and prostrate.

At this moment the Angelus rang out from the village belfry; the waves of mellowed air brought up the sound in gusts, announcing that at this hour all Christendom was repeating the words spoken by the angel to the woman who made reparation for the sins of her sex. This evening the *Ave Maria* came to us as a greeting from heaven. The prophecy was so sure, the event so near, that we melted into tears.

The murmurous sounds of the evening—a melodious breeze in the leaves, the last twitter of the birds, the buzz and hum of insects, the voice of waters, the plaintive cry of the tree-frog—all the land was taking leave of the loveliest lily of this valley and her simple, rural life. The religious poetry of the scene, added to all this natural poetry, so well expressed a chant of departure that our sobs began again.

Though the bedroom door was open, we were so lost in this terrible contemplation, trying to stamp on our minds the memory of it for ever, that we did not observe all the servants of the house kneeling in a group outside and putting up fervent prayers. All these poor souls, accustomed to hope, had thought they should still keep their mistress, and these unmistakable signs overwhelmed them. At a sign from the Abbé Birotteau the old huntsman went to fetch the curé of Saché. The doctor, standing by the bed, as calm as science, holding his patient's torpid hand, had signed to the confessor to express that this sleep was the last hour of ease that was given to the recalled angel. The moment had come for administering the last sacraments of the church.

At nine o'clock she gently awoke and looked at us in mild surprise; we saw our idol in all the beauty of her best days.

"Mother, you are too beautiful to die; life and health are coming back to you!" cried Madeleine.

"My dear daughter, I shall live—but in you," said she, with a smile.

Then came heart-rending farewells from the mother to the children and from the children to the mother. Monsieur de Mortsauf kissed his wife piously on the brow. The Countess flushed as she saw me.

"Dear Félix," said she, "this is, I believe, the only grief I shall ever have given you! But forget all I may have said to you, poor crazed thing as I was!" She held out her hand; I took it to kiss, and she said with a smile of virtue—
"As of old, Félix!"

We all left the room, and remained in the drawing-room while the sick woman made her last confession. I sat down next to Madeleine. In the presence of them all she could not avoid me without being rude; but, as her mother used, she looked at no one and kept silence, without once raising her eyes to mine.

"Dear Madeleine," said I in a low voice, "what grievance have you against me? Why such coldness when, in the presence of death, we ought to be friends?"

"I fancy I can hear what my mother is saying at this

moment," replied she, putting on the expression that Ingres had given to his "Mother of God," the mourning Virgin preparing to protect the world in which her Son is about to perish.

"Then you condemn me at the moment when your mother is absolving me, supposing me to be guilty."

"You, and always you!" She spoke with unreasoning hatred, like that of a Corsican, as implacable as all judgments are that are pronounced by those who, not knowing life, admit no extenuation of the sins committed against the laws of the heart.

An hour passed in utter silence. The Abbé Birotteau came in after hearing the Comtesse de Mortsauf's general confession, and we all went into her room again. Henriette, in obedience to one of the ideas that occur to noble souls, all sisters in purpose, had been robed in a long garment that was to serve as her winding-sheet. We found her sitting up in bed, beautiful with expiation and hope. I saw in the fireplace the black ashes of my letters which had just been burnt; a sacrifice she would not make, the confessor told me, till she was at the point of death. She smiled at us all—her old smile. Her eyes, moist with tears, were, we saw, finally unsealed; she already saw the celestial joys of the promised land.

"Dear Félix," she said, holding out her hand and pressing mine. "Stay. You must be present at one of the closing scenes of my life, which will not be one of the least painful of all, but in which you are intimately concerned."

She made a sign, and the door was shut. By her desire the Count sat down; the Abbé Birotteau and I remained standing. With Manette's assistance the Countess got up and knelt down before the astonished Count, insisting on remaining there. Then, when Manette had left the room, she raised her head, which she had bent, resting it on his knees.

"Though I have always been a faithful wife to you," said

she in a broken voice, "I have, perhaps, monsieur, failed in my duties. I have prayed to God to give me strength to ask your forgiveness of my faults. I have perhaps devoted to the cares of a friendship outside my home attentions more affectionate than I owed even to you. Perhaps I have annoyed you by the comparisons you may have drawn between those cares, those thoughts, and such as I have given to you. I have known," she said in a very low voice, "a great friendship, which no one, not even he who was its object, ever wholly knew. Though I have been virtuous by all human law, a blameless wife to you, thoughts—voluntary or involuntary—have found their way into my mind and I fear I may have cherished them too gladly. But as I have always loved you truly, and have been your obedient wife, as the clouds passing across the sky have never darkened its clearness, you behold me craving your blessing with an unsullied brow. I can die without a bitter pang if I may hear from your lips one loving word for your Blanche, the mother of your children, and if you will forgive all these things, which she did not forgive herself till she had received the absolution of the tribunal to which we all bow."

"Blanche, Blanche," cried the old man, suddenly bursting into tears over his wife's head, "do you want to kill me?"

He raised her in his arms with unwonted strength, and clasping her to him, "Have I no forgiveness to ask?" he went on. "Have I not often been harsh? Are you not magnifying a child's scruples?"

"Perhaps," she answered. "But be tender, my dear, to the weakness of the dying; soothe my soul. When you are in the hour of death you will remember that I blessed you as we parted.

"Will you allow me to leave to our friend here this pledge of deep regard?" said she, pointing to a letter on the chimney-shelf. "He is now my adopted son, nothing more. The heart, my dear Count, has its bequests to make; my last words are to impress on our dear Félix certain duties to be carried out; I do not think I have expected too much of him —grant that I may not have expected too much of you in allowing myself to bequeath to him a few thoughts. I am still a woman," she said, bowing her head with sweet melancholy; "after being forgiven, I ask a favor. Read it, but not until after my death," she added, handing me the mysterious manuscript.

The Count saw his wife turn paler; he lifted her, and himself carried her to the bed, where we gathered round her.

"Felix," said she, "I may have done you some wrong. I may often have given you pain by leading you to hope for joys I dared not give; but is it not to my courage as a wife and as a mother that I owe the comfort of dying reconciled to you all? So you, too, will forgive me, you who have so often accused me, and whose injustice was a pleasure to me."

The Abbé Birotteau put his finger to his lips. At this hint the dying woman bowed her head; weakness was too much for her; she waved her hands to express that the priest, the children, and the servants were to be admitted; then, with a commanding gesture to me, she pointed to the Count, quite crushed, and her children as they entered. The sight of that father, whose insanity none knew save herself and me, the guardian now of these delicate creatures, inspired her with mute entreaties which fell on my soul like sacred fire. Before receiving extreme unction she begged pardon of her servants for being sometimes rough with them, she asked their prayers, and commended each separately to the Count. She nobly confessed that, during the past few months, she had uttered complaints little worthy of a Christian, which might have scandalized her dependents. She had been cold to her children, and had given way to unseemly sentiments; but she ascribed to her intolerable sufferings this want of submission to the will of God.

Finally, she publicly thanked the Abbé Birotteau, with touching and heartfelt effusiveness, for having shown her the vanity of all earthly things.

When she ceased speaking all began to pray, and the curé of Saché administered the viaticum. A few minutes later her breathing became difficult, a cloud dimmed her eyes, though she presently opened them again to give me a last look, and she died in the presence of us all, hearing perhaps the chorus of our sobs.

At the moment when she breathed her last sigh—the last pang of a life that was one long pain, I felt myself struck by a blow which paralyzed all my faculties.

The Count and I remained by the bed of death all night, with the two abbés and the curé, watching the dead by the light of the tapers, as she lay on the mattress, calm now, where she had suffered so much.

This was my first personal knowledge of death. I sat the whole night through, my eyes fixed on Henriette, fascinated by the pure expression given by the stilling of every tempest, by the pallor of the face in which I still read numberless affections, which could no longer respond to my love.

What majesty there is in that silence and coldness! How many reflections do they utter! What beauty in that perfect repose, what command in that motionless sleep! All the past is there, and the future has begun. Ah! I loved her as well in death as I had in life.

In the morning the Count went to bed, the three weary priests fell asleep at that hour of exhaustion, so well known to all who have watched through a night. And then, alone with her, I could, unseen, kiss her brow with all the love she had never allowed me to express.

On the next day but one, in a cool autumn morning, we followed the Countess to her last home. She was borne to the grave by the old huntsman, the two Martineaus, and Manette's husband. We went down the road I had so gleefully come up on the day when I returned to her. We crossed the valley of the Indre to reach the little graveyard of Saché—a humble village cemetery, lying at the back of the church on the brow of a hill, where she had desired to be buried, out of Christian humility, with a plain cross of black wood, like a poor laboring woman, as she had said.

When, from the middle of the valley, I caught sight of the village church and the graveyard, I was seized with a convulsive shudder. Alas! we each have a Golgotha in our life, where we leave our first three and thirty years, receiving then a spear-thrust in our heart, and feeling on our head a crown of thorns in the place of the crown of roses: this hill was to me the Mount of Expiation.

We were followed by an immense crowd that had collected to express the regrets of the whole valley where she had silently buried endless acts of benevolence. We knew from Manette, whom she trusted entirely, that she economized in dress to help the poor when her savings were insufficient. Naked children had been clothed, baby-linen supplied, mothers rescued, sacks of corn bought of the millers in winter for helpless old men, a cow bestowed on a poverty-stricken household; in short, all the good works of a Christian, a mother, a lady bountiful; and sums of money given to help loving couples to marry, or to provide substitutes for young men drawn by the conscription, touching gifts from the loving soul that had said: "The happiness of others becomes the joy of those who can no longer be happy."

These facts, talked over every evening for the last three days, had brought together a vast throng. I followed the bier with Jacques and the two abbés. According to custom neither Madeleine nor the Count were present; they remained alone at Clochegourde. Manette insisted on coming.

"Poor madame! poor madame! she is happy now!" I heard many times spoken through sobs.

At the moment when the procession turned off from the road to the hills there was a unanimous groan, mingled with weeping, that was enough to make one think that the valley had lost its soul.

The church was full of people. After the service we went to the cemetery where she was to be buried close to the cross. When I heard the stones and gravel rattle on the coffin my strength failed me. I had to ask the Martineaus to support me and they led me half-dead to the Château of Saché; there the owners politely offered me shelter, which I accepted. I confess I could not endure to return to Clochegourde; I would not go to Frapesle whence I could see Henriette's home. Here I was near her.

I spent some days in a room whose windows overlooked the tranquil and solitary coombe of which I have spoken; it is a deep ravine in the hills, overgrown with ancient oaks, and down it a torrent rushes in heavy rains. The scene was suited to the severe and solemn meditations to which I gave myself up.

In the course of the day following that fatal night, I had seen how intrusive my presence at Clochegourde would be. The Count had given way to violent feelings at Henriette's death; still, the dreadful event was expected, and in the depths of his heart there was a prepared calmness verging on indifference. I had more than once seen this, and when the Countess had given me the letter I dared not open, when she spoke of her affection for me, this man, suspicious as he was, had not given me the fulminating glance I had expected. He had ascribed his wife's words to the excessive delicacy of her conscience, which he knew to be so pure.

This selfish insensibility was but natural. The souls of these two beings had been no more wedded than their bodies, they had never had that incessant intimacy which renews feeling; they had no communion of griefs or joys, those close ties which, when they are broken, leave us sore at so many points, because they are one with every fibre, because they are rooted in every fold of the heart, while soothing the soul which sanctions every such tie.

Madeleine's hostility closed Clochegourde to me. This stern young thing was not inclined to come to terms with her aversion over her mother's grave; and I should have been dreadfully uncomfortable between the Count, who would have talked of himself, and the mistress of the house, who would have made no secret of her invincible dislike. And to live on such terms there—where of old the very flowers had caressed me, where the terrace steps were eloquent, where all my memories lent poetry to the balconies, the parapets, the balustrades and terraces, to the trees, and to every point of view; to be hated where all had been love! I could not endure the thought. So my mind was made up from the first. This then, alas! was the end of the strongest love that ever dwelt in the heart of man. In the eyes of strangers my conduct would seem blameworthy, but it had the sanction of my conscience.

This is the outcome of the finest sentiments, the greatest dramas of youth. We all set forth one fine morning, as I had started from Tours for Clochegourde, annexing the world, our hearts craving for love; then, when our treasure has been through the crucible, when we have mixed with men, and known events, it all seems unaccountably small, we find no little gold among the ashes. Such is life—life in its reality! —a great deal of aspiration, a small result.

I meditated on myself at great length, wondering what I could do after a blow that had cut down all my flowers. I determined to rush into politics and science, by the tortuous paths of ambition, to cut women out of my life entirely, and be a statesman—cold, passionless, faithful to the saint I had loved. My thoughts went far away, out of sight, while my eyes were fixed on the glorious background of golden oaks with their sombre heads and feet of bronze. I asked myself whether Henriette's virtue had not been mere ignorance, whether I was really guilty of her death. I struggled against the burden of remorse. At last, one limpid autumn day, under one of heaven's latest smiles, so lovely in Touraine, I read the letter which, by her instructions, I was not to open before her death—and I read as follows:

Madame de Mortsauf to the Vicomte Félix de Vandenesse.

"Félix, friend too much beloved, I must now open my heart to you, less to tell you how well I love you than to show you the extent of your obligations, by revealing the depth and severity of the wounds you have made in it. At this moment, when I am dropping, exhausted by the fatigues of the journey, worn out by the strokes I have received in the fight, the woman, happily, is dead, the mother alone survives. You will see, my dear, how you were the first cause of my woes. Though I afterward submitted, not unwillingly, to your blows, I am now dying of a last wound inflicted by you; but there is exquisite delight in feeling one's self crushed by the man one loves.

"Before long my sufferings will, no doubt, rob me of my strength, so I take advantage of the last gleam of intelligence to implore you, once more, to fill the place toward my children of the heart you have robbed them of. If I loved you less, I should lay this charge on you authoritatively, but I would rather leave you to assume it out of saintly repentance, and also as a perpetuation of your love for me. Has not our love been always mingled with repentant reflections and expiatory fears? And we love each other still, I know it.

"Your fault is fatal, not so much through your own act as through the importance I have given it in my own heart. Did I not tell you that I was jealous—jealous unto death? Well, I am dying. Yet, be comforted. We have satisfied human law. The church, through one of its purest speakers, has assured me that God will show mercy to those who have sacrificed their natural weakness to the commandments. So let me, my beloved, tell you all, for I would not keep a single thought from you. What I shall confess to God in my last hour, you too must know who are the king of my heart, as he is the King of Heaven.

"Until the ball given to the Duc d'Angoulême, the only one I ever went to, marriage had left me in the perfect ignorance which gives a maiden's soul its angelic beauty. I was, indeed, a mother, but love had given me none of its permitted pleasures. How was it that this happened? I know not; nor do I know by what law everything in me was changed in an instant. Do you still remember your kisses? They mastered my life, they burnt into my soul. The fire in your blood awoke the fire in mine; your youth became one with my youth; your longing entered into my heart. When I stood up so proudly, I felt a sensation for which I know no word in any language, for children have found no word to express the marriage of their eyes to the light or the kiss of life on their lips. Yes, it was indeed the sound that first aroused the echo, the light flashing in darkness, the impulse given to the universe—at least, it was as instantaneous as all these; but far more beautiful, for it was life to a soul! I understood that there was in the world something I had never known, a power more glorious than thought; that it was all thought, all power, a whole future in a common emotion. I was now no more than half a mother. This thunderbolt, falling on my heart, fired the desires that slept there unknown to me; I suddenly understood what my aunt had meant when she used to kiss my brow and say, 'Poor Henriette!'

"On my return to Clochegourde, the springtime, the first leaves, the scent of flowers, the pretty fleecy clouds, the Indre, the sky, all spoke to me in a tongue I had never yet understood, and which restored to my soul some of the impetus you had given to my senses. If you have forgotten those terrible kisses, I have never been able to efface them from my memory; I am dying of them!

"Yes, every time I have seen you since, you have revived the impression; I have thrilled from head to foot when I saw you, from the mere presentiment of your coming. Neither time nor my firm determination has been able to quench this insistent rapture. I involuntarily wondered, What then must pleasure be? Our exchange of glances, your respectful kisses on my hands, my arm resting in yours, your voice in its tender tones; in short, the veriest trifles disturbed me so violently that a cloud almost always darkened my sight, and the hum of my rebellious blood sang in my ears. Oh! if in those moments when I was colder to you than ever, you had taken me in your arms, I should have died of happiness. Sometimes I have longed that you might be overbold—but prayer soon drove out that evil thought. Your name spoken by my children filled my heart with hotter blood which mounted in a flush to my face, and I would lay snares for poor little Madeleine, to make her mention it, so dearly did I love the surge of that emotion.

"How can I tell you all? Your writing had its charms; I gazed at your letters as we study a portrait. And if from that first day you had such a fateful power over me, you may imagine, my friend, that it must have become infinite when you allowed me to read to the bottom of your soul. What ecstasy was mine when I found you so pure, so perfectly true, gifted with such great qualities, capable of such great things, and already so sorely tried! A man and a child, timid and brave! What joy it was to find that we had been dedicated to a common suffering!

"From that evening when we confided in each other, to lose you was death to me; I kept you near me out of selfishness. I was deeply touched to find that Monsieur de la Berge was certain that I should die of your absence; he then had read my heart. He decided that I was indispensable to my children and to the Count; he desired me not to forbid you the house, for I promised him to remain pure in deed and thought. 'Thought is involuntary,' he said, 'but it may be guarded in the midst of torments.' 'If I think,' said I, 'all will be lost; save me from myself! He must stay near me, but I must remain virtuous—help me!'

"The good old man, though most severe, was indulgent to my honest purpose: 'You can love him as a son, and look forward to his marrying your daughter,' he replied.

"I bravely took up a life of endurance that I might not lose you, and suffered gladly when I was sure that we were called to bear the same burden. Ah, God! I remained neutral, faithful to my husband, and never allowing you, Félix, to take a step in your dominion. The frenzy of my passions reacted on my faculties. I regarded the trials inflicted on me by Monsieur de Mortsauf as expiations, and endured them with pride to outrage my guilty wishes. Of old I had been prone to discontent, but after you came to be near us I recovered some spirit, which was a satisfaction to Monsieur de Mortsauf. But for the strength you lent me I should long ago have sunk under the inward life I have told you of. Yes, you have counted for much in the doing of my duty. It is the same with regard to the children; I felt I had robbed them of something, and I feared I could never do enough for them. Henceforth my life was one continued anguish that I cherished. Feeling myself less a mother, less a faithful wife, remorse made its abode in my heart, and for fear of failing in my duties I constantly overdid them. Hence, to save myself, I set Madeleine between us, intending you for each other, and thus raising a barrier between you and me. An unavailing barrier! Nothing could repress the stress of feeling you gave me. Absent or present your power was the same. I loved Madeleine more than Jacques, because Madeleine was to be yours.

"Still, I could not yield to my daughter without a struggle;

I told myself that I was but twenty-eight when I first met you, and that you were nearly twenty-two. I abridged distances, I allowed myself to indulge false hopes. Oh, my dear Félix, I make this confession to spare you some remorse; partly, perhaps, to show you that I was not insensible, that our sufferings in love were cruelly equalized, and that Arabella was in nothing my superior. I, too, was one of those daughters of the fallen race whom men love so well.

"There was a time when the conflict was so fearful that I wept all the night, and night after night; my hair fell out— you have that hair! You remember Monsieur de Mortsauf's illness. Your magnanimity at that time, far from raising me, made me fall lower. Alas! there was a time when I longed to throw myself into your arms as the reward of so much heroism; but that madness was brief. I laid it at the footstool of God during that mass which you refused to attend. Then Jacques' illness and Madeleine's ill health seemed to me as threats from God, who was trying thus to recall the erring sheep. And your love for that Englishwoman, natural as it was, revealed to me secrets of which I knew nothing; I loved you more than I knew I did. I lost sight of Madeleine.

"The constant agitations of this storm-tossed life, the efforts I made to subdue myself with no help but that of religion, have laid the seeds of the disease I am dying of. That dreadful blow brought on attacks of which I would say nothing. I saw in death the only possible conclusion to this unrevealed tragedy.

"I lived a whole life of passion, jealousy, fury, during the two months between the news given me by my mother of your connection with Lady Dudley and your arrival here. I wanted to go to Paris, I thirsted for murder, I longed for the death of that woman, I was insensible to the affection of my children. Prayer, which until then had been a balm to me, had no further effect on my spirit. It was jealousy that made the breach through which death entered in. Still, I maintained a placid front; yes, that time of conflict was a secret between God and me.

"When I was quite sure that I was as much loved by you as you were by me, and that it was nature only and not your heart that had made you faithless, I longed to live—but it was too late. God had taken me under His protection, in pity no doubt for a being true to herself, true to Him, whose sufferings had so constantly brought her to the gates of the sanctuary. My best-beloved, God has judged me, Monsieur de Mortsauf will no doubt forgive me, but you—will you be merciful? Will you listen to the voice which at this moment reaches you from my tomb? Will you make good the disasters for which we both are responsible—you, perhaps, less than I? You know what I would ask of you. Be to Monsieur de Mortsauf what a sister of charity is to a sick man; listen to him, love him—no one will love him. Stand between him and his children as I have always done. Fill that vacant place.

"The task will not be a long one. Jacques will soon leave home to live in Paris with his grandfather, and you have promised to guide him among the rocks of the world. As to Madeleine, she will marry; would that she might some day accept you! She is all myself, and she is also strong in the will that I lack, in the energy needed in the companion of a man whose career must carry him through the storms of political life; she is clever and clear-sighted. If your destinies were united she would be happier than her mother has been. By acquiring a right to carry on my work at Clochegourde you would wipe out such errors as have been insufficiently atoned for, though forgiven in heaven and on earth, for he is generous and will forgive.

"I am still egotistical, you see; but is not that a proof of overweening love? I want you to love me in those that belong to me. Never having been yours by right, I bequeath to you my cares and duties. If you will not marry Madeleine, at least you will secure the repose of my soul by making Monsieur de Mortsauf as happy as it is possible for him to be.

"Farewell, dear son of my heart; this is a perfectly rational leave-taking, still full of life; the adieux of a soul on which you have bestowed joys so great that you should feel no remorse over the catastrophe they have led to. And I say this as I remember that you love me; for I am going to the home of rest, a victim to duty, and—which makes me shudder—I cannot go without a regret! God knows better than I can whether I have obeyed His holy laws in the spirit. I have often stumbled, no doubt, but I never fell, and the most pressing cause of my errors lay in the temptations that surrounded me. The Lord will see me, quaking quite as much as though I had yielded.

"Once more farewell—such a farewell as I yesterday bade our beloved valley, in whose lap I shall soon be lying, and to which you will often come, will you not?

"HENRIETTE."

I sat, sunk in a gulf of meditations as I here saw the unknown depths of her life lighted up by this last flash. The clouds of my selfishness vanished. So she had suffered as much as I—more, since she was dead. She had believed that everybody else must be kind to her friend; her love had so effectually blinded her that she had never suspected her daughter's animosity. This last proof of her affection was a painful thing; poor Henriette wanted to give me Clochegourde and her daughter!

Natalie, since the dreadful day when, for the first time I entered a graveyard, following the remains of that noble creature, whom you now know, the sun has been less warm and bright, the night has been blacker, action has been less prompt with me, thought a greater burden. We lay many to rest under the earth, but some of them, especially dear, have our hearts for their winding-sheets, their memory is perpetually one with its throbs; we think of them as we breathe; they dwell in us by a beautiful law of metempsychosis peculiar to love. There is a soul within my soul. When I do any good thing, when I speak a noble word, it is that soul which speaks and acts; all that is good in me emanates from that tomb as from a lily whose scent embalms the air. Mockery, evil speaking, all you blame in me, is myself.

And now, when a cloud dims my eyes and they look up to heaven after long resting on the earth, when my lips make no response to your words or your kindness, do not henceforth ask me, "What are you thinking about?"

Dear Natalie, I had ceased writing for some little time; these reminiscences had agitated me too painfully. I must now relate the events that followed on this misfortune. They can be told in a few words. When a life consists only of action and stir it is soon recorded; but when it is spent in the loftiest regions of the soul the story must be diffuse.

Henriette's letter showed me one bright star of hope. In this tremendous shipwreck I saw an island I might reach. To live at Clochegourde with Madeleine and devote my life to her was a lot to satisfy all the ideas that tossed my soul; but I must first learn Madeleine's true opinions. I had to take leave of the Count; I went to Clochegourde to call on him, and met him on the terrace. There we walked together for some time.

At first he spoke of his wife as a man who understood the extent of his loss, and all the ruin it had wrought in his home life. But after that first cry of sorrow, he was evidently more anxious about the future than about the present. He was afraid of his daughter, who was not, he said, so gentle as her mother. Madeleine's firm temper and a tinge of something heroical, mingling in her with her mother's gracious nature, terrified the old man, accustomed as he was to Henriette's tender kindness; he foresaw meeting a will which nothing could bend. Still, what comforted him in his loss was the certainty of joining his wife ere long; the agitations and grief of the last few days had increased his malady and brought on his old pains; the conflict he foresaw between his authority as the father and his daughter's as the mistress of the house would fill his last days with bitterness, for in cases where he could contend with his wife he would have to give way to his child. And then his son would go away, his daughter would marry—what sort of son-in-law should he have?

In the course of an hour, while he talked of nothing but himself, claiming my friendship for his wife's sake, I clearly saw before me the grandiose figure of the *émigré*, one of the most impressive types of our century. In appearance he was frail and broken, but life still clung to him by reason of his simple habits and agricultural occupations.

At this moment, when I write, he still lives.

Though Madeleine could see us pacing the terrace, she did not come down; she came out to the steps and went in again several times, to mark her disdain of me. I seized a moment when she had come out to beg the Count to go up to the house; I wanted to speak to Madeleine, and I made a pretext of a last request left by the Countess—I had no other way of seeing her; the Count went to fetch her, and left us together on the terrace.

"Dear Madeleine," said I, "I must speak a word with you. Was it not here that your mother used to listen to me when she had less to blame me for than the circumstances of her life? My life and happiness are, as you know, bound up with this spot, and you banish me by the coldness you have assumed instead of the brotherly regard which used to unite us and which death has made closer by a common sorrow. Dear Madeleine, for you I would this instant give my life without any hope of reward, without your knowing it even, for so truly do we love the children of the women who have been good to us in their lifetime—you know nothing of the scheme which your adored mother had cherished for the last seven years, and which may perhaps affect your views—but I will take no advantage of that! All I beseech of you is that you will not deprive me of the right of coming to breathe the air on this terrace, and to wait until time has modified your ideas of social life. At this moment I would not shock them for the world. I respect the grief that misleads you, for it deprives me, too, of the power of judging fairly of the position in which I find myself. The saint who is now watching over us will approve of the reserve I maintain when I only ask you to remain neutral as between your own feelings and myself.

"I love you too truly, in spite of the aversion you show for me, to lay a proposal before the Count which he would hail with eager satisfaction. Be free. But, by-and-by, consider that you will never know anybody in the world so well as you know me, that no man can bear in his heart feelings more devoted——"

So far Madeleine had listened with downcast eyes, but she stopped me with a gesture.

"Monsieur," she said in a voice tremulous with agitation, "I, too, know all your mind. But I can never change in feeling toward you, and I would rather drown myself in the Indre than unite myself with you. Of myself I will not speak, but if my mother's name can still influence you, in her name I beg you never to come to Clochegourde so long as I am here. The mere sight of you occasions me such distress as I cannot describe, and I shall never get over it."

She bowed to me with much dignity and went up to the house, never looking back; as rigid as her mother had been once, and once only, and quite pitiless. The girl's clear sight had, though only of late, seen to the bottom of her mother's heart, and her hatred of the man who seemed to her so fatal was increased, perhaps, by some regret at her own innocent complicity.

Here was an impassable gulf. Madeleine hated me without

choosing to ascertain whether I was the cause or the victim of her griefs; and she would, I dare say, have hated both her mother and me if we had been happy. So this fair castle of promised happiness was in ruins.

I alone was ever to know the whole life of this noble unknown woman, I alone was in the secret of her feelings. I alone had studied her soul in its complete grandeur. Neither her mother, nor her father, nor her husband, nor her children had understood her.

It is a strange thing! I can turn over that pile of ashes, and take pleasure in spreading them before you; we may all find among them something of what has been dearest to us. How many families have their Henriette! How many noble creatures depart from earth without having met with an intelligent friend to tell their story, and to sound their hearts, and measure their depth and height! This is human life in its stern reality; and often mothers know no more of their children than the children know of them. And it is the same with married couples, lovers, brothers and sisters. Could I foresee that the day would come when, over my father's grave, I should go to law with Charles de Vandenesse, the brother to whose advancement I had so largely contributed? Good heavens! How much may be learned from the simplest tale!

When Madeleine had disappeared into the house I came away heart-broken, took leave of my hospitable friends, and set out for Paris along the right bank of the Indre—the road by which I had come down the valley for the first time. I was sad enough as I rode through the village of Pont du Ruan. And yet I was now rich; political life smiled upon me; I was no longer the weary wayfarer of eighteen hundred and fourteen. Then my heart had been full of desires, now my eyes were full of tears; then I had to fill up my life, now I felt it a desert. I was still quite young—twenty-nine—and my heart was crushed. A few years had been enough to rob the landscape of its pristine glory and to disgust me with life. You may conceive then of my emotion when, on looking back, I discerned Madeleine on the terrace.

Wholly possessed by absorbing sorrow, I never thought of the end of my journey. Lady Dudley was far from my mind when I found that I had unconsciously entered her courtyard. The blunder once made, I could but act it out.

My habits in the house were quite marital; I went upstairs, gloomy in anticipation of a vexatious rupture. If you have ever understood the character of Lady Dudley you can imagine how disconcerted I felt when her butler showed me, as I was, in traveling dress, into a drawing-room where she sat splendidly dressed with a party of five visitors. Lord Dudley, one of the most noteworthy of English statesmen, was standing in front of the fire—elderly, starch, arrogant, cold, with the satirical expression he must wear in the House; he smiled on hearing my name. With their mother were Arabella's two boys, astonishingly like de Marsay, one of the nobleman's natural sons, who was sitting on the sofa by the Marchioness.

Arabella, as soon as she saw me, assumed a lofty air, and stared at my traveling cap as if she were on the point of inquiring what had brought me to see her. She looked at me from head to foot, as she might have done at some country 'squire just introduced to her. As to our intimacy, our eternal passion, her vows that she must die if ever I ceased to love her—all the phantasmagoria of Armida—it had vanished like a dream. I had never held her hand, I was a stranger, she did not know me!

I was startled, in spite of the diplomatic coolness I was beginning to acquire; and any man in my place would have been no less so. De Marsay smiled as he looked at his boots, examining them with obvious significance.

I made up my mind at once. From any other woman I would have submissively accepted my discomfiture; but enraged at finding this heroine, who was to die of love, alive and well, after laughing to scorn the woman who had died, I determined to meet insolence with insolence. She knew of Lady Brandon's wreck; to remind her of it would be to stab her to the heart, even if it should turn the edge of the dagger.

"Madame," said I, "you will forgive me for coming to you in so cavalier a manner when I tell you that I have this instant arrived from Touraine, and that Lady Brandon gave me a message for you which allows of no delay. I feared I might find that you had started for Lancashire; but since you are not leaving Paris, I await your orders at the hour when you will condescend to receive me."

She bowed and I left the room.

From that day I have never seen her excepting in company, where we exchange friendly bows, with sometimes a repartee. I rally her about the inconsolable women of Lancashire, and she retorts about the Frenchwomen who do credit to their broken hearts by attacks of dyspepsia. Thanks to her good offices I have a mortal foe in de Marsay, whom she makes much of; and I, in return, say she has married father and son.

Thus my disaster was complete.

I took up the plan of life I had decided on during my retirement at Saché. I threw myself into hard work; I took up science, literature, and politics. On the accession of Charles X., who abolished the post I had filled under the late King, I made diplomacy my career. From that hour I vowed never to pay any attention to a woman, however beautiful, witty, or affectionate she might be. This conduct was a wonderful success. I gained incredible peace of mind, great powers of work, and I learned that women waste men's lives and think they have indemnified them by a few gracious words.

However, all my fine resolutions have come to nothing— you know how and why.

Dearest Natalie, in relating my whole life without reserve or concealment, as I should to myself, in confessing to you feelings in which you had no part, I may perhaps have vexed some tender spot of your jealous and sensitive heart. But what would infuriate a vulgar woman will be, to you, I am sure, a fresh reason for loving me. The noblest women have a sublime part to play toward suffering and aching souls, that of a sister of mercy who dresses their wounds, of the mother who forgives her children. Nor are artists and poets the only sufferers. Men who live for their country, for the future of nations, as they widen the circle of their passions and their thoughts, often find themselves in cruel solitude. They long to feel that by their side is some pure and devoted love. Believe me, they will know its greatness and its value.

To-morrow I shall know whether I have made a mistake in loving you.

To Monsieur le Comte Félix de Vandenesse.

" Dear Count, you received as you tell me, a letter from poor Madame de Mortsauf which has been of some use in guiding you through the world, a letter to which you owe your high fortunes. Allow me to finish your education.

"I implore you to divest yourself of an odious habit. Do not imitate certain widows who are always talking of their first husband and throwing the virtues of the dear departed in the teeth of the second. I, dear Count, am a Frenchwoman; I should wish to marry the whole of the man I loved; now I really cannot marry Madame de Mortsauf.

"After reading your narrative with the attention it deserves—and you know what interest I feel in you—it strikes me that you must have bored Lady Dudley very considerably by holding up to her Madame de Mortsauf's perfections, while deeply wounding the Countess by expatiating on the various resources of English love-making. You have now failed in tact toward me, a poor creature who can boast of no merit but that of having attracted your liking; you have implied that I do not love you as much as either Henriette or Arabella. I confess my deficiencies. I know them; but why make me feel them so cruelly?

"Shall I tell you whom I pity? The fourth woman you may love. She will inevitably be required to hold her own against three predecessors; so, in your interest as much as in hers, I must warn you against the perils of your memory.

"I renounce the laborious honor of loving you. I should require too many catholic or anglican virtues, and I have no taste for fighting ghosts. The virtues of the Virgin of Clochegourde would reduce the most self-confident woman to despair; and your dashing horsewoman discourages the boldest dreams of happiness. Do what she may, no woman can hope to give you satisfaction in proportion to her ambition. Neither heart nor senses can ever triumph over your reminiscences. You have forgotten that we often ride out together. I have not succeeded in warming up the sun that was chilled by your Henriette's decease; you would shiver by my side.

"My friend—for you will always be my friend—beware of repeating these confidences which strip your disenchantment bare, dishearten love, and compel a woman to doubt her powers. Love, my dear friend, lives on mutual trustfulness. The woman who, before she says a word or mounts her horse, stops to ask herself whether a heavenly Henriette did not speak better, or a horsewoman like Arabella did not display more grace, that woman, take my word for it, will have a trembling tongue and knees.

"You made me wish that I might receive some of your intoxicating nosegays—but you say you will make no more. Thus it is with a hundred things you no longer dare do, with thoughts and enjoyments which can never again be yours. No woman, be very sure, would choose to dwell in your heart elbowing the corpse you cherish there.

"You beseech me to love you out of Christian charity. I could, I own, do much out of charity—everything but love.

"You are sometimes dull and tiresome; you dignify your gloom by the name of melancholy, well and good; but it is intolerable and fills the woman who loves you with cruel anxieties. I have come across that saint's tomb too often standing between us; I have reflected, and I have concluded that I have no wish to die like her. If you exasperated Lady Dudley, a woman of the first distinction, I, who have not her furious passions, fear I should even sooner grow cold.

"Put love out of the question as between you and me, since you no longer find happiness but with the dead, and let us be friends; I am willing.

"Why, my dear Count, you began by loving an adorable woman, a perfect mistress, who undertook to make your fortune, who procured you a peerage, who loved you to distraction—and you made her die of grief! Why, nothing can be more monstrous. Among the most ardent and the most luckless youths who drag their ambitions over the pavements of Paris, is there one who would not have behaved himself for ten years to obtain half the favors which you failed to recognize? When a man is so beloved, what more does he want?

"Poor woman! she suffered much; and you, when you have made a few sentimental speeches, think you have paid your debt over her bier. This, no doubt, is the prize that awaits my affection for you. Thank you, dear Count, but I desire no rival on either side of the grave.

"When a man has such a crime on his conscience, the least he can do is not to tell!

"I asked you a foolish question; it was in my part as a woman, a daughter of Eve. It was your part to calculate the results of the answer. You ought to have deceived me; I should have thanked you for it later. Have you understood wherein lies the merit of men who are liked by women? Do you not perceive how magnanimous they are when they swear that they have never loved before, that this is their first love? Your programme is impossible. Lady Dudley and Madame de Mortsauf in one! Why, my dear friend, you might as well try to combine fire and water. Do you know nothing of women? They are as they are; they must have the defects of their qualities.

"You met Lady Dudley too soon to appreciate her, and the evil you say of her seems to me the revenge of your wounded vanity; you understood Madame de Mortsauf too late'; you punished each for not being the other; what then would become of me, being neither one nor the other?

"I like you well enough to have reflected very seriously on your future prospects. Your look, as of the Knight of the Rueful Countenance, has always interested me (and I believe in the constancy of melancholy men), but I did not know that you had begun your career in the world by killing the loveliest and most virtuous of women. Well, I have been considering what remains for you to do; I have thought it out. I think you had better marry some Mrs. Shandy, who will know nothing of love or passion, who will never trouble her head about Lady Dudley or Madame de Mortsauf, nor about those spells of dullness which you call melancholy—when you are as amusing as a rainy day—and who will be the worthy sister of charity you long for.

"As to love—thrilling at a word, knowing how to wait for happiness, how to give and take it, feeling the myriad storms of passion, making common cause with the little vanities of the woman you love—my dear Count, give it up. You have followed the advice of your good angel too exactly; you have avoided young women so effectually that you know nothing about them. Madame de Mortsauf was wise in getting you to a front place at once; every woman would have been against you and you would never have reached one. It is too late now to begin your training, to learn to say the things we like to hear, to be noble at appropriate moments, to worship our triviality when we have a fancy to be trivial. We are not such simpletons as you think us. When we love, we set the man of our choice above all else. Anything that shakes our faith in our own supremacy shakes our love. By flattering us, you flatter yourselves.

"If you want to live in the world and mingle on equal terms with women, conceal with care all you have told me; they do not care to strew the flowers of their affections on stones or lavish their tender caresses to heal a wounded heart. Every woman will at once discern the shallowness of your heart and you will be constantly more unhappy. Very few will be frank enough to tell you what I have told you, or good-natured enough to dismiss you without rancor and offer you their friendship, as she now does who still remains your sincere friend.

"NATALIE DE MANERVILLE."

PARIS, *October*, 1835.

ANOTHER STUDY OF WOMAN.

(*L'Autre Étude de Femme.*)

Translated by CLARA BELL.

To Leon Gozlan as a Token of Literary Good-fellowship.

AT Paris there are almost always two separate parties going on at every ball and rout. First, an official party, composed of the persons invited, a fashionable and much-bored circle. Each one grimaces for his neighbor's eye; most of the younger women are there for one person only; when each woman has assured herself that for that one she is the handsomest woman in the room, and that the opinion is perhaps shared by a few others, a few insignificant phrases are exchanged, such as: "Do you think of going away soon to La Crampade?" "How well Madame de Portenduère sang!" "Who is the little woman with such a load of diamonds?" Or, after firing off some smart epigrams, which give transient pleasure and leave wounds that rankle long, the groups thin out, the mere lookers-on go away, and the wax-lights burn down to the sconces.

The mistress of the house then waylays a few artists, amusing people or intimate friends, saying, "Do not go yet; we will have a snug little supper." These collect in some small, cozy room. The second, the real party, now begins; a party where, as of old, every one can hear what is said, conversation is general, each one is bound to be witty, and to contribute to the amusement of all. Everything is made to tell, honest laughter takes the place of the gloom which in company saddens the prettiest faces. In short, where the rout ends pleasure begins.

The rout, a cold display of luxury, a review of self-conceits in full dress, is one of those English inventions which tend to *mechanize* other nations. England seems bent on seeing the whole world as dull as itself—and dull in the same way. So this second party is, in some French houses, a happy protest on the part of the old spirit of our light-hearted people. Only, unfortunately, so few houses protest; and the reason is a simple one. If we no longer have many suppers nowadays, it is because never, under any rule, have there been fewer men placed, established, and successful than under the reign of Louis Philippe, when the revolution began again, lawfully. Everybody is on the march some whither, or trotting at the heels of Fortune. Time has become the costliest commodity, so no one can afford the lavish extravagance of going home to-morrow morning and getting up late. Hence, there is no second soiree now but at the houses of women rich enough to entertain, and since July, 1830, such women may be counted in Paris.

In spite of the covert opposition of the Faubourg Saint-Germain, two or three women, among them Madame d'Espard and Mademoiselle des Touches, have not chosen to give up the share of influence they exercised in Paris and have not closed their houses.

The salon of Mademoiselle des Touches is noted in Paris as being the last refuge where the old French wit has found a home, with its reserved depths, its myriad subtle byways, and its exquisite politeness. You will there still find grace of manner notwithstanding the conventionalities of courtesy, perfect freedom of talk notwithstanding the reserve which is natural to persons of breeding, and, above all, a liberal flow of ideas. No one there thinks of keeping his thought for a play; and no one regards a story as material for a book. In short, the hideous skeleton of literature at bay never stalks there on the prowl for a clever sally or an interesting subject.

The memory of one of these evenings especially dwells

with me, less by reason of a confidence in which the illustrious de Marsay opened up one of the deepest recesses of woman's heart, than on account of the reflections to which his narrative gave rise, as to the changes that have taken place in the Frenchwoman since the fateful revolution of July.

On that evening chance had brought together several persons whose indisputable merits have won them European reputations. This is not a piece of flattery addressed to France, for there were a good many foreigners present. And, indeed, the men who most shone were not the most famous. Ingenious repartee, acute remarks, admirable banter, pictures sketched with brilliant precision, all sparkled and flowed without elaboration, were poured out without disdain, but without effort, and were exquisitely expressed and delicately appreciated. The men of the world especially were conspicuous for their really artistic grace and spirit.

Elsewhere in Europe you will find elegant manners, cordiality, genial fellowship, and knowledge; but only in Paris, in this drawing-room, and those to which I have alluded, does the particular wit abound which gives an agreeable and changeful unity to all these social qualities, an indescribable river-like flow which makes this profusion of ideas, of definitions, of anecdotes, of historical incidents, meander with ease. Paris, the capital of taste, alone possesses the science which makes conversation a tourney in which each type of wit is condensed into a shaft, each speaker utters his phrase and casts his experience in a word, in which every one finds amusement, relaxation, and exercise. Here, then, alone, will you exchange ideas; here you need not, like the dolphin in the fable, carry a monkey on your shoulders; here you will be understood, and will not risk staking your gold-pieces against base metal.

Here, again, secrets neatly betrayed, and talk, light or deep, play and eddy, changing their aspect and hue at every phrase. Eager criticism and crisp anecdotes lead on from one to the next. All eyes are listening, a gesture asks a question, and an expressive look gives the answer. In short, and in a word, everything is wit and mind.

The phenomenon of speech, which, when duly studied and well handled, is the power of the actor and the story-teller, had never so completely bewitched me. Nor was I alone under the influence of its spell; we all spent a delightful evening. The conversation had drifted into anecdote, and brought out in its rushing course some curious confessions, several portraits, and a thousand follies, which make this enchanting improvisation impossible to record; still, by setting these things down in all their natural freshness and abruptness, their elusive divarications, you may perhaps feel the charm of a real French evening, taken at the moment when the most engaging familiarity makes each one forget his own interests, his personal conceit, or, if you like, his pretensions.

At about two in the morning, as supper ended, no one was left sitting around the table but intimate friends, proved by an intercourse of fifteen years, and some persons of great taste and good breeding, who knew the world. By tacit agreement, perfectly carried out, at supper every one renounced his pretensions to importance. Perfect equality set the tone. But indeed there was no one present who was not very proud of being himself.

Mademoiselle des Touches always insists on her guests remaining at table until they leave, having frequently remarked the change which a move produces in the spirit of a party. Between the dining-room and the drawing-room the charm is destroyed. According to Sterne, the ideas of an author after shaving are different from those he had before. If Sterne is right, may it not be boldly asserted that the frame of mind of a party at table is not the same as that of the same persons returned to the drawing-room? The new atmosphere is not heady, the eye no longer contemplates the brilliant disorder of the dessert, lost are the happy effects of that laxness of mood, that benevolence which comes over us while we remain in the humor peculiar to the well-filled man, settled comfortably on one of the springy chairs which are made in these days. Perhaps we are more ready to talk face to face with the dessert and in the society of good wine, during the delightful interval when every one may sit with an elbow on the table and his head resting on his hand. Not only does every one like to talk then, but also to listen. Digestion, which is almost always attent, is loquacious or silent, as the various characters differ. Then every one finds his opportunity.

Was not this preamble necessary to make you know the charm of the narrative, by which a celebrated man, now dead, depicted the innocent jesuitry of woman, painting it with the subtlety peculiar to persons who have seen much of the world, and which makes statesmen such delightful story-tellers when, like Prince Talleyrand and Prince Metternich, they vouchsafe to tell a story?

De Marsay, prime minister for some six months, had already given proofs of superior capabilities. Those who had known him long were not indeed surprised to see him display all the talents and various aptitudes of a statesman; still it might yet be a question whether he would prove to be a solid politician, or had merely been moulded in the fire of circumstance. This question had just been asked by a man whom he had made préfet, a man of wit and observation, who had for a long time been a journalist, and who admired de Marsay without infusing into his admiration that dash of acrid criticism by which, in Paris, one superior man excuses himself from admiring another.

"Was there ever," said he, "in your former life, any event, any thought or wish which told you what your vocation was?" asked Emile Blondet; "for we all, like Newton, have our apple, which falls and leads us to the spot where our faculties develop——"

"Yes," said de Marsay; "I will tell you about it."

Pretty women, political dandies, artists, old men, de Marsay's intimate friends—all settled themselves comfortably, each in his favorite attitude, to look at the minister. Need it be said that the servants had left, that the doors were shut, and the curtains drawn over them? The silence was so complete that the murmurs of the coachmen's voices could be heard from the courtyard, and the pawing and champing made by horses when asking to be taken back to their stable.

"The statesman, my friends, exists by one single quality," said the minister, playing with his gold and mother-of-pearl dessert knife. "To wit: the power of always being master of himself; of profiting more or less, under all circumstances, by every event, however fortuitous; in short, of having within himself a cold and disinterested other self, who looks on as a spectator at all the chances of life, noting our passions and our sentiments, and whispering to us in every case the judgment of a sort of moral ready-reckoner."

"That explains why a statesman is so rare a thing in France," said old Lord Dudley.

"From a sentimental point of view, this is horrible," the minister went on. "Hence, when such a phenomenon is seen in a young man—Richelieu, who, when warned overnight by a letter of Concini's peril, slept till midday, when his benefactor was to be killed at ten o'clock—or say Pitt, or Napoleon—he is a monster. I became such a monster at a very early age, thanks to a woman."

"I fancied," said Madame de Montcornet with a smile, "that more politicians were undone by us than we could make."

"The monster of which I speak is a monster just because he withstands you," replied de Marsay, with a little ironical bow.

"If this is a love story," the Baronne de Nucingen interposed, "I request that it may not be interrupted by any reflections."

"Reflection is so antipathetic to it!" cried Joseph Bridau.

"I was seventeen," de Marsay went on; "the restoration was being consolidated; my old friends know how impetuous and fervid I was then. I was in love for the first time, and I was—I may say so now—one of the handsomest young fellows in Paris. I had youth and good looks, two advantages due to good fortune, but of which we are all as proud as of a conquest. I must be silent as to the rest. Like all youths, I was in love with a woman six years older than myself. No one of you here," said he, looking carefully round the table, "can suspect her name or recognize her. Ronquerolles alone, at the time, ever guessed my secret. He has kept it well, but I should have feared his smile. However, he is gone," said the minister, looking around.

"He would not stay to supper," said Madame de Nucingen.

"For six months, possessed by my passion," de Marsay went on, "but incapable of suspecting that it had overmastered me, I had abandoned myself to that rapturous idolatry which is at once the triumph and the frail joy of the young. I treasured *her* old gloves; I drank an infusion of the flowers *she* had worn; I got out of bed at night to go and gaze at *her* window. All my blood rushed to my heart when I inhaled the perfume she used. I was miles away from knowing that woman is a stove with a marble casing."

"Oh! spare us your terrible verdicts," cried Madame de Montcornet with a smile.

"I believe I should have crushed with my scorn the philosopher who first uttered this terrible but profoundly true thought," said de Marsay. "You are all far too keen-sighted for me to say any more on that point. These few words will remind you of your own follies.

"A great lady, if ever there was one; a widow without

children—oh! all was perfect—my idol would shut herself up to mark my linen with her hair; in short, she responded to my madness by her own. And how can we fail to believe in passion when it has the guarantee of madness?

"We each devoted all our minds to concealing a love so perfect and so beautiful from the eyes of the world; and we succeeded. And what charm we found in our escapades! Of her I will say nothing. She was perfection then, and to this day is considered one of the most beautiful women in Paris; but at that time a man would have endured death to win one of her glances. She had been left with an amount of fortune sufficient for a woman who loved and was adored; but the restoration, to which she owed renewed lustre, made it seem inadequate in comparison with her name. In my position I was so fatuous as never to dream of a suspicion. Though my jealousy would have been of a hundred and twenty Othello-power, that terrible passion slumbered in me as gold in the nugget. I would have ordered my servant to thrash me if I had been so base as ever to doubt the purity of that angel—so fragile and so strong, so fair, so artless, pure, spotless, and whose blue eye allowed my gaze to sound it to the very depths of her heart with adorable submissiveness. Never was there the slightest hesitancy in her attitude, her look, or word; always white and fresh and ready for the Beloved like the Oriental Lily of the 'Song of Songs!' Ah! my friends!" sadly exclaimed the minister, grown young again, "a man must hit his head very hard on the marble to dispel that poem!"

This cry of nature, finding an echo in the listeners, spurred the curiosity he had excited in them with so much skill.

"Every morning, riding Sultan—the fine horse you sent me from England," de Marsay went on, addressing Lord Dudley—"I rode past her open carriage, the horses' pace being intentionally reduced to a walk, and read the order of the day signaled to me by the flowers of her bouquet in case we were unable to exchange a few words. Though we saw each other almost every evening in society and she wrote to me every day, to deceive the curious and mislead the observant we had adopted a scheme of conduct: never to look at each other; to avoid meeting; to speak ill of each other. Self-admiration, swagger, or playing the disdained swain—all these old manœuvres are not to compare on either part with a false passion professed for an indifferent person and an air of indifference toward the true idol. If two lovers will only play that game the world will always be deceived; but then they must be very secure of each other.

"Her stalking-horse was a man in high favor, a courtier, cold and sanctimonious, whom she never received at her own house. This little comedy was performed for the benefit of simpletons and drawing-room circles, who laughed at it. Marriage was never spoken of between us; six years' difference of age might give her pause; she knew nothing of my fortune, of which, on principle, I have always kept the secret. I, on my part, fascinated by her wit and manners, by the extent of her knowledge and her experience of the world, would have married her without a thought. At the same time, her reserve charmed me. If she had been the first to speak of marriage in a certain tone, I might perhaps have noted it as vulgar in that accomplished soul.

"Six months, full and perfect—a diamond of the purest water! That has been my portion of love in this base world.

"One morning, attacked by the feverish stiffness which marks the beginning of a cold, I wrote her a line to put off one of these secret festivals which are buried under the roofs of Paris like pearls in the sea. No sooner was the letter sent than remorse seized me: she will not believe that I am ill! thought I. She was wont to affect jealousy and suspiciousness. When jealousy is genuine," said de Marsay, interrupting himself, "it is the visible sign of a unique passion."

"Why?" asked the Princess de Cadignan eagerly.

"Unique and true love," said de Marsay, "produces a sort of corporeal apathy attuned to the contemplation into which one falls. Then the mind complicates everything; it works on itself, pictures its fancies, turns them into reality and torment; and such jealousy is as delightful as it is distressing."

A foreign minister smiled as, by the light of memory, he felt the truth of this remark.

"Beside," de Marsay went on, "I said to myself, why miss a happy hour? Was it not better to go, even though feverish? And then, if she learns that I am ill, I believe her capable of hurrying here and compromising herself. I made an effort; I wrote a second letter and carried it myself, for my confidential servant was now gone. The river lay between us. I had to cross Paris; but at last, within a suitable distance of her house, I caught sight of a messenger; I charged him to have the note sent up to her at once, and I had the happy idea of driving past her door in a hackney cab to see whether she might not by chance receive the two letters together. At the moment when I arrived it was two o'clock; the great gate opened to admit a carriage. Whose? That of the stalking-horse!

"It is fifteen years since—well, even while I tell the tale, I, the exhausted orator, the minister dried up by the friction of public business, I still feel a surging in my heart and the hot blood about my diaphragm. At the end of an hour I passed once more; the carriage was still in the courtyard! My note no doubt was in the porter's hands. At last, at half-past three, the carriage drove out. I could observe my rival's expression; he was grave, and did not smile; but he was in love, and no doubt there was business in hand.

"I went to keep my appointment; the queen of my heart met me. I saw her calm, pure, serene. And here I must confess that I have always thought that Othello was not only stupid, but showed very bad taste. Only a man who is half a negro could behave so: indeed Shakespeare felt this when he called his play 'The Moor of Venice.' The sight of the woman we love is such a balm to the heart that it must dispel anguish, doubt, and sorrow. All my rage vanished. I could smile again. Hence this cheerfulness, which at my age now would be the most atrocious dissimulation, was the result of my youth and my love. My jealousy once buried, I had the power of observation. My ailing condition was evident; the horrible doubts that had fermented in me increased it. At last I found an opening for putting in these words: 'You have had no one with you this morning?' making a pretext of the uneasiness I had felt in the fear lest she should have disposed of her time after receiving my first note. 'Ah!' she exclaimed, 'only a man could have such ideas! As if I could think of anything but your suffering. Till the moment when I received your second note I could think only of how I could really contrive to go to see you.' 'And you were alone?' 'Alone,' said she, looking at me with a face of innocence so perfect that it must have been his distrust of such a look as that which made the Moor kill Desdemona. As she lived alone in the house, the word was a fearful lie. One single lie destroys the absolute confidence which to some souls is the very foundation of happiness.

"To explain to you what passed in me at that moment it must be assumed that we have an internal self of which the exterior *I* is but the husk; that this self, as brilliant as light, is as fragile as a shade—well, that beautiful self was in me thenceforth for ever shrouded in crape. Yes; I felt a cold and fleshless hand cast over me the winding-sheet of experience, dooming me to the eternal mourning into which the first betrayal plunges the soul. As I cast my eyes down that she might not observe my dizziness, this proud thought somewhat restored my strength: 'If she is deceiving you she is unworthy of you!'

"I ascribed my sudden reddening and the tears which

started to my eyes to an attack of pain, and the sweet creature insisted on driving me home with the blinds of the cab drawn. On the way she was full of a solicitude and tenderness that might have deceived the Moor of Venice whom I have taken as a standard of comparison. Indeed, if that great child were to hesitate two seconds longer, every intelligent spectator feels that he would ask Desdemona's forgiveness. Thus, killing the woman is the act of a boy. She wept as we parted, so much was she distressed at being unable to nurse me herself. She wished she were my valet, in whose happiness she found a cause of envy, and all this was as elegantly expressed, oh! as Clarissa might have written in her happiness. There is always a precious ape in the prettiest and most angelic woman!"

At these words all the women looked down as if hurt by this brutal truth so brutally stated.

"I will say nothing of the night nor the week I spent," de Marsay went on. "I discovered that I was a statesman."

It was so well said that we all uttered an admiring exclamation.

"As I thought over the really cruel vengeance to be taken on a woman," said de Marsay, continuing his story, "with infernal ingenuity—for, as we had loved each other, some terrible and irreparable revenges were possible—I despised myself, I felt how common I was, I insensibly formulated a horrible code—that of indulgence. In taking vengeance on a woman, do we not in fact admit that there is but one for us, that we cannot do without her? And, then, is revenge the way to win her back! If she is not indispensable, if there are other women in the world, why not grant her the right to change which we assume?

"'This, of course, applies only to passion; in any other sense it would be socially wrong. Nothing more clearly proves the necessity for indissoluble marriage than the instability of passion. The two sexes must be chained up, like wild beasts as they are, by inevitable law, deaf and mute. Eliminate revenge and infidelity in love is nothing. Those who believe that for them there is but one woman in the world must be in favor of vengeance, and then there is but one form of it—that of Othello.

"Mine was different."

The words produced in each of us the imperceptible movement which newspaper writers represent in parliamentary reports by the words: "Great sensation."

"Cured of my cold, and of my pure, absolute, divine love, I flung myself into an adventure, of which the heroine was charming and of a style of beauty utterly opposed to that of my deceiving angel. I took care not to quarrel with this clever woman who was so good an actress, for I doubt whether true love can give such gracious delights as those lavished by such a dexterous fraud. Such refined hypocrisy is as good as virtue. I am not speaking to you Englishwomen, my lady," said the minister suavely, addressing Lady Barimore, Lord Dudley's daughter. "I tried to be the same lover.

"I wished to have some of my hair worked up for my new angel so I went to a skilled artist, who at that time dwelt in the Rue Boucher. The man had a monopoly of capillary keepsakes, and I mention his address for the benefit of those who have not much hair; he has plenty of every kind and every color. After I had explained my order he showed me his work. I then saw achievements of patience surpassing those which the story books ascribe to fairies, or which are executed by prisoners. He brought me up to date as to the caprices and fashions governing the use of hair. 'For the last year,' said he, 'there has been a rage for marking linen with hair; happily I had a fine collection of hair and skilled needlewomen.' On hearing this a suspicion flashed upon me; I took out my handkerchief and said, 'So this was done in your shop, with false hair?' He looked at the handkerchief, and said, 'Ay! that lady was very particular, she insisted on veri-

"WHEN ARE YOU TO MARRY THE DUKE?"

fying the tint of the hair. My wife herself marked those handkerchiefs. You have there, sir, one of the finest pieces of work we have ever executed.' Before this last ray of light I might have believed something—might have taken a woman's word. I left the store still having faith in pleasure, but where love was concerned I was as atheistical as a mathematician.

"Two months later I was sitting by the side of the ethereal being in her boudoir, on her sofa; I was holding one of her hands—they were very beautiful—and we scaled the Alps of sentiment, culling their sweetest flowers, and pulling off the daisy-petals; there is always a moment when one pulls daisies to pieces, even if it is in a drawing-room and there are no daisies. At the intensest moment of tenderness and when we are most in love, love is so well aware of its own short duration that we are irresistibly urged to ask, 'Do you love me? Will you love me always?' I seized the elegiac moment, so warm, so flowery, so full-blown, to lead her to tell her most delightful lies, in the enchanting language of rapturous exaggeration and high-flown poetry peculiar to love. Charlotte displayed her choicest allurements: She could not live without me; I was to her the only man in the world; she feared to weary me, because my presence bereft her of all her wits; with me all her faculties were lost in love; she was indeed too tender to escape alarms; for the last six months she had been seeking some way to bind me to her eternally, and God alone knew that secret; in short, I was her god!"

The women who heard de Marsay seemed offended by seeing themselves so well acted, for he seconded the words by airs, and sidelong attitudes, and mincing grimaces which were quite illusory.

"At the very moment when I might have believed these adorable falsehoods, as I still held her right hand in mine, I said to her, 'When are you to marry the Duke?'

"The thrust was so direct, my gaze met hers so boldly, and her hand lay so tightly in mine, that her start, slight as it was, could not be disguised; her eyes fell before mine, and a faint blush colored her cheeks. 'The Duke! What do you mean?' she said, affecting great astonishment. 'I know everything,' I replied; 'and, in my opinion, you should delay no longer; he is rich; he is a duke; but he is more than devout, he is religious! I am sure, therefore, that you have been faithful to me, thanks to his scruples. You cannot imagine how urgently necessary it is that you should compromise him with himself and with God; short of that you will never bring him to the point.' 'Is this a dream?' said she, pushing her hair from her forehead, fifteen years before Malibran, with the gesture which Malibran has made so famous. 'Come, do not be childish, my angel,' I said, trying to take her hands; but she folded them before her with a little prudish and indignant mien. 'Marry him, you have my permission,' said I, replying to this gesture by using the formal *vous* (you) instead of *tu* (thou). 'Nay, better, I beg you will do so.' 'But,' cried she, falling at my knees, 'there is some horrible mistake; I love no one in the world but you; you may demand any proofs you please.' 'Rise, my dear,' said I, 'and do me the honor of being truthful.' 'As before God.' 'Do you doubt my love?' 'No.' 'Nor my fidelity?' 'No.' 'Well, I have committed the greatest crime,' I went on. 'I have doubted your love and your fidelity. Between two intoxications I looked calmly about me.' 'Calmly!' sighed she. 'That is enough, Henri; you no longer love me.'

"She had at once found, you perceive, a loophole for escape. In scenes like these an adverb is dangerous. But, happily, curiosity made her add: 'And what did you see? Have I ever spoken of the Duke excepting in public? Have you detected in my eyes——?' 'No,' I said, 'but in his. And you have eight times made me go to Saint-Thomas d'Aquin to see you listening to the same mass as he.' 'Ah!' she exclaimed, 'then I have made you jealous!' 'Oh! I only wish I could be!' said I, admiring the pliancy of her quick intelligence, and these acrobatic feats which can only be successful in the eyes of the blind. 'But by dint of going to church I have become very incredulous. On the day of my first cold, and your first treachery, when you thought I was in bed, you received the Duke, and you told me you had seen no one.' 'Do you know that your conduct is infamous?' 'In what respect? I consider your marriage to the Duke an excellent arrangement; he gives you a great name, the only rank that suits you, a brilliant and distinguished position. You will be one of the queens of Paris. I should be doing you a wrong if I placed any obstacle in the way of this prospect, this distinguished life, this splendid alliance. Ah! Charlotte, some day you will do me justice by discovering how unlike my character is to that of other young men. You would have been compelled to deceive me; yes, you would have found it very difficult to break with me, for he watches you. It is time that we should part, for the Duke is rigidly virtuous. You must turn prude; I advise you to do so. The Duke is vain; he will be proud of his wife.' 'Oh!' cried she, bursting into tears, 'Henri, if only you had spoken! Yes, if you had chosen'—it was I who was to blame, you understand—'we would have gone to live all our days in a corner, married, happy, and defied the world.' 'Well, it is too late now,' said I, kissing her hands and putting on a victimized air. 'Good God! But I can undo it all!' she said. 'No, you have gone too far with the Duke. I ought indeed to go a journey to part us more effectually. We should both have reason to fear our own affection——' 'Henri, do you think the Duke has any suspicions?' I was still 'Henri,' but the *tu* was lost forever. 'I do not think so,' I replied, assuming the manner of a friend; 'but be as devout as possible, reconcile yourself to God, for the Duke waits for proofs; he hesitates, you must bring him to the point.'

"She arose and walked twice round the boudoir in real or

affected agitation; then she no doubt found an attitude and a look beseeming the new state of affairs, for she stopped in front of me, held out her hand, and said in a voice broken by emotion, 'Well, Henri, you are loyal, noble, and a charming man; I shall never forget you.'

"These were admirable tactics. She was bewitching in this transition of feeling, indispensable to the situation in which she wished to place herself in regard to me. I fell into the attitude, the manners, and the look of a man so deeply distressed that I saw her too newly assumed dignity giving way; she looked at me, took my hand, drew me along almost, threw me on to the sofa, but quite gently, and said after a moment's silence, 'I am dreadfully unhappy, my dear fellow. Do you love me?' 'Oh! yes.' 'Well, then, what will become of you?'"

At this point the women all looked at each other.

"Though I can still suffer when I recall her perfidy, I still laugh at her expression of entire conviction and sweet satisfaction that I must die, or at any rate sink into perpetual melancholy," de Marsay went on. "Oh! do not laugh yet!" he said to his listeners; "there is better to come. I looked at her very tenderly after a pause, and said to her, 'Yes, that is what I have been wondering.' 'Well, what will you do?' 'I asked myself that the day after my cold.' 'And——?' she asked with eager anxiety. 'And I have made advances to the little lady to whom I was supposed to be attached.'

"Charlotte started up from the sofa like a frightened doe, trembling like a leaf, gave me one of those looks in which women forego all their dignity, all their modesty, their refinement, and even their grace; the sparkling glitter of a hunted viper's eye when driven into a corner, and ejaculated, 'And I have loved this man! I have struggled! I have——' On this last thought, which I leave you to guess, she made the most impressive pause I ever heard. 'Good God!' she cried, 'how unhappy are we women! we never can be loved. To you there is nothing serious in the purest feelings. But never mind; when you cheat us you still are our dupes!' 'I see that plainly,' said I, with a stricken air; 'you have far too much wit in your anger for your heart to suffer from it.' This modest epigram increased her rage; she found some tears of vexation. 'You disgust me with the world and with life,' she said; 'you snatch away all my illusions; you deprave my heart.'

"She said to me all that I had a right to say to her, and with a simple effrontery, an artless audacity, which would certainly have nailed any man but me on the spot. 'What is to become of us poor women in a state of society such as Louis XVIII.'s charter has made it?' (Imagine how her words had run away with her.) 'Yes, indeed, we are born to suffer. In matters of passion we are always superior to you, and you are beneath all loyalty. There is no honesty in your hearts. To you love is a game in which you always cheat.' 'My dear,' I answered, 'to take anything serious in society nowadays would be like making romantic love to an actress.' 'What a shameless betrayal! It was deliberately planned!' 'No, only a rational issue.' 'Good-by, Monsieur de Marsay,' she said; 'you have deceived me horribly.' 'Surely,' I replied, taking up a submissive attitude, 'Madame la Duchesse will not remember Charlotte's grievances?' 'Certainly,' she aswered bitterly. 'Then, in fact, you hate me?' She bowed, and I said to myself, 'There is something still left!'

"The feeling she had when I parted from her allowed her to believe that she still had something to avenge. Well, my friends, I have carefully studied the lives of men who have had great success with women, but I do not believe that the Maréchal de Richelieu, or Lauzun, or Louis de Valois ever effected a more judicious retreat at the first attempt. As to my mind and heart, they were cast in a mould then and there, once for all, and the power of control I thus acquired over the thoughtless impulses which make us commit so many follies gained me the admirable presence of mind you all know."

"How deeply I pity the second!" exclaimed the Baronne de Nucingen.

A scarcely perceptible smile on de Marsay's pale lips made Delphine de Nucingen color.

"How we do forget!" said the Baron de Nucingen.

The great banker's simplicity was so extremely droll that his wife, who was de Marsay's "second," could not help laughing like every one else.

"You are all ready to condemn the woman," said Lady Dudley. "Well, I quite understand that she did not regard her marriage as an act of inconstancy. Men will never distinguish between constancy and fidelity. I know the woman whose story Monsieur de Marsay has told us, she is one of the last of your truly great ladies."

"Alas! my lady, you are right," replied de Marsay. "For very nearly fifty years we have been looking on at the progressive ruin of all social distinctions. We ought to have saved our women from this great wreck, but the civil code has swept its leveling influence over their heads. However terrible the words, they must be spoken: Duchesses are vanishing, and marquises too! As to the baronesses—I must apologize to Madame de Nucingen, who will become a countess when her husband is made a peer of France—baronesses have never succeeded in getting people to take them seriously."

"Aristocracy begins with the viscountess," said Blondet with a smile.

"Countesses will survive," said de Marsay. "An elegant woman will be more or less of a countess—a countess of the empire or of yesterday, a countess of the old block, or, as they say in Italy, a countess by courtesy. But as to the great lady, she died out with the dignified splendor of the last century, with powder, patches, high-heeled slippers, and stiff bodices with a delta stomacher of bows. Duchesses in these days can pass through a door without any need to widen it for their hoops. The empire saw the last of gowns with trains! I am still puzzled to understand how a sovereign who wished to see his drawing-room swept by ducal satin and velvet did not make indestructible laws. Napoleon never guessed the results of the code he was so proud of. That man, by creating duchesses, founded the race of our 'ladies' of to-day—the indirect offspring of his legislation."

"It was logic, handled as a hammer by boys just out of school and by obscure journalists, which demolished the splendors of the social state," said the Comte de Vandenesse. "In these days every rogue who can hold his head straight in his collar, cover his manly bosom with half an ell of satin by way of a cuirass, display a brow where apocryphal genius gleams under curling locks, and strut in a pair of patent-leather pumps graced by silk socks which cost six francs, screws his eyeglass into one of his eye-sockets by puckering up his cheek, and whether he be an attorney's clerk, a contractor's son, or a banker's bastard, he stares impertinently at the prettiest duchess, appraises her as she walks downstairs, and says to his friend—dressed by Buisson, as we all are, and mounted in patent-leather like any duke himself—'There, my boy, that is a perfect lady.'"

"You have not known how to form a party," said Lord Dudley; "it will be a long time yet before you have a policy. You talk a great deal in France about organizing labor, and you have not yet organized property. So this is what happens: Any duke—and even in the time of Louis XVIII. and Charles X. there were some left who had two hundred thousand francs a year, a magnificent residence, and a sumptuous train of servants—well, such a duke could live like a great lord. The last of these great gentlemen in France was the Prince de Talleyrand. This duke leaves four children, two of them girls. Granting that he has great luck in marrying them all well, each of these descendants will have but sixty or eighty thousand francs a year now; each is the father or mother of children, and consequently obliged to live with the strictest economy in a flat on the first floor or second floor of a large house. Who knows if they may not even be hunting a fortune? Henceforth the eldest son's wife, a duchess in name only, has no carriage, no people, no opera-box, no time to herself. She has not her own rooms in the family mansion, nor her fortune, nor her pretty toys; she is buried in marriage as a wife in the Rue Saint-Denis is buried in trade; she buys socks for her dear little children, nurses them herself, and keeps an eye on her girls, whom she no longer sends to school at a convent. Thus your noblest dames have been turned into worthy brood-hens."

"Alas! it is true," said Joseph Bridau. "In our day we cannot show those beautiful flowers of womanhood which graced the golden ages of the French monarchy. The great lady's fan is broken. A woman has nothing now to blush for; she need not slander or whisper, hide her face or reveal it. A fan is of no use now but for fanning herself. When once a thing is no more than what it is, it is too useful to be a form of luxury."

"Everything in France has aided and abetted the 'perfect lady,'" said Daniel d'Arthez. "The aristocracy has acknowledged her by retreating to the recesses of its landed estates, where it has hidden itself to die—emigrating inland before the march of ideas, as of old to foreign lands before that of the masses. The women who could have founded European *salons*, could have guided opinion and turned it inside out like a glove, could have ruled the world by ruling the men of art or of intellect who ought to have ruled it, have committed the blunder of abandoning their ground; they were ashamed of having to fight against the citizen class drunk with power, and rushing out on to the stage of the world, there to be cut to pieces perhaps by the barbarians who are at its heels. Hence, where the middle class insists on seeing princesses, these are really only lady-like young women. In these days princes can find no great ladies whom they may compromise; they cannot even confer honor on a woman taken up at random. The Duc de Bourbon was the last prince to avail himself of this privilege."

"And God alone knows how dearly he paid for it!" said Lord Dudley.

"Nowadays princes have lady-like wives, obliged to share their opera-box with other ladies; royal favor could not raise them higher by a hair's-breadth; they glide unremarkable between the waters of the citizen class and those of the nobility—not altogether noble nor altogether middle class," said the Marquise de Rochegude acridly.

"The press has fallen heir to the woman," exclaimed Rastignac. "She no longer has the quality of a spoken *feuilleton**—delightful calumnies graced by elegant language. We read *feuilletons* written in a dialect which changes every three years, society papers about as mirthful as an undertaker's mute, and as light as the lead of their type. French conversation is carried on from one end of the country to the other in a revolutionary jargon, through long columns of type printed in old mansions where a press groans in the place where formerly elegant company used to meet."

"The knell of the highest society is tolling," said a Russian Prince. "Do you hear it? And the first stroke is your modern word *lady*."

"You are right, Prince," said de Marsay. "The 'perfect lady,' issuing from the ranks of the nobility, or sprouting from the citizen class, and the product of every soil, even of the provinces, is the expression of these times, a last remaining embodiment of good taste, grace, wit, and distinction, all combined, but dwarfed. We shall see no more great ladies in France, but there will be 'ladies' for a long time, elected by public opinion to form an upper chamber of women, and

* The light gossip of a newspaper.

who will be among the fair sex what a 'gentleman' is in England."

"And that they call progress!" exclaimed Mademoiselle des Touches. "I should like to know where the progress lies."

"Why in this," said Madame de Nucingen. "Formerly a woman might have the voice of a fish-seller, the walk of a grenadier, the face of an impudent courtesan, her hair too high on her forehead, a large foot, a thick hand—she was a great lady in spite of it all; but in these days, even if she was a Montmorency—if a Montmorency could ever be such a creature—she would not be a lady."

"But what do you mean by a 'perfect lady?'" asked Count Adam Laginski.

"She is a modern product, a deplorable triumph of the elective system as applied to the fair sex," said the minister. "Every revolution has a word of its own which epitomizes and depicts it."

"You are right," said the Russian, who had come to make a literary reputation in Paris. "The explanation of certain words added from time to time to your beautiful language would make a magnificent history. *Organize*, for instance, is the word of the empire, and sums up Napoleon completely."

"But all that does not explain what is meant by a lady!" the young Pole exclaimed, with some impatience.

"Well, I will tell you," said Emile Blondet to Count Adam. "One fine morning you go for a saunter in Paris. It is past two, but five has not yet struck. You see a woman coming toward you; your first glance at her is like the preface to a good book, it leads you to expect a world of elegance and refinement. Like a botanist over hill and dale in his pursuit of plants, among the vulgarities of Paris life you have at last found a rare flower. This woman is attended by two very distinguished-looking men, of whom one, at any rate, wears an order; or else a servant out of livery follows her at a distance of ten yards. She displays no gaudy colors, no open-worked stockings, no over-elaborate waist-buckle, no embroiderd frills to her drawers fussing round her ankles. You will see that she is shod with prunella slippers, with sandals crossed over extremely fine cotton stockings, or plain gray silk stockings; or perhaps she wears shoes of the most exquisite simplicity. You notice that her gown is made of a neat and inexpensive material, but made in a way that surprises more than one woman of the middle class; it is almost always a long pelisse, with bows to fasten it, and neatly bound with fine cord or an imperceptible braid. The unknown has a way of her own in wrapping herself in her shawl or mantilla; she knows how to draw it around her from her hips to her neck, outlining a carapace, as it were, which would make an ordinary woman look like a turtle, but which in her sets off the most beautiful forms while concealing them. How does she do it? This secret she keeps, though unguarded by any patent.

"As she walks she gives herself a little concentric and harmonious twist, which makes her supple or dangerous slenderness writhe under the stuff, as a snake does under the green gauze of trembling grass. Is it to an angel or a devil that she owes the graceful undulation which plays under her long, black silk cape, stirs its lace frill, sheds an airy balm, and what I should like to call the breeze of a Parisienne? You may recognize over her arms, round her waist, about her throat, a science of drapery recalling the antique Mnemosyne, mother of the Muses.

"Oh! how thoroughly she understands the *cut* of her gait —forgive the expression. Study the way she puts her foot forward, moulding her skirt with such a decent preciseness that the passer-by is filled with admiration, mingled with desire, but subdued by deep respect. When an Englishwoman attempts this step she looks like a grenadier marching forward to attack a redoubt. The women of Paris have a genius for walking. The municipality really owed them asphalt sidewalks.

"Our unknown jostles no one. If she wants to pass, she waits with proud humility till some one makes way. The distinction peculiar to a well-bred woman betrays itself, especially in the way she holds her shawl or cloak crossed over her bosom. Even as she walks she has a little air of serene dignity, like Raphael's Madonnas in their frames. Her aspect, at once quiet and disdainful, makes the most insolent dandy step aside for her.

"Her bonnet, remarkable for its simplicity, is trimmed with crisp ribbons; there may be flowers in it, but the cleverest of such women wear only bows. Feathers demand a carriage; flowers are too showy. Beneath it you see the fresh unworn face of a woman who, without conceit, is sure of herself; who looks at nothing, and sees everything; whose vanity, satiated by being constantly gratified, stamps her face with an indifference which piques your curiosity. She knows that she is looked at; she knows that everybody, even women, turn round to see her again. And she threads her way through Paris like a gossamer, spotless and pure.

"This delightful species affects the hottest latitudes, the cleanest longitudes of Paris; you will meet her between the 10th and 110th arcade of the Rue de Rivoli; along the line of the boulevards from the equator of the Passage des Panoramas, where the products of India flourish, where the warmest creations of industry are displayed, to the cape of the Madeleine; in the least muddy districts of the citizen quarters, between No. 30 and No. 130 of the Rue du Faubourg Saint-Honoré. During the winter she haunts the terrace of the Feuillants, but not the asphalt pavement that lies parallel. According to the weather, she may be seen flying in the avenue of the Champs-Élysées, which is bounded on the east by the Place Louis XV., on the west by the Avenue de Marigny, to the south by the road, to the north by the gardens of the Faubourg Saint-Honoré. Never is this pretty variety of woman to be seen in the hyperborean regions of the Rue Saint-Denis, never in the Kamtschatka of miry, narrow, commercial streets; never anywhere in bad weather. These flowers of Paris, blooming only in Oriental weather, perfume the highways; and after five o'clock fold up like morning-glory flowers. The women you will see later, looking a little like them, trying to ape them, are would-be ladies; while the fair unknown, your Beatrice of a day, is a 'perfect lady.'

"It is not very easy for a foreigner, my dear Count, to recognize the differences by which the old observer distinguishes them—women are such consummate actresses; but they are glaring in the eyes of Parisians: hooks ill fastened, strings showing loops of rusty-white tape through a gaping slit in the back, rubbed shoe-leather, ironed bonnet-strings, an overfull skirt, an overtight waist. You will see a certain effort in the intentional droop of the eyelid. There is something conventional in the attitude.

"As to the middle class, the citizen womankind, she can not possibly be mistaken for the lady; she is an admirable foil to her, she accounts for the spell cast over you by the unknown. She is bustling, and goes out in all weathers, trots about, comes, goes, gazes, does not know whether she will or will not go into a store. Where the lady knows just what she wants and what she is doing, the townswoman is undecided, tucks up her skirts to cross a gutter, dragging a child by the hand, which compels her to look out for the vehicles; she is a mother in public, and talks to her daughter; she carries money in her bag, and has open-work stockings on her feet; in winter, she wears a boa over her fur cloak; in summer, a shawl and a scarf; she is accomplished in the redundancies of dress.

"You will meet the fair unknown again at the Italiens, at the opera, at a ball. She will then appear under such a different aspect that you would think them two beings devoid of any analogy. The woman has emerged from those mysterious garments like a butterfly from its silky cocoon. She serves up, like some rare dainty, to your ravished eyes, the forms which her bodice scarcely revealed in the morning. At the theatre she never mounts higher than the second tier, excepting at the Italiens. You can there watch at your leisure the studied deliberateness of her movements. The enchanting deceiver plays off all the little political artifices of her sex so naturally as to exclude all idea of art or premeditation. If she has a royally beautiful hand, the most perspicacious beholder will believe that it is absolutely necessary that she should twist, or refix, or push aside the ringlet or curl she plays with. If she has some dignity of profile, you will be persuaded that she is giving irony or grace to what she says to her neighbor, sitting in such a position as to produce the magical effect of the 'lost profile,' so dear to great painters, by which the cheek catches the high light, the nose is shown in clear outline, the nostrils are transparently rosy, the forehead squarely modeled, the eye has its spangle of fire, but fixed on space, and the white roundness of the chin is accentuated by a line of light. If she has a pretty foot, she will throw herself on a sofa with the coquettish grace of a cat in the sunshine, her feet outstretched without your feeling that her attitude is anything but the most charming model ever given to a sculptor by lassitude.

"Only the perfect lady is quite at her ease in full dress; nothing inconveniences her. You will never see her, like the woman of the citizen class, pulling up a refractory shoulder-strap, or pushing down a rebellious whalebone, or looking whether her tucker is doing its office of faithful guardian to two treasures of dazzling whiteness, or glancing in the mirrors to see if her head-dress is keeping its place. Her toilet is always in harmony with her character; she has had time to study herself, to learn what becomes her, for she has long known what does not suit her. You will not find her as you go out;

she vanishes before the end of the play. If by chance she is to be seen, calm and stately, on the stairs, she is experiencing some violent emotion; she has to bestow a glance, to receive a promise. Perhaps she goes down so slowly on purpose to gratify the vanity of a slave whom she sometimes obeys. If your meeting takes place at a ball or an evening party, you will gather the honey, natural or affected, of her insinuating voice; her empty words will enchant you, and she will know how to give them the value of thought by her inimitable bearing."

"To be such a woman, is it not necessary to be very clever?" asked the Polish Count.

"It is necessary to have great taste," replied the Princesse de Cadignan.

"And in France taste is more than cleverness," said the Russian.

"This woman's cleverness is the triumph of a purely plastic art," Blondet went on. "You will not know what she said, but you will be fascinated. She will toss her head, or gently shrug her white shoulders; she will gild an insignificant speech with a charming pout and smile; or throw a Voltairean epigram into an 'Indeed!' an 'Ah!' a 'What then!' A jerk of her head will be her most pertinent form of questioning; she will give meaning to the movement by which she twirls a vinaigrette hanging to her finger by a ring. She gets an artificial grandeur out of superlative trivialities; she simply drops her hand impressively, letting it fall over the arm of her chair as dewdrops hang on the cup of a flower, and all is said —she has pronounced judgment beyond appeal, to the apprehension of the most obtuse. She knows how to listen to you; she gives you the opportunity of shining, and—I ask your modesty—those moments are rare?"

The candid simplicity of the young Pole, to whom Blondet spoke, made all the party shout with laughter.

"Now, you will not talk for half-an-hour with a *bourgeoise* without her alluding to her husband in one way or another," Blondet went on with unperturbed gravity; "whereas, even if you know that your lady is married, she will have the delicacy to conceal her husband so effectually that it will need the enterprise of Christopher Columbus to discover him. Often you will fail in the attempt single-handed. If you have had no opportunity of inquiring, toward the end of the evening you detect her gazing fixedly at a middle-aged man wearing a decoration, who bows and goes out. She has ordered her carriage, and goes.

"You are not the rose, but you have been with the rose, and you go to bed under the golden canopy of a delicious dream, which will last perhaps after sleep, with his heavy finger, has opened the ivory gates of the temple of dreams.

"The lady, when she is at home, sees no one before four; she is shrewd enough always to keep you waiting. In her house you will find everything in good taste; her luxury is for hourly use, and duly renewed; you will see nothing under glass shades, no rags of wrappings hanging about, and looking like a pantry. You will find the staircase warmed. Flowers on all sides will charm your sight—flowers, the only gift she accepts, and those only from certain people, for nosegays live but a day; they give pleasure, and must be replaced; to her they are, as in the East, a symbol and a promise. The costly toys of fashion lie about, but not so as to suggest a museum or a curiosity shop. You will find her sitting by the fire in a low chair, from which she will not rise to greet you. Her talk will not now be what it was at the ball; there she was our creditor; in her own home she owes you the pleasure of her wit. These are the shades of which the lady is a marvelous mistress. What she likes in you is a man to swell her circle, an object for the cares and attentions which such women are now happy to bestow. Therefore, to attract you to her drawing-room, she will be bewitchingly charming. This especially is where you feel how isolated women are nowadays, and why they want a little world of their own to which they may seem a constellation. Conversation is impossible without generalities."

"Yes," said de Marsay, "you have truly hit the fault of our age. The epigram—a volume in a word—no longer strikes, as it did in the eighteenth century, at persons or at things, but at squalid events, and it dies in a day."

"Hence," said Blondet, "the intelligence of the lady, if she has any, consists in casting doubts on everything, while the *bourgeoise* uses hers to affirm everything. Here lies the great difference between the two women; the townswoman is certainly virtuous; the lady does not know yet whether she is, or whether she always will be; she hesitates and struggles where the other refuses point-blank and falls full length. This hesitancy in everything is one of the last graces left to her by our horrible times. She rarely goes to church, but she will talk to you of religion; and if you have the good taste to affect freethought, she will try to convert you, for you will have opened a way for the stereotyped phrases, the head-shaking and gestures understood by all these women: 'For shame! I thought you had too much sense to attack religion. Society is tottering, and you deprive it of its support. Why, religion at this moment means you and me; it is property, and the future of our children! Ah! let us not be selfish! Individualism is the disease of the age and religion is the only remedy; it unites families which your laws put asunder,' and so forth. Then she plunges into some neo-Christian speech sprinkled with political notions which is neither catholic nor protestant but—moral? Oh! deuced moral!—in which you may recognize a fag-end of every material woven by modern doctrines, at loggerheads together."

The women could not help laughing at the airs by which Blondet illustrated his satire.

"This explanation, dear Count Adam," said Blondet, turning to the Pole, "will have proved to you that the 'perfect lady' represents the intellectual no less than the political muddle, just as she is surrounded by the showy and not very lasting products of an industry which is always aiming at destroying its work in order to replace it by something else. When you leave her you say to yourself: 'She certainly has superior ideas!' And you believe it all the more because she will have sounded your heart with a delicate touch and have asked you your secrets; she affects ignorance, to learn everything; there are some things she never knows, not even when she knows them. You alone will be uneasy, you will know nothing of the state of her heart. The great ladies of old flaunted their love-affairs with newspapers and advertisements; in these days the lady has her little passion neatly ruled like a sheet of music with its crotchets and quavers and minims, its rests, its pauses, its sharps to sign the key. A mere weak woman, she is anxious not to compromise her love, or her husband, or the future of her children. Name, position, and fortune are no longer flags so respected as to protect all kinds of merchandise on board. The whole aristocracy no longer advances in a body to screen the lady. She has not, like the great lady of the past, the demeanor of lofty antagonism; she can crush nothing under foot, it is she who would be crushed. Thus she is apt at Jesuitical *mezzo termine* (middle courses); she is a creature of equivocal compromises, of guarded proprieties, of anonymous passions steered between two reef-bound shores. She is as much afraid of her servants as an Englishwoman who lives in dread of a trial in the divorce court. This woman—so free at a ball, so attractive out walking—is a slave at home; she is never independent but in perfect privacy, or theoretically. She must preserve herself in her position as a lady. This is her task.

"For in our day a woman repudiated by her husband, reduced to a meagre allowance, with no carriage, no luxury, no opera-box, none of the divine accessories of the toilet, is no longer a wife, a maid, or a townswoman; she is adrift, and becomes a chattel. The Carmelites will not receive a married woman; it would be bigamy. Would her lover still have anything to say to her? That is the question. Thus your perfect lady may perhaps give occasion to calumny, never to slander."

" It is all horribly true," said the Princesse de Cadignan.

"And so," responded Blondet, " our ' perfect lady ' lives between English hypocrisy and the delightful frankness of the eighteenth century—a bastard system, symptomatic of an age in which nothing that grows up is at all like the thing that has vanished, in which transition leads nowhere, everything is a matter of degree; all the great figures shrink into the background, and distinction is purely personal. I am fully convinced that it is impossible for a woman, even if she was born close to a throne, to acquire before the age of five-and-twenty the encyclopædic knowledge of trifles, the practice of manœuvring, the important small things, the musical tones and harmony of coloring, the angelic bedevilments and innocent cunning, the speech and the silence, the seriousness and the banter, the wit and the obtuseness, the diplomacy and the ignorance which make up the perfect lady."

" And where, in accordance with the sketch you have drawn," said Mademoiselle des Touches to Emile Blondet, " would you class the female author? Is she a perfect lady—a woman *comme il faut?*" (as she should be).

" When she has no genius, she is a woman *comme il n'en faut pas* " (who is not as she should be), Blondet replied, emphasizing the words with a stolen glance, which might make them seem praise frankly addressed to Camille Maupin. " This epigram is not mine, but Napoleon's," he added.

" You need not owe Napoleon any grudge on that score," said Canalis, with an emphatic tone and gesture. " It was one of his weaknesses to be jealous of literary genius—for he had his mean points. Who will ever explain, depict, or understand Napoleon? A man represented with his arms folded, and who did everything, who was the greatest force ever known, the most concentrated, the most mordant, the most acid of all forces; a singular genius who carried armed civilization in every direction without fixing it anywhere; a man who could do everything because he willed everything; a prodigious phenomenon of will conquering an illness by a battle, and yet doomed to die of disease in bed after living in the midst of ball and bullets; a man with a code and a sword in his brain, word and deed; a clear-sighted spirit that foresaw everything but his own fall; a capricious politician who risked men by handfuls out of economy, and who spared three heads—those of Talleyrand, of Pozzo di Borgo, and of Metternich, diplomatists whose death would have saved the French empire, and who seemed to him of greater weight than thousands of soldiers; a man to whom nature, as a rare privilege, had given a heart in a frame of bronze; mirthful and kind at midnight amid women, and next morning manipulating Europe as a young girl might amuse herself by splashing the water in her bath! Hypocritical and generous; loving tawdriness and simplicity; devoid of taste, but protecting the arts; and, in spite of these antitheses, really great in everything by instinct or by temperament; Cæsar at five-and-twenty, Cromwell at thirty; and then, like my grocer buried in Père Lachaise, a good husband and a good father. In short, he improvised public works, empires, kings, codes, verses, a romance—and all with more range than precision. Did he not aim at making all Europe France? And, after making us weigh on the earth in such a way as to change the laws of gravitation, he left us poorer than on the day when he first laid hands on us; while he, who had taken an empire by his name, lost his name on the frontier of his empire in a sea of blood and soldiers. A man all thought and all action, who comprehended Desaix and Fouché."

"All despotism and all justice at the right moments. The true king?" said de Marsay.

"Ah! vat a pleashre it is to dichest vile you talk," said Baron de Nucingen.

"But do you suppose that the treat we are giving you is a common one?" asked Joseph Bridau. "If you had to pay for the charms of conversation as you do for those of dancing or of music, your fortune would be inadequate! There is no second performance of the same flash of wit."

"And are we really so much deteriorated as these gentlemen think?" said the Princesse de Cadignan, addressing the women with a smile at once skeptical and ironical. "Because, in these days, under a régime which makes everything small, you prefer small dishes, small rooms, small pictures, small articles, small newspapers, small books, does that prove that women too have grown smaller? Why should the human heart change because you change your coat? In all ages the passions will remain the same. I know cases of beautiful devotion, of sublime sufferings, which lack the publicity— the glory, if you choose—which formerly gave lustre to the errors of some women. But though one may not have saved a King of France, one is not the less an Agnes Sorel. Do you believe that our dear Marquise d'Espard is not the peer of Madame Doublet or Madame du Deffant, in whose rooms so much evil was spoken and done? Is not Taglioni a match for Camargo? or Malibran the equal of Saint-Huberti? Are not our poets superior to those of the eighteenth century? If at this moment, through the fault of the grocers who govern us, we have not a style of our own, had not the empire its distinguishing stamp as the age of Louis XV. had, and was not its splendor fabulous? Have the sciences lost anything?"

"I am quite of your opinion, madame; the women of this age are truly great," replied the Comte de Vandenesse. "When posterity shall have followed us, will not Madame Récamier appear in proportions as fine as those of the most beautiful women of the past? We have made so much history that historians will be lacking! The age of Louis XIV. had but one Madame de Sévigné; we have a thousand now in Paris who certainly write better than she did, and who do not publish their letters. Whether the Frenchwoman be called 'perfect lady' or great lady, she will always be *the* woman among women.

"Emile Blondet has given us a picture of the fascinations of a woman of the day; but, at need, this creature who bridles or shows off, who chirps out the ideas of Mr. This and Mr. That, would be heroic. And it must be said, your faults, mesdames, are all the more poetical, because they must always, and under all circumstances, be surrounded by greater perils. I have seen much of the world, I have studied it perhaps too late; but in cases where the illegality of your feelings might be excused, I have always observed the effects of I know not what chance—which you may call providence—inevitably overwhelming such as we consider light women."

"I hope," said Madame de Vandenesse, "that we can be great in other ways——"

"Oh, let the Comte de Vandenesse preach to us!" exclaimed Madame de Sérizy.

"With all the more reason because he has preached a great deal by example," said the Baronne de Nucingen.

"On my honor!" said General de Montriveau, "in all the dramas—a word you are very fond of," he said, looking at Blondet—"in which the finger of God has been visible, the most frightful I ever knew was very near being by my act——"

"Well, tell us all about it!" cried Lady Barimore; "I love to shudder!"

"It is the taste of a virtuous woman," replied de Marsay, looking at Lord Dudley's lovely daughter.

"During the campaign of 1812," General de Montriveau began, "I was the involuntary cause of a terrible disaster which may be of use to you, Doctor Bianchon," turning to the doctor, "since, while devoting yourself to the human body, you concern yourself a good deal with the mind; it may tend to solve some of the problems of the will.

"I was going through my second campaign; I enjoyed danger, and laughed at everything, like the young and foolish lieutenant of artillery that I was. When we reached the Beresina, the army had, as you know, lost all discipline and had forgotten military obedience. It was a medley of men of all nations, instinctively making their way from north to south. The soldiers would drive a general in rags and barefoot away from their fire if he brought neither wood nor victuals. After the passage of this famous river disorder did not diminish. I had come quietly and alone, without food, out of the marshes of Zembin, and was wandering in search of a house where I might be taken in. Finding none, or driven away from those I came across, happily toward evening I perceived a wretched little Polish farm, of which nothing can give you any idea unless you have seen the wooden houses of Lower Normandy, or the poorest farm-buildings of la Beauce. These dwellings consist of a single room, with one end divided off by a wooden partition, the smaller division serving as a storeroom for forage.

"In the darkness of twilight I could just see a faint smoke rising above this house. Hoping to find there some comrades more compassionate than those I had hitherto addressed, I boldly walked as far as the farm. On going in, I found the table laid. Several officers, and with them a woman—a common sight enough—were eating potatoes, some horseflesh broiled over the charcoal, and some frozen beet-roots. I recognized among the company two or three artillery captains of the regiment in which I had first served. I was welcomed with a shout of acclamation, which would have amazed me greatly on the other side of the Beresina; but at this moment the cold was less intense; my fellow-officers were resting, they were warm, they had food, and the room, strewn with trusses

of straw, gave the promise of a delightful night. We did
not ask for so much in those days. My comrades could be
philanthropists *gratis*—one of the commonest ways of being
philanthropic. I sat down to eat on one of the bundles of
straw.

"At the end of the table, by the side of the door opening
into the smaller room full of straw and hay, sat my old
colonel, one of the most extraordinary men I ever saw among
all the mixed collection of men it has been my lot to meet.
He was an Italian. Now, whenever human nature is truly
fine in the lands of the south, it is really sublime. I do not
know whether you have ever observed the extreme fairness of
Italians when they are fair. It is exquisite, especially under
an artificial light. When I read the fantastical portrait of
Colonel Oudet sketched by Charles Nodier, I found my own
sensations in every one of his elegant phrases. Italian, then,
as were most of the officers of his regiment, which had, in
fact, been borrowed by the Emperor from Eugène's army,
my colonel was a tall man, at least eight or nine inches above
the standard, and admirably proportioned—a little stout perhaps, but prodigiously powerful, active, and clean-limbed as a
greyhound. His black hair in abundant curls showed up his
complexion, as white as a woman's; he had small hands, a
shapely foot, a pleasant mouth, and an aquiline nose delicately
formed, of which the tip used to become naturally pinched
and white whenever he was angry, as happened often. His
irascibility was so far beyond belief that I will tell you nothing
about it; you will have the opportunity of judging of it. No
one could be calm in his presence. I alone, perhaps, was not
afraid of him; he had indeed taken such a singular fancy to
me that he thought everything I did right. When he was in
a rage his brow was knit and the muscles of the middle of his
forehead set in a delta, or, to be more explicit, in Redgaunt-
let's horseshoe. This mark was, perhaps, even more terrify-
ing than the magnetic flashes of his blue eyes. His whole

frame quivered, and his strength, great as it was in his normal state, became almost unbounded.

"He spoke with a strong guttural roll. His voice, at least as powerful as that of Charles Nodier's Oudet, threw an incredible fullness of tone into the syllable or the consonant in which this burr was sounded. Though this faulty pronunciation was at times a grace, when commanding his men or when he was excited, you cannot imagine, unless you had heard it, what force was expressed by this accent, which at Paris is so common. When the colonel was quiescent, his blue eyes were sweetly angelic, and his smooth brow had a most charming expression. On parade or with the army of Italy, not a man could compare with him. Indeed, d'Orsay himself, the handsome d'Orsay, was eclipsed by our colonel on the occasion of the last review held by Napoleon before the invasion of Russia.

"Everything was in contrasts in this exceptional man. Passion lives on contrast. Hence you need not ask whether he exerted over women the irresistible influences to which our nature yields"—and the general looked at the Princesse de Cadignan—"as vitreous matter is moulded under the pipe of the glassblower; still, by a singular fatality—an observer might perhaps explain the phenomenon—the colonel was not a lady-killer, or was indifferent to such successes.

"To give you an idea of his violence, I will tell you in a few words what I once saw him do in a paroxysm of fury: We were dragging our guns up a very narrow road, bordered by a somewhat high slope on one side and by thickets on the other. When we were half-way up we met another regiment of artillery, its colonel marching at the head. This colonel wanted to make the captain who was at the head of our foremost battery back down again. The captain, of course, refused; but the colonel of the other regiment signed to his foremost battery to advance, and, in spite of the care the driver took to keep among the scrub, the wheel of the first gun struck our captain's right leg and broke it, throwing him over on the near-side of his horse. All this was the work of a moment. Our colonel, who was but a little way off, guessed that there was a quarrel; he galloped up, riding among the guns at the risk of falling with his horse's four feet in the air, and reached the spot, face to face with the other colonel, at the very moment when the captain fell, calling out 'Help!' No, our Italian colonel was no longer human! Foam like the froth of champagne rose to his lips; he roared inarticulately like a lion. Incapable of uttering a word, or even a cry, he made a terrific signal to his antagonist, pointing to the wood and drawing his sword. The two colonels went aside. In two seconds we saw our colonel's opponent stretched on the ground, his skull split in two. The soldiers of his regiment backed—yes, by heaven, and pretty quickly too!

"The captain, who had been so nearly crushed, and who lay yelping in the puddle where the gun carriage had thrown him, had an Italian wife, a beautiful Sicilian of Messina, who was not indifferent to our colonel. This circumstance had aggravated his rage. He was pledged to protect the husband, bound to defend him as he would have defended the woman herself.

"Now, in the hovel beyond Zembin, where I was so well received, this captain was sitting opposite to me, and his wife was at the other end of the table, facing the colonel. This Sicilian was a little woman named Rosina, very dark, but with all the fire of the southern sun in her black almond-shaped eyes. At this moment she was deplorably thin; her face was covered with dust, like fruit exposed to the drought of a high-road. Scarcely clothed in rags, exhausted by marches, her hair in disorder, and clinging together under a piece of a shawl tied close over her head, still she had the graces of a woman; her movements were engaging, her small rosy mouth and white teeth, the outline of her features and figure, charms which misery, cold, and neglect had not altogether defaced, still suggested love to any man who could think of a woman. Rosina had one of those frames which are fragile in appearance, but wiry and full of spring. Her husband, a gentleman of Piedmont, had a face expressive of ironical simplicity, if it is allowable to ally the two words. Brave and well informed, he seemed to know nothing of the connection which had subsisted between his wife and the colonel for three years past. I ascribed this unconcern to Italian manners, or to some domestic secret; yet there was in the man's countenance one feature which always filled me with involuntary distrust. His under lip, which was thin and very restless, turned down at the corners instead of turning up, and this, as I thought, betrayed a streak of cruelty in a character which seemed so phlegmatic and indolent.

"As you may suppose, the conversation was not very sparkling when I went in. My weary comrades ate in silence; of course, they asked me some questions, and we related our misadventures, mingled with reflections on the campaign, the generals, their mistakes, the Russians, and the cold. A minute after my arrival the colonel, having finished his meagre meal, wiped his mustache, bade us good-night, shot a black look at the Italian woman, saying, 'Rosina?' and then, without waiting for a reply, went into the little barn full of hay to bed. The meaning of the colonel's utterance was self-evident. The young wife replied by an indescribable gesture, expressing all the annoyance she could not but feel at seeing her thraldom thus flaunted without human decency, and the offense to her dignity as a woman and to her husband. But there was, too, in the rigid setting of her features and the tight knitting of her brows a sort of presentiment; perhaps she foresaw her fate. Rosina remained quietly in her place.

"A minute later, and apparently when the colonel was snug in his couch of straw or hay, he repeated, 'Rosina?'

"The tone of this second call was even more brutally

questioning than the first. The colonel's strong burr, and the length which the Italian language allows to be given to vowels and the final syllable, concentrated all the man's despotism, impatience, and strength of will. Rosina turned pale, but she rose, passed behind us, and went to the colonel.

"All the party sat in utter silence; I, unluckily after looking at them all, began to laugh, and then they all laughed too. '*Tu ridi ?*—you laugh?' said the husband.

"'On my honor, old comrade,' said I, becoming serious again, 'I confess that I was wrong; I ask your pardon a thousand times, and if you are not satisfied by my apologies I am ready to give you satisfaction.'

"'Oh! it is not you who are wrong, it is I!' he replied coldly.

"Thereupon we all lay down in the room and before long all were sound asleep.

"Next morning each one, without rousing his neighbor or seeking companionship, set out again on his way, with that selfishness which made our rout one of the most horrible dramas of self-seeking, melancholy, and horror which ever was enacted under heaven. Nevertheless, at about seven or eight hundred paces from our shelter we, most of us, met again and walked on together, like geese led in flocks by a child's willful tyranny. The same necessity urged us all.

"Having reached a knoll whence we could still see the farmhouse where we had spent the night, we heard sounds resembling the roar of lions in the desert, the bellowing of bulls—no, it was a noise which can be compared to no known cry. And yet, mingling with this horrible and ominous roar, we could hear a woman's feeble scream. We all looked round, seized by I know not what impulse of terror; we no longer saw the house, but a huge bonfire. The farmhouse had been barricaded, and was in flames. Swirls of smoke borne on the wind brought us hoarse cries and an indescribable pungent smell. A few yards behind the captain was quietly approaching to join our caravan; we gazed at him in silence, for no one dared question him; but he, understanding our curiosity, pointed to his breast with the forefinger of his right hand, and, waving the left in the direction of the fire, he said, '*Son' io.*'

"We all walked on without saying a word to him."

"There is nothing more terrible than the revolt of a sheep," said de Marsay.

"It would be frightful to let us leave with this horrible picture in our memory," said Madame de Montcornet. "I shall dream of it——"

"And what was the punishment of Monsieur de Marsay's 'First?'" asked Lord Dudley, smiling.

"When the English are in jest, their foils have the buttons on," said Blondet.

"Monsieur Bianchon can tell us, for he saw her dying," replied de Marsay, turning to me.

"Yes," said Bianchon, "her end was one of the most beautiful I ever saw. The Duke and I spent the night by the dying woman's pillow; pulmonary consumption, in the last stage, left no hope; she had taken the sacrament the day before. The Duke had fallen asleep. The Duchess, waking at about four in the morning, signed to me in the most touching way, with a friendly smile, to bid me leave him to rest, and she meanwhile was about to die. She had become incredibly thin, but her face had preserved its really sublime outline and features. Her pallor made her skin look like porcelain with a light within. Her bright eyes and color contrasted with this languidly elegant complexion, and her countenance was full of impressive calm. She seemed to pity the Duke, and the feeling had its origin in a lofty tenderness which, as death approached, seemed to know no bounds. The silence was absolute. The room, softly lighted by a lamp, looked like every sick-room at the hour of death.

"At this moment the clock struck. The Duke awoke, and

was in despair at having fallen asleep. I did not see the gesture of impatience by which he manifested the regret he felt at having lost sight of his wife for a few of the last minutes vouchsafed to him; but it is quite certain that any one but the dying woman might have misunderstood it. A busy statesman, always thinking of the interests of France, the Duke had a thousand-odd ways on the surface, such as often lead to a man of genius being mistaken for a madman, and of which the explanation lies in the exquisiteness and exacting needs of their intellect. He came to seat himself in an armchair by his wife's side, and looked fixedly at her. The dying woman put her hand out a little way, took her husband's and clasped it feebly; and in a low but agitated voice she said, 'My poor dear, who is left to understand you now?' Then she died, looking at him."

"The stories the doctor tells us," said the Comte de Vandenesse, "always leave a deep impression."

"But a sweet one," said Mademoiselle des Touches, as she arose.

PARIS, *June*, 1839-42.

THE GREAT BRETÊCHE.

(*Sequel to "Another Study of Woman."*)

Translated by CLARA BELL.

"AH! madame," replied the doctor, "I have some appalling stories in my collection. But each one has its proper hour in a conversation—you know the pretty jest recorded by Chamfort, and said to the Duc de Fronsac: 'Between your sally and the present moment lie ten bottles of champagne.'"

"But it is two in the morning, and the story of Rosina has prepared us," said the mistress of the house.

"Tell us, Monsieur Bianchon," was the cry on every side.

The obliging doctor bowed, and silence reigned.

"At about a hundred paces from Vendôme, on the banks of the Loire," said he, "stands an old brown house, crowned with very high roofs, and so completely isolated that there is nothing near it, not even a fetid tannery or a squalid tavern, such as are commonly seen outside small towns. In front of this house is a garden down to the river, where the box-shrubs, formerly clipped close to the edge of the walks, now straggle at their own will. A few willows, rooted in the stream, have grown up quickly like an enclosing fence and half-hide the house. The wild plants we call weeds have clothed the bank with their beautiful luxuriance. The fruit trees, neglected for these ten years past, no longer bear a crop, and their suckers have formed a thicket. The espaliers are like a copse. The paths, once graveled, are overgrown with purslane; but, to be accurate, there is no trace of a path.

"Looking down from the hill-top, to which cling the ruins of the old castle of the Dukes of Vendôme, the only spot whence the eye can see into this enclosure, we think that at a time, difficult now to determine, this spot of earth must have been the joy of some country gentleman devoted to roses and tulips—in a word, to horticulture—but, above all, a lover of choice fruit. An arbor is visible, or rather the wreck of an arbor, and under it a table still stands not entirely destroyed by time. At the aspect of this garden that is no more, the negative joys of the peaceful life of the provinces may be divined as we divine the history of a worthy tradesman when we read the epitaph on his tomb. To complete the mournful and tender impressions which seize the soul, on one of the walls is a sundial graced with this homely Christian motto, '*Ultimam cogita.*'

"The roof of this house is dreadfully dilapidated; the outside shutters are always closed; the balconies are hung with swallows' nests; the doors are for ever shut. Straggling grasses have outlined the flagstones of the steps with green; the ironwork is rusty. Moon and sun, winter, summer, and snow have eaten into the wood, warped the boards, peeled off the paint. The dreary silence is broken only by birds and cats, polecats, rats, and mice, free to scamper around, and fight, and eat each other. An invisible hand has written over it all: 'Mystery.'

"If, prompted by curiosity, you go to look at this house from the street, you will see a large gate, with a round-arched top; the children have made many holes in it. I learned later that this door had been blocked for ten years. Through these irregular breaches you will see that the side toward the courtyard is in perfect harmony with the side toward the garden. The same ruin prevails. Tufts of weeds outline the paving stones; the walls are scored by enormous cracks, and the blackened coping is laced with a thousand festoons of pellitory. The stone steps are disjointed; the bell-cord is rotten; the gutter-spouts broken. What fire from heaven can have fallen there? By what decree has salt been sown on this dwelling? Has God been mocked here? Or was France betrayed? These are the questions we ask ourselves. Reptiles crawl over it, but give no reply. This empty and deserted house is a vast enigma of which the answer is known to none.

"It was formerly a little domain, held in fief, and is known as La Grande Bretèche. During my stay at Vendôme, where Despleins had left me in charge of a rich patient, the sight of this strange dwelling became one of my keenest pleasures. Was it not far better than a ruin? Certain memories of indisputable authenticity attach themselves to a ruin; but this house, still standing, though being slowly destroyed by an avenging hand, contained a secret, an unrevealed thought. At the very least it testified to a caprice. More than once in the evening I boarded the hedge, run wild, which surrounded the enclosure. I braved scratches, I got into this ownerless garden, this plot which was no longer public or private; I lingered there for hours gazing at the disorder. I would not, as the price of the story to which this strange scene no doubt was due, have asked a single question of any gossiping native. On that spot I wove delightful romances, and abandoned myself to little debauches of melancholy which enchanted me. If I had known the reason—perhaps quite commonplace—of this neglect, I should have lost the unwritten poetry which intoxicated me. To me this refuge represented the most various phases of human life, shadowed by misfortune; sometimes the calm of a cloister without the monks; sometimes the peace of the graveyard without the dead, who speak in the language of epitaphs; one day I saw in it the home of lepers; another, the house of the Atridæ; but, above all, I found there provincial life, with its contemplative ideas, its hour-glass existence. I often wept there; I never laughed.

"More than once I felt involuntary terrors as I heard overhead the dull hum of the wings of some hurrying wood-pigeon. The earth is dank; you must be on the watch for lizards, vipers, and frogs, wandering about with the wild freedom of nature; above all, you must have no fear of cold, for in a few minutes you feel an icy cloak settle on your shoulders, like the commendatore's hand on Don Giovanni's neck.

"One evening I felt a shudder; the wind had turned an old rusty weathercock, and the creaking sounded like a cry from the house, at the very moment when I was finishing a gloomy drama to account for this monumental embodiment of woe. I returned to my inn, lost in gloomy thoughts. When I had supped, the hostess came in to my room with an air of mystery, and, apologetically, said, 'Monsieur, here is Monsieur Regnault.'

"'Who is Monsieur Regnault?'

"'What, sir, do you not know Monsieur Regnault? Well, that's odd,' said she, leaving the room.

"On a sudden I saw a man appear, tall, slim, dressed in black, hat in hand, who came in like a ram ready to butt his opponent, showing a receding forehead, a small pointed head, and a colorless face of the hue of a glass of dirty water. You would have taken him for an usher. The stranger wore an old coat, much worn at the seams; but he had a diamond in his shirt frill and gold rings in his ears.

"'Monsieur,' said I, 'whom have I the honor of addressing?' He took a chair, placed himself in front of my fire, put his hat on my table, and answered while he rubbed his hands: 'Dear me, it is very cold. Monsieur, I am Monsieur Regnault.'

"I was encouraging myself by saying to myself, 'Here good dog! Seek!'

"'I am,' he went on, 'notary at Vendôme.'

"'I am delighted to hear it, monsieur,' I exclaimed. 'But I am not in a position to make a will for reasons best known to myself.'

"'One moment!' said he, holding up his hand as though to gain silence. 'Allow me, monsieur, allow me! I am informed that you sometimes go to walk in the garden of La Grande Bretêche.'

"'Yes, monsieur.'

"'One moment!' said he, repeating his gesture. 'That constitutes a misdemeanor. Monsieur, as executor under the will of the late Comtesse de Merret, I come in her name to beg you to discontinue the practice. One moment! I am not a Turk, and do not wish to make a crime of it. And, beside, you are free to be ignorant of the circumstances which compel me to leave the finest mansion in Vendôme to fall into ruin. Nevertheless, monsieur, you must be a man of education, and you should know that the laws forbid, under heavy penalties, any trespass on enclosed property. A hedge is the same as a wall. But the state in which the place is left may be an excuse for your curiosity. For my part, I should be quite content to make you free to come and go in the house; but being bound to respect the will of the testatrix, I have the honor, monsieur, to beg that you will go into the garden no more. I myself, monsieur, since the will was read, have never set foot in the house, which, as I had the honor of informing you, is part of the estate of the late Madame de Merret. We have done nothing there but verify the number of doors and windows to assess the taxes I have to pay annually out of the funds left for that purpose by the late Madame de Merret. Ah! my dear sir, her will made a great commotion in the town.'

"The good man paused to blow his nose. I respected his volubility, perfectly understanding that the administration of Madame de Merret's estate had been the most important event of his life, his reputation, his glory, his restoration. As I was forced to bid farewell to my beautiful reveries and romances, I was to reject learning the truth on official authority.

"'Monsieur,' said I, 'would it be indiscreet if I were to ask you the reasons for such eccentricity?'

"At these words an expression, which revealed all the pleasure which men feel who are accustomed to ride a hobby, overspread the lawyer's countenance. He pulled up the collar of his shirt with an air, took out his snuff-box, opened it and offered me a pinch; on my refusing, he took a large one. He was happy! A man who has no hobby does not know all the good to be gotten out of life. A hobby is the happy medium between a passion and a monomania. At this very moment I understood the whole bearing of Sterne's charming passion, and had a perfect idea of the delight with which my Uncle Toby, encouraged by Trim, bestrode his hobby-horse.

"'Monsieur,' said Monsieur Regnault, 'I was the head clerk in Monsieur Roguin's law office, in Paris. A first-rate house, which you, perhaps, have heard mentioned? No! An unfortunate bankruptcy made it famous. Not having money enough to purchase a practice in Paris at the price to which they were run up in 1816, I came here and bought my predecessor's business. I had relations in Vendôme; among others, a wealthy aunt, who allowed me to marry her daughter. Monsieur,' he went on after a little pause, 'three months after being licensed by the keeper of the seals, one evening, as I was going to bed—it was before my marriage—I was sent for by Madame la Comtesse de Merret, to her château of Merret. Her maid, a good girl, who is now a servant in this inn, was waiting at my door with the Countess' own carriage. Ah! one moment! I ought to tell you that Monsieur le Comte de Merret had gone to Paris to die two months before I came here. He came to a miserable end, flinging himself into every kind of dissipation. You understand?

"'On the day when he left, Madame la Comtesse had quitted La Grande Bretèche, having dismantled it. Some people even say that she had burnt all the furniture, the hangings—in short, all the chattels and furniture whatever used in furnishing the premises now let by the said M. (Dear! what am I saying? I beg your pardon, I thought I was dictating a lease.) In short, that she burnt everything in the meadow at Merret. Have you been to Merret, monsieur? No,' said he, answering himself. 'Ah, indeed, it is a very fine place.

"'For about three months previously,' he went on, with a jerk of his head, 'the Count and Countess had lived in a very eccentric way; they admitted no visitors; madame lived on the first floor and monsieur on the second floor. When the Countess was left alone, she was never seen excepting at church. Subsequently, at home, at the château, she refused to see the friends, whether gentlemen or ladies, who went to call on her. She was already very much altered when she left La Grande Bretèche to go to Merret. That dear lady—I say dear lady, for it was she who gave me this diamond, but indeed I saw her but once—that kind lady was very ill; she had, no doubt, given up all hope, for she died without choosing to send for a doctor; indeed, many of our ladies fancied she was not quite right in her head. Well, sir, my curiosity was strangely excited by hearing that Madame de Merret had need of my services. Nor was I the only person who took an interest in the affair. That very night, though it was already late, all the town knew that I was going to Merret.

"'The waiting-woman replied but vaguely to the questions I asked her on the way; nevertheless, she told me that her mistress had received the sacrament in the course of the day at the hands of the curé of Merret, and seemed unlikely to live through the night. It was about eleven when I reached the château. I went up the great staircase. After crossing some large, lofty, dark rooms, diabolically cold and damp, I reached the state bedroom where the Countess lay. From the rumors that were current concerning this lady (monsieur, I should never end if I were to repeat all the tales that were told about her), I had imagined her a coquette. Imagine, then, that I had great difficulty in seeing her in the great bed whereon she was lying. To be sure, to light this enormous room, with old-fashioned heavy cornices and so thick with dust that merely to see it was enough to make you sneeze, she had only an old argand lamp. Ah! but you have not been to Merret. Well, the bed is one of those old-world beds, with a high tester hung with flowered chintz. A small table stood by the bed, on which I saw an "Imitation of Christ," which, by the way, I bought for my wife, as well as the lamp. There were also a deep armchair for her confidential maid, and two small chairs. There was no fire in the large old-fashioned grate. That was all the furniture; not enough to fill ten lines in an inventory.

"'My dear sir, if you had seen, as I then saw, that vast room, papered and hung with brown, you would have felt yourself transported into a scene of a romance. It was icy; nay more, funereal,' and he lifted his hand with a theatrical gesture and paused.

"'By dint of seeking, as I approached the bed, at last I saw Madame de Merret, under the glimmer of the lamp, which fell on the pillows. Her face was as yellow as wax and as narrow as two folded hands. The Countess had a lace cap showing abundant hair, but as white as linen thread. She was sitting up in bed, and seemed to keep upright with great difficulty. Her large black eyes, dimmed by fever, no doubt, and half-dead already, hardly moved under the bony arch of her eyebrows. There,' he added, pointing to his own brow. 'Her forehead was clammy; her fleshless hands were like bones covered with soft skin; the veins and muscles were perfectly visible. She must have been very handsome; but at this moment I was startled into an indescribable emotion at the sight. Never, said those who wrapped her in her shroud, had any living creature been so emaciated and lived. In short, it was awful to behold! Sickness had so consumed that woman that she was no more than a phantom. Her lips, which were pale violet, seemed to me not to move when she spoke to me.

"'Though my profession has familiarized me with such spectacles, by calling me not unfrequently to the bedside of the dying to record their last wishes, I confess that families in tears and the agonies I have seen were as nothing in comparison with this lonely and silent woman in her vast château. I heard not the least sound, I did not perceive the movement which the sufferer's breathing ought to have given to the sheets that covered her, and I stood motionless, absorbed in looking at her in a sort of stupor. In fancy I am there still. At last her large eyes moved; she tried to raise her right hand, but it fell back on the bed, and she uttered these words, which came like a breath, for her voice was no longer a voice: "I have waited for you with the greatest impatience." A bright flush rose to her cheeks. It was a great effort to her to speak.

"'"Madame," I began. She signed to me to be silent. At that moment the old housekeeper arose and said in my ear, "Do not speak; Madame la Comtesse is not in a state to bear the slightest noise, and what you would say might agitate her."

"'I sat down. A few instants after, Madame de Merret collected all her remaining strength to move her right hand and slipped it, not without infinite difficulty, under the bolster; she then paused a moment. With a last effort she withdrew her hand, and, when she brought out a sealed paper, drops of perspiration rolled from her brow. "I place my will in your hands. Oh! God! Oh!" and that was all. She clutched a crucifix that lay on the bed, lifted it hastily to her lips, and died.

"'The expression of her eyes still makes me shudder as I think of it. She must have suffered much! There was joy in her last glance, and it remained stamped on her dead eyes.

"'I brought away the will, and when it was opened I

found that Madame de Merret had appointed me her executor. She left the whole of her property to the hospital at Vendôme excepting a few legacies. But these were her instructions as relating to La Grande Bretêche: She ordered me to leave the place, for fifty years counting from the day of her death, in the state in which it might be at the time of her decease, forbidding any one, whoever he might be, to enter the apartments, prohibiting any repairs whatever, and even settling a salary to pay watchmen if it were needful to secure the absolute fulfillment of her intentions. At the expiration of that term, if the will of the testatrix has been duly carried out, the house is to become the property of my heirs, for, as you know, a notary cannot take a bequest. Otherwise La Grande Bretêche reverts to the heirs-at-law, but on condition of fulfilling certain conditions set forth in a codicil to the will, which is not to be opened until the expiration of the said term of fifty years. The will has not been disputed, so——'
And without finishing his sentence, the lanky notary looked at me with an air of triumph; I made him quite happy by offering him my congratulations.

"'Monsieur,' I said in conclusion, 'you have so vividly impressed me that I fancy I see the dying woman whiter than her sheets; her glittering eyes frighten me; I shall dream of her to-night. But you must have formed some idea as to the instructions contained in that extraordinary will.'

"'Monsieur,' said he, with comical reticence, 'I never allow myself to criticise the conduct of a person who honors me with the gift of a diamond.'

"However, I soon loosened the tongue of the discreet notary of Vendôme, who communicated to me, not without long digressions, the opinions of the deep politicians of both sexes whose judgments are law in Vendôme. But these opinions were so contradictory, so diffuse, that I was near falling asleep in spite of the interest I felt in this authentic history. The notary's ponderous voice and monotonous accent, accustomed no doubt to listen to himself and to make himself listened to by his clients or fellow-townsmen, were too much for my curiosity. Happily, he soon went away.

"'Ah, ha, monsieur,' said he on the stairs, 'a good many persons would be glad to live five-and-forty years longer; but —one moment!' and he laid the first finger of his right hand to his nostril with a cunning look, as much as to say, 'Mark my words! To last as long as that—as long as that, you must not be past sixty now.'

"I closed my door, having been roused from my apathy by this last speech, which the notary thought very funny; then I sat down in my armchair, with my feet on the fire-dogs. I had lost myself in a romance *à la* Radcliffe, constructed on the juridical base given me by Monsieur Regnault, when the door, opened by a woman's cautious hand, turned on the hinges. I saw my landlady come in, a buxom, florid dame, always good-humored, who had missed her calling in life. She was a Fleming, who ought to have seen the light in a picture by Teniers.

"'Well, monsieur,' said she, 'Monsieur Regnault has no doubt been giving you his history of La Grande Bretêche?'

"'Yes, Madame Lepas.'

"'And what did he tell you?'"

"I repeated in a few words the creepy and sinister story of Madame de Merret. At each sentence my hostess put her head forward, looking at me with an innkeeper's keen scrutiny, a happy compromise between the instinct of a police constable, the astuteness of a spy, and the cunning of a dealer.

"'My good Madame Lepas,' said I, as I ended, 'you seem to know more about it. Heh? If not, why have you come up to me?'

"'On my word as an honest woman——'

"'Do not swear; your eyes are big with a secret. You knew Monsieur de Merret; what sort of man was he?'

"'Monsieur de Merret—well, you see he was a man you never could see the top of, he was so tall! A very good gentleman, from Picardy, and who had, as we say, his head close to his cap. He paid for everything down, so as never to have difficulties with any one. He was hot-tempered, you see! All our ladies liked him very much.'

"'Because he was hot-tempered?' I asked her.

"'Well, may be,' she said; 'and you may suppose, sir, that a man had to have something to show for a figure-head before he could marry Madame de Merret, who, without any reflection on others, was the handsomest and richest heiress in our parts. She had about twenty thousand francs a year. All the town was at the wedding; the bride was pretty and sweet-looking, quite a gem of a woman. Oh, they were a handsome couple in their day!'

"'And were they happy together?'

"'Hm, hm! so-so—so far as can be guessed, for, as you may suppose, we of the common sort were not hail-fellow-well-met with them. Madame de Merret was a kind woman and very pleasant, who had no doubt sometimes to put up with her husband's tantrums. But though he was rather haughty, we were fond of him. After all, it was his place to behave so. When a man is a born nobleman, you see——'

"'Still, there must have been some catastrophe for Monsieur and Madame de Merret to part so violently?'

"'I did not say there was any catastrophe, sir. I know nothing about it.'

"'Indeed. Well, now, I am sure you know everything.'

"'Well, sir, I will tell you the whole story. When I saw Monsieur Regnault go up to see you, it struck me that he would speak to you about Madame de Merret as having to do with La Grande Bretêche. That put it into my head to ask your advice, sir, seeming to me that you are a man of good judgment and incapable of playing a poor woman like me false—for I never did any one a wrong and yet I am tormented by my conscience. Up to now I have never dared to say a word to the people of these parts; they are all chatter-mags, with tongues like knives. And never till now, sir, have I had any traveler here who stayed so long in the inn as you have, and to whom I could tell the history of the fifteen thousand francs——'

"'My dear Madame Lepas, if there is anything in your story of a nature to compromise me,' I said, interrupting the flow of her words, 'I would not hear it for all the world.'

"'You need have no fears,' said she; 'you will see.'

"Her eagerness made me suspect that I was not the only person to whom my worthy landlady had communicated the secret of which I was to be sole possessor, but I listened.

"'Monsieur,' said she, 'when the Emperor sent the Spaniards here, prisoners of war and others, I was required to lodge at the charge of the government a young Spaniard sent to Vendôme on parole. Notwithstanding his parole, he had to show himself every day to the sub-prefect. He was a Spanish grandee—neither more nor less. He had a name in *os* and *dia*, something like Bagos de Férédia. I wrote his name down in my books, and you may see it if you like. Ah! he was a handsome young fellow for a Spaniard, who are all ugly, they say. He was not more than five feet two or three in height, but so well made; and he had little hands that he kept so beautifully! Ah! you should have seen them. He had as many brushes for his hands as a woman has for her toilet. He had thick, black hair, a flame in his eye, a somewhat coppery complexion, but which I admired all the same. He wore the finest linen I have ever seen, though I have had princesses to lodge here, and, among others, General Bertrand, the Duc and Duchesse d'Abrantés, Monsieur Descazes, and the King of Spain. He did not eat much, but he had such polite and amiable ways that it was impossible to owe him a grudge for that. Oh! I was very fond of him, though he did not say four words to me in a day, and it was impossible to have the least bit of talk with him; if he was spoken to, he did not answer; it is a way, a mania they all have, it would seem.

"'He read his breviary like a priest, and went to mass and all the services quite regularly. And where did he post himself?—we found this out later. Within two yards of Madame de Merret's chapel. As he took that place the very first time he entered the church no one imagined that there was any purpose in it. Beside, he never raised his nose above his book, poor young man! And then, monsieur, of an evening he went for a walk on the hill among the ruins of the old castle. It was his only amusement, poor man; it reminded him of his native land. They say that Spain is all hills!

"'One evening, a few days after he was sent here, he was out very late. I was rather uneasy when he did not come in till just on the stroke of midnight; but we all got used to his whims; he took the key of the door, and we never sat up for him. He lived in a house belonging to us in the Rue des Casernes. Well, then, one of our stable-boys told us one evening that, going down to wash the horses in the river, he fancied he had seen the Spanish grandee swimming some little way off, just like a fish. When he came in, I told him to be careful of the weeds, and he seemed put out at having been seen in the water.

"'At last, monsieur, one day, or rather one morning, we did not find him in his room; he had not come back. By hunting through his things, I found a written paper in the drawer of his table, with fifty pieces of Spanish gold of the kind they call doubloons, worth about five thousand francs; and in a little sealed box ten thousand francs' worth of diamonds. The paper said that in case he should not return, he left us this money and these diamonds in trust to found masses to thank God for his escape and for his salvation.

"'At that time I still had my husband, who ran off in search of him. And this is the queer part of the story: he brought back the Spaniard's clothes, which he had found under a big stone on a sort of breakwater along the river-bank, nearly opposite La Grande Bretêche. My husband went so early that no one saw him. After reading the letter, he burned the clothes, and, in obedience to Count Férédia's wish, we announced that he had escaped.

"'The sub-prefect set all the constabulary at his heels; but, pshaw! he was never caught. Lepas believed that the Spaniard had drowned himself. I, sir, have never thought so; I believe, on the contrary, that he had something to do with the business about Madame de Merret, seeing that Rosalie told me that the crucifix her mistress was so fond of that she had it buried with her was made of ebony and silver; now in the early days of his stay here, Monsieur Férédia had one of ebony and silver which I never saw later. And now, monsieur, do not you say that I need have no remorse about the Spaniard's fifteen thousand francs? Are they not really and truly mine?'

"'Certainly. But have you never tried to question Rosalie?' I asked.

"'Oh, to be sure I have, sir. But what is to be done? That girl is like a wall. She knows something, but it is impossible to make her talk.'

"After chatting with me for a few minutes, my hostess left me a prey to vague and sinister thoughts, to romantic curiosity, and a religious dread, not unlike the deep emotion which comes upon us when we go into a dark church at night and discern a feeble light glimmering under a lofty vault—a dim figure glides across—the sweep of a gown or of a priest's cassock is audible—and we shiver! La Grande Bretêche, with its rank grasses, its shuttered windows, its rusty ironwork, its locked doors, its deserted rooms, suddenly rose before me in fantastic vividness. I tried to get into the mysterious dwelling to search out the heart of this solemn story, this drama which had killed three persons.

"Rosalie became in my eyes the most interesting being in Vendôme. As I studied her, I detected signs of an inmost thought, in spite of the blooming health that glowed in her dimpled face. There was in her soul some element of ruth or of hope; her manner suggested a secret, like the expression of devout souls who pray in excess, or of a girl who has killed her child and for ever hears its last cry. Nevertheless, she was simple and clumsy in her ways; her vacant smile had nothing criminal in it, and you would have pronounced her innocent only from seeing the large red and blue checked kerchief that covered her stalwart bust, tucked into the tight-laced square bodice of a lilac- and white-striped gown. 'No,' said I to myself, 'I will not quit Vendôme without knowing the whole history of La Grande Bretêche. To achieve this end, I will make love to Rosalie if it proves necessary.'

"'Rosalie!' said I, one evening.

"'Your servant, sir?'

"'You are not married?' She started a little.

"'Oh! there is no lack of men if ever I take a fancy to be miserable!' she replied, laughing. She got over her agitation at once; for every woman, from the highest lady to the inn-servant inclusive, has a native presence of mind.

"'Yes; you are fresh and good-looking enough never to lack lovers! But tell me, Rosalie, why did you become an inn-servant on leaving Madame de Merret? Did she not leave you some little annuity?'

"'Oh yes, sir. But my place here is the best in all the town of Vendôme.'

"This reply was such a one as judges and attorneys call evasive. Rosalie, as it seemed to me, held in this romantic affair the place of the middle square of the chess-board; she was at the very centre of the interest and of the truth; she appeared to me to be tied into the knot of it. It was not a case for ordinary love-making; this girl contained the last chapter of a romance, and from that moment all my attentions were devoted to Rosalie. By dint of studying the girl, I observed in her, as in every woman whom we make our ruling thought, a variety of good qualities; she was clean and neat; she was handsome, I need not say; she soon was possessed of every charm that desire can lend to a woman in whatever rank of life. A fortnight after the notary's visit, one evening, or rather one morning, in the small hours, I said to Rosalie—

"'Come, tell me all you know about Madame de Merret.'

"'Oh!' she cried in terror, 'do not ask me that, Monsieur Horace!'

"Her handsome features clouded over, her bright coloring grew pale, and her eyes lost their artless, liquid brightness.

"'Well,' she said, 'I will tell you; but keep the secret carefully.'

"'All right, my child; I will keep all your secrets with a thief's honor, which is the most loyal known.'

"'If it is all the same to you,' she said, 'I would rather it should be with your own.'

"Thereupon she set her head-kerchief straight, and settled herself to tell the tale; for, there is no doubt, a particular attitude of confidence and security is necessary to the telling of a narrative. The best tales are told at a certain hour—just as we are all here at table. No one ever told a story well standing up or fasting.

"If I were to reproduce exactly Rosalie's diffuse eloquence, a whole volume would scarcely contain it. Now, as the event of which she gave me a confused account stands exactly midway between the notary's gossip and that of Madame Lepas, as precisely as the middle term of a rule-of-three sum stands between the first and third, I have only to relate it in as few words as may be. I shall therefore be brief:

"The room at La Grande Bretêche in which Madame de Merret slept was on the first floor; a little wardrobe in the wall, about four feet deep, served her to hang her dresses in.

Three months before the evening of which I have to relate the events, Madame de Merret had been seriously ailing, so much so that her husband had left her to herself, and had his own bedroom on the second floor. By one of those accidents which it is impossible to foresee, he came in that evening two hours later than usual from the club, where he went to read the papers and talk politics with the residents in the neighborhood. His wife supposed him to have come in, to be in bed and asleep. But the invasion of France had been the subject of a very animated discussion; the game of billiards had waxed vehement; he had lost forty francs, an enormous sum at Vendôme, where everybody is thrifty, and where social habits are restrained within the bounds of a simplicity worthy of all praise, and the foundation, perhaps, of a form of true happiness which no Parisian would care for.

"For some time past Monsieur de Merret had been satisfied to ask Rosalie whether his wife was in bed; on the girl's replying always in the affirmative, he at once went to his own room, with the good faith that comes of habit and confidence. But this evening, on coming in, he took it into his head to go to see Madame de Merret, to tell her of his ill-luck and perhaps to find consolation. During dinner he had observed that his wife was very becomingly dressed; he reflected as he came home from the club that his wife was certainly much better, that convalescence had improved her beauty, discovering it, as husbands discover everything, a little too late. Instead of calling Rosalie, who was in the kitchen at the moment watching the cook and the coachman playing a puzzling hand at cards, Monsieur de Merret made his way to his wife's room by the light of his lantern, which he set down on the lowest step of the stairs. His step, easy to recognize, rang under the vaulted passage.

"At the instant when the gentleman turned the key to enter his wife's room, he fancied he heard the door shut of the closet of which I have spoken; but, when he went in,

"Madame de Merret was alone, standing in front of the fireplace. The unsuspecting husband fancied that Rosalie was in the cupboard; nevertheless, a doubt, ringing in his ears like a peal of bells, put him on his guard; he looked at his wife and read in her eyes an indescribably anxious and hunted expression.

"'You are very late,' she said. Her voice, usually so clear and sweet, struck him as being slightly husky.

"Monsieur de Merret made no reply, for at this moment Rosalie came in. This was like a thunderclap. He walked up and down the room, going from one window to another at a regular pace, his arms folded.

"'Have you had bad news or are you ill?' his wife asked him timidly, while Rosalie helped her to undress. He made no reply.

"'You can go, Rosalie,' said Madame de Merret to her maid; 'I can put in my curl-papers myself.' She scented disaster at the mere aspect of her husband's face, and wished to be alone with him. As soon as Rosalie was gone, or supposed to be gone, for she lingered a few minutes in the passage, Monsieur de Merret came and stood facing his wife, and said coldly, 'Madame, there is some one in your cupboard!' She looked at her husband calmly, and replied quite simply, 'No, monsieur.'

"This 'No' wrung Monsieur de Merret's heart; he did not believe it; and yet his wife had never appeared purer and more saintly than she seemed to be at this moment. He rose to go and open the closet door. Madame de Merret took his hand, stopped him, looked at him sadly, and said in a voice of strange emotion, 'Remember, if you should find no one there, everything must be at an end between you and me.'

"The extraordinary dignity of his wife's attitude filled him with deep esteem for her and inspired him with one of those resolves which need only a grander stage to become immortal.

"'No, Josephine,' he said, 'I will not open it. In either

event we should be parted for ever. Listen; I know all the purity of your soul, I know you lead a saintly life, and would not commit a deadly sin to save your life.' At these words Madame de Merret looked at her husband with a haggard stare—'See, here is your crucifix,' he went on. 'Swear to me before God that there is no one in there; I will believe you—I will never open that door.'

"Madame de Merret took up the crucifix and said, 'I swear it.'

"'Louder,' said her husband; 'and repeat: I swear before God that there is nobody in that closet.' She repeated the words without flinching.

"'That will do,' said Monsieur de Merret coldly. After a moment's silence: 'You have there a fine piece of work which I never saw before,' said he, examining the crucifix of ebony and silver, very artistically wrought.

"'I found it at Duvivier's; last year when that troop of Spanish prisoners came through Vendôme, he bought it of a Spanish monk.'

"'Indeed,' said Monsieur de Merret, hanging the crucifix on its nail; and he rang the bell.

"He had not to wait for Rosalie. Monsieur de Merret went forward quickly to meet her, led her into the bay of the window that looked on to the garden, and said to her in an undertone—

"'I know that Gorenflot wants to marry you, that poverty alone prevents your setting up house, and that you told him you would not be his wife until he found means to become a master mason. Well, go and fetch him; tell him to come here with his trowel and tools. Contrive to wake no one in his house but himself. His reward will be beyond your wishes. Above all, go out without saying a word—or else!' and he frowned.

"Rosalie was going, and he called her back. 'Here, take my latch-key,' said he.

"'Jean!' Monsieur de Merret called in a voice of thunder down the passage. Jean, who was both coachman and confidential servant, left his cards and came.

"'Go to bed, all of you,' said his master, beckoning him to come close; and the gentleman added in a whisper, 'When they are all asleep—mind, *asleep*—you understand?—come down and tell me.'

"Monsieur de Merret, who had never lost sight of his wife while giving his orders, quietly came back to her at the fireside and began to tell her the details of the game of billiards and the discussion at the club. When Rosalie returned she found Monsieur and Madame de Merret conversing amiably.

"Not long before this Monsieur de Merret had had new ceilings made to all the reception-rooms on the first floor. Plaster is very scarce at Vendôme; the price is enhanced by the cost of carriage; the gentleman had therefore had a considerable quantity delivered to him, knowing that he could always find purchasers for what might be left. It was this circumstance which suggested the plan he carried out.

"'Gorenflot is here, sir,' said Rosalie in a whisper.

"'Tell him to come in,' said her master aloud.

"Madame de Merret turned paler when she saw the mason.

"'Gorenflot,' said her husband, 'go and fetch some bricks from the coach-house; bring enough to wall up the door of this cupboard; you can use the plaster that is left for cement.' Then, dragging Rosalie and the workman close to him—'Listen, Gorenflot,' said he, in a low voice, 'you are to sleep here to-night; but to-morrow morning you shall have a passport to take you abroad to a place I will tell you of. I will give you six thousand francs for your journey. You must live in that town for ten years; if you find you do not like it, you may settle in another, but it must be in the same country. Go through Paris and wait there till I join you. I will there give you an agreement for six thousand francs more, to be paid to you on your return, provided you have carried out the conditions of the bargain. For that price you are to keep perfect silence as to what you have to do this night. To you, Rosalie, I will secure ten thousand francs, which will not be paid to you until your wedding-day, and on condition of your marrying Gorenflot; but, to get married, you must hold your tongue. If not, no wedding-gift!'

"'Rosalie,' said Madame de Merret, 'come and brush my hair.'

"Her husband quietly walked up and down the room, keeping an eye on the door, on the mason, and on his wife, but without any insulting display of suspicion. Gorenflot could not help making some noise. Madame de Merret seized a moment when he was unloading some bricks, and when her husband was at the other end of the room, to say to Rosalie: 'My dear child, I will give you a thousand francs a year if only you will tell Gorenflot to leave a crack at the bottom.' Then she added aloud quite coolly: 'You had better help him.'

"Monsieur and Madame de Merret were silent all the time while Gorenflot was walling up the door. This silence was intentional on the husband's part; he did not wish to give his wife the opportunity of saying anything with a double meaning. On Madame de Merret's side it was pride or prudence. When the wall was half built up the cunning mason took advantage of his master's back being turned to break one of the two panes in the top of the door with a blow of his pick. By this Madame de Merret understood that Rosalie had spoken to Gorenflot. They all three then saw the face of a dark, gloomy-looking man, with black hair and flaming eyes.

"Before her husband turned round again the poor woman had nodded to the stranger, to whom the signal was meant to convey, 'Hope.'

"At four o'clock, as day was dawning, for it was the month of September, the work was done. The mason was placed in charge of Jean, and Monsieur de Merret slept in his wife's room.

"Next morning when he got up he said with apparent carelessness, 'Oh, by the way, I must go to the mayor for the passport.' He put on his hat, took two or three steps toward the door, paused, and took the crucifix. His wife was trembling with joy.

"'He will go to Duvivier's,' thought she.

"As soon as he had left, Madame de Merret rang for Rosalie, and then in a terrible voice she cried: 'The pick! Bring the pick! and set to work. I saw how Gorenflot did it yesterday; we shall have time to make a gap and build it up again.'

"In an instant Rosalie had brought her mistress a sort of cleaver; she, with a vehemence of which no words can give an idea, set to work to demolish the wall. She had already gotten out a few bricks, when, turning to deal a stronger blow than before, she saw behind her Monsieur de Merret. She fainted away.

"'Lay madame on her bed,' he said coldly.

"Foreseeing what would certainly happen in his absence, he had laid this trap for his wife; he had merely written to the mayor and sent for Duvivier. The jeweler arrived just as the disorder in the room had been repaired.

"'Duvivier,' asked Monsieur de Merret, 'did you not buy some crucifixes of the Spaniards who passed through the town?'

"'No, monsieur.'

"'Very good; thank you,' said he, flashing a tiger's glare at his wife. 'Jean,' he added, turning to his confidential valet, 'you can serve my meals here in Madame de Merret's room. She is ill, and I shall not leave her until she recovers.'

"The cruel man remained in his wife's room for twenty days. During the earlier time, when there was some little noise in the closet, and Josephine wanted to intercede for the dying man, he said, without allowing her to utter a word, 'You swore on the cross that there was no one in there.'"

After this story all the ladies arose from the table, and thus the spell under which Bianchon had held them was broken. But there were some among them who had almost shivered at the last words.

A MAN OF BUSINESS.

Translated by ELLEN MARRIAGE.

To Monsieur le Baron James de Rothschild, Banker and Austrian Consul-General at Paris.

THE word *lorette* is a euphemism invented to describe the status of a personage, or a personage of a status, of which it is awkward to speak; the French Académie, in its modesty, having omitted to supply a definition out of regard for the age of its forty members. Whenever a new word comes in to supply the place of an unwieldy circumlocution, its fortune is assured; the word *lorette* has passed into the language of every class of society, even where the lorette herself will never gain an entrance. It was only invented in 1840, and derived beyond a doubt from the agglomeration of such swallows' nests about the church of Our Lady of Loretto. This information is for etymologists only. Those gentlemen would not be so often in a quandary if mediæval writers had only taken such pains with details of contemporary manners as we take in these days of analysis and description.

Mlle. Turquet, or Malaga, for she is better known by her pseudonym,* was one of the earliest parishioners of that charming church. At the time to which this story belongs, that light-hearted and lively damsel gladdened the existence of a notary with a wife somewhat too bigoted, rigid, and frigid for domestic happiness.

Now, it so fell out that one carnival evening Master Cardot was entertaining guests at Mlle. Turquet's house—Desroches the attorney, Bixiou of the caricatures, Lousteau the jour-

* See "The Imaginary Mistress."

nalist, Nathan, and others; it is quite unnecessary to give any further description of these personages, all bearers of illustrious names in the "Comédie Humaine." Young La Palférine, in spite of his title of Count and his great descent, which, alas! means a great descent in fortune likewise, had honored the notary's little establishment with his presence.

At dinner, in such a house, one does not expect to meet the patriarchal beef, the skinny fowl and salad of domestic and family life, nor is there any attempt at the hypocritical conversation of drawing-rooms furnished with highly respectable matrons. When, alas! will respectability be charming? When will the women in good society vouchsafe to show rather less of their shoulders and rather more wit or geniality? Marguerite Turquet, the Aspasia of the Cirque-Olympique, is one of those frank, very living personalities to whom all is forgiven, such unconscious sinners are they, such intelligent penitents; of such as Malaga one might ask, like Cardot—a witty man enough, albeit a notary—to be well "deceived." And yet you must not think that any enormities were committed. Desroches and Cardot were good fellows grown too gray in the profession not to feel at ease with Bixiou, Lousteau, Nathan, and young La Palférine. And they on their side had too often had recourse to their legal advisers and knew them too well to try to "draw them out," in lorette language.

Conversation, perfumed with seven cigars, at first was as fantastic as a kid let loose, but finally it settled down upon the strategy of the constant war waged in Paris between creditors and debtors.

Now, if you will be so good as to recall the history and antecedents of the guests, you will know that in all Paris you could scarcely find a group of men with more experience in this matter; the professional men on one hand and the artists on the other were something in the position of magistrates and criminals hobnobbing together. A set of Bixiou's drawings to illustrate life in the debtors' prison led the conversation to take this particular turn; and from debtors' prisons they went to debts.

It was midnight. They had broken up into little knots around the table and before the fire, and gave themselves up to the burlesque fun which is only possible or comprehensible in Paris and in that particular region which is bounded by the Faubourg Montmartre, the Rue Chaussée d'Antin, the upper end of the Rue de Navarin and the line of the boulevards.

In ten minutes' time they had come to an end of all the deep reflections, all the moralizings, small and great, all the bad puns made on a subject already exhausted by Rabelais three hundred and fifty years ago. It is not a little to their credit that the pyrotechnic display was cut short with a final squib from Malaga.

"It all goes to the shoemakers," she said. "I left a milliner because she failed twice with my hats. The vixen has been here twenty-seven times to ask for twenty francs. She did not know that we never have twenty francs. One has a thousand francs, or one sends to one's notary for five hundred; but twenty francs I have never had in my life. My cook and my maid may, perhaps, have so much between them; but for my own part, I have nothing but credit, and I should lose that if I took to borrowing small sums. If I were to ask for twenty francs, I should have nothing to distinguish me from my colleagues that walk the boulevard."

"Is the milliner paid?" asked La Palférine.

"Oh, come now, are you turning stupid?" she said, with a wink. "She came this morning for the twenty-seventh time, that is how I came to mention it."

"What did you do?" asked Desroches.

"I took pity upon her, and—ordered a little hat that I have just invented, a quite new shape. If Mademoiselle Amanda succeeds with it, she will say no more about the money, her fortune is made."

"In my opinion," put in Desroches, "the finest things that I have seen in a duel of this kind give those who know Paris a far better picture of the city than all the fancy portraits that they paint. Some of you think that you know a thing or two," he continued, glancing round at Nathan, Bixiou, La Palférine, and Lousteau, "but the king of the ground is a certain Count, now busy ranging himself. In his time, he was supposed to be the cleverest, adroitest, canniest, boldest, stoutest, most subtle, and experienced of all the pirates, who, equipped with fine manners, yellow kid gloves, and cabs, have ever sailed or ever will sail upon the stormy sea of Paris. He fears neither God nor man. He applies in private life the principles that guide the English cabinet. Up to the time of his marriage, his life was one continual war, like—Lousteau's, for instance. I was and am still his attorney."

"And the first letter of his name is Maxime de Trailles," said La Palférine.

"For that matter, he has paid every one and injured no one," continued Desroches. "But as our friend Bixiou was saying just now, it is a violation of the liberty of the subject to be made to pay in March when you have no mind to pay till October. By virtue of this article of his particular code, Maxime regarded a creditor's scheme for making him pay at once as a swindler's trick. It was long since he had grasped the significance of the bill of exchange in all its bearings, direct and remote. A young man once, in my place, called a bill of exchange the 'asses' bridge' in his hearing. 'No,' said he, 'it is the Bridge of Sighs; it is the shortest way to an execution.' Indeed, his knowledge of commercial law was so complete that a professional could not have taught him anything. At that time he had nothing, as you know. His carriage and horses were jobbed; he lived in his valet's house; and, by the way, he will be a hero to his valet to the end of the chapter, even after the marriage that he proposes to make. He belonged to three clubs, and dined at one of them whenever he did not dine out. As a rule, he was to be found very seldom at his own address——"

"He once said to me," interrupted la Palférine, "'My own affectation is the pretense that I make of living in the Rue Pigalle.'"

"Well," resumed Desroches, "he was one of the combatants; and now for the other. You have heard more or less talk of one Claparon?"

"Had hair like this!" cried Bixiou, ruffling his locks till they stood on end. Gifted with the same talent for mimicking absurdities which Chopin the pianist possesses to so high a degree, he proceeded forthwith to represent the character with startling truth.

"He rolls his head like this when he speaks; he was once a commercial traveler; he has been all sorts of things——"

"Well, he was born to travel, for at this minute, as I speak, he is on the sea on his way to America," said Desroches. "It is his only chance, for in all probability he will be condemned by default as a fraudulent bankrupt next session."

"Very much at sea!" exclaimed Malaga.

"For six or seven years this Claparon acted as man of straw, cat's-paw, and scapegoat to two friends of ours, du Tillet and Nucingen; but in 1829 his part was so well known that——"

"Our friends dropped him," put in Bixiou.

"They left him to his fate at last, and he wallowed in the mire," continued Desroches. "In 1833 he went into partnership with one Cérizet——"

"What! he that promoted a joint-stock company so nicely that the Sixth Chamber cut short his career with a couple of years in jail?" asked the lorette.

"The same. Under the restoration, between 1823 and 1827, Cérizet's occupation consisted in first putting his name intrepidly to various paragraphs, on which the public prosecutor fastened with avidity, and subsequently marching him off to prison. A man could make a name for himself with small expense in those days. The liberal party called their provincial champion 'the courageous Cérizet,' and toward 1828 so much zeal received its reward in 'general interest.'

"'General interest' is a kind of civic crown bestowed on the deserving by the daily press. Cérizet tried to discount the 'general interest' taken in him. He came to Paris, and, with some help from capitalists in the opposition, started as a broker, and conducted financial operations to some extent, the capital being found by a man in hiding, a skillful gambler who overreached himself, and in consequence, in July, 1830, his capital foundered in the shipwreck of the government."

"Oh! it was he whom we used to call the System," cried Bixiou.

"Say no harm of him, poor fellow," protested Malaga. "D'Estourny was a good sort."

"You can imagine the part that a ruined man was sure to play in 1830 when his name in politics was 'the courageous Cérizet.' He was sent off into a very snug little sub-prefecture. Unluckily for him, it is one thing to be in opposition —any missile is good enough to throw, so long as the fight lasts; but quite another to be in office. Three months later he was obliged to send in his resignation. Had he not taken it into his head to attempt to win popularity? Still, as he had done nothing as yet to imperil his title of 'courageous Cérizet,' the government proposed by way of compensation that he should manage a newspaper; nominally an opposition paper, but ministerialist *in petto*. So the fall of this noble nature was really due to the government. To Cérizet, as manager of the paper, it was rather too evident that he was as a bird perched on a rotten bough; and then it was that he promoted that nice little joint-stock company and thereby secured a couple of years in prison; he was caught, while more ingenious swindlers succeeded in catching the public."

"We are acquainted with the more ingenious," said Bixiou;

"let us say no ill of the poor fellow; he was nabbed; Couture allowed them to squeeze his cash-box; who would ever have thought it of him?"

"At all events, Cérizet was a low sort of fellow, a good deal damaged by low debauchery. Now for the duel I spoke about. Never did two tradesmen of the worst type, with the worst manners, the lowest pair of villains imaginable, go into partnership in a dirtier business. Their stock-in-trade consisted of the peculiar idiom of the man about town, the audacity of poverty, the cunning that comes of experience, and a special knowledge of Parisian capitalists, their origin, connections, acquaintances, and intrinsic value. This partnership of two 'dabblers' (let the stock exchange term pass, for it is the only word which describes them), this partnership of dabblers did not last very long. They fought like famished curs over every bit of garbage.

"The earlier speculations of the firm of Cérizet and Claparon were, however, well planned. The two scamps joined forces with Barbet, Chaboisseau, Samanon, and usurers of that stamp and bought up hopelessly bad debts.

"Claparon's place of business at that time was a cramped entresol in the Rue Chabannais—five rooms at a rent of seven hundred francs at most. Each partner slept in a little closet, so carefully closed from prudence that my head clerk could never get inside. The furniture of the other three rooms— an antechamber, a waiting-room, and a private office—would not have fetched three hundred francs altogether at a distress-warrant sale. You know enough of Paris to know the look of it; the stuffed horsehair-covered chairs, a table covered with a green cloth, a trumpery clock between a couple of candle sconces, growing tarnished under glass shades, the small gilt-framed mirror over the chimney-piece, and in the grate a charred stick or two of firewood which had lasted them for two winters, as my head clerk put it. As for the office, you can guess what it was like—more letter-files than business letters, a set of common pigeon-holes for either partner, a cylinder desk, empty as the cash-box, in the middle of the room, and a couple of armchairs on either side of a coal fire. The carpet on the floor was bought cheap at second-hand (like the bills and bad debts). In short, it was the mahogany furniture of furnished apartments which usually descends from one occupant of chambers to another during fifty years of service. Now you know the pair of antagonists.

"During the first three months of a partnership dissolved four months later in a bout of fisticuffs, Cérizet and Claparon bought up two thousand francs' worth of bills bearing Maxime's signature (since Maxime is his name), and filled a couple of letter-files to bursting with judgments, appeals, orders of the court, distress-warrants, application for stay of proceedings, and all the rest of it; to put it briefly, they had bills for three thousand two hundred francs odd centimes, for which they had given five hundred francs; the transfer being made under private seal, with special power of attorney, to save the expense of registration. Now it so happened at this juncture, Maxime, being of ripe age, was seized with one of the fancies peculiar to the man of fifty——"

"Antonia!" exclaimed La Palférine. "That Antonia whose fortune I made by writing to ask for a tooth-brush!"

"Her real name is Chocardelle," said Malaga, not over well pleased by the fine-sounding pseudonym.

"The same," continued Desroches.

"It was the only mistake Maxime ever made in his life. But what would you have, no vice is absolutely perfect?" put in Bixiou.

"Maxime had still to learn what sort of a life a man may be led into by a girl of eighteen when she is minded to take a header from her honest garret into a sumptuous carriage; it is a lesson that all statesmen should take to heart. At this time, de Marsay had just been employing his friend, our friend de Trailles, in the high comedy of politics. Maxime had looked high for his conquests; he had no experience of untitled women; and at fifty years he felt that he had a right to take a bite of a little so-called wild fruit, much as a sportsman will halt under a peasant's apple tree. So the Count found a reading-room for Mademoiselle Chocardelle, a rather smart little place to be had cheap, as usual——"

"Pooh!" said Nathan. "She did not stay in it six months. She was too handsome to keep a reading-room."

"Perhaps you are the father of her child?" suggested the lorette.

Desroches resumed:

"Since the firm bought up Maxime's debts, Cérizet's likeness to a bailiff's officer grew more and more striking, and one morning after seven fruitless attempts he succeeded in penetrating into the Count's presence. Suzon, the old manservant, albeit he was by no means in his novitiate, at last mistook the visitor for a petitioner, come to propose a thousand crowns if Maxime would obtain a license to sell postage stamps for a young lady. Suzon, without the slightest suspicion of the little scamp, a thoroughbred Paris street-boy into whom prudence had been rubbed by repeated personal experience of the police courts, induced his master to receive him. Can you see the man of business, with an uneasy eye, a bald forehead, and scarcely any hair on his head, standing in his threadbare jacket and muddy shoes——"

"What a picture of a dun!" cried Lousteau.

"Standing before the Count, that image of flaunting debt, in his blue flannel dressing-gown, slippers worked by some marquise or other, trousers of white woollen stuff, and a dazzling shirt? There he stood, with a gorgeous cap on his black dyed hair, playing with the tassels at his waist——"

"'Tis a bit of genre for anybody who knows the pretty little morning room, hung with silk and full of valuable paintings, where Maxime breakfasts," said Nathan. "You tread on a Smyrna carpet, you admire the sideboards filled with curiosities, ornaments, and rarities fit to make a King of Saxony envious——''

"Now for the scene itself," said Desroches, and the deepest silence followed.

"'Monsieur le Comte,' began Cérizet, 'I have come from a Monsieur Charles Claparon, who used to be a banker——'

"'Ah! poor devil, and what does he want with me?'

"'Well, he is at present your creditor for a matter of three thousand two hundred francs, seventy-five centimes, principal, interest, and costs——'

"'Coutelier's business?' put in Maxime, who knew his affairs as a pilot knows his coast.

"'Yes, Monsieur le Comte,' said Cérizet with a bow. 'I have come to ask your intentions.'

"'I shall only pay when the fancy takes me,' returned Maxime, and he rang for Suzon. 'It was very rash of Claparon to buy up bills of mine without speaking to me beforehand. I am sorry for him, for he did so very well for such a long time as a man of straw for friends of mine. I always said that a man must really be weak in his intellect to work for men that stuff themselves with millions, and to serve them so faithfully for such low wages. And now here he gives me another proof of his stupidity! Yes, men deserve what they get. It is your own doing whether you get a crown on your forehead or a bullet through your head; whether you are a millionaire or a porter, justice is always done you. I cannot help it, my dear fellow; I myself am not a king, I stick to my principles. I have no pity for those that put me to expense or do not know their business as creditors. Suzon! my tea! Do you see this gentleman?' he continued when the man came in. 'Well, you have allowed yourself to be taken in, poor old boy. This gentleman is a creditor; you ought to have known him by his shoes. No friend nor foe of mine, nor those that are neither and want something of me, come to see me on foot. My dear

Monsieur Cérizet, do you understand? You will not wipe your shoes on my carpet again' (looking as he spoke at the mud that whitened the enemy's soles). 'Convey my compliments and sympathy to Claparon, poor buffer, for I shall file this business under the letter Z.'

"All this with an easy good-humor fit to give a virtuous citizen the colic.

" 'You are wrong, Monsieur le Comte,' retorted Cérizet, in a slightly peremptory tone. 'We shall be paid in full, and that in a way which you may not like. That was why I came to you first in a friendly spirit, as is right and fit between gentlemen——'

" 'Oh! so that is how you understand it?' began Maxime, enraged by this last piece of presumption. There was something of Talleyrand's wit in the insolent retort, if you have quite grasped the contrast between the two men and their costumes. Maxime scowled and looked full at the intruder; Cérizet not merely endured the glare of cold fury, but even returned it, with an icy, cat-like malignance and fixity of gaze.

" 'Very good, sir, go out——'

" 'Very well, good-day, Monsieur le Comte. We shall be quits before six months are out.'

" 'If you can steal the amount of your bill, which is legally due I own, I shall be indebted to you, sir,' replied Maxime. 'You will have taught me a new precaution to take. I am very much your servant.'

" 'Monsieur le Comte,' said Cérizet, 'it is I, on the contrary, who am yours.'

"Here was an explicit, forcible, confident declaration on either side. A couple of tigers confabulating, with the prey before them and a fight impending, would have been no finer and no shrewder than this pair; the insolent fine gentleman as great a blackguard as the other in his soiled and mud-stained clothes.

"Which will you lay your money on?" asked Desroches, looking round at an audience, surprised to find how deeply it was interested.

"A pretty story!" cried Malaga. "My dear boy, go on, I beg of you. This goes to one's heart."

"Nothing commonplace could happen between two fighting-cocks of that calibre," added La Palférine.

"Pooh!" cried Malaga, "I will wager my cabinet-maker's invoice (the fellow is dunning me) that the little toad was too many for Maxime."

"I bet on Maxime," said Cardot. "Nobody ever caught him napping."

Desroches drank off a glass that Malaga handed to him.

"Mademoiselle Chocardelle's reading-room," he continued, after a pause, "was in the Rue Coquenard, just a step or two from the Rue Pigalle where Maxime was living. The said Chocardelle lived at the back on the garden-side of the house, beyond a big, dark place where the books were kept. Antonia left her aunt to look after the business——"

"Had she an aunt even then?" exclaimed Malaga. "Hang it all, Maxime did things handsomely."

"Alas! it was a real aunt," said Desroches; "her name was—let me see——"

"Ida Bonamy," said Bixiou.

"So as Antonia's aunt took a good deal of the work off her hands, she went to bed late and lay late of a morning, never showing her face at the desk until the afternoon, some time between two and four. From the very first her appearance was enough to draw custom. Several elderly men in the quarter used to come, among them a retired coach-builder, one Croizeau. Beholding this miracle of female loveliness through the window-panes, he took it into his head to read the newspapers in the beauty's reading-room; and a sometime custom-house officer, named Denisart, with a ribbon in his button-hole, followed the example. Croizeau chose to look upon Denisart as a rival. '*Môsieur*,' he said afterward, 'I did not know what to buy for you!'

"That speech should give you an idea of the man. The Sieur Croizeau happens to belong to a particular class of old man which should be known as 'Coquerels' since Henri Monnier's time; so well did Monnier render the piping voice, the little mannerisms, little queue, little sprinkling of powder, little movements of the head, prim little manner, and tripping gait in the part of Coquerel in 'La Famille Improvisée.' This Croizeau used to hand over his halfpence with a flourish and a 'There, fair lady!'

"Madame Ida Bonamy the aunt was not long in finding out through the servant that Croizeau, by popular report of the neighborhood of the Rue de Buffault, where he lived, was a man of exceeding stinginess, possessed of forty thousand francs per annum. A week after the installment of the charming librarian he was delivered of a pun—

"'You lend me books (*livres**), but I give you plenty of francs in return,' he said.

"A few days later he put on a knowing little air, as much as to say, 'I know you are engaged, but my turn will come one day; I am a widower.'

"He always came arrayed in fine linen, a cornflower blue coat, a paduasoy waistcoat, black trousers, and black ribbon bows on the double-soled shoes that creaked like an abbé's; he always held a fourteen-franc silk hat in his hand.

"'I am old and I have no children,' he took occasion to confide to the young lady some few days after Cérizet's visit to Maxime. 'I hold my relations in horror. They are peasants born to work in the fields. Just imagine it, I came up from the country with six francs in my pocket, and made my fortune here. I am not proud. A pretty woman is my equal. Now would it not be nicer to be Madame Croizeau for some years to come than to do a Count's pleasure for a twelvemonth?

* Livre: masculine, book; feminine, franc.

He will go off and leave you some time or other; and when that day comes, you will think of me—your servant, my pretty lady!'

"All this was simmering below the surface. The slightest approach at love-making was made quite on the sly. Not a soul suspected that the trim little old fogey was smitten with Antonia; and so prudent was the elderly lover, that no rival could have guessed anything from his behavior in the reading-room. For a couple of months Croizeau watched the retired custom-house official; but before the third month was out he had good reason to believe that his suspicions were groundless. He exerted his ingenuity to scrape an acquaintance with Denisart, came up with him in the street, and at length seized his opportunity to remark, 'It is a fine day, sir!'

"Whereupon the retired official responded with, 'Austerlitz weather, sir. I was there myself—I was wounded indeed; I won my cross on that glorious day.'

"And so from one thing to another the two drifted wrecks of the empire struck up an acquaintance. Little Croizeau was attached to the empire through his connection with Napoleon's sisters. He had been their coach-builder, and had frequently dunned them for money; so he gave out that he 'had had relations with the imperial family.' Maxime, duly informed by Antonia of the 'nice old man's' proposals (for so the aunt called Croizeau), wished to see him. Cérizet's declaration of war had so far taken effect that he of the yellow kid gloves was studying the position of every piece, however insignificant, upon the board; and it so happened that at the mention of that 'nice old man,' an ominous tinkling sounded in his ears. One evening, therefore, Maxime seated himself among the bookshelves in the dimly lighted back room, reconnoitred the seven or eight customers through the chink between the green curtains, and took the little coach-builder's measure. He gauged the man's infatuation, and was very well satisfied to find that the varnished doors of a tolerably sumptuous future were ready to turn at a word from Antonia so soon as his own fancy had passed off.

"'And that other one yonder?' he asked, pointing out the stout, fine-looking elderly man with the cross of the Legion of Honor. 'Who is he?'

"'A retired custom-house officer.'

"'The cut of his countenance is not reassuring,' said Maxime, beholding the Sieur Denisart.

"And, indeed, the old soldier held himself upright as a steeple. His head was remarkable for the amount of powder and pomatum bestowed upon it; he looked almost like a postillion at a fancy ball. Underneath that felted covering, moulded to the top of the wearer's cranium, appeared an elderly profile, half-official, half-soldierly, with a comical admixture of arrogance, altogether something like caricatures of the 'Constitutionnel.' The sometime official finding that age, and hair-powder, and the conformation of his spine made it impossible to read a word without spectacles, sat displaying a very creditable expanse of chest with all the pride of an old man with a mistress. Like old General Montcornet, that pillar of the Vaudeville, he wore ear-rings. Denisart was partial to blue; his roomy trousers and well-worn great-coat were both of blue cloth.

"'How long is it since that old fogey came here?' inquired Maxime, thinking that he saw danger in the spectacles.

"'Oh, from the beginning,' returned Antonia, 'pretty nearly two months ago now.'

"'Good,' said Maxime to himself, 'Cérizet only came to me a month ago. Just get him to talk,' he added in Antonia's ear; 'I want to hear his voice.'

"'Pshaw,' she replied, 'that is not so easy. He never says a word to me.'

"'Then why does he come here?' demanded Maxime.

"'For a queer reason,' returned the fair Antonia. 'In the first place, although he is sixty-nine, he has a fancy; and because he is sixty-nine, he is as methodical as a clock-face. Every day at five o'clock the old gentleman goes to dine with *her* in the Rue de la Victoire. (I am sorry for her.) Then at six o'clock he comes here, reads steadily at the papers for four hours, and goes back at ten o'clock. Daddy Croizeau says that he knows Monsieur Denisart's motives, and approves his conduct; and, in his place, he would do the same. So I know exactly what to expect. If ever I am Madame Croizeau, I shall have four hours to myself between six and ten o'clock.'

"Maxime looked through the directory and found the following reassuring item:

"'DENISART, * retired custom-house officer, Rue de la Victoire.'

"His uneasiness vanished.

"Gradually the Sieur Denisart and the Sieur Croizeau began to exchange confidences. Nothing so binds two men together as a similarity of views in the matter of womankind. Daddy Croizeau went to dine with 'Monsieur Denisart's fair lady,' as he called her. And here I must make a somewhat important observation.

"The reading-room had been paid for half in cash, half in bills signed by the said Mlle. Chocardelle. The *quart d'heure de Rabelais* (Rabelais' 'instant of action') arrived; the Count had no money. So the first bill of three thousand-franc bills was met by the amiable coach-builder; that old scoundrel Denisart having recommended him to secure himself with a mortgage on the reading-room.

"'For my own part,' said Denisart, 'I have seen pretty doings from pretty women. So, in all cases, even when I have lost my head, I am always on my guard with a woman. There is this creature, for instance; I am madly in love with her; but this is not her furniture; no, it belongs to me. The lease is taken out in my name.'

"You know Maxime! He thought the coach-builder uncommonly green. Croizeau might pay all three bills, and get nothing for a long while; for Maxime felt more infatuated with Antonia than ever."

"I can well believe it," said La Palférine. "She is the *bella imperia* (imperial beauty) of our day."

"With her rough skin?" exclaimed Malaga; "so rough, that she ruins herself in bran baths?"

"Croizeau spoke with a coach-builder's admiration of the sumptuous furniture provided by the amorous Denisart as a setting for his fair one, describing it all in detail with diabolical complacency for Antonia's benefit," continued Desroches. "The ebony chests inlaid with mother-of-pearl and gold wire, the Brussels carpets, a mediæval bedstead worth three thousand francs, a boule clock, candelabra in the four corners of the dining-room, silk curtains, on which Chinese patience had wrought pictures of birds, and hangings over the doors, worth more than the portress that opened them.

"'And that is what *you* ought to have, my pretty lady. And that is what I should like to offer you,' he would conclude. 'I am quite aware that you scarcely care a bit about me; but, at my age, we cannot expect too much. Judge how much I love you; I have lent you a thousand francs. I must confess that, in all my born days, I have not lent anybody *that* much——'

"He held out his penny as he spoke, with the important air of a man that gives a learned demonstration.

"That same evening at the Variétés, Antonia spoke to the Count.

"'A reading-room is very dull, all the same,' said she; 'I feel that I have no sort of taste for that kind of life, and I see no future in it. It is only fit for a widow that wishes to keep body and soul together, or for some hideously ugly thing that fancies she can catch a husband with a little finery.'

"'It was your own choice,' returned the Count. Just at that moment in came Nucingen, of whom Maxime, king of lions (the 'yellow kid gloves' were the lions of that day), had won three thousand francs the evening before. Nucingen had come to pay his gaming debt.

"'Ein writ of attachment haf shoost peen served on me by der order of dot teufel Glabaron,' he said, seeing Maxime's astonishment.

"'Oh, so that is how they are going to work, is it?' cried Maxime. 'They are not up to much, that pair——'

"'It makes not,' said the banker, 'bay dem, for dey may apply demselfs to oders pesides, und do you harm. I dake dees bretty voman to vitness dot I haf baid you dees morning, long pefore dat writ was serfed.'"

"Queen of the boards," smiled La Palférine, looking at Malaga, "thou art about to lose thy bet."

"Once, a long time ago, in a similar case, resumed Desroches, a too honest debtor took fright at the idea of a solemn declaration in a court of law, and declined to pay Maxime after notice was given. That time we made it hot for the crditor by piling on writs of attachment, so as to absorb the whole amount in costs——"

"Oh, what is that?" cried Malaga; "it all sounds like gibberish to me. As you thought the sturgeon so excellent at dinner, let me take out the value of the sauce in lessons in chicanery."

"Very well," said Desroches. "Suppose that a man owes you money, and your creditors serve a writ of attachment upon him; there is nothing to prevent all your other creditors from doing the same thing. And now what does the court do when all the creditors make application for orders to pay? *The court divides the whole sum attached, proportionately among them all.* That division, made under the eye of a magistrate, is what we call a *contribution*. If you owe ten thousand francs, and your creditors issue writs of attachment on a debt due to you of a thousand francs, each one of them gets so much per cent., 'so much in the franc,' in legal phrase; so much (that means) in proportion to the amounts severally claimed by the creditors. But—the creditors cannot touch the money without a special order from the clerk of the court. Do you guess what all this work drawn up by a judge and prepared by attorneys must mean? It means a quantity of stamped paper full of diffuse lines and blanks, the figures almost lost in vast spaces of completely empty ruled columns. The first proceeding is to deduct the costs. Now, as the costs are precisely the same whether the amount attached is one thousand or one million francs, it is not difficult to eat up three thousand francs (for instance) in costs, especially if you can manage to raise counter-applications."

"And an attorney always manages to do it," said Cardot. "How many a time one of you has come to me with, 'What is there to be got out of the case?'"

"It is particularly easy to manage it if the debtor eggs you on to run up costs till they eat up the amount. And, as a rule, the Count's creditors took nothing by that move, and were out of pocket in law and personal expenses. To get money out of so experienced a debtor as the Count, a creditor should really be in a position uncommonly difficult to reach; it is a question of being creditor and debtor both, for then you are legally entitled to work the confusion of rights, in law language——"

"To the confusion of the debtor?" asked Malaga, lending an attentive ear to this discourse.

"No, the confusion of rights of debtor and creditor, and pay yourself through your own hands. So Claparon's innocence in merely issuing writs of attachment eased the Count's mind. As he came back from the Variétés with Antonia, he was so much the more taken with the idea of selling the reading-room to pay off the last two thousand francs of the purchase-money, because he did not care to have his name made public as a partner in such a concern. So he adopted Antonia's plan. Antonia wished to reach the higher ranks of her calling, with splendid rooms, a maid, and a carriage;

in short, she wanted to rival our charming hostess, for instance——"

"She was not woman enough for that," cried the famous beauty of the circus; "still, she ruined young d'Esgrignon very neatly."

"Ten days afterward, little Croizeau, perched on his dignity, said almost exactly the same thing, for the fair Antonia's benefit," continued Desroches.

"'Child,' said he, 'your reading-room is a hole of a place. You will lose your complexion; the gas will ruin your eyesight. You ought to come out of it; and, look here, let us take advantage of an opportunity. I have found a young lady for you that asks no better than to buy your reading-room. She is a ruined woman with nothing before her but a plunge into the river; but she has four thousand francs in cash, and the best thing to do is to turn them to account, so as to feed and educate a couple of children. This is the place for her.'

"'Very well. It is kind of you, Daddy Croizeau,' said Antonia.

"'Oh, I shall be much kinder before I have done. Just imagine it, poor Monsieur Denisart has been worried into the jaundice! Yes, it has gone to the liver, as it usually does with susceptible old men. It is a pity he feels things so. I told him so myself; I said, "Be passionate, there is no harm in that, but as for taking things to heart—draw the line at that! It is the way to kill yourself." Really, I would not have expected him to take on so about it; a man that has sense enough and experience enough to keep away as he does while he digests his dinner——'

"'But what is the matter?' inquired Mademoiselle Chocardelle.

"'That little baggage with whom I dined has cleared out and left him! Yes. Gave him the slip without any warning but a letter, in which the spelling was all to seek.'

"'There, Daddy Croizeau, you see what comes of boring a woman——'

"'It is indeed a lesson, my pretty lady,' said the guileful Croizeau. 'Meanwhile, I have never seen a man in such a state. Our friend Denisart cannot tell his left hand from his right; he will not go back to look at the "scene of his happiness," as he calls it. He has so thoroughly lost his wits that he proposes that I should buy all Hortense's furniture (Hortense was her name) for four thousand francs.'

"'A pretty name,' said Antonia.

"'Yes. Napoleon's step-daughter was called Hortense. I built carriages for her as you know,' said the stricken ex-coach-maker.

"'Very well, I will see,' said cunning Antonia; 'begin by sending this young woman to me.'

"Antonia hurried off to see the furniture, and came back fascinated. She brought Maxime under the spell of antiquarian enthusiasm. That very evening the Count agreed to the sale of the reading-room. The establishment, you see, nominally belonged to Mademoiselle Chocardelle. Maxime burst out laughing at the idea of little Croizeau's finding him a buyer. The firm of Maxime and Chocardelle was losing two thousand francs, it is true, but what was the loss compared with four glorious thousand-franc notes in hand? 'Four thousand francs of live coin! there are moments in one's life when one would sign bills for eight thousand to get them,' as the Count said to me.

"Two days later the Count must see the furniture himself, and took the four thousand francs upon him. The sale had been arranged; thanks to little Croizeau's diligence, he pushed matters on; he had 'come round' the widow, as he expressed it. It was Maxime's intention to have all the furniture removed at once to a lodging in a new house in the Rue Tronchet, taken in the name of Madame Ida Bonamy; he did not trouble himself much about the nice old man that was about to lose his thousand francs. But he had sent beforehand for several big furniture vans.

"Once again he was fascinated by the beautiful furniture which a wholesale dealer would have valued at six thousand francs. By the fireside sat the wretched owner, yellow with jaundice, his head tied up in a couple of printed handkerchiefs, and a cotton night-cap on the top of them; he was huddled up in wrappings like a chandelier, exhausted, unable to speak, and altogether so knocked to pieces that the Count was obliged to transact his business with the manservant. When he had paid down the four thousand francs, and the servant had taken the money to his master for a receipt, Maxime turned to tell the man to call up the vans to the door: but even as he spoke, a voice like a rattle sounded in his ears:

"'It is not worth while, Monsieur le Comte. You and I are quits; I have six hundred and thirty francs fifteen centimes to give you!'

"To his utter consternation, he saw Cérizet, emerged from his wrappings like a butterfly from the chrysalis, holding out the accursed bundle of documents.

"'When I was down on my luck I learned to act on the stage,' added Cérizet. 'I am as good as Bouffé at old men.'

"'I have fallen among thieves!' shouted Maxime.

"'No, Monsieur le Comte, you are in Mademoiselle Hortense's house. She is a friend of old Lord Dudley's; he keeps her hidden away here; but she has the bad taste to like your humble servant.'

"'If ever I longed to kill a man,' so the Count told me afterward, 'it was at that moment; but what could one do? Hortense showed her pretty face, one had to laugh. To keep my dignity, I flung her the six hundred francs. "There's for the girl," I said.'"

"That is Maxime all over!" cried La Palférine.

"More especially as it was little Croizeau's money," added Cardot the profound.

"Maxime scored a trump," continued Desroches, "for Hortense exclaimed, 'Oh! if I had only known that it was you.'"

"A pretty 'confusion' indeed!" put in Malaga. "You have lost, milord," she added, turning to the notary.

And in this way the cabinet-maker, to whom Malaga owed a hundred crowns, was paid.

PARIS, 1845.

www.ingramcontent.com/pod-product-compliance
Lightning Source LLC
Chambersburg PA
CBHW030549300426
44111CB00009B/916